1st
Edition
1970

of 10.00

W9-BZK-707

HISTORY'S CARNIVAL

LEONID PLYUSHCH

With a contribution by Tatyana Plyushch

Edited and translated by Marco Carynnyk

HISTORY'S CARNIVAL

A Dissident's Autobiography

A Helen and Kurt Wolff Book

Harcourt Brace Jovanovich

New York and London

WITHDRAWN

Copyright © 1977 by Editions du Seuil
English translation copyright © 1979
by Harcourt Brace Jovanovich, Inc., and
William Collins Sons & Co. Ltd.

All rights reserved. No part of this publication may be
reproduced or transmitted in any form or by any means,
electronic or mechanical, including photocopy, recording,
or any information storage and retrieval system,
without permission in writing from the publisher.

The poetry excerpt on page 251 is from *The Bedbug and
Selected Poetry* by Vladimir Mayakovsky, translated by Max Hayward and
George Reavey, edited by Patricia Blake (The World Publishing Company),
© 1960 by Harper & Row, Publishers, Inc., and is
reprinted by permission of the publisher.

Printed in the United States of America

Library of Congress Cataloging in Publication Data

Pliushch, Leonyd Ivanovych, 1939–
History's Carnival.

Translated from the author's manuscript: V karnavale istorii.
"A Helen and Kurt Wolff Book."
Includes index.
1. Russia—Politics and government—1953–
2. Pliushch, Leonid Ivanovich, 1939–
3. Political prisoners—Russia—Biography.
4. Psychiatric hospitals—Russia.
I. Pliushch, Tania.
II. Title.
DK274.P5413   364.1'3 [B]   77-92544
ISBN 0-15-141614-1

First edition

B C D E

MILSTEIN
DK
274
.P5413

He's God's fool, they say. God's fool!
Maybe—so what. He—means me.
I'm God's fool man. . . .
I'm God's free-man!
Good night, then, my freedom!

Lina Kostenko, "Van Gogh"

CONTENTS

IV THE EPICENTER

V THE OUTER ZONE

By Tatyana Plyushch (Zhitnikova)

MARXIST METANOIA

> Carnival festivities and the comic spectacles and ritual
> connected with them had an important place in the life
> of medieval man. . . . They were sharply distinct from the
> serious official, ecclesiastical, feudal, and political cult
> forms and ceremonials. They offered a completely differ-
> ent, nonofficial, extraecclesiastical, and extrapolitical
> aspect of the world, of man, and of human relations; they
> built a second world and a second life outside official-
> dom. . . .
>
> Mikhail Bakhtin, *Rabelais and His World*

As newsmen pressed forward with cameras and tape recorders, a pale,
slight, but puffy man with hesitant gait and glazed eyes stepped down
from a train in the Austrian border town of Marchegg on the morning of January 10, 1976. Supported by his wife and two sons, who
stroked his trembling hands as if he were a child, he muttered, "It
was a horror." The man was Leonid Plyushch—"the dissident
Ukrainian mathematician Plyushch," as the press had been calling
him—and his arrival in the West was the *dénouement* of a protracted
and intense campaign to win his release from the Soviet psychiatric
hospital where he had been doped and abused for two and a half
years. *History's Carnival* is his account of how he found himself at
Marchegg.

Plyushch's run-in with the Soviet authorities had begun long before he was committed to a psychiatric institution. The draconian
trials of dissenters that began in the mid-1960's, along with the Warsaw Pact occupation of Czechoslovakia in 1968, smashed hopes that
the post-Stalin liberalization would continue. Like so many of his
colleagues, Plyushch was moved to voice his opposition by dashing
off protest letters, attending trials, and contributing reports to the
uncensored journals—*Chronicle of Current Events* and *Ukrainian*

Herald. Fired from his job as a mathematician and blacklisted from other work, Plyushch reluctantly became a professional dissident. "Politics struck me as vanity," he writes, "an overcoming of obstacles rather than an unfolding of one's abilities. Yet forgetting, moving away, shutting my eyes and ears, and remaining silent were also impossible. Above all, as an oppositionist I would not need to lie or to play the double role of 'building the brilliant future' and opposing the dismal present."

Undeterred by the surveillance, harassment, questioning, and arrests and trials of his friends, Plyushch continued to sign appeals and support his fellow dissidents until he himself was arrested in January 1972, when the KGB determined to wipe out clandestine literature in Ukraine by carrying out a wave of house searches and arrests. Others arrested in the sweep were sentenced to labor camps and internal exile; Plyushch, however, was singled out for special treatment. He was held for investigation long beyond the permitted term, denied his right to defense counsel, and subjected to three psychiatric examinations by KGB-appointed psychiatrists.

The first panel concluded that Plyushch had a psychopathic personality but was mentally competent to stand trial. The second one reported that Plyushch was suffering from schizophrenia with "symptoms of paranoid disorder, ideas of reformism, [and] elements of messianism." Plyushch was deemed nonresponsible and therefore in need of treatment in a special psychiatric hospital, that is, a prisonlike institution for housing persons who have committed serious crimes and have been diagnosed as suffering from a mental illness. The third panel announced that Plyushch suffered from a "sluggish form of schizophrenia," but now with "changes toward emotional-volitional disorder [and] loss of the urgency of ideas of reformism and transformation of them into ideas of inventiveness in the field of psychology." This time treatment in an ordinary psychiatric hospital was recommended.

Plyushch was finally brought to trial at the Kiev Provincial Court on January 25, 1973. The court session was closed: neither the accused, nor his attorney, nor his relatives were permitted to be present. Witnesses were told from the outset that Plyushch was insane, and testimony about his mental state was taken from people who barely knew him. Plyushch's wife, Tatyana, and sister, Ada, on the other hand, were allowed to enter only for the reading of the verdict, although Soviet law requires the verdict to be announced in public even in those few cases where the trial may be held *in camera.* Adding insult to injury, the judge refused to give Plyushch's wife a copy of the verdict.*

At the trial, Plyushch was charged—under the infamous and frequently invoked law forbidding "anti-Soviet agitation and propaganda"—with possessing and distributing the *Chronicle of Current Events* and *Ukrainian Herald*; preparing, possessing, and distributing slanderous, anti-Soviet manuscripts; signing anti-Soviet letters to the United Nations as a member of the Initiative Group for the Defense of Human Rights in the USSR; and, finally, conducting anti-Soviet conversations. Ruling that he had committed these actions in a state of mental nonresponsibility, the court chose the harsher recommendation of the second panel and dispatched Plyushch to a special psychiatric hospital in the provincial Ukrainian town of Dnipropetrovsk.

Why was Plyushch committed to a psychiatric institution instead of being bundled off to a labor camp? There was, first of all, his refusal to cooperate with the KGB investigators. Had they given him a full-scale trial, he might well have turned the prisoner's dock into a political podium. Secondly, a ruling of insanity was useful in discrediting the opposition as a bunch of crackpots. The KGB had for some time been circulating rumors that Plyushch was "as crazy as General Grigorenko," that other famous dissident who spent long terms in psychiatric hospitals. Then there was the possibility that Plyushch might have an undesirable influence: in a labor camp he would have had dealings with normal people and made friends. Finally, even the longest labor-camp sentence is finite, whereas psychiatric commitment is indefinite. No strait jacket would be needed, either: several shots of tranquilizers and the most rebellious mind would be "corrected."

The psychiatric myrmidons assiduously carried out their assignment to impose what Tatyana Khodorovich called "punishment by madness." Concealing their surnames and insisting to Plyushch's distraught wife that they were acting in his best interests, they confined him with genuinely disturbed patients and pumped him again and again with drugs that made him bloated, immobile, severely depressed, and intellectually deadened. The "treatment" was making

---

* The numerous violations of Soviet law in Plyushch's case are discussed by Tatyana Khodorovich in her article "Nakazaniye bezumiyem" ["Punishment by Madness"] in Tatyana Khodorovich, ed., *Istoriya bolezni Leonida Plyushcha* (Amsterdam: Herzen Foundation, 1974), pp. 160–81. The book has been translated as *The Case of Leonid Plyushch* (London: C. Hurst; Boulder: Westview Press, 1976), but without this article.

Plyushch gravely ill. No wonder that Arkadiy Levin said in an appeal for his friend that the Soviet regime was practicing menticide on Plyushch, and Tatyana Plyushch called Andrey Snezhnevsky, the chief psychiatrist of the Soviet Ministry of· Health, her husband's executioner.*

Proving herself to be a stubborn and persistent fighter, Tatyana Plyushch sent a steady stream of letters and appeals, first to every possible Soviet authority and then to the Western public. Apolitical herself, she firmly supported her husband's right to his convictions and resisted threats, blackmail, personal indignities, and even the loss of her job. It is no exaggeration to say that the KGB was more afraid of Tatyana Plyushch than of her husband and that she deserves the credit for crafting his release.

The incarceration of the young scientist evoked a wide response abroad. Inquiries and interventions poured into Moscow from the American Red Cross, the American Medical Association, Amnesty International, and Ukrainian organizations. Such distinguished leaders of the struggle for civil rights in Eastern Europe as Pavel Litvinov, Yuriy Orlov, Tatyana Khodorovich, and Jiří Pelikan put out one appeal after another for Plyushch. In response to an appeal from Andrey Sakharov in February 1974, French mathematicians unified their efforts for two colleagues interned in mental hospitals by forming the International Committee for the Defense of Yuriy Shikhanovich and Leonid Plyushch. Moved by another appeal from Sakharov, the International Congress of Mathematicians in Vancouver in August 1974 called for Plyushch's release.

The case acquired even broader resonance when French mathematicians joined with Amnesty International to sponsor an International Day for Leonid Plyushch on April 23, 1975. On October 23, 1975, a public meeting was held in Paris. Attended by some five thousand people, including representatives of socialist organizations, it was the largest rally ever sponsored for a Soviet prisoner of conscience. Fearful of losing electoral support, the French Communist Party declared two days later in *L'Humanité*, "If it is true that [Plyushch] is interned in a psychiatric hospital solely because he has taken a stand against some aspects of Soviet policy or against the regime itself, we can only confirm with the greatest clarity our total disapproval and demand that he be liberated as quickly as possible."

* The savaging of Plyushch was not an isolated incident, of course. The extensive evidence on Soviet psychiatric abuses, including Plyushch's case, is presented and discussed in Sidney Bloch and Peter Reddaway, *Psychiatric Terror: How Soviet Psychiatry Is Used to Suppress Dissent* (New York: Basic Books, 1977).

The end of the long nightmare was in sight: late in 1975 reports circulated that Plyushch and his family would be permitted to leave the Soviet Union. In January 1976 Tatyana Plyushch was given exit visas for her family, and the Soviet news agency Tass announced that since Plyushch's health had improved considerably because of the treatment he had received, he could now be permitted to emigrate to Israel. Arriving in Austria, the Plyushch family proceeded to settle in France.

Many books by and about Soviet dissidents have appeared, but none is quite like Plyushch's. For *History's Carnival* is both a political autobiography and an account of a remarkable intellectual development. An insider's observations of the Democratic Movement are interspersed with reflections on Soviet society and state. A Christian in his childhood, Plyushch describes for us his conversion to atheism. Brought up in a Russian environment and encouraged by official policies to be a Russian chauvinist and an anti-Semite, he becomes a Judeophile, discovers his Ukrainian heritage, and supports oppressed religious and national groups. A Stalinist who works zealously in the Komsomol and offers his services to the KGB, he becomes a neo-Marxist concerned with justice, equality, and dignity.

As a promising young mathematician at the Institute of Cybernetics in Kiev, where he specialized in the computer simulation of biochemical processes (he is disarmingly offhanded about his work in this area), Plyushch published several articles on mathematical modeling. But his intellectual interests ranged beyond mathematics and cybernetics to logic, psychiatry, structural linguistics, philosophy, and above all ethics and human relations. He has always been particularly interested—both as a political creature and as a thinker— in Stalinism as a historical and psychological phenomenon. Despite the tensions and uncertainties of involvement in the Democratic Movement, he managed to write several important essays, including "The Heirs of Stalin," which is only part of a larger work on the meaning of life that he hopes to write.

For Plyushch is a philosopher above all else. Democratization is the major problem facing the Soviet Union. A country that has had a social revolution, it has not yet had the bourgeois revolution that would establish democratic freedoms. Society must be changed, Plyushch realizes, but the means with which the end is to be attained must always be kept in mind. Social progress must be determined by the development of human consciousness and not by economic necessity. Drawing on Tolstoy, Saint-Exupéry, and the unjustly neglected

Russian writer Mikhail Prishvin, Plyushch develops an original theory of human relations. True Communism becomes defined for him
as an opposition to everything boorish and demeaning of human
dignity.

The intelligentsia has played a major role first in establishing the
Soviet regime and then in leading an opposition to it. But neither
Soviet Communism nor the attempts to reform it have succeeded. Although Czechoslovak and Polish spokesmen for human rights have
had some success in bringing about an amelioration in their countries, Soviet dissidents on the whole have not. In purely political
terms, the Democratic Movement of the 1960's has been a failure, and
the hopes of persuading the Soviet government to adhere to the legality enunciated in its own constitution have proved to be illusory.

In moral terms, however, the Democratic Movement has won an
immeasurable victory. Acting as spiritual witnesses who demonstrate that it is possible to live without lies and Orwellian double-
think, the Soviet democrats have reminded us that freedom is the
principle issue we must address. The virtues that emerge from
Plyushch's self-portrait are sincerity (he never poses or attempts to
conceal his weaknesses), goodness of heart, and concern for his fellow
man. These are also the virtues of the Democratic Movement, and
Plyushch is their best embodiment. At the price of four years as a
hounded dissident and four as a tortured prisoner, Leonid Plyushch
has achieved inner freedom.

As editor I have pruned Leonid Plyushch's manuscript with the
English-speaking reader in mind, in some cases rearranging the material and supplementing it with passages from Plyushch's interviews
and speeches, and supplied chapter titles and end notes. For transliter-
ating Slavic names I have used the system of the United States Board
on Geographic Names. Ukrainian names are transcribed directly from
the original, and not via Russian (as, for example, Lviv instead of
Lvov and Kharkiv instead of Kharkov). At Plyushch's request I have
retained without translation *psikhushka*, the Soviet slang term for a
special psychiatric hospital, in the hope that it will achieve as wide
a currency as *Gulag, samizdat*, and *zek*. I am grateful to Herbert
Marshall for translating the epigraph to this book, from Lina Kostenko's poem "Van Gogh," and to Gerry Smith for allowing me to
use his translations of Alexander Galich's poems.

Marco Carynnyk

xiv

PREFACE

The thought of writing a book such as this one first occurred to me in the summer of 1968 at a birthday party for Pavel Litvinov. Late in the evening, when the guests had left, I found myself alone with Vladimir Dremlyuga, a young worker who had been expelled from Leningrad University for "unreliability." We struck up a typically Russian discussion about all the "eternal" problems. When we came down to earth and told each other about our personal lives, we were astonished to see how different we were. Our characters, our social backgrounds, and our activities at school and university were all radically different. And yet our paths had crossed, and we were both facing imprisonment. (We couldn't even imagine then that after prison we would both go into emigration.)

Dremlyuga and I agreed that it would be valuable to analyze how people come to speak out against the Soviet regime and what unites the members of the Democratic Movement despite their differences of opinion. I thought much about this latter point at the *psikhushka* in Dnipropetrovsk, and the answer is clear to me now. It is illustrated by a legend about the Indian mystic Ramakrishna, who saw a peasant being flogged so severely that bloody lines were left on his back. Identical lashmarks appeared on Ramakrishna's back. This naked, defenseless conscience prevents a man from adapting to the society around him and retreating behind some clever ideology that conceals the sufferings of his fellow men.

Soviet psychiatrists and secret-police men are not entirely wrong when they claim that anyone who dares to speak out against the regime is mentally disturbed. A naked, abnormal conscience, an inability to live with lies, and a poor adaptation to a society where falsehood and evil prevail are all signs that the patient has crossed the borders of conformism and philistine values. It is no accident that the Democratic Movement—like any popular, religious, or political movement—includes genuine hysterics, psychopaths, and schizophrenics. The secret police tries to profit from the mental illness of some members of the Democratic Movement and to obtain from them evidence it can use to discredit the opposition. For thinking people such exploitation testifies to the immorality of the Soviet regime.

Thus the book before you is neither a confession nor a literary autobiography. It is an account of one more road to freedom, a description of how the Soviet Union appears in the eyes of a citizen whose fanatical faith in the Soviet system gave way to a struggle to free himself of its illusions, slavery, and terror. I have tried to show what my comrades in the Soviet Union are fighting for and how they are persecuted.

I should not want my testimony about the reality of "socialism" to serve as a moral justification for all sorts of fascist scum, because my enemy's enemy is not necessarily my friend. Barbarity is barbarity no matter what its ideological hue. Nor should I want my book to be used as evidence at trials of people who remain in the Soviet Union. I have therefore rearranged some events, changed certain names, and in some cases combined several real people into one. My wife has done the same in her part of the book. We are grateful to those friends whose identities we have concealed. But for this new edition of the book I have restored the real names of certain people who have died, emigrated, or come out into the open. I have also exposed the identities of several scoundrels and cowards, on Solzhenitsyn's principle that a country must know its informers.

I had intended to conclude the account with my impressions of the West. But how can I say anything serious, even after I have seen a great deal here, when I still do not know any Western languages? I am convinced, however, that one of the most important freedoms is the opportunity to see the world with one's own eyes. When one looks benevolently at another country, one better understands the virtues and vices of one's own. How I wish that my friends could see both the "hell" here, which is not at all like the hell depicted by Soviet propaganda, and the "heaven," which so many of them long for in protest against the heaven they know.

Here in the "free West" (the Western reader knows that its freedom is qualified), I see only one duty for myself: to testify, as if in court, about the Marxist hell that I, a Marxist, have witnessed in my mother Ukraine and stepmother Russia, as well as in other republics of the USSR. By doing so I hope to combat inhuman actions by all governments in the West and the East jointly with Amnesty International, the International Committee Against Repressions, and honest and thinking parties, trade unions, and churches.

I want to dedicate this book to humanitarians. I am not certain that they will be victorious, but only in their struggle does human life in the twentieth century find its full expression.

Paris   L. P.
August 15, 1977

I

SETTING

OUT

1

A SANATORIUM CHILDHOOD

I was born into a Ukrainian working-class family in 1939 at Naryn in the Kirghiz Republic in Central Asia. My father, a railway foreman, was killed at the front in 1941.

At the end of the war my mother, my sister, Ada, and I moved from Frunze, the capital of the Kirghiz Republic, to my father's native town of Borzna in Ukraine to live with my grandmother. What can I say about the life we led then? With the exception of the bureaucratic elite, the entire country lived in various degrees of famine. In Frunze in 1943 my mother had sent my sister and me to a hospital, although we were perfectly healthy, so that we'd have something to eat. After the war we ate beet soup for half a year, and then soup with beans. We children went out into the fields to gather the spikes of grain left from the harvest. Grownups couldn't go, because they'd be arrested for stealing government property. We would crawl into the melon plantation to steal tomatoes, cucumbers, watermelons, and canteloupes. The guard shot salt at us, but he always missed. Grandmother brought firewood from the forest on her back. It must have been hard for her: even I could barely lift the branches. We were all afraid of the warden—he'd fine us for stealing—but what were we to burn in the stove during the winter? Peat doesn't burn without wood.

The whole town was talking about a soldier who had come back from a prisoner-of-war camp. People said that the English took all our prisoners in the German camps and sent them to their own camps in Africa. When someone tried to escape, he was tied to a tree, and African ants would eat him to the bone. Grandmother cried and cursed the English for letting Father be eaten by ants. I could clearly see his skeleton: I had recently found the remains of a lizard in an anthill. I began to hate the English more than the Germans.

3

"We have to smash them the way we smashed the Germans!" I declared. Thus my first accusation against the regime: Comrade Stalin gave Father a pistol and sent him to fight German tanks, and then spread rumors about Anglo-American camps where our soldiers were being held.

Grandmother was a devout believer, and my sister and I also became believers. I remember how I trembled at the age of six when I read a children's book about Jesus. Mother tried to convince us that God does not exist, but all her arguments came to naught in the face of our experience. Grandmother was a sorceress. She would utter incantations for children who were ill with the "infant disease" (as I understand it now, it was of a neurotic nature), "fright," and the "evil eye." (I still don't understand this illness; it was produced by a look from a person with "dangerous eyes.") Mother ridiculed Grandmother's medicine but could not deny an obvious fact: almost all the children she treated recovered, and the doctors at the hospital where Mother worked learned to recognize "Grandmother's disease" and referred all such patients to her.

In the second grade, at the age of eight, I contracted tuberculosis of the bone. My mother wrote to Nikita Khrushchev, who was First Secretary of the Communist Party of Ukraine at this time, requesting that I be sent to a sanatorium because the local doctors had not been able to help. I was admitted to one, and my mother is still deeply grateful to Khrushchev. I am not: in a country where medical treatment is free, admission to a sanatorium should be a matter of course.

My stay at the sanatorium did not begin auspiciously. I was brought into the ward just as dinner was being served—borsch, mashed potatoes, and grapes, which looked like a feast after the semi-starvation I had known at home. I had never seen grapes and so immediately ate them all. Then I set about devouring the borsch. Suddenly a slice of bread landed in my dish, then another, and then grape seeds. I looked around in confusion for my enemy. When I finally spotted him among the many children, I crawled over to his bed and began to pummel him. What could he do to me when I was a village boy firm on my legs and he had been bedridden for years?

The nurse dashed in to drag me away to the isolation ward. I burst into tears and explained that it wasn't my fault, but the nurse scolded both of us and left. From all the beds I began to hear, over and over, "Darkie! Darkie!" I sensed a threat in this and asked the boy with the most likable face to explain. He told me that the older boys would come during the night, cover me with a blanket, and beat me with their crutches because I was a *seksot*.

4

"What's that?" I asked.

"An informer."

I knew this word. I tried to convince him that it wasn't fair, that the others were at fault. Grownups are always against children and one mustn't help them punish children, he patiently explained. I agreed with this, but I also insisted that I should be forgiven because I hadn't known. He didn't see my point.

All evening I waited in horror for the night. My only salvation, it seemed to me, was to hide under the bed. But before I could do so a group of big boys—aged ten or eleven and armed with crutches—rushed into the room. Instead of descending on me, they went straight to the boy who had most vehemently called for a "darkie." They tapped him jokingly with their crutches and left. Talking to the boy with the likable face had borne fruit.

I learned what *seksot* means only when I grew up. It is a contraction of *sekretny sotrudnik*—a secret collaborator of the police or the KGB.[1]

The administration at the sanatorium waged an intensive campaign of atheist propaganda. Coming from villages, we children were almost all believers. The teacher in charge of the campaign was an intelligent man. He would visit us after lessons and explain very reasonably why God does not exist. Everyone would quickly admit that the leader was right. I didn't argue with him, but when he had left I would tell the boys about various miracles, including my grandmother's. At the next discussion the teacher would see, to his surprise, that all the children believed in God again and were offering new arguments. Finally he realized that I was his chief opponent. He deftly broke down my resistance in regard to the miracles of Christ and self-renewing icons but found it difficult to dispose of my grandmother. He would leave, promising to explain a particular phenomenon the next time. Now I know that he went to read up on the matter. All my arguments were eventually shattered by the theory of suggestion and hypnosis. But I hated to lose and ruminated until I found new evidence. My grandmother cured babies who were still breast-feeding. How can anything be suggested to an infant, I asked the teacher. He was visibly perplexed and promised to explain later. Many days went by before he could do so. In a case such as this, he said, the mother responds to suggestion. She begins to believe that her child will recover, which brings about a great improvement in her milk. As a result the baby recovers.

Under such instruction I became an atheist. I sent my grandmother a diplomatic letter explaining that God does not exist and

5

asking her forgiveness for my new-found atheism. My grandmother had hoped to pass on her magical incantations to me, but now she had to pass them on to my aunt, who had no intention of becoming a sorceress.

Life at the sanatorium was not very interesting: dreams of family and freedom, conversations, books, and studies. It was much like a prison, but with kindliness and compassion from the staff and decent food. We were being educated in an incubator and learned about the world only through books and discussions with the teachers. Hence words, thoughts, and ideas played a major role in our lives. The ideology that informed our education was humane. We accepted it in its pure form because we never saw it tested by life. I saw no conflict between the ethical principles of my Christian childhood and the new ones.

At the beginning of the seventh grade I fell in love for the first time. The girls in the adjacent ward had been brought in on their beds to play with us. We played post office, sending one another letters without revealing our names. Those who received letters had to reply anonymously. To attract attention I sent the girls rude remarks, which were returned in kind. Finally everyone guessed that I was the sender. Now the girls sent me rude remarks. A girl named Masha reciprocated with particular venom. She had tuberculosis of the hip joint. We pitied such girls even more than the ones with hunchbacks, because we knew they'd never bear children. I fell in love with Masha and suggested that we be friends. She agreed.

At the end of the seventh grade I was made to leave the sanatorium and moved to another part of town. Masha did not reply when I wrote to her. I decided to go see her by streetcar, though I didn't know how to go about it. I possessed three rubles but had no idea whether this was enough for the fare or where to buy a ticket. I set out on foot, cursing writers for failing to describe how streetcar tickets are purchased. We had been taught, after all, that literature is a primer for life.

At the sanatorium I asked for Masha. After a long wait she appeared and dropped a note explaining that a girl had recently received a letter from a boy that had been intercepted by a teacher. The girl was thereupon ridiculed in front of the others for being "in love." Masha asked me not to see her or to write letters. I went home, reviling young girls for their perfidy.

Hypocrisy in sex is intimately connected with the political hypocrisy of official ideology. In the second or third grade I had begun to think about the problem of procreation as it related to the leaders of the Revolution. Lenin had had a wife but no children. That meant that Lenin was virtuous. Comrade Stalin had children—the teacher had told us about them. That meant . . . It was terrible to think about. . . . I failed to find justification for Stalin. Only in the seventh grade was I able to forgive him such a terrible sin.

My stay at the sanatorium ended in expulsion. A twenty-year-old boy in my class wielded a strong influence over the other pupils. He played around with the nurses and told us all the details. We listened with rapture and wished we were his age. The nurses brought him wine, which he shared with us. Under his influence discipline in the class was disintegrating, to the point where a pupil threw an inkwell at a teacher. I myself was never rowdy, but to my misfortune we were studying the Constitution of the USSR. When I learned that every citizen is entitled to freedom of speech, I began to practice this right. As soon as the teacher had made what I thought was a mistake, I would raise my hand and politely correct him. Seizing upon the teacher's every inaccuracy in his arguments with the rowdy pupils, I systematically contributed to the dissolution of discipline.

A school conference ruled to give me bad marks for "rudeness to the staff" and to issue a public reprimand to the boy who had thrown the inkwell. I was upset by the disproportion in the punishments and began to behave even more rudely. Just then a new head physician was appointed. He was obsessed with quick cures for tuberculosis and embarked on a series of operations that left the afflicted joint immobile. (Several years later a new head physician introduced a diametrically opposite method of treatment: constant movement of the joint.) The question of an operation was put to me. The choice seemed clear: spending several more years of confinement in the sanatorium or becoming a cripple and living in freedom. Many years later I was faced with a similar dilemma: several more years in a psychiatric prison within my country or freedom outside it. The second time I hesitated much longer.

Some months after the operation I was allowed to walk. I hadn't been on my feet for five years and decided to go outside. The sanatorium was under quarantine, and we were not permitted to go out. A nurse caught me on the stairs and took me to the head physician. As luck would have it, we were joined on the way by my teacher, who was going to complain that I was debauching the other children by playing cards with them. The head physician listened to both of them and then told me that I was cured and could go home.

The sanatorium gave me a poor reference: intelligent, but lazy, distrustful, and rude to the staff. Returning to Frunze, I took the reference to a normal school. The principal said that he had had enough of bad pupils and would not admit me. I explained that I had been given such a reference for insisting on freedom of speech. The principal consented to take me if I would make my remarks to teachers in private and avoid disrupting discipline. I agreed with him.

In Frunze in the early 1950's boys and girls could not walk about the streets in the evening. Everyone belonged to a gang. My friends and I organized our own gang with an arsenal of one dagger. We intended to go to the militia and offer our services against the thieves and rowdies. Naturally I was the commissar of our gang.

At the Pioneer Palace I was the monitor of the zoology club. Catching field mice in winter, we saw a hand protruding from a snowdrift. I ran to get the militia. Every station refused to go out: "It isn't our district." Finally militiamen arrived from the city. It was a case of rape and murder. The militia captain who came out with me immediately pointed to a Gypsy encampment nearby. I believed him. Everyone knew that Gypsies were thieves and murderers.

I believed the old wives' tales about the Chechens, Ingush, Kurds, Kabardins, and other small nationalities resettled on the outskirts of Frunze: they had betrayed their motherland to the Germans.[2] Now they were not permitted to live in the cities, and militiamen arrested them on sight. All the children—and the adults, too—believed that these "traitors" were in the habit of murdering Russian and Ukrainian children. My friends and I went into the hills armed with a hunting rifle.

In school we were required to study the Kirghiz language. At first I proudly refused. I despised the Kirghiz teacher and had no use for the language. Then I started to study the language and make fun of the Kirghiz children. I knew only a dozen Kirghiz words, but I could effortlessly answer questions on grammar. For some reason the Kirghiz children found grammar difficult, and I always got better marks than they. No one was deliberately bringing me up to hate the natives, but prejudice was in the air. The Kirghiz and Uzbeks were not yet called "animals," but already half the population was Russian and Ukrainian. (The Ukrainians were dispossessed kulaks who tended to live on the outskirts.[3]) The whites were better educated and had better jobs. They were the bearers of everything progressive and cultured.

This, too, I hold against the regime: inculcating children with chauvinism, anti-Semitism, and KGBism. It took me, a Ukrainian boy, and made me a Russian chauvinist, an oppressor of Chechens,

Kurds, and Kirghizians, a white racist blinded by his mission as a *Kulturträger*. Today, when nationalism raises its head in Kirghizia, all my sympathy is on its side, even when it explodes as hatred of the Russian colonizers. The Ukrainians there are in a particularly sad and difficult position. At a time when their own land is being Russified, Ukrainians are forced to Russify Central Asia.

I had barely become acquainted with the new school when we were shaken by terrible news. Our leader Stalin had died on March 5, 1953. The teachers and pupils wept. I understood the horror of what had happened and wondered how the country would survive in a capitalist encirclement. My torments were heightened by pangs of conscience: everyone was weeping, but I couldn't force a single tear. I realized that my country was the most beautiful in the world and that Stalin had been the wisest leader of all times. But at the same time I knew that I came from the lower class. My mother earned thirty rubles a month as a cook and could not support both my sister and me. When we moved to Odessa, Ada stayed behind in Frunze with Mother's relatives, and I grew up hardly knowing her. In Odessa my mother and I huddled on a bed in a women's dormitory. Sailors and militiamen visited the girls in the evenings and stayed to sleep with them. My mother tried unsuccessfully to drown out unpleasant sounds, the way foreign radio stations are jammed in the Soviet Union. I saw a similar poverty all around me, and some of my schoolmates were even worse off. Unlike them, I could go to my mother in the kitchen and eat the patients' leftovers.

The ideology I was taught in school and the life I knew were in glaring contradiction. I could not bring myself to doubt my books and teachers and had to find another way to resolve the contradiction. The population does not know what standard of living the rulers enjoy, because it is a state secret. But we did encounter a section of the population that lived better than we did: salesclerks (they were paid little but made it up by stealing), teachers, doctors, and health-resort visitors. In Odessa at that time most of these well-to-do people were Jews. It was natural to become an anti-Semite. Blind national and social protest has often led to anti-Semitism. Engels called anti-Semitism the "socialism of fools."

I was an excellent pupil and thought that anyone who did badly in his studies was a loafer. We, the activists in the class, struggled against the loafers in a twofold fashion. At Komsomol meetings [4] I would pull out a special notebook and read the names of pupils who gave others answers, used cribs, or copied from their neighbors. The bad pupils nicknamed me the "gendarme of the school." I was proud of the title. If pupils dared to reproach me to my face, I would speak up about them at Komsomol meetings, arguing that I was right and demanding that they rebut my arguments. They would remain silent, and I would mock their cowardly behavior. The meeting would pass a resolution condemning the cheaters. I also stayed behind after classes to help the backward pupils with their mathematics.

The teachers' praise went to my head. I developed an inordinate pride and ambition, aggravated by the fact that most of the teachers were remarkably stupid: of the teachers I got to know in ten years of school, I feel love and gratitude for only three. I was certain that I knew the subjects better than they did, and I dreamed of accomplishing a revolution in mathematics and philosophy. I set forth my dreams in a diary that the KGB seized in 1972. My foolish adolescent dreams served as a basis for their accusing me of having had a "reformist mania." The country was in the grip of a cult of leaders—strong and brilliant men who were leading us to the radiant heights of Communism. No wonder that my idols were Robespierre, Napoleon, Karmalyuk (a Ukrainian Robin Hood), and Dzerzhinsky (the founder of the Soviet secret police).

My favorite writers in school were Nikolay Ostrovsky, Alexander Fadeyev, and Maxim Gorky.[5] I thought that Gorky's prose poem "Man" was sublime, and I also liked his romantic "Song of the Falcon," "Song of the Stormy Petrel," and "The Legend of Danko." Comrade Stalin had told us that "The Maiden and Death" surpassed Goethe's *Faust*. I didn't read *Faust* and took Stalin at his word but found "The Maiden and Death" boring. It was upsetting to realize that my tastes differed from those of the great leader, and I consoled myself by saying that I would eventually learn to appreciate the profound thoughts in "The Maiden and Death."

I say "thoughts" because we were not taught any other aspect of literature. The "artistic characteristics" of the various writers we discussed in school referred only to forms of expression and were as boring as classifications of syllogisms in logic. Epithets, synonyms, metaphors, and other devices appeared to resemble mathematical concepts but did not contain any problems that had to be solved. Without such problems the classification of "artistic characteristics" seemed meaningless. In literature I looked only for thoughts that had a mathematical clarity and were, in Mayakovsky's phrase, "as simple as a moo." [6]

When I was in the ninth grade, I visited my grandmother in Borzna. I saw her cure sick children again, and all the old problems came back to me. I remembered the theory of the beneficial mother's

10

milk and took to reading books about suggestion and hypnosis and hypnotizing my friends. But suggestion and hypnosis still could not explain how breast-fed infants were cured. During my first year at the university I came across a prerevolutionary book about telepathy. My grandmother's cures began to make sense. I became keen on telepathy, and then yoga.

Reading Diderot led me to conclude: Down with shame in sexual matters! We had to make morality rational by discarding formal proprieties and prejudices. Natural shame was keeping the new morality from becoming rooted in daily life. My moral quest was dictated both by a desire to mathematicize morality and by a protest against the hypocrisy of adults.

At the end of the ninth grade one of my classmates gave birth to a baby. We learned about this at the start of the following school year. All her friends stopped seeing her and angrily condemned her "misdemeanor." I proposed that we summon a Komsomol meeting. The teacher is usually present at such meetings, but I told our teacher that his presence would only hinder an honest discussion. I generally behaved with considerable impudence toward the teachers, but they forgave me because I was the best pupil.

At the meeting I spoke up against the behavior of the offender's friends. Sex, I said, is a private matter; the girl had behaved foolishly, of course, but most of the girls in our class had avoided her fate only by luck, since they were quite free with sailors. The meeting unanimously adopted a resolution to help the young mother.

I had a great deal of energy, not all of which was absorbed by studies, books, and Komsomol activities. By now I had thoroughly assimilated the Leninist axiom that a Communist must identify the "main link" in society and focus his attention on it. Odessa is a border city, and espionage seemed to pose a serious threat. It was natural to arrive at the conclusion that a prime mission was to help catch spies. "Brigades of Assistance to Border Guards," made up of young people, were already in existence. They were instructed in the use of firearms, trained to catch spies, and sent out to patrol the border at night. It was all a bit boring, but I joined because the work corresponded to my views on my task in life.

My involvement in the brigade ended sadly. One night in November 1955 we were summoned to the post and told that a spy was expected to land. We were distributed among the border guards within eyeshot of one another and ordered to wait. Several hours later three figures appeared. "Stop! Who goes there?" I shouted. Two border guards had abandoned their posts and were leading their thoroughly drunk commander. My first reaction was to report the commander. My second was to doubt the expediency of our brigade.

Some months later a warrant officer in the navy visited my family. He mentioned that Lenin had been a very good man, but Stalin had been bad. I blew up and threatened to report him to the authorities if he went on with such rot. Soon afterward I requested, by letter, admission to the KGB school. My aim was simple. The "main link" was war. My tuberculosis would keep me from military service, but I could hunt spies.

Summoned to the KGB, I explained in great detail that I was an exemplary pupil and an active Komsomol member, and that I wanted to become an investigator. I was told that investigators could be hired only after they had completed military service, and tuberculosis ruled this out. I insisted that I was ready to do any sort of work if only I could join the KGB. My mathematical abilities qualified me as a code expert, or I could serve as a translator since I had A's in German. Again I was turned down, because of my tuberculosis. With hindsight I understand that the KGB had no use for me. It was 1956, and they were all frantically wondering how to escape going to jail for their crimes. They might have suggested that I become an informer for them. I think I should have agreed with satisfaction.

The moment that was central in my intellectual development occurred in that same year. A close friend came up to me after classes one day. The daughter of a border-guard officer, she was my "comrade in arms" in various Komsomol projects. She had an important secret to tell me: Khrushchev had made a speech at the Twentieth Party Congress, denouncing Stalin for his crimes.[7] My friend told me less than a tenth of what Khrushchev had said, but even this was enough to shake the foundations of my ideology—faith in Comrade Stalin's brilliance and endless kindness toward workers.

I walked the streets till evening in extreme agitation, then called on a friend and told him what I had heard. I could tell him everything, I felt, because he, too, had high ideals. We wandered about all night, discussing the revelations from every possible angle and concluding "they're all scoundrels." If our leaders knew what Stalin had done but remained silent, they were cowards and not Communists. We also decided that if Stalin was a blackguard, his wrongdoings should be corrected without public discussion. Later I met many adult imbeciles who took the same position.

In the tenth grade I took part in a mathematics competition. The smartest and best-educated boys were Jews. I became friendly with them, and a close relationship with one boy made the first breach in my anti-Semitism. I started to protest when others displayed anti-Semitic attitudes. When I was submitting my application for the university, I overheard two clerks. "Ukrainian? You can tell by her mug that she's Jewish. She won't hide from us. We'll flunk her in the entrance exams!" These words had a profound effect on me. Anti-Semites were running the country. As a private citizen I allowed myself to be anti-Semitic, but the rulers were Communists and had no such right.

2

WHORES AND
HORSEMEN

University studies came easily to me, and I had a good deal of free time after lectures. Komsomol work at the university was limited to campaigns for progress in studies and excursions to the theater or movies. Several of us students read that a mathematics study group had been set up at Moscow University, and we requested of our professors that a similar group be set up at our university. Permission was granted, but the group was led by a stupid woman who gave us boring assignments from textbooks, and it soon disintegrated.

My attitude toward the Komsomol at this time was not favorable. I protested against the demagoguery, the blind optimism, and the fact that membership meant little more than paying dues. But a friend convinced me that instead of criticizing the Komsomol we should try to reform it. He saw such an opportunity in the "Light Cavalry." Made up of students and young workers, the Cavalry was assigned to catch prostitutes, thieves, and currency speculators. It was particularly persistent in hunting *stilyaga*s, young men with long hair, loud shirts, tight trousers, and thick-soled shoes. When they stopped a *stilyaga* on the street, the cavalrymen would appeal to his conscience. If this didn't work, his hair would be cut and his trousers slit. I despised the *stilyaga*s for their vacuity but objected to the reprisals against them. In this respect I succeeded: the Cavalry stopped hunting them.

When we caught a profiteer, we would seize his merchandise, lock it in a safe, and hand him over to the militia. We had no right to confiscate merchandise, but the militia encouraged us to do so. If the profiteer tried to conceal the evidence, we would take him to our headquarters, an old bomb shelter, for a beating. Those of us with weak nerves would leave the room, the air-raid siren would be turned on, and the beating would begin. We had no right to beat anyone,

14

either, but the militia advised us to do so when we needed to obtain evidence. Several of us students objected to the beatings, but the majority argued quite logically that we were decadent intellectuals and that these scoundrels needed good thrashings. We were made to feel ashamed of our tender sensibilities.

I was placed in charge of the retail-trade section. We'd go into a restaurant and order food and drinks. Then we'd tell the waiter to weigh the portions he had served. Usually they would be considerably below the norm. We would fill out a report. The manager or the head cook would call us into another room and offer us vodka, fancy food, or even his own watch. As high-minded Komsomol members, we would report the bribe. The manager would be fired.

Most of our work involved profiteers. I suggested that we put up in our headquarters a sign with Lenin's saying "The profiteer is the enemy of the people." The general belief in the magical power of words was so strong that I assumed most profiteers would realize how low they had fallen and would immediately reform simply from reading Lenin.

After the Moscow Youth Festival in 1957 many Negroes, Arabs, and other foreigners appeared in Odessa. Our Cavalry brigade was thrown into the campaign against prostitution, which had increased sharply. We'd walk around the parks looking for couples in the bushes. It was very embarrassing, but what could we do? That was our job. One girl whom we caught we took to the Komsomol district headquarters. The district secretary read her a crushing speech about the honor of Soviet girls, emphasizing that she was undermining the country's reputation. The girl stubbornly insisted that her sexual organs belonged only to her, and that her use of them was none of the Komsomol's business. (She expressed this much more crudely, of course.) But as she was threatened with prison, she caved in and pleaded guilty.

In our group was a working-class boy who was very good at appealing to the conscience of offenders. Once we had caught a girl student as she was amusing herself in the park with a soldier. Our orator took her aside to lecture her about pride and honor. We listened through the door, splitting our sides with laughter because of his trite and bookish phrases, yet the girl was soon in tears. We then warned her that if we caught her again, she would be reported to her school and expelled; she swore that she was cured of such behavior.

One of my friends caught three men red-handed stealing carloads of construction materials and took two of them to a militia station, demanding an immediate report. The militia promised to send investigators to the construction site, but it took them a month to get there. They found no evidence of theft, of course.

Our work at headquarters intensified when my friend became the secretary there, until one day our chief offered her a pair of imported shoes confiscated from a profiteer and hinted that he would supply her with even costlier items. Naturally she refused the bribe. The investigation we started revealed that the chief and his assistant were reselling confiscated goods and, afraid that my friend would find out about this, tried to conciliate her with gifts.

When exam time came, we stopped going to headquarters. Then, unexpectedly, we learned that the chief and his assistant had dragged a prostitute into headquarters and raped her. To keep the story from spreading, the district committee disbanded our unit without even calling a meeting of the members. Neither rapist was brought to account. My belief that the abominations in our society were controllable was dealt a stiff blow.

Shortly before the meeting of the Twelfth Congress of the Komsomol, several Komsomol members in the mathematics department and I wrote a letter to the Congress, describing the formalism of Komsomol activities and the way in which most members were discrediting the organization in their private lives. Our main proposal was to purge the Komsomol of petit-bourgeois good-for-nothings and raise admission standards. We also proposed various foolish projects for making Komsomol work more exciting, including the collection of funds to build a spaceship.

We anxiously awaited a reply. We were told that our letter was being discussed by the Central Committee and would be brought up at the Congress. But the Congress didn't mention the issues we had raised even in passing. Instead it abounded in drum rolls and fanfares about the great accomplishments of the Komsomol in opening up the virgin lands in the East.[1] We knew from friends who had gone to those virgin lands that most of the press reports about the campaign were sheer demagoguery.

When our teacher of party history proposed a discussion of the resolutions of the Congress, I immediately denounced it as a "congress of good-for-nothings." The teacher took me aside and warned me of the trouble I could get into for such talk, to which I replied proudly that the Stalinist period was past, and now everyone had the right to speak his mind. The teacher merely shrugged his shoulders.

The Twentieth Congress of the Communist Party and the Hungarian Revolution in 1956 instigated a wave of free thinking at all the larger universities. Clandestine or semiclandestine organizations were founded in Moscow, Leningrad, and Kiev. But we at Odessa University judged the events in Hungary according to what we read in the newspapers. The free thinking among our students manifested itself in the form of a wall newspaper called *Thought*, with the motto "*Cogito ergo sum.*" The newspaper discussed jazz and poetry. Two issues appeared. I wrote an article for the third, but rumors reached us that the party members in the department had condemned the newspaper for its bourgeois ideology. One of the arguments against it was its motto. "Why not 'Workers of the world unite'?" the party members asked. I heatedly challenged the secretary of the departmental Komsomol bureau about the banning of *Thought*. He countered that the editors were *stilyagas* connected with profiteers. The answer satisfied me. In the senior classes meetings were held at which the editors were expelled from the Komsomol and the university.

In my third year at the university I was elected secretary of my class's Komsomol group. I was able to achieve little at this post, but I did make many interesting friends, including my former logic teacher, Yakiv Sikorsky, who had given up teaching and joined the Writers' Union.[2] His writing was undistinguished, and his views were a mixture of Ukrainian nationalism and official demagoguery. His nationalism, the first I had encountered, shocked me, although I now realize that some of his points were justified; the official demagoguery seemed even more repulsive. Yet Sikorsky was an intelligent man, and I enjoyed arguing with him. In one such discussion I expressed doubt about Lenin's definition of matter in *Materialism and Empiriocriticism* [3] and Engels's definition of life. I also told Sikorsky about a friend who was knowledgeable in various idealistic philosophies.

A month later I was summoned to the personnel office of the university. The director of the office—these are usually former KGB men, but I didn't know it then—greeted me warmly and proceeded to interrogate me about my plans for the future. Not knowing what he wanted, I replied curtly. Finally I asked point-blank why he had summoned me. All my teachers considered me to be a remarkable student, he explained, and he had wanted to meet me. This was obviously not true, and I pricked up my ears.

The director began to discuss my views. I replied cautiously, although I saw no danger for myself. Stalinism, I was convinced, had irrevocably receded into the past. Then he asked whether I had any friends who were idealist philosophers. At once everything became clear. Sikorsky, the only person who knew about my friend, had denounced me. I sighed with relief. Sikorsky didn't know my friend's name. Now I understood what my tactic should be—playing the part

17

of a vain prattler. I proceeded to expound everything I had read
about Marxism. The director pretended that he was captivated by
my erudition but kept throwing in leading questions to steer me to
what interested him. Then he brought up the question of friends
again. I explained that I was so busy with my studies that I didn't
have time for friends.

"But there must be people you discuss philosophy with. Some of
them are no doubt intelligent. I should like to meet them."

"Very well. I have a writer friend whose name is Sikorsky. I often
see him to discuss philosophy."

The director asked for Sikorsky's address and then inquired what
sort of problems we discussed.

"Whether there's life on Mars," I replied. "Sikorsky argues that
there isn't, and I argue that there is." I went on to explain why my
position was Marxist. The director agreed with me. Now I think that
I behaved badly then, since I couldn't be certain that Sikorsky had
informed on me.

The director asked whether I had tried to meet any famous people.
I decided to have some fun at his expense and told him about my
visit to Gleb Krzhizhanovsky,[4] a former associate of Lenin's who had
spoken out against Stalin; I had wanted to know how a Leninist explains Stalinism. When I arrived at Krzhizhanovsky's, the door was
opened by an old woman who said, "I am their servant. Gleb Maksimilianovich is severely ill and is being treated at the Kremlin clinic."
I was so shocked to discover that a Leninist had a servant that I lost
all interest in meeting him.

I didn't mention to the director that Krzhizhanovsky had been a
friend of Lenin's. The director's eyes shone with satisfaction. He
asked me for the name and address. When he had written everything
down, I mentioned innocently that Krzhizhanovsky was an Old Bolshevik. The director's jaw dropped for a second. He concluded that I
was a harmless fool and rushed to end the interview. We stood at the
door, heartily shaking hands. My first interrogation had taken place.
In 1964 I tried to repeat the tactic of playing a harmless prattler, but
this time the interrogators were more intelligent, and I was not
successful.

My other experience with Sikorsky was also amusing. I read a new
novel of his in which he related how a simple Soviet boy had become
a theology student and was morally corrupted. To my great surprise,
I recognized myself in the student. Many of his ideas were ones I had
expounded to Sikorsky. I was outraged to see that he had combined
my words with contradictory ones. Sikorsky's daughter, whom I knew

from the university, confirmed that her father was convinced that I would turn to religion and come to a bad end. (I had just become interested in the meaning of life, which was officially regarded as a purely religious problem.)

I attended a lecture by priests who had renounced religion. They talked about their studies at the seminary and their service as priests. The highlight of the lecture was an account of the sexual escapades of Biblical saints and present-day priests. Although I considered myself an atheist, I was shocked by the scabrous stories. The response of the women in the audience was particularly vile. They giggled lasciviously at all the piquant moments.

After the lecture I approached Sikorsky to ask about his novel, but I was interrupted by a young girl who announced that she had recognized herself in the theology student. Citing several quotations of her words in the novel, she angrily listed all the ideas she had never espoused. I broke into laughter and explained to her where these ideas had come from. Sikorsky tried to justify himself by talking about the mysteries of the creative process and the "synthetic image" of the theology student. The girl and I told him that mixing up contradictory ideas is a crude way of discrediting an opponent. Sikorsky prophesied a dismal future for us. I wonder what has since happened to that girl.

3

COUNTRY SCHOOLTEACHERS

Upon completing my third year at the university I began to consider an occupation. The notion I had had in the tenth grade of finding the main link remained unchanged. To this I added the idea that everyone should do an honest job in his own place. What link was most important? The serious backwardness of agriculture was being discussed at length at the time. I had seen with my own eyes the beggarly lives of the collective farmers. The school situation was also very bad. Scant wages and the lack of creative opportunities keep young people away from teaching. In the cities at least some of the teachers are energetic and intelligent, but only passive and stupid ones go to teach in the villages. I had energy and mathematical abilities and made my decision quickly: I would teach in a village school and try to improve the lot of the peasants. I went to the provincial Department of Education and asked for an assignment to a village school. The director looked at me as if I were mad but drew up the papers.

The tiny village was sixty kilometers from Odessa. Its school had pupils from neighboring villages as well and was called a "growing school" because it had started with four grades, now had six, and later was to have eight. My subjects were arithmetic, geometry, and physics in the fifth and sixth grades. My salary was fifty rubles a month, half of which I gave to the woman I boarded with. My bed was paid for by the collective farm.

I was immediately struck by the poverty of the villagers. A third of them had tuberculosis. Some peasants had their own cows but had to give all the milk to the collective farm. My landlady had a daughter of six who almost never drank milk. Living standards, I must say, improved greatly after 1964: the peasants acquired television sets and in some cases even cars. This is probably the only accomplishment of the Khrushchev era.

The principal of the school often arrived drunk. My pupils and I were husking corn one day when we saw him fall off his bicycle. "Bardyuh is drunk again," the pupils commented matter-of-factly. He frequently interfered in the teaching and demanded that even the worst pupils be given good marks. My colleagues were boring. The men talked about drinking, and the women discussed clothes and the plots of land assigned to them by the collective farm. Only Alla Mikhaylovna, the Russian and German teacher, provided relief. She had graduated from a teachers' college and, like me, was in her first year of teaching. We spent many evenings together, talking about literature, our pupils, and the primitive conditions at the school.

In the autumn classes were disrupted when the pupils had to help gather the harvest. Discipline was poor, and the classrooms were filled with commotion. Some pupils came to school drunk, and few of them responded to the teachers' admonishments. "I'll break your other leg!" one pupil in the fifth grade threatened when I made a remark to him. I myself was partly responsible for the lack of discipline. Unable to find the proper balance between severity and kindness, I believed that I should only influence the children's minds and assist their intellectual development. They liked me for my jokes but did not obey me.

Each class had some backward children. In the fifth grade there was a girl of eighteen, in the sixth a boy and girl of nineteen. (I was twenty.) The latter two had missed several years of school because of tuberculosis; the girl in the fifth grade was simply lazy and stupid. One day, when the class was working on a test, she stood up and handed in a blank sheet of paper. "I can't understand this crap!" she announced to me. I turned red and pretended to be studying the roll book. The class fell silent and waited for my response. Finally I asked the girl to leave the room. She refused. I attempted to push her out. She smiled insolently and tried to touch me with her breasts.

The school had no scientific equipment, and the principal paid no heed to my requests to buy any. At one lesson I had to explain connecting vessels. I demonstrated them with my hands and then pointed to a sixteen-year-old boy who often came to school drunk. He goes into his father's cellar, I explained, inserts a hose into a barrel of wine, and drinks. The boy and the barrel are connecting vessels. My pupils were delighted with such physics. My colleagues comforted me after the lesson. "You see, you can get along perfectly well without scientific apparatuses."

At the end of the first quarter I gave five D's in the fifth grade. The Russian teacher gave ten. The tests in Russian were terrible, and some pupils made seventy mistakes or more. Alla Mikhaylovna and I spoke to our colleagues about the need for a change, but of the nine teachers only four supported us. We then wrote letters to the district party committee and the Department of Education, explaining how matters stood at the school. When the principal heard about this, he threatened that we would suffer for them, but that it wasn't too late to retract them. My landlady woke me up one morning. "Officials from town came to see Bardyuh yesterday and were up the whole night drinking wine." It was clear that we had lost.

The inspectors came to our classes, but not the other teachers', and ordered us to give tests. In the evening Alla Mikhaylovna and I sat down to grade them. When a paper has seventy or eighty mistakes, one person cannot spot all of them. She would read a paper and pass it to me, and then I to her. Despite this triple check we missed some mistakes, for which she was blamed. The next day a teachers' conference was called. Alla Mikhaylovna and I were isolated. All the others either remained neutral or spoke out against us. We were accused of causing trouble and, more significantly, not following standard methods. In my case the charge had a basis to it. I hadn't studied teaching methods at the university, and many of the methods suggested by the principal had struck me as ridiculous. But in Alla Mikhaylovna's case the charge was groundless. She had always received high marks in her practice teaching at college. In the end the conference issued a resolution to enter reprimands into our records, as well as the principal's. Later we learned that his reprimand was only oral.

Alla Mikhaylovna argued that we should leave the school. I replied that we did not have a moral right to abandon our pupils, but she had come to hate the pupils almost as much as the teachers. She was pregnant and found it difficult to handle the disturbances in the classroom. When I tried to get the children to read literature, she ridiculed my attempts. In the end she left. When I visited her later in Odessa, she looked terrible. Her child had been stillborn, apparently because of nervous strain, and she became thoroughly misanthropic. Her experience taught me a lesson: we can't put the blame for social conditions on individuals. When I was sent to the *psikhushka*, I thought of her and told myself not to lose my temper.

After Alla Mikhaylovna departed, her classes were reassigned to the remaining teachers. The principal offered the physical-education class to me, but I explained that I had been exempted from physical education at school. Then he offered military preparation, singing, and drawing, on the assumption that I would be more tractable if I had a bigger salary. I turned down these subjects, too. Finally I was offered the German class. I knew very little German, but the other teachers knew even less, so I agreed to take it. Suddenly the botany teacher stormed into the faculty room and accused me of taking away her classes. The principal made a Solomonic decision: she would have three German classes in the sixth grade, and I would have two classes in the fifth.

I had given only a few German lessons when the botany teacher suggested that we trade places and asked me to help her prepare her first lesson in the fifth grade. I agreed and went to see her at home. She placed a bottle of wine on the table, and we set about preparing the lesson. I discovered that she had studied German at school and English at college and as a result knew neither. I choked with laughter when I saw that she knew only the vowels *a*, *e*, *i*, and *o* in the German alphabet. She wrote out the German words in Russian letters and added translations from a dictionary. Liking jokes, I asked her to let me attend her class.

In the classroom I watched as she began to read the text, making one mistake after another, and the pupils corrected her. Soon the entire class was badgering her at every opportunity. The boy beside me nudged me with his elbow. "She doesn't know anything!" I gave him a stern look but was unable to answer. After such a fiasco I expected that the teacher would return the German class to me. Instead she asked during recess, "Well, how was it?" I was dumfounded by her imperturbable stupidity and barely managed to say, "It was all right for a first time, only it's a bit awkward to have pupils correct their teacher."

"What am I to do?" she asked.

I hesitated for a moment. "Tell them that you're deliberately making mistakes to test their knowledge."

The next day the fifth-graders came up to me at recess and announced in a chorus how sly their teacher was and how she tried to trick them by making mistakes.

After Alla Mikhaylovna left, the situation became completely unbearable. Classes took up only two or three hours a day, and my preparations required no more than half an hour. Unable to afford books on my salary, I had little to read, and there was no one to talk to until two young specialists, an agronomist and a veterinarian, arrived at the collective farm. They would meet after work, bone weary, to discuss grandiose plans for transforming the farm. I envied their fatigue as well as their enthusiasm. Vasiliy Aksyonov had just published a novella, *Colleagues,* that dealt with young technicians who heroically overcame various obstacles.[1] My new friends cited the novella and put me to shame for losing heart.

I also became friendly with a tenth-grade pupil who took an interest in many things. He didn't know very much, but he loved to listen and even to argue with me. I talked to him about mathematics, philosophy, telepathy, and literature and taught him games. He and all his family had pulmonary tuberculosis. His girl friend was a sixth-grade pupil of mine. She was an intelligent girl of nineteen who hadn't been able to attend school regularly because of tuberculosis. We would gather at her house in the evening to play games and tell stories.

I advised the girl to cram her seventh-grade subjects and pass the exams so that she could enter the technical school the following year. I tutored her in algebra, geometry, and Russian. At first she made twenty or thirty mistakes in each dictation, but later these were reduced to two or three. She passed all her exams with good marks.

At the end of the school year the teacher with whom I had had the row about German classes gave her pupils a final exam that was to be sent to the district Department of Education. The principal apparently suspected what the results would be and asked me to help her mark the papers. I was astounded to discover that every longer word had two or three mistakes in it and even the best pupils had made many mistakes, a sure sign that the mistakes were the teacher's. All the nouns, for example, began with small letters, although German uses capitals. When I explained this to the principal, he ordered a repetition of the test. I suspect that this time the teacher wrote the answers on the blackboard and let the pupils copy them.

How could I have agreed to such cheating when I had begun my career by objecting to overly high marks? A whole year had passed, and I had been able to observe the principal and the school. I concluded that the principal was not entirely at fault. We had demanded, for example, that two older boys be removed from the fifth grade because they were corrupting their classmates. But the class would have been left with only nine pupils and would have had to be closed. This might have led to the closing of the entire school. The children would have had to attend a school ten kilometers away, as the pupils in the seventh to tenth grades already did. The children had to walk because the collective farm had refused to detail a vehicle for their transportation, and many of them smoked and brawled on the way or played hooky. This would have a very bad effect on the youngsters in the first through sixth grades. If marks were given fairly, to cite another example, all the teachers would be dismissed because of the pupils' poor progress. New teachers would arrive, but they would be just as poor, and nothing would change.

The principal himself was bored to death by his job and had no illusions about making improvements. His drinking was an attempt to escape from a sad and pointless life. No, it was not the principal or the teachers who had to be replaced, but the entire system of education, which was based on demagoguery, deception, and concern for high marks. The educational system could not be improved without a change in society, and I did not see anyone trying to change society. I had also realized how limited my own education was, how narrow my conception of art and philosophy. Fully aware that this action could be called escapism, I decided to go back to the university. A year later my friends the agronomist and veterinarian also fled from what Marx called "the idiocy of rural life."

4

IN THE CRYSTAL PALACE

My career as a teacher over, I got married, moved to Kiev, and entered the fourth year of the mathematics program at Kiev University. The teaching was on a higher level than in Odessa. The lecturer in my course on dialectical materialism was intelligent and did not teach straight from the book, and there were heated discussions at the philosophy seminars. In the course on the political economy of capitalism, the early chapters of Marx's *Capital* proved to be very interesting, but then I got bored, because the lecturer was stupid and I didn't have the patience to work through the book on my own. At the political-economy seminars, several of us continually expressed discontent by posing the lecturer tricky questions and drawing parallels between capitalism and the socialism in which we lived.

Eager to study telepathy and yoga, I went to Moscow for a month and got a pass to the Lenin Library, where I discovered vast riches in the fields that interested me. I soon had my fill of mysticism. The human imagination is limited, and the lack of realistic frames of reference in mystical writings makes them groundless. Since then I have been interested only in the artistic aspects of mystical literature. Most of the books on telepathy and clairvoyance also proved to be unscientific, but yoga did teach me about the unconscious (which was never discussed in Soviet Pavlovian psychology), gave me insights into the psychology of daily life, and revealed a subtle analysis of man's relations with himself, others, and God. The notion that the mind must be guided and developed seemed particularly important to me. I immediately saw a connection with the Marxist idea that a society must be created in which progress will be determined by human consciousness and not by the mechanical laws of political economy.

The practical sides of yoga—hatha-yoga, physical exercise, and

26

yoga medicine—were not of interest to me. I did practice raja-yoga concentration for two weeks but noticed at a lecture that I had been concentrating on one thought so intensely that I had lost all ties with reality. Realizing that I could damage my mind without an experienced guide, I backed off in fear. The yoga thesis that the body is the temple of the soul and must be carefully tended is opposed to the traditional Christian disregard and even contempt for the body. Although by nature I am closer to Christianity in this respect, the yoga attitude toward the body has always seemed more scientific to me.

My interest in yoga and science fiction—Ray Bradbury, Stanisław Lem, and Arkadiy and Boris Strugatsky [1]—led to a friendship with an engineer. He was keen on abstract art, though I found it incomprehensible no matter how he explained it to me. But I had learned by then to respect the tastes and interests of others and did develop a passion for Mikhail Vrubel, Nicholas Roerich, Mikalojus Čiurlionis,[2] and the late Van Gogh. I had finally appreciated that intuitive apprehension precedes thought and that attempts to comprehend beauty only with the intellect are doomed to failure.

My interest in paranormal phenomena grew as I read more widely in the literature on telepathy. Several students and I proposed to the psychology department of the university to set up a telepathy study group. A psychology lecturer promised to help us, saying, "All right, an interest in telepathy is better than some of the other interests students have." To attract specialists from various fields to the group, I gave lectures on telepathy at several scientific institutes. The first articles on telepathy were appearing in the Soviet press, and I learned that Bernard Kazhinsky, who had worked on telepathic experiments in the 1920's and 1930's, was living in Moscow.[3] I got in touch with Kazhinsky and went to see him. He received me warmly, because he thought of me as one of the young people who would resume the prewar research on telepathy.

Four of us sat around the table at his house—Kazhinsky, his wife, a young medical student named Eduard Naumov, and I.[4] In a whispered aside Naumov suggested that I help him in a telepathic experiment by nudging him with my foot. Kazhinsky tried to figure out the trick, but we managed to deceive him, and he seriously believed that he had performed telepathy. My interest in Kazhinsky vanished, and I drew a conclusion that I later always applied to parapsychology: an investigator performing an experiment must set it up in such a way as to rule out deception.

I also went to Leningrad, to see the parapsychologist Leonid Vasilyev, who told me about the interesting experiments he had conducted before the war and the devastation wreaked by Stalin in Soviet parapsychology.[5] I asked him about the telepathic experiments on the American submarine *Nautilus,* which had been mentioned in the Soviet press.[6] The reports had been fabricated by Western reporters, Vasilyev explained, but he thought it expedient to cite them. The authorities were sure to set up their own telepathic laboratories if they learned that the American military had become involved in telepathy. Several secret laboratories were in fact established.

Toward the end of 1961 Milan Ryzl, a Czechoslovak parapsychologist, wrote to me that he was coming to Kiev for three days and wanted to give a lecture and exchange views on parapsychology.[7] The secretary of the Komsomol office in my class, to whom I mentioned this, became quite agitated and referred me to the party organizer in the department. The party organizer was just as flustered and called party headquarters. The people there didn't know what to do, either, and called the KGB. The latter knew precisely what to do.

I was summoned to the dean's office to meet Yuriy Nikiforov, an officer in the KGB. He questioned me about my correspondence with Ryzl and then explained that although Czechoslovakia is a socialist country, Ryzl was a foreigner and could be an "unknown quantity." He asked me to phone him every day while Ryzl was in Kiev to report where we were and what Ryzl said, and not to leave Ryzl's side even for a moment. I had no intention of reporting my conversations with Ryzl, but I did agree to call Nikiforov. My moral principles were still "socialist" then.

Ryzl's first words to me were "I'm here for only three days and want us to spend all this time together." I laughed to myself. The KGB, Ryzl, and I had the identical wish. Ryzl proved to be a very likable person who was passionately enthusiastic about parapsychology and cared nothing for politics. I tried to start up political discussions with him, but he turned a deaf ear. The three days flew by as we wandered around Kiev, talking about parapsychology and admiring the architecture of the city.

I noticed by chance that we kept running into one man. When I was seeing Ryzl off at the station, I saw the man again. This was my first experience with a secret agent. I found it exciting, as if I were in a detective story. The day after Ryzl left, Nikiforov listened to my description of him—a parapsychologist who talks only about his field —and asked whether I had noticed anything suspicious about him. I felt an urge to make fun of this dolt and told him that a man had constantly followed us; I suspected that he was a British or an American spy. Nikiforov replied that I had probably imagined this and suggested that I write a memorandum on parapsychology for the KGB. I agreed. Finally Nikiforov asked whether I knew a certain student. I guessed that he was trying to enlist me as an informer and firmly replied that I did not. He asked about another student. I gave the same answer. He realized my position and ended the conversation.

In the memorandum I tried to explain the present state of knowledge in parapsychology and gave a negative opinion of clairvoyance and telekinesis. I placed particular emphasis on the possible military applications of telepathy. I had realized by then that I was living in a bad society but believed that imperialist countries might go to war against us and therefore everything had to be done to increase Soviet military strength. Now I find it very pleasant to think that my ideas about the military applications of telepathy were impractical. In "Report from the Beria Reserve" Valentyn Moroz writes about a KGB captain who wished he could read the minds of political prisoners.[8] Telepathy, thank God, will be of no use here.

I continued to correspond with Ryzl for several years. He ran a parapsychological laboratory in Prague and won the McDougall Award of the Parapsychology Association at Duke University for developing a method of training telepathic abilities. But the government limited his funds and interfered with his research. In 1966 Moscow parapsychologists told me that Ryzl had fled to the United States; apparently he wanted to devote himself completely to his work. At Christmas I received a card from him, but I had become involved in *samizdat* by then and did not want to attract the attention of the police by replying. Nor did I reply to letters from American and Indian parapsychologists. If these letters had come after 1968, I would have replied to them, because by then I had begun to speak out openly.

In my fifth year at the university I studied historical materialism and the political economy of socialism. The latter struck me as being thoroughly unscientific. There were no profound postulates, no statistics, no logically justified laws. At the seminars we expressed our discontent even more openly than in the previous year. We were joined in this by the nephew of Nikolay Bulganin, who told us about the life the party leaders enjoyed.[9] He had once asked his uncle why he needed such luxurious apartments and villas. The luxury sickened him, his uncle replied, but he had to show foreign visitors that we are civilized and know how to live.

We studied Lenin's *The State and Revolution*.[10] Students are usually told to make abstracts of a chapter. What student reads more than he is assigned? In earlier years I had read Lenin without pleasure. His constant repetitions, digressions, party squabbles, and attention to trivialities had irritated me. But in my fourth and fifth years I came to love Lenin's style. The persistent repetition of an idea is a way of examining it from all sides and developing it dialectically. The Ukrainian critic Yevhen Sverstyuk has compared Lenin's method of presenting his thought to a spiral that bores into the reader's mind.[11] In this way Lenin managed to convey very complicated ideas to the masses. Stalin—and Mao Tse-tung even more—replaced this method with simple syllogisms which are repeated like hypnotic formulas.

Marx and Lenin show the profound connection between a thought and the form in which it is presented. When I read Marx's *Economic and Philosophic Manuscripts of 1844*, I was struck by his artistic profundity.[12] His style is radically different from the allegorical style of Christ or of Nietzsche, who is also a remarkably profound artist. Marx's dialectical style has a flexibility which reflects the dialectical flexibility of thought, which in turn reflects the dialectics of nature and society. The formula "Religion is the opium of the people," for example, is taken in Soviet atheistic propaganda to refer only to the narcotic, stupefying function of religion. This is certainly a valid interpretation. Tolstoy came to a similar conclusion about church religion: he spoke of chloroform. But opium is also an anesthetic. Marx developed his thought and said that religion is the "heart of a heartless world," but this idea has never been studied in Soviet ideology.

After I had read *The State and Revolution* several times, I was most impressed by Lenin's demand that government officials be paid salaries no higher than the average wages of a worker. At that time I did not understand this demand's political significance for socialist states, although Lenin explains it quite clearly, but the demand was in such sharp contradiction to Soviet practice that I continually raised the question at our seminars on political economy. The lecturer always avoided the subject, and his only reply was that I should not take all of Lenin's ideas as absolutely true.

The course on historical materialism was even more primitive than the course on the political economy of socialism, and I attended only a few lectures and seminars. One day the lecturer bumped into me in the hall and asked why I wasn't attending his classes. Historical materialism was such an important subject that I couldn't bear to see it profaned, I replied. He gave me an unsatisfactory mark on the exam. I had answered all the obligatory and optional questions but

30

stumbled over a question about the people's democracies. I had read the theses of a conference of workers' and Communist parties on this subject but could not remember the definition of a people's democracy and so answered—entirely correctly, I learned later—on the basis of the name. When I asked the lecturer why he had given me the low mark, he replied, "You should have attended the lectures and seminars."

I had to redo the exam. The questions were the same. I answered them as before and received a good mark. Nevertheless, I lost my scholarship. This was a severe blow, because my wife, Tanya, had a salary of only sixty rubles a month, of which half went to pay for the room we rented in a private home. In this manner I learned how important matter is for a true understanding of the spirit of Marxism.

In my last year the question of a degree thesis came up. Mathematicians I knew at the Institute of Physiology suggested that I write about mathematical methods in diagnosing mental illness. The assistant director of the laboratory of mathematical modeling proposed that I develop a mathematical model of concept formation. He and I would then build a cybernetic machine capable of forming concepts and destroy various links in the machine to see how mistakes in concepts occurred. This would be a model of mentally disturbed concept formation. By comparing machine diseases with human ones we could discover the mechanism of mental illness. At that time I had read very little about cybernetics, but I was struck by this fantastic scheme. Constructing an adequate model of concept formation would require years of work by an entire institute.

Yet the subject interested me, and three of us mathematicians went to the Pavlov Psychiatric Hospital to see for ourselves how mental illness is diagnosed. Professor Frumkin, an honest and intelligent man, invited us to attend a meeting of the panel that issued diagnoses.

First we were acquainted with the case history of a woman gynecologist who had worked at the Pavlov for many years. Her patients had begun to complain about her lewd sexual proposals a year or so before. The complaints were dismissed as ravings, but when they increased the administration looked into them and found a sad picture. Besides her sexual pathology, the woman suffered from a persecution complex. She claimed that her neighbors were spies who had been assigned by the British imperialists to slip blue bugs with long tails into her apartment.

Then the patient was brought in. Her face was emaciated, and she appeared frightened and confused. The doctors asked her to explain why she was in the hospital. She replied with a pitiful smile that she had worked at the hospital until her health deteriorated and her colleagues decided that she needed a rest. Even we mathematicians could see that she was avoiding the question and concealing the unpleasant fact that she was mentally ill. When a doctor asked why she was not in an ordinary hospital, she replied that getting into one was difficult and her colleagues had been good enough to admit her to the Pavlov. The doctor then asked the woman to tell us about her neighbors. She gave a brief but warm description. We exchanged glances. Only when I myself was sent to a psychiatric prison did I understand that patients often intuitively sense what should not be mentioned to doctors to avoid giving them evidence for a diagnosis.

Frumkin asked the patient to explain a proverb, "not to see the forest for the trees." She replied without hesitation that if you stand too close to a tree it will block your view of other trees. Later I learned that this explanation was evidence of "concrete thinking," but even then it struck me as an obvious symptom of illness. The next question to her was to solve a riddle, "a coal bag, but white." We exchanged glances again—none of us understood the riddle. The patient replied that she didn't know. Afterward we asked Frumkin about the riddle. It refers to a bag of flour, he explained. One of us whispered a suspicion that psychiatrists themselves are somewhat abnormal. I often remembered this when I was at the *psikhushka*.

The patient was asked to subtract thirteen from eighty-one. She gave the correct answer before we could do the subtraction in our heads. Then she had to subtract thirteen from the result. Again she gave the correct answer more quickly than we mathematicians could arrive at it. The third time she refused to answer because she was fed up.

The woman was led away, and the doctors began to discuss her case. Frumkin announced that she suffered from schizophrenia. I had read about schizophrenia in a popular magazine and so understood that there are many varieties of the disease. Saying that a patient has schizophrenia is not enough to determine the subsequent course of treatment. The next doctor to speak refuted Frumkin and argued that the patient was a typical manic depressive. A third doctor insisted that she had progressive paralysis. Frumkin summed it up for us: "Now you see what state psychiatry is in today." We realized that a particularly complex case had been chosen to persuade us mathematicians to become involved in psychiatry. Nevertheless, we got quite a somber impression. It did not occur to me then that one day I would find myself in the hands of psychiatrists, but more ignorant and unscrupulous ones than these.

I did not like Tolstoy when I first read him at school, but when I later came across his *Confession*, I was struck by his merciless criticism of modern science, art, religion, and industry, and his brilliant formulation of the problem of life's meaning.[13] I read many of his other philosophical works, and my admiration for him as a philosopher grew. I wondered why Lenin, who admired Tolstoy's literary works, was so disdainful of him as a philosopher. Rereading Lenin's articles about Tolstoy, I found them unconvincing. I sensed an affinity with Tolstoy's striving for a system, for precision in definitions, for an ethic based on reason and an aversion to mysticism.

My passion for Tolstoy waned after about three years, and the things I did not like about him gradually came to the forefront. At first I had paid no attention to his concept of nonviolent resistance to evil, but when I studied the question, I concluded that Tolstoy had not in fact refuted his opponents' essential objections. Nonviolent resistance has some relevance if the evil is directed against me personally. But what am I to do if I see someone beating a woman? I reason with him. He tells me to go to hell. I continue to reason with him. He knocks me away and goes on beating the woman. There is no policeman at hand, but it wouldn't do to summon the police anyway: the rowdy would be punished with greater violence than if I beat him up. Besides, there is the commandment "Do not judge!" No matter how many times I posed this problem to Tolstoyans, they could never give me a satisfactory answer.

I felt a greater affinity with the Hindu philosopher Vivekananda, who also preached nonviolent resistance but recognized the necessity of violence in exceptional cases. Could peaceful measures have been applied to Nazi Germany, for example? No, violence or threat of violence was needed. Later I was struck by Tolstoy's ideological intolerance, which reminded me of Christian intolerance in the Middle Ages. I was also shocked by Tolstoy's attitude toward sex. He was so frenzied in his attacks against lechery and used such cynical images in his exposure of sexual vices that I could not stand to read him. When I became acquainted with psychoanalysis, I realized that a frenzied struggle for sexual purity indicates an attempt to overcome one's own unconscious sexual inclinations. I was and still am in agreement with Tolstoy's demand that sexual urges be limited by moral barriers or taboos, but his militant opposition to the act of procreation, as in *The Kreutzer Sonata*, strikes me as a monstrous ethical maximalism.[14]

Finally, there is the question of God, who, practically speaking, does not exist for Tolstoy. God is an empty word for him, and he may be said to have an ethic, but not a religion. Tolstoy's lack of religion is closely linked with the rationalist tendency of his philosophy. He is a last Mohican of the Enlightenment, when people believed that society will turn toward goodness and beauty if education is based on rational principles.

In my first year at the university I had read Sergey Yesenin, who had very recently been accepted as a Soviet poet.[15] He made the first breach in my search for clear, simple thoughts in literature. His bewilderment and longing for truth echoed the feelings of my generation, which was starting life with its faith in society shattered. When Erich Maria Remarque began to be published, almost all of us rushed to read him. The lost generation of the West extended a hand to us, the lost generation in the Soviet Union. The repugnance for official morality and politics and the desire to see such purely human aspects of life as unsanctimonious love, friendship, illness, and death cleansed of verbal dross were all very familiar to us. With the exception of *The Old Man and the Sea*, however, Hemingway was too complicated for me, and I grew to like him only in 1972 and 1973, when I was at the KGB prison in Kiev.

The stories of Vasiliy Aksyonov and plays of Victor Rozov began to appear in the early 1960's.[16] They presented an accurate portrait of my generation, but I was attracted by only one aspect of them— the corrupted, slangy Russian spoken by the young characters. I myself was hardly touched by this plague, but most of my friends suffered through it. The reason for the popularity of slang was quite simple: the protest against a mendacious literature and press turned into a protest against the language in which they expressed their lies. Words such as "love," "friendship," "socialism," and "patriotism" seemed thoroughly false and were replaced by slang and thieves' cant. Vulgar behavior and speech concealed a chaste desire to shield one's feelings from the filth and falseness of society.

Konstantin Paustovsky, whom I read at this time, seemed completely new in comparison with the rest of Soviet literature.[17] From Gorky's militant romanticism I had passed to a more sophisticated romanticism. Socialist romanticism is more artistic than socialist realism. Realistic art requires an adequate reflection of reality, but the romantic writer is not hampered by such cruel restrictions. He is free to select particularly vivid phenomena and images and can introduce fairy tales, legends, and what should be instead of what is. The socialist realist depicts reality in two dimensions, juggling with the facts to make them fit his scheme. His flat and unreal images distort reality and clash with the language and the realistic elements in the work. The romantic, however, elevates all the elements of his work above daily life. The logic and the proportions may be unrealistic, but they satisfy the requirements of verisimilitude because all the elements are coordinated with one another according to the special rules of romantic art. Coordination with reality is present, but only with its romantic aspects, and not with life as a whole. Socialist realists manage to write satisfactory works only when they depict heroic reality, as in Ostrovsky's *How the Steel Was Tempered* or Fadeyev's *The Young Guard*, but in such cases they are in fact adopting a romantic position. No wonder Lenin disliked the first socialist-realist writings and reproached Gorky for idealizing the intelligentsia (the working class, too, one might add).

Turning to Alexander Grin, I saw Paustovsky's virtues and failings more clearly.[18] Paustovsky's romanticism is bookish, and only a few of his stories are successful. Most of his writings are marred by the jarring mixture of reality and fantasy. Grin's subject is the same as Remarque's: simple human feelings and relations. Both reject everything that stands over man—ideology, the state, and God. Grin was the idol of Soviet youth for many years, and Scarlet Sails clubs, named after his most popular novel, were formed in many cities. For most young people a love for Grin is the first protest, whether conscious or not, against the falsehoods of adults. Grin represents for them a childhood miraculously transferred into adult life.

When the Ukrainian critic Ivan Svitlychny [19] gave me Antoine de Saint-Exupéry's *The Little Prince*, it immediately became my favorite book.[20] I reread it dozens of times and always discovered new levels of meaning. Some parts I still do not understand. I sense the sad beauty of the little prince's departure for his own planet, for example, but I cannot grasp it intellectually.

The scene where the little prince tames the fox strikes me as particularly profound. A concept as primitive as taming contains a deep insight into the psychology of love and friendship. Later, at Lefortovo Prison, I read Prishvin's "The Root of Life" and "The Thaw" and was struck by his approach to the concept of taming.[21] Prishvin draws a distinction between taming and appropriation. Appropriation is the usual form of man's relations with other men or with things. In appropriating a thing, man deprives it of its value and

35

makes it into a mechanical appendage of himself. In the Russian fairy tale "The Frog Princess," a frog loves a prince so much that it throws off its skin and turns into a girl. The prince burns the skin; that is, he intrudes into the frog princess's independent existence. He loses the princess because he cannot tame her with his love. Taming is a lengthy process in which a man gradually comes out of his skin and enters the spiritual world of the tamer, but without losing his individuality and self-sufficiency. In taming another, man is enriched by his spiritual approach to the other. He transcends the confines of his ego and to some extent becomes the other, just as the other becomes part of him. But when he appropriates another and thus deprives him or it of self-sufficiency, he leaves only his or its utilitarian value.

The other idea in *The Little Prince* that had a great influence on my views was that "what is essential is invisible to the eye," which I understood as an assertion that one must respect the infinity of the universe and the potential infinity of man's spiritual life. This is not a refusal to create rational models of such infinity, but we must be modest and understand that our models are only crude slices of reality, approximations of the truth, but not truth itself. In my encounters with scientists and intellectuals I saw that the great accomplishments of the natural sciences have led to an inordinate pride. Our formulas and machines can accomplish anything, scientists say. Down with ideology! We shall use mathematics and science to solve all the world's problems! It is true that mankind must base its further development on a rational scientific effort. But such irrational things as morality and ethics must grow in importance. Marx said that in the future a naturalistic science of man and a human science of nature must develop and then become one.

My reflections on Saint-Exupéry went hand in hand with meditations on the Bible. Tolstoy had forced me to read the Gospels, and the parables of the yogis prepared me for the parables of the Bible. I concluded that socialist realism is unsuccessful partly because literature is allegorical by nature. Only those artistic images that contain many meanings survive for any length of time. Each generation finds its own meaning in such images and may even discover meanings of which the author never dreamed.

Soviet atheistic propaganda continually harps on the contradictions in the Bible. If we pay attention only to them, we have to conclude that our predecessors revered an absurd and illogical book. But both Christianity and the Bible contain profound contradictions which reflect the dialectics of nature and society. I was particularly drawn to the parable of the loaves of bread that Christ distributed. One wonders why our predecessors, some of whom, like Saint Thomas Aquinas, were profound thinkers, did not see how absurd the story is. How could Christ feed thousands of people with several loaves and still have several baskets of crumbs left? This would be a glaring violation of the law of conservation. I decided that one has to find in nature a phenomenon to which the laws of conservation do not apply. Such a phenomenon is information. When a professor reads a lecture to his students, they obtain new information, while he does not lose the information he has given them.

An even more significant contradiction occurs in the Gospel according to Saint Matthew, when Christ says, "Think not that I come to destroy the law, or the prophets: I am not come to destroy, but to fulfill." Yet in the same chapter Christ speaks against the law of Moses: "Ye have heard that it hath been said, An eye for an eye, and a tooth for a tooth. But I say unto you, That ye resist not evil." Since the contradiction occurs within one chapter, Matthew, or one of the editors or compilers of the Gospels, could not have failed to see the contradiction and therefore must also have seen a resolution of it. I struggled with the problem for a long time until I found an answer for myself. Christianity appeared at a time when the Roman Empire was undergoing a disintegration. Moral and social bonds were becoming weaker. An unrestrained egoism and desire of enjoyment for enjoyment's sake appeared. Desire was not restrained, and the mind kept finding new ways of satisfying it. Every social class had become corrupt and decadent, and not one of them was capable of revitalizing society by transforming productive relations. A new morality was needed to give a universal meaning to life and to restrain egoism. Such a new morality could not develop from nothing and had to be a dialectical negation of the previous morality. Christianity brought the new morality, just as Buddhism and Mohammedanism brought a new morality to the East. The three religions have essential differences, but they also have a common feature: they are systems of moral taboos placed like chains on man's egoism. How realistic the new morality was and how it handled its social functions are a different matter.

When I graduated from Kiev University in 1962, I was assigned to teach mathematics in a high school. I had no desire to return to teaching and set about looking for jobs at scientific research institutes. At one of my lectures on telepathy I had met Yuriy Antomonov, the director of a laboratory that applied mathematical and technical models to biology and medicine at the Institute of Cybernetics of the Academy of Sciences of the Ukrainian Republic. Antomonov now suggested that I join him, promising freedom in the selection of my projects and support for setting up telepathic research in my spare time.

I noticed that Antomonov was hesitating about something while we were discussing the job. I asked him point-blank whether it was a question of item five. (Item five on Soviet identity cards, which are called "passports," records the citizen's "nationality," that is, membership in a recognized national group such as Russian, Jewish, Armenian, or Ukrainian.) Embarrassed, he confirmed my guess. I assured him that I didn't have a single drop of Jewish blood, and we exchanged jokes about the authorities' anti-Semitism. When I was working at the laboratory, I frequently witnessed similar incidents. A man who looked Jewish would come for a job interview. The boss was too liberal to study the applicant's passport and would ask him to come back in a week. Afterward all the people present would try to guess whether he was a Jew. If they decided that he was, they would inform him the following week that there were no openings. I expressed my outrage at this practice, but most people thought that orders from above had to be followed even if they weren't right.

The research at the laboratory proved to be uninteresting. We worked on the mathematical analysis of the level of blood sugar, the biopotential of acupuncture points, and voice identification.* The more I learned about these subjects, the more disillusioned I became. Mathematics has only limited applications in biology and psychology. Take the construction of differential equations for changes of sugar level in the blood. The estimates of the sugar level were extremely crude, and the equations themselves were selected empirically and based on primitive biological conceptions (more complex conceptions could not be subjected to mathematical analysis). We wrote in our articles about placing the treatment of diabetes on a mathematical basis, but I realized that the claim was not justified. The theoretical significance of our work was just as negligible. Data can be formally established only after the phenomenon itself has been studied. This is how physics developed and how other sciences must develop. In cybernetics one frequently sees the opposite: formulas are arbitrarily constructed and then experimental data are fitted into them.

Most of the works I read by Western cyberneticists on biology and

---

* Solzhenitsyn's *The First Circle* shows that similar experiments had been conducted under Stalin, but on a higher scientific level and with greater success than today.

psychology differ little from Soviet works. For example, information theory is used to calculate the informational capacity of the cerebral cortex. The number of neurons and the number of states of a neuron are elements in these calculations. But no one knows how the neurons interact, or even what role electrical charges play in transmitting information. The calculations are based not on detailed electrophysiological studies, but on arbitrary theoretical models, and no one knows what relation these models have to the actual functioning of the brain. Over the years I became convinced that psychology requires a new mathematical apparatus, because the present one was developed in response to the needs of physics and is suitable only for physical phenomena.

The Twenty-second Congress of the Communist Party took place during my first year at the Institute of Cybernetics. Stalinism was openly discussed at the Congress, and many facts about the tragic history of the October Revolution were made public for the first time. Many people realized that Trotsky, Bukharin, Zinovyev, Kamenev, and other close associates of Lenin had been slandered. Official historiography is marked by a ridiculous contradiction even today. On the one hand, Lenin was implacable toward his enemies; on the other, almost all his associates were anti-Communists, revisionists, and opportunists.

The unmasking of Molotov's gang—the "antiparty group," as it was called—was gratifying, but the fact that these men were eliminated secretly without being given an opportunity to express their views in public showed that the party's internal methods had not changed essentially.[22] I vividly remember how I first heard about the antiparty group when I was living in Odessa. I didn't understand why these people had been dismissed, but I sided with them out of a desire to be contradictory. When I went to vote, I crossed out the party candidates on the ballot and wrote in Molotov's name. Afterward I asked an acquaintance who had been a scrutineer whether anything untoward had occurred at the election. "No," she replied, "the party candidates were elected unanimously."

A month later a historian told me in detail about Molotov's activities under Stalin. I realized that voting in elections was ridiculous if you could not know for whom you were voting, could not organize support for your candidate (such an organization would be deemed anti-Soviet), and could not scrutinize voter registration. After that I never went to vote for or against the "bloc of Communists and nonparty members."

I was also outraged that the Twenty-second Congress devoted its attention to the murder of prominent party and government leaders, and not to the killing of millions of ordinary people. The "cult of personality," as Stalinism was officially called, seemed a thoroughly un-Marxist concept. Stalinism cannot be explained in terms of the leader's personal qualities or by such "objective" reasons as the isolation of the country and the need to struggle against the opposition. Stalinism was obviously not simply a cult, but a rebirth of autocracy on a new class basis. It was necessary to study the class roots of the degeneration of the Revolution instead of placing the blame on "individual distortions" in the leadership of the party and the country. Guarantees that the Constitution would be observed were needed, and the principles of a new constitution had to be developed.

The Congress declared that the USSR was no longer a dictatorship of the proletariat but, rather, a state of all the people. In terms of classical Leninism this was nonsense, and a Marxist analysis of this new concept was needed. After all, the state is a machine that one class uses to oppress other classes. A state of all the people would be equivalent to a round square.

Political writings began to appear in *samizdat* in 1962. One of the first works that I read was Admiral Fyodor Raskolnikov's letter to Stalin, which included facts not mentioned in the official press.[23] I was most disturbed by Raskolnikov's thesis that the famine of 1933 in Ukraine had been deliberately engineered, and set about finding people who had witnessed it. My grandfather told me that in 1933 he had seen a mountain of corpses in a village in one of the most prosperous provinces. He asked his boss, a Latvian sharpshooter in the Civil War, about the corpses. "That was a kulak demonstration," the man replied coolly.

An acquaintance of mine who had been involved in the collectivization campaign in Siberia returned to Ukraine in 1933. The population of his native village was almost extinct, and his house stood empty. From his younger brother he learned that the survivors were eating bark, grass, and hares. "What will you do when the hares are gone?" my acquaintance asked his brother. "Mother said that we should eat her if she dies," came the reply. I heard from him about several cases of cannibalism he encountered then, too terrible to relate. The famine, he explained, had begun in 1931, when the more prosperous peasants refused to join the collective farms that were being established. The party began to hold daily meetings, which all the peasants were forced to attend. They were faced with the statement: "Anyone opposed to the collective farm is opposed to the Soviet government. Let's vote. Who is against the collective farm?" Very few peasants were bold enough to vote against the collectives, and more than ninety percent joined.

Knowing that they would have to turn their horses and cattle over to the collectives, the peasants slaughtered their livestock. Many took pity on their horses and turned them out. Herds of starving horses ran wild throughout Ukraine. In response to such "sabotage" the government reinforced its economic and police terror. Special taxes were levied by the village councils on top of the regular taxes. The chairman of the council would frequently pile up taxes on his personal enemies regardless of their income. If the peasants did not turn in enough grain to pay the taxes, activists would conduct searches. If grain was found, the chimney on the house would be demolished as a sign that this was the house of a kulak or a "kulak's henchman" who was sabotaging the government's measures. Peasants were often taxed until all their grain was gone. The grain thus collected was guarded by troops in special granaries. If hungry peasants tried to break in, the soldiers would shoot at them. Much grain rotted, and much was exported. In 1933 the situation was made even worse by drought and crop failure. Starving peasants fled to the cities and to other republics. Troops were stationed at the borders of Ukraine to prevent them from leaving. In the cities bread was issued in small rations so that the city dwellers would not be able to help the peasants. Many city dwellers sympathized with the peasants, but some maliciously reminded them of the Civil War, when the cities had been starving and the peasants had either refused to sell bread or had bartered it for prized possessions. Writing about the famine was forbidden, and people who mentioned it in letters were often sent to prison for anti-Soviet propaganda. Parcels of food to Ukraine were frequently sent back.

While the famine was in progress Ukrainian writers were dispatched to write reports about the peasants' prosperous life in the new collective farms. Many writers who saw the reality joined the ranks of the opposition. Others were so frightened that they became fellow travelers (the Ukrainian phrase is more colorful—"tagalongs") and then active "builders of Communism." Iona Yakir, the famous Red Army commander, went to Moscow to demand that the grain collected by the government be distributed to the hungry peasants.[24] Stalin told him that a military officer should stay out of politics.

The information that I gathered about the famine was so stunning that it reduced to insignificance the purge of almost the entire party, government, trade unions, and armed forces in the 1930's. No one knows exactly how many people perished in the famine, but party members cite a figure of five or six million—as many as the number of Jews killed by the Nazis—and others speak about ten million victims. The true figure probably lies in between. In the 1960's people began to say that the Bolsheviks had got what was coming to them. The Bolsheviks murdered by Stalin were, after all, guilty of crimes against the people. But why did millions of innocent ordinary people have to die? A single death is terrible, and the inequality $1,000,000 > 1$ does not hold true for ethics, but the mere thought of millions of victims defies all attempts to comprehend. Leftists in the capitalist world must remember this; they must think about the means by which they intend to construct what Dostoyevsky called the crystal palace of the future.

5

ANTI-SOVIET SPIRITS

As a member of the Komsomol bureau at the Institute of Cybernetics, I was assigned to serve as a propagandist and to conduct philosophy seminars. Propagandists have the job of organizing political-information sessions on domestic and international affairs. I took on this unrewarding task because propagandists at the Academy of Sciences were given lectures by professional propagandists, speakers from the Central Committee, professors of history, and specialists from abroad. Such lectures often included facts unmentionable in the press. In my own political-information sessions I never commented on these facts. My audience was sufficiently intelligent to draw its own conclusions, and comments could only lead to a charge of conducting hostile propaganda.

At the philosophy seminars I was, amusingly enough, the only member to defend a materialist standpoint on ethics and esthetics. The lone party member at the institute, bored by our arguments, did not attend the seminars, and the other participants preached Tolstoyism or the Vedanta or merely asked questions. Mainly we discussed the meaning of life, but we also examined esthetics and the philosophical implications of attempts to model life and thought.

In our free moments a friend and I tried to develop telepathic abilities by using hypnosis and the methods of Milan Ryzl. After considerable difficulties we found volunteers, in a few of whom we were able to induce deep hypnosis. But they quickly lost interest in our sessions, because they expected miracles and none were forthcoming. We thought of paying our volunteers, but no funds were available. Official research groups had been set up in several cities, but these were soon classified as secret. At first we, too, wanted to receive government support, but then we came to see the immorality of the government's aims in this field.

The press was overflowing at this time with encomiums to Nikita Khrushchev. In *Our Dear Nikita Sergeyevich,* a film released in 1963, Khrushchev was shown to have helped Stalin and also to have saved us from him. Khrushchev was a brilliant leader, both at war and on the labor front. The new cult of personality was growing stronger. Less bloody than the previous one, it was nonetheless just as abhorrent. It became clear that a cult of personality was essential to Soviet society. The cults had begun even before the Revolution, when the people placed their trust in the "good tsars," their defenders against the cruel landowners. The transcripts of the party congress that took place just before Lenin died show that almost all the party leaders endlessly praised Lenin, a deification of the leader that paved the way for the Stalin cult. Only Trotsky and Stalin showed self-respect and did not toady to Lenin. Although I despise Stalin, I must admit that his formal attitude toward the dying leader was dignified.*

By June 1963 there were abundant signs that the harvest that year would be a failure. A Ukrainian writer whom I knew went back to his native village and was surprised by the peasants' indifference. When he questioned the party organizer at the collective farm, he was told that there had been a good harvest in 1962, but the state had taken almost all the grain. Now the peasants didn't care what came of their labor: they knew that they would get little one way or the other.

Toward the end of the year the shops began to sell bread made of corn or rye mixed with peas. White bread was available only on a doctor's prescription or through connections. Flour had been difficult to obtain for many years and was sold only for holidays at places of work. Scarce items had to be bought in combination with items nobody wanted—canned fish, for example. At holidays oranges and herrings would sometimes be added to the rations. Outside Kiev the situation was much worse, and bread was often completely unavailable. Food supplies remained unchanged only in Moscow, but the Muscovites grumbled, too. The raptures in the press about the party's wise leadership in agriculture abated slightly, but not a word was said about the true situation. Western radio broadcasts told us that the government had begun to buy wheat from Canada. The news was both sad and funny: a country that had exported grain before the Revolution now had to import it.

In our intellectual life the journal *Novy mir* was becoming in-

---

* I say "formal" because documents published in the fifth edition of Lenin's works show that he was aware of the harm Stalin could inflict on the Revolution and formed an alliance with Trotsky against Stalin.

creasingly important.[1] Its artistic level was not very high, but it offered a bit of truth and published some genuine literature. After decades of socialist realism the return to simple realism seemed to be a step forward. Solzhenitsyn's *One Day in the Life of Ivan Denisovich* made an overwhelming but contradictory impression on me.[2] Brought up on Soviet-Christian sanctimony, I found the obscenities grating to my ear. A more significant objection was that Solzhenitsyn had chosen to make Ivan Denisovich, and not Captain Buynovsky, the hero of his tale. The captain, it seemed to me, was a true Communist and intellectual, an invincible champion of justice who could understand the course of the Revolution and explain to the reader why Stalinism had emerged. Ivan Denisovich had lived like a workhorse before he was sent to the camps, and little had changed for him. As an intellectual and a Komsomol member inculcated with Stalin's contempt for the masses, I assumed that the true tragedy of the October Revolution could not be seen through Ivan Denisovich's eyes.

Another reason for objecting to the adulation of Solzhenitsyn was that Vladimir Dudintsev's *Not by Bread Alone* had recently been hauled over the coals by the Khrushchev press.[3] Though of little literary merit, the novel criticized Stalinism from party positions and had given us hope for the future. I had a vague sense that *Ivan Denisovich* was anti-Soviet and could only lead to despair. Solzhenitsyn was revealing the falsehood on which the Soviet system was based, and not simply showing how Stalin had distorted that system. It was strange to hear praise for Solzhenitsyn and abuse for Dudintsev, and I wanted to write a letter to *Literaturnaya gazeta* [*Literary Gazette*] about this paradox in official criticism. I am glad that I did not make this mistake, because the following year I began to appreciate the literary merits of *Ivan Denisovich*.

Novy mir also published *The Diary of Nina Kosterin.*[4] Nina was killed by the Nazis during the war. Her father, Aleksey Kosterin, had been convicted as an "enemy of the people" in 1938.[5] We understood Nina's sincere faith in her society, her suffering when her father was arrested, and her willingness for self-sacrifice despite the monstrous crime against her father. Several years later I read Aleksey Kosterin's *samizdat* articles about Stalinism and the Crimean Tatars. When I was in Moscow during the summer of 1968, I learned many details about his life that increased my respect for him. Petro Grigorenko's wife, Zinaida, suggested that we go visit him, but I chose to attend some business meetings instead, thinking that I would have many other opportunities to meet him.[6]

But in November I heard that Aleksey Kosterin had died. I went to the funeral. A crowd had gathered at the mortuary, and an official urged us to speed up: other people were waiting, as if in a line for bread or beer. There were agents everywhere. I hadn't learned to distinguish them yet, but friends pointed them out. Petro Grigorenko delivered the eulogy.[7] His pathos was not jarring to the ear precisely because we were surrounded by the KGB. The mortuary official stood petrified—such sincere revolutionary words had not been heard in the country for a long time. An agent ran up to whisper in the official's ear, and he again shouted at us to make room for the next funeral.

Afterward some of us went back to the Grigorenkos', where more eulogies were delivered by Chechens, Jews, and Russians. The Chechen writer Khalid Oshaev told us how Kosterin had fought as a guerrilla during the Civil War in the Chechen-Ingush Autonomous Republic. Kosterin's widow sat at the table weeping. I was introduced to her as being "from Ukraine." It was awkward to be taken as a Ukrainian representative and not simply as a person.

A year later I met Aleksey Kosterin's daughter Yelena, who told me about her father's death. He had been extremely disturbed by the invasion of Czechoslovakia and finally returned his party membership card to the Central Committee; he had lost all hope that the party could be regenerated. When Yelena told this to her mother, she replied: "That will kill him." A week later Kosterin was dead. I asked Yelena whether this could be explained as fanaticism. No, she answered, but when you see in your old age that your lifelong ideals have been shattered, the blow is unbearable. Kosterin had kept his faith in the healthy forces within the party even when he was sent to the labor camps, but the rebirth of Stalinism in the 1960's destroyed his last illusions.

In 1963 many articles and books appeared criticizing the Stalin era. Ilya Ehrenburg's memoirs, *People, Life, Years*, which brilliantly depicted the destruction of prominent party leaders and artists, made a strong impression on me.[8] Solzhenitsyn's *The Gulag Archipelago* had not been published yet, and Ehrenburg's memoirs served to deepen our knowledge of the years euphemistically called "the period of the personality cult." Ehrenburg wrote, "We knew but remained silent." This may not have been an entirely moral position, but at least it was an honest admission. Most people active in "unmasking" the cult had either supported it or lain low, and few afterward confessed to any guilt.

A story went around intellectual circles that Ehrenburg was mor-

ally responsible for repressions against Jewish wri
during the anti-Semitic campaign of 1947–53, when
politanism" was castigated in much the same way a
day.[9] According to the rumors, Ehrenburg was floode
protest in response to an article he published urging
late; all the letter writers were sent to camps and pr
determine how just this charge was and concluded
himself had not passed the letters on to the secret
they had been intercepted at the post office. The per
Ehrenburg showed at that time was a common pl
should not be judged harshly.

Komsomolskaya pravda attacked Yevgeniy Yevtu
and betrayal of party principles in an article entitle
less Bragging Leads To." I obtained Yevtushenko's
ography, which had so angered the newspaper, a
although egocentric and boastful, it was also sincere
lost his sincerity in the late 1960's, when he became
ognized "oppositionist" who traveled abroad and h
demonstrate its liberality.

The press also published a speech by Leonid Ilich
of the Ideological Commission at the Central Comm
agely attacked formalism, abstract art, and the po
Volpin.[11] We all smelled another witch hunt. By the
with writers and poets who kept me informed about

On March 8, 1963, Khrushchev gave a speech in
other things, he charged Victor Nekrasov with two
travel essays "On Both Sides of the Ocean," Nekraso
conversation with a journalist who advised him n
United States only in gloomy colors.[12] "Maintain a
fifty," the journalist advised. "Show the good ar
America." This theory of "fifty-fifty" infuriated Khr
lack of party-mindedness. Nekrasov also praised a r
in Marlen Khutsiyev's film *Ilich's Gate*. The son of
in the war sees his father's ghost and asks him how
Instead of replying the father asks his son how old
three" is the reply. "I am twenty-one," the father say
est spectator understood that the father is advising h
own answers. Khrushchev missed the point and an;
that even dogs teach their pups. The intelligentsia
the party leader's obtuseness and insolent interferen

The Ukrainian leaders followed Moscow's examp
gorny, then First Secretary of the Ukrainian party, a

47

ekrasov. Other leaders censured Ivan Drach, Vitaliy Korotych, and ykola Vinhranovsky.[13] My wife, Tanya, and I knew almost nothing out the new Ukrainian poetry and were grateful to the party critics r revealing that something fresh and honest had appeared in krainian culture. We were not disappointed in the poets who had en criticized, and Drach struck me as much more gifted than Yevshenko, my idol until then.

As the cultural controls tightened, Solzhenitsyn's nomination for e Lenin Prize in December 1963 sounded like a sinister joke. I was rticularly angered by the references to Ivan Denisovich as a true ro of the people and to the nobility of slave labor. The mainspring my protest against the praise of Solzhenitsyn, however, was that he as admired by Khrushchev. It took me another year to understand y mistake, but from then on I tried to avoid judging art or life from e viewpoint of the current political situation.

After my move to Kiev I still kept in touch with several friends in dessa. Kolya, as I shall call him, had been my best friend for many ars. Having grown up in even greater poverty than I, he was much ore intolerant of the Soviet bourgeoisie. In the ninth and tenth ades Kolya supported his mother by working as a night watchman a fishing collective. In the tenth grade he unmasked and helped pture a real spy. Together he and I belonged to the Light Cavalry, udied at the university, and suffered when our friends "betrayed" s by giving up social work for studies or family life.

In the summer of 1964 my wife and I visited Kolya in Odessa. Then we discussed the Khrushchev era, Kolya defended Khrushchev nd cited his accomplishments in opening up the virgin lands. Buyng grain abroad, he said, was necessary only because of drought. We xchanged heated words about the possibility of returning to Leninm. Kolya also attacked Yevtushenko for being a braggart, for abanoning the party line, and for indulging in formalist "idiosyncrasies" nat obscured the meaning. Knowing that Kolya admired Mayaovsky, I reminded him of the influence the futurist Khlebnikov[14] ad exerted on Mayakovsky. Imperceptibly we passed over to the gnificance of the Briks[15] in Mayakovsky's life, and then to Jews.

Kolya cited case after case of money grubbing, corruption, currency eculation, and bribe taking by Jews. I admitted that such cases uld be true but tried to show how close Kolya was to anti-Semitism. fter all, the fascists also tried to turn individual cases to account. In iev Ukrainian and Russian Komsomol girls had replaced the old ewish saleswomen. They soon began to steal and give short weight customers. In some respects things became even worse. The pre-

vious saleswomen had at least been polite when they cheated you; the new ones were insolent. Just try to tell a racially pure Komsomol saleswoman that she has cheated you. She'll raise such a stink that you'll be glad to get away alive. "As a Marxist," I said to Kolya, "you must understand that the causes of theft and corruption are social, not national. Salesclerks are paid such low wages that they can't help stealing. Khrushchev must take credit for the fact that they steal."

The argument grew more heated every day. When we parted, I called Kolya a Soviet fascist, and he called me a Soviet petit bourgeois. I suffered over the breakup of our friendship and tried to explain to myself why we had quarreled. Kolya and I had become friends because of our similar backgrounds, and our anti-Semitism had its origins in social conditions. Until our third year at the university our development had run a parallel course: protests against official lies and attempts to combat evil in the ranks of the Komsomol. Now Kolya had become an apologist for the regime and remained an anti-Semite, while I had become an opponent of the regime and a philo-Semite.

I remember our first years of friendship. I had loved Lermontov and Lesya Ukrayinka's *The Forest Song*;[16] he had loved Mayakovsky. Our arguments about poetry had revolved around "coarse honesty and directness," "beauty," "the consumptive spittle of the world" licked by Mayakovsky, and my objection to Mayakovsky's advertising jingles and propaganda. Now we had reversed positions. I admired Yevtushenko's anti-Stalinist jingles (with their hint at being anti-Khrushchevian), and Kolya was in favor of a return to "Leninist norms." But we had also retained some of our earlier convictions. I emphasized the artistic merits in some of Yevtushenko's "capers," and Kolya insisted on "correct" contents.

Our arguments about esthetics ceased for a year or two. Kolya fell in love with a girl and became very fond of Yesenin, Grin, and Saint-Exupéry. Then he broke up with the girl and was unhappy in a very touching and unproletarian way. Unexpectedly he resumed his previous convictions: scorn for ethics, esthetics, and intellectual "prattle." His world view was based on a lack of culture, a blind social protest, an inability to think dialectically, and a vulgar materialism. After Khrushchev's downfall I tried to renew my friendship with Kolya. After all, the facts had shown that I was right. Alas, Kolya recognized Khrushchev's political mistakes but remained an anti-Semite, although he did not object to the bureaucracy and even began to study Hegel in order to understand the philosophical roots of Stalinism and Khrushchevism. Kolya had some trouble with the party committee at the university, and the matter almost ended up with his commitment to a mental hospital. But then things turned out all right for him because he dropped philosophy and Komsomol work and concentrated on being an anti-Semite.

The social protest of the masses often turns into an apology for the system. I knew a very honest and intelligent teacher of Russian who was always in trouble with the directors of his school. The Jews on the staff persecuted my friend and finally drove him from the school. When I met him again, he hated Jews. I tried to remind him that he was a party member and a Communist, but this did not help. "The Jews are responsible for the regime's perversions," he insisted. I pointed out that the "Jewish clique" at his school had also persecuted a teacher of Russian who was a Jewess. "Only because she betrayed the Jews and loves Russian culture," my friend rebutted. "I am not accusing all Jews. I have a Jewish friend. . . ."

The arguments ended the way they had with Kolya: we pinned labels on each other. I was very fond of the teacher, but both of us found it difficult to maintain our relationship. The teacher's daughter also suffered at the hands of the "Jewish clique" at her school when her marks were lowered. Her father was forced to threaten the clique with court and a collective letter from the parents to the Central Committee of the party. The clique backed down.

After this the daughter also became an anti-Semite. I often argued with her, because she was sincere and intelligent and I wanted her to change her views. I explained to her why the "clique" had appeared: the stifling atmosphere in the country, the low morale in the Department of Education, and the Stalinist methods of fighting for good jobs. Unlike her father, she partly understood my explanations but tried to justify herself by citing bribes given for admission to the medical school in Odessa. "Your sister was rejected by the medical school only because she was poor and wasn't Jewish," my friend said. I described to her similar cases at other universities, where both Jews and poor people had difficulty being admitted. She told me about Jewish solidarity, corruption, and lack of patriotism. I cautiously asked her whether she had heard about a world-wide Jewish conspiracy. No, she hadn't, but she didn't exclude the possibility. I brought up *The Protocols of the Elders of Zion*, in which this notion is clearly developed.[17] But even the parallel with fascism did not have an effect on her, and her hatred of the Jews remained unabated. I decided to appeal to emotion. Maria declared during one discussion that I was dishonest. I was defending Jews because my wife was half Jewish. Just then my infant son cried out in his cradle. "Shut your

Yid trap!" I shouted at him. "Fouling things up for the Russians again, are you? Lousy little Jew!" Maria burst into tears. Who likes to admit to being close to fascism? Calming down, she accused me of being cruel and using unfair debating tactics. I replied that one cannot speak politely with fascists. I would leave that to Stalin, Khrushchev, and Brezhnev. The argument forced Maria to think. She became a research scientist, ran into official anti-Semitism, and began to understand certain things. Swearing off Jews and the government, she retreated to the purity of scientific formulas.

In 1961 or 1962 *Literaturnaya gazeta* published a letter entitled "Down with the Chatterbox Fly" concerning a fairy tale by Korney Chukovsky in which a fly marries a mosquito.[18] A spider tries to eat the fly, but the mosquito rescues his wife, and all the insects live happily ever after. Like Chukovsky's other stories, "The Chatterbox Fly" belongs to the best in Soviet children's literature. The author of the letter complained that he had seen his child reading the story and was horrified to discover what children were reading on the advice of their teachers. The country was struggling to eradicate flies because they transmit disease, and here Chukovsky had made a fly into a positive hero, not to mention a mosquito, which drinks human blood and transmits malaria. Furthermore, the letter writer hinted (Soviet people do not mention such terrible things aloud) that the marriage of a fly and a mosquito was thoroughly unnatural and might give children nasty ideas. Chukovsky replied that he had at first taken the letter for a bad joke, but then other readers had protested to him that he was making disease carriers into heroes.

One might think that the letters only serve to prove that Russia has its share of fools, but several months after the exchange in *Literaturnaya gazeta*, the Ministry of Education of the Ukrainian Republic discussed a new program for kindergartens. My wife was employed then as a specialist in preschool education in the Ministry's Office of Methodology and was working on the selection of children's literature. In a discussion of recommended books for preschool children, an employee of the Ministry announced that unfortunately fairy tales praise agricultural pests—mice, rabbits, gophers, and even wolves, which kill livestock. Lecturers at the teachers' college supported the argument, and a heated discussion broke out. By a narrow majority agricultural pests won their right to exist in fairy tales, but their victory was Pyrrhic: a resolution was passed to reduce their significance in fairy tales and to stress instead little Volodya, who grew up to become Lenin.

Literaturnaya gazeta also published an article by a reader who had been horrified to discover that his son was eagerly reading *Tom Sawyer,* which praised the ne'er-do-well Tom and ridiculed his brother, Sid, a conscientious pupil. The guardian of literary morality concluded his article by asking: What sort of examples are our children being brought up on? The newspaper editors replied with a humorous article. Inspired by the reader's zeal, they had decided to examine world literature and had discovered, to their horror, that from ancient Greek literature to Pushkin all sorts of immoral people appeared as protagonists.

In 1969 or 1970 *Literaturnaya Rossiya* [*Literary Russia*] published an article entitled "What Does Vysotsky Sing About?" The author, a party specialist in cultural affairs, argued that Vladimir Vysotsky ridicules the Russian people (he has a song about the Russian spirit crawling out of a bottle of vodka) and glorifies hooligans, thieves, and alcoholics.[19] This time it was too dangerous to reply to the cultural arm of the law. Sinyavsky and Daniel had recently been sentenced, and the prosecution had identified their views with those of their satirical characters.

These anecdotes illustrate the demands socialist realism places on art. Socialism does not exist in the country, but the rulers insist that it exist in literature. Yes, the theory says, there are individual shortcomings in the country, but they are relics of the past or caused by the rotten West, the cult of Stalin, or voluntarism. Socialist realism claims that how well an artist writes is less important than what he writes about. Literature must be popular and accessible to all. Literature must be party-minded and conform to the instructions issued by each new set of rulers. Literature must instruct by providing positive characters and creating a cult of heroes and cogs in the mechanism of the state. Finally, literature must depict life in its revolutionary development by portraying what exists in newspapers, but not in reality.

We must, however, distinguish between the theory and practice of socialist realism. If we set aside the excessive rationalism and the lack of an esthetic definition of the new art, we find that the theory is not entirely bad. After all, if the contents are new, then the esthetic form should also be new. This was understood by many people in the 1920's, who were then punished for it in the 1930's. In a broad sense literature is always ideological, because it reflects the aspirations, consciousness, subconscious, and esthetics of a specific nation, class, or group. Yet there is no direct correlation between a writer's affiliations and what he writes about. Marx's observation on Balzac is well known: without intending to, by virtue of his genius, Balzac expressed the psychoideology of part of the bourgeoisie. As if anticipating his followers' stupidity, Marx wrote that a poet is like a nightingale: you cannot keep him in a golden cage if you want him to sing.

The official thesis about the national character [narodnost'] of literature is not entirely stupid, because it expresses the fact that every major writer finds inspiration both in himself and in his language, history, and surroundings. Thus he expresses both himself and something common to his nation. But a writer does not have to strive to be national; if he is gifted he cannot help being national. Second, he does not express simple, widely accessible ideas but, rather, something new and original. His national spirit is refracted in his soul.

The Soviet demand for realism, which in practice amounts to varnished naturalism, prevents a profound understanding of reality. The theater of the absurd is realistic because it depicts the absurd aspects of the world, but this does not negate the realism of Solzhenitsyn's higher naturalism. The socialist-realist insistence on positive heroes is ridiculous because certain genres, such as satire, simply cannot have a positive hero; certain writers have a talent only for depicting negative phenomena; and in certain historical periods no positive direction for social development is evident. Gogol's inability to write the second volume of Dead Souls is highly instructive. He tried to invent a positive hero because he did not see one in life. Given a different predisposition, he would have been able to imagine a utopian or fairy-tale hero. The early Gogol depicted fairy-tale heroes because he saw them in Ukrainian folk culture. After his move to bureaucratic Saint Petersburg, Gogol could not find an optimistic fairy tale, and a pessimistic one would no longer have been a fairy tale.

Fairy tales remind me of an event that had a seminal influence on Tanya's and my intellectual development. We met Iryna Avdiyeva, who had been an actress in the Berezil Theater of the brilliant Ukrainian producer Les Kurbas.[20] Russian by nationality, Avdiyeva loved Ukraine and Ukrainian culture. But her interests were truly international, and she loved French and Japanese art as well and was knowledgeable in all styles, from primitive to abstract. I emphasize her Ukrainian interests because under her influence my interest in my own people and culture developed beyond a fondness for Ukrainian songs, Lesya Ukrayinka, and Taras Shevchenko.[21] Avdiyeva showed me that Ukrainians have a great spiritual potential which has been revealed in part by the poet Pavlo Tychyna, the playwright Mykola Kulish, the film director and screenwriter Alexander Dovzhenko, and the artists Fedir Krychevsky, Anatol Petrytsky, Mykhaylo Boychuk, and Ivan Padalka.[22]

Avdiyeva had no interest in philosophy or politics—the latter always repelled her—but her esthetic concerns were enriched by a profound intellect and even wisdom. I was startled to learn, after I left the *psikhushka*, that the KGB considered Avdiyeva guilty of inculcating young people, including Tanya and myself, with an anti-Soviet spirit. If the KGB believes that a love of beauty, or of the Ukrainian and Russian people, is anti-Soviet, then it is right, of course. But it is not right where Tanya and I are concerned. Even before meeting Avdiyeva we had been developing an appreciation for beauty and realizing how significant folk culture is even for the most refined, elitist art. Avdiyeva was a catalyst in my growth; she helped me to shatter more quickly the chains of shallow, soulless rationalism.

II

THE
TURNING
POINT

6

A LETTER TO THE PARTY

In October 1964 Nikita Khrushchev was overthrown at a plenary meeting of the Central Committee. I was so elated by the news that I came to work drunk. "Idiot," a colleague commented. "I think things will get worse."

"Perhaps, but the more often they overthrow one another, the faster the regime will collapse," I replied. Alas, I was to see once again how pointless it is to prophesy. My colleague guessed correctly, only because a Cassandra is right more often than an optimist.

We propagandists were summoned to a lecture about Khrushchev at the Higher Party School. Because we were scientists, the lecturer directed his attention to Khrushchev's interference in scientific matters. He had, for example, used purely political considerations in setting the Soviet space center a deadline for launching a spacecraft. Thus the lecturer hinted that Khrushchev was to blame for the deaths of the three cosmonauts because their flight had not been properly prepared. Khrushchev had also intended to deprive the Academy of Sciences of its autonomy and had supported Lysenko against the geneticists.[1] The Soviet government was concerned that scientists have material security and be able to devote themselves to science, but Khrushchev had wanted to cancel the bonuses given for advanced degrees. Because many of the people in the audience were Ukrainians, the lecturer stressed that Khrushchev had exploited Ukraine, particularly the peasants, by sending all its grain to Russia. Then the lecturer referred to Khrushchev's way of life: he had had thirty-three dachas throughout the country, none of which could be called modest. I sent the lecturer two questions. Was there not a certain regularity in the development of new cults? And why were the reasons for Khrushchev's dismissal not set forth in the press? I waited for an answer in vain.

I wrote a letter to the party's Central Committee.[2] In the first part, titled "Enough," I argued that the Soviet government had brought enough shame on the country. We had had enough of cults, voluntarism, and anti-Semitism. In the second part, headed "We Demand!," I insisted that bureaucrats must be paid no more than an average worker's wages, that the Russification of non-Russian soldiers must be discontinued, and that the army must be reorganized on a territorial basis to avoid a repetition of the strike at Novocherkassk, when soldiers from Central Asia and the Caucasus were forced to fire on a crowd of workers after Russian and Ukrainian soldiers had refused to do so.[3] These were all demands that had been put forth by the Bolsheviks before the Revolution. Attaching a scribbled postscript to the letter—"Add or subtract what you like; if you think it more expedient, we can circulate the letter as an unsigned proclamation at the university and the polytechnical school"—I sent it through an acquaintance to my friend Eduard Nedoroslov in Odessa.

Three or four weeks later I received a telegram from Eduard: "Do not do anything. Details by letter." The next day Yuriy Nikiforov, my old friend from the KGB, appeared at the laboratory with a good-natured smile on his face. My heart skipped a beat, but I smiled in return and inquired what he wanted. Nikiforov asked me to accompany him for a talk. I replied that I would be finished in five minutes, and he went out. I quickly concealed the *samizdat* I had been working on. Outside, plainclothesmen walked up from both sides and smilingly escorted me to a car. Nikiforov was waiting inside. When I asked him what we were to talk about, he began to question me about my research and my experiments in telepathy. I sighed with relief—they had finally decided to set up a secret laboratory. At KGB headquarters Nikiforov took me into an office where another man joined us. "Leonid Ivanovych, could you please tell us about your plans and the problems that interest you?"

I began with telepathy. The KGB agents soon became bored and asked me about my interests in philosophy. I told them about the seminar I was conducting, but again they rapidly became bored. They tossed me a leading question on Tolstoy. I perked up. Someone had reported my enthusiasm about Tolstoy's philosophy. I explained in detail what I thought was valuable in Tolstoy, omitting any criticism. The agents asked what the shortcomings of Soviet youth were, to my mind. I cited the growth of crime and what I thought were the reasons: increased leisure time, an ideological vacuum, boring propaganda, and a paucity of cultural values. I thought it best to keep silent about the social causes for crime, merely pointing out that the children of affluent bureaucrats were particularly vulnerable to moral corruption. When I was asked to cite facts, I mentioned several sensational cases which the press had ignored but which all Kiev knew about. As the discussion went on, I noticed that my finger was trembling. I found this disturbing, because on a conscious level I was confident that the KGB had no serious evidence against me.

After two hours I was taken to another office and asked about wages for bureaucrats and workers. I realized that they had my letter. My finger immediately stopped trembling, and my voice grew firm. A real danger is less frightening than an uncertain one. I quoted Lenin: bureaucrats ought not to be paid more than an average worker's wages. Nikiforov rebutted that not everything Lenin had said was correct. I naturally agreed with this bold statement by a functionary of the secret police but parried by saying that Lenin had emphasized the primacy of this principle for the state. It provides a material guarantee against the pursuit of ranks and sinecures and against the bureaucratization of the socialist system. The KGB man smiled broadly. "But it's naïve to want a cook to be paid more than a minister."

My heart jumped with joy. Now I would teach this guardian of socialism and Leninism a thing or two. " 'The reduction of the remuneration of high state officials seems to be "simply" a demand of naïve, primitive democracy. One of the "founders" of modern opportunism, the ex-Social Democrat Eduard Bernstein, has more than once repeated the vulgar bourgeois jeers at "primitive democracy.' [4] So you see what dubious company you've found yourself in," I finished, unable to repress a smile.

Nikiforov put an end to the discussion by placing my letter on the table. "Why did you write this?"

"I had thought of sending it to the Central Committee."

"Only to the Central Committee?"

"No, if my friend had thought that stupid, I would have distributed the letter to students."

"Why?"

"I explained that in the letter. How long will you go on mocking the people and the ideals of Communism?"

Nikiforov avoided an answer by taking up particular passages in the letter. "What workers' demonstration are you referring to?"

"The one in Novocherkassk."

"How do you know about it?"

"Friends of mine went there and heard about it from eyewitnesses."

"What exactly did they say?"

"Meat prices were raised throughout the country. In Novocherkassk, factory workers had their wages decreased at the same time. The workers went out to demonstrate, and the local party committee sent in troops against them. The garrison commander telephoned Khrushchev to ask whether he could disobey the party committee's order to shoot. Khrushchev ordered him to obey. The commander put a bullet in his own head. The Russian and Ukrainian soldiers and officers refused to shoot. Then troops from Central Asia and the Caucasus were called in. Their shots broke up the demonstration, and the instigators were arrested soon after."

"Who told you this?" Nikiforov asked.

"Friends."

"What friends?"

"I don't want to answer that."

"You're a mathematician. How can you believe what *someone* said?"

"It's not my fault that such important events are either not reported or falsified in the press. In such cases I try to obtain information from various people with different points of view. I have to work and don't have the money to go to Novocherkassk. Some of my facts may be incorrect, but the whole country knows that a peaceful demonstration was broken up by gunfire."

"Tell me now. How can a letter based on unconfirmed facts be sent to the Central Committee?"

"I insist that the shooting took place and that Ukrainian and Russian soldiers refused to fire. That's all I claimed in the letter to the Central Committee."

"Now here you write that freedom of the press is lacking. But you know that our press is party-minded and cannot publish anti-Soviet articles."

"Lenin wrote that under socialism everyone is free to speak and write anything he likes without the slightest restrictions on freedom of speech and press."

"You're a dogmatist, Leonid Ivanovych. You've pulled one phrase by Lenin out of context and not read his article about party-minded literature."

My spirits picked up again. I was winning this round, too, and in a minute the KGB man would be flat on his back. "The point is that I've quoted precisely this article."

"How can that be? Even the title of the article indicates that Lenin had the opposite view."

"You've misunderstood the article. First of all, Lenin wrote that any book, no matter what its contents, is party-minded in the sense that it reflects the views of a particular group, class, or nation. Secondly, Lenin said that you cannot advocate anti-Communist views if you are a member of the Communist Party. But if you are not a member of the party, you are free to say whatever you like. That's recorded in the Constitution."

Nikiforov changed the subject. "Where have you witnessed anti-Semitism?"

"When I was applying to the university. Later, at the institute, I learned about it from lecturers at the university. I know young Jews who were refused admission to universities even when they were very able."

"Leonid Ivanovych, we live in Ukraine and have to guard against Jews predominating at the universities." With that, Nikiforov ended the interrogation. He announced that the KGB office hours were over and that I should come back the next day, and cautioned me to keep our conversation an absolute secret.

At home I learned that Tanya had also been called in by the KGB. She was asked whether she knew about my letter and agreed with the idea of writing it. "No," she replied, "I think such letters are useless."

"Do you agree with the contents of the letter?"

"With certain thoughts, yes. The Khrushchev cult should not be repeated. I've also encountered anti-Semitism. But I am not interested in politics and so cannot comment on my husband's views."

The following day, I was asked who had helped me write the letter and who knew about it. I mentioned only the people the KGB already knew of: my wife, my friend Eduard in Odessa, and the girl who had taken the letter from him. Then the agents questioned me in detail concerning my views on the established order. I replied eagerly, as most novices to police interrogation do. It is hard to believe that the man smiling at you is a scoundrel or an idiot, and you are sure that you can convince him that your views are right, or at least that you're honest and not anti-Soviet.

The KGB men demanded statistics in support of my thesis about the poverty of the workers and peasants. I replied that statistics are classified in the Soviet Union.

"Have you looked for them?" an agent asked.

"Yes, I have."

"Where?"

"In the library of the Academy of Sciences."

The agent argued that I had done a poor job of research. "How strange that you, a mathematician, refuse to use figures about wages and the state of the economy."

"Well, then, help me find these data," I replied.

"You know we have a lot of work as it is. We advise you not to rush to conclusions and not to write without proper statistical research."

As a mathematician I had to agree. But no matter how hard I looked, I never found the relevant data; at best I unearthed generalized figures unfit for a comparative analysis of the wages of bureaucrats, workers, and peasants. Still, I did discover amusing things about the methods of Soviet statistics. I learned, for example, that the production of sugar in the United States had declined. I made inquiries and found that the figures were correct: the Americans had achieved the level of sugar production necessary to satisfy their needs. The rate of steam-locomotive construction, to take another example, is much higher in the USSR than in the West, but only because the West has moved ahead to diesel locomotives, electric locomotives, and automotive transport. When Soviet statisticians cite the decrease in the Soviet crime rate, they probably quote a correct percentage of decrease, but they take as the base of their calculations the immediate postwar years, when banditry, theft, currency speculation, and hooliganism were naturally high. The statistics give only percentages, not actual figures. Still, this does not prevent the preparation of two sets of statistics—one for the Central Committee, the Supreme Soviet, the Council of Ministers, the Ministry of Internal Affairs (MVD), and the KGB, and another for public consumption.

After my KGB interview a meeting was called at my laboratory. My colleagues did not try to convince me of errors in my letter. Instead they argued that such letters were futile and endanger the entire laboratory. We should stick to professional matters and not get involved in areas where we were dilettantes. I asked whether I would be permitted to go on conducting the seminar and political-information sessions.

"But you don't speak out against the regime as a propagandist, do you?" my colleagues replied. "We shall insist that you remain a propagandist." All of them saw the paradox that I, the only Marxist at the laboratory, was also the only unreliable employee. My more intelligent co-workers laughed at the situation; the less intelligent ones wondered why I was dissatisfied if I agreed with the official ideology.

The girl who had taken my letter to Odessa returned to Kiev and threw light on the reasons for our KGB interrogation. Eduard had a stepmother who disapproved of his going off to the virgin lands, instead of applying to the university, and later becoming a factory worker.

"Where's Eduard?" our messenger asked his stepmother. "I've brought a letter for him."

"I'll give it to him."

"No, I want to give it to him myself."

The messenger then took the letter to Eduard, who read it and put it in his pocket. His stepmother searched all his things, found the letter, and gave it to his father, an officer in the border guards. At the insistence of his wife, Eduard's father, much against his grain, took the letter to friends at the KGB.

The KGB interrogated Eduard on two consecutive days, each time for seven hours. He was asked the same questions as I had been. The telegram I had received was sent by the KGB, who were afraid I would have time to circulate my letter.

After this incident I decided to be more cautious in writing on political subjects, to be certain of the facts, assemble statistics, and study Marxist philosophy and party history. I also resolved to write for *samizdat* only under a pseudonym. I began by rereading Lenin's *The State and Revolution*. At first it seemed to me that for a socialist state the most important economic principle was payment according to work performed. The most important political principle was guarantees against the bureaucracy: appointments by election, removability, wages no higher than those of an average worker, freedom to criticize the government, and a gradual withering away of the state. I tried to calculate how much money was consumed by the party bosses and found that the amount was not great. Where was the surplus value going? It was being spent on armament, propaganda (including the space program), the police apparatus, and unprofitable enterprises.

Then I turned my attention to Marx. His writings contained the most cogent arguments I had ever encountered for freedom of speech, press, trade unions, and assembly. It became clear to me that these freedoms could help prevent the degeneration of the socialist revolution. From Marx's *Economic and Philosophic Manuscripts of 1844* I learned that everything created by man has a tendency to escape his control and to become alien and hostile to him. This includes alienated ideas, labor, and products of labor, as well as organizations and the state. When Lenin speaks about the state as an instrument that one class uses to oppress another, he sees only the most striking function of the exploitative society. Marx and Engels had a more profound conception of the state. Marx cited historical periods when the state transcended classes and became more or less autonomous, balancing class contradictions and drawing support from several mutually hostile classes.

My first work for *samizdat* was titled *Letters to a Friend* and was signed with the rather transparent pseudonym "Loza." [5] It consisted of ten letters or chapters. My main theses were that democracy is essential for socialism; the Soviet state functions as an abstract capitalist; economically the USSR is a state-capitalist society; in its form it is an ideocracy that has become an idolocracy.[6] The bureaucrats are not new exploiters but, rather, servants of an abstract capitalist—the state—that shares its profits with them.

Not having access to data about the salaries paid to the bureaucrats, I pointed out the unofficial benefits and privileges our rulers enjoy. High-ranking bureaucrats can buy goods of a much better quality at a price two or three times lower than the normal one, in special retail establishments that are concealed from the populace. My wife worked with two women who could shop at such establishments since their husbands were employed by the Council of Ministers of the Ukrainian Republic. One woman envied the other because her husband was qualified for admission to an establishment of a higher category, and the two boasted about their acquisitions without regard for their co-workers.

A professor of physiology with whom I was friendly once got drunk and poured out his troubles. He had been the student of a prominent Pavlovian and, thanks to this, was employed in a clinic reserved for the Central Committee, the Supreme Soviet, and the Council of Ministers of Ukraine. By simply asking one of his patients he could get anything his heart desired—cars, dachas, and passes to resorts and closed shops. But a battle was under way in Soviet physiology between two of Pavlov's students, one of whom was quite orthodox and the other less so. My friend's teacher, who was one of the opponents, lost the battle. Things looked bad for my friend until his patients came to the rescue. He even went up the ladder and was given access to a secret brothel reserved for the Central Committee. ("Shall we go visit the girls?" my friend interjected. "They're classy broads!") Alas, the brothel led to his downfall. One of the Central

Committee girls became pregnant, and my friend was asked to claim paternity. He proudly refused, because he hadn't made use of the girl's charms. The victim of the "servants of the people" was Polish. A letter in which my friend called her a "Polish tart" was intercepted. The girl complained to the Polish writer Wanda Wasilewska,[7] and charges of chauvinism and "ideological diversion" in physiology were brought against my friend. But the times were liberal, and he got off with an oral reprimand. I can still hear my friend's drunken comments: "Why do they need a brothel? All the broads are at their disposal anyway. But they're too old to get it up and have to use imported stimulants. The most potent one is from Burma. They pay huge sums for it, not out of their own pockets, of course. Shall I get some for you? I'm getting four hundred rubles a month now. I understand you. I hate the bourgeoisie, too. They bought me. I used to feel like shitting on their money, but now I drink it away. After all, I've got a conscience, too!"

Tanya and I had a friend who worked in a Moscow kindergarten for the children of the party bigwigs. Party and government leaders are divided into two groups: child-loving and non-child-loving. The latter send their children and grandchildren to boarding schools and see them only on weekends. Our friend taught at a kindergarten for "child-loving" parents, where the children were kept only eight hours a day. Each class had its own bus, and the children were taken on excursions to museums and the countryside. Fresh fruit and vegetables were flown in for them every day from the Crimea. The kindergarten had every imaginable toy and game, of course. This could be called microcommunism, invented for the children of those who are struggling to establish the Communist heaven on earth.

Our friend paid for her many benefits by being under constant pressure. The children were well aware of their own importance. When the grandson of Andrey Gromyko, the Minister of Foreign Affairs, was given a reprimand, he would fly into a rage and shout, "My grandpapa will put you in prison!" On one occasion a boy whose parents were lower in rank slammed the door on the finger of Gromyko's grandson. There were tears and screams. The victim's grandmother arrived and took her darling to one of the best doctors, who failed to discover anything but prescribed treatment. A menacing cloud gathered over the staff, but they got off lightly: only one teacher was fired.

As a minor official in the Ministry of Education, Tanya attended a ceremony at which a day-care center attached to a candy factory was awarded a medal for exemplary work. At the banquet after the ceremony the factory bosses served sweets to their comrades from the Ministry. They had the same labels as items sold in ordinary shops, but the quality was much higher. Even honey for the "servants of the people" is gathered from beehives located in orchards and fields that are not sprayed with insecticides.

At a conference on the state of nursery schools in rural areas, held in Mykolayiv in southeast Ukraine, the delegates were shown nursery schools where the play equipment had been manufactured in nearby concentration camps. Once again prisoners were used to help build the Potyomkin villages of socialism. These and many other, similar facts led me to conclude that the Soviet Union had become a new form of exploitative society, and it was on such firsthand information that I now based my writing.

Samizdat in the early 1960's was largely literary, philosophical, and religious, and my first work was not widely distributed. Several years later I learned that someone had been caught with a copy of my essay and given a prison sentence because of its harsh criticism. In all my subsequent writings I tried to put criticism in euphemistic terms. Why say that Yuriy Andropov, the chief of the KGB, is a bandit and that Nuremberg longs for him, when you can say that his organization is anti-Soviet and unconstitutional? The sense is the same, but the reader who is caught with such a document may get a lighter sentence.

At the Institute of Physiology I met a professor who was studying the biopotential of acupuncture points. He discovered that when an internal organ was diseased, the point associated with it showed a marked increase in potential. In trying to develop a method of diagnosing disease on this basis he ran into certain constant obstacles. The potential in the acupuncture points was affected by magnetic storms on the sun. The professor asked me to prove statistically that such a connection exists. I began by trying to determine whether the chakras—the centers of vital energy in yoga theory—are similar to acupuncture points, and discovered twelve points along the spine with heightened potentials. The professor gave me data for magnetic storms and for potentials in various points. I found a marked correlation.

At about that time, the Academy of Sciences received a brochure from a North Korean scientist. Guided by the wise Kim Il Sung, the brochure began, Korean scientists had united ancient Korean and contemporary scientific achievements and were thus able to explain acupuncture. By performing histological cross sections, the author of the brochure had established that in addition to the nervous, circu-

66

latory, and lymphatic systems, the body contains a fourth system which links its energy centers. I excitedly urged the professor to investigate the Korean research so that we could use new data in studying ancient Chinese and Indian medicine. He countered that the brochure was on a very low scientific level. "All the more reason for you to investigate it," I said.

Soon after, the professor attended a conference on acupuncture. He returned in a humorous mood. The latest achievements of Korean socialist physiology had turned out to be a fake. The photographs offered as evidence in the brochure revealed nothing. One had to wear dialectical-materialist eyeglasses to see the fourth connecting system. The conference ended in laughter, but the party ordered that nothing be published, to avoid harming relations with North Korea.

A year later we received a second brochure from the Korean scientist, this time in English ("He thinks it will be more scientific in English," the professor cracked), with further evidence of the existence of a fourth system. The Korean scientist had injected radioactive elements into the acupuncture points and taken photographs that showed the trajectories of the marked atoms. The trajectories were roughly similar to lines on ancient Chinese diagrams of the human body. The professor remarked with surprise that the text was much more scientific than the previous one. I insisted that we repeat the Korean experiments, but the professor was afraid that his colleagues would laugh him down if he were to confirm the Korean theory. After the first brochure everyone was convinced that this was all nonsense.

Soon afterward a highly secret biocybernetic laboratory was set up in Kiev. Kyy and Kolesnykov, the directors, conceived the idea of transmitting the biopotential of a healthy organ to the corresponding organ of a sick person. In this way a man could be made to move a paralyzed leg or regain his sexual potency. Kyy and Kolesnykov even dreamed of implanting electrodes in a man's brain and controlling his behavior through radio signals. I had once read about similar experiments by an American scientist and told Kyy about them. He and Kolesnykov thereupon informed the Central Committee that the Americans might find a way of controlling masses of people by radio. The Soviet Union could not afford to lag behind, so the Central Committee issued the appropriate directives. The more sober scientists at the institute tried to cool down the young enthusiasts and to prepare a scientifically sound work plan, but Kyy and Kolesnykov had such strong support from the Central Committee that they were given a free hand. They started to scheme against their colleagues, to the point of fighting over the washroom. Large sums of money were appropriated to their research, rather than to the institute. They were finally thrown out, but they set up their own laboratory, which was shrouded in secrecy. Even their lowly technicians would hardly speak to us. Finally, a committee was appointed to inspect Kyy and Kolesnykov's laboratory, of which my boss, Antomonov, was a member. It was found that the laboratory had signed an agreement with the Ministry of Defense and bought huge quantities of expensive equipment. One piece, an ultramodern spectroscope bought at great cost in West Germany, later migrated to my laboratory. I asked Kolesnykov's co-workers what it was for. They had thought they might investigate some sort of body radiations but had no idea what kind.

The investigating committee further established that under the cover of secrecy Kyy and Kolesnykov had been writing ridiculous articles full of war fantasies. The articles were read only by army officers, who liked the fantasies and left the scientific nonsense to the scientists. At the conclusion of the investigation a joint meeting of the staffs at the two laboratories was held, but the findings were not revealed. A representative of the institute's party bureau summed up all the complaints and proposed that the two laboratories be merged. "And now we shall have a closed party meeting," he announced. "All Communists will stay behind." We almost broke up with laughter: only those who had just been defeated remained behind. In the end, Kyy and Kolesnykov were dismissed from the laboratory for "adventurism in science."

I became friendly with several of Kolesnykov's former co-workers. One of them told me about his experiences with him. Kolesnykov had once called him in and said, "You've been meeting regularly with a Jew. Don't you have any Russian or Ukrainian friends?"

"What difference does his nationality make? He's an interesting scientist."

"Jews work only for themselves. Even Einstein didn't have a school of his own."

Kolesnykov had served in the NKVD troops after the war and took part in the campaign against the Banderites.[8] When he was drunk, he would reminisce about NKVD tactics. A list of the guerrillas in a village would be drawn up. Soldiers would storm into a house and ask, "Is Ivan at home?"

"No, I'm his brother."

The soldiers would shoot the brother and put an X beside Ivan's name. Sometimes Ivan would be killed three or four times.

Oddly enough, Kolesnykov despised the Soviet regime, Communist ideology, and workers and peasants, whom he called "cattle." But he lived according to his favorite proverb: "When in Rome, do as the Romans do." My boss, Antomonov, who was honest to a degree, tried to persuade Kolesnykov that his methods in dealing with scientific competitors were not entirely clean. Kolesnykov always replied by citing the proverb.

Not long before my arrest I learned that Kolesnykov had set himself up in a biological institute and Kyy had got a job in another department at the Institute of Cybernetics. They were still faithful to the party's general line. I do not want to defame all Soviet intellectuals, and I must admit that most of them are more intelligent and honest than Kolesnykov. Yet it is no accident that few writers supported Solzhenitsyn and almost no academicians supported Sakharov.

7

REMEMBERING
THE PAST

In recent years Soviet intellectuals have increasingly refused to collaborate in the crimes of the state. Honest and thoughtful scientists try not to lie in their research or to help the military industry. Conscientious teachers prefer to teach natural science, because it requires less lying than literature or the social sciences. Tanya was very pleased when she was able to transfer from the Office of Preschool Education to the Office of Games and Toys, because she thought she'd be able to stop lying in her work: no ideology is involved in chess and dolls. Solzhenitsyn's appeal to avoid lies has become an unshakable tenet of the Democratic Movement.

Yet applying this principle to daily life in the Soviet Union is almost impossible. Once Tanya had mastered the theory of learning through games, she realized that games, too, can be used to lie. Until recently Soviet educators discouraged toy rifles, tanks, and cannons, but now they have begun to encourage "military-patriotic education," both in the classroom and in games and toys. Soviet ideologists have made patriotism almost synonymous with militarism. They deride the militarization of schools in China and the abundance of military toys in the United States and at the same time conduct war games in all Soviet schools. Older teachers continue from habit to reject military toys, but they are reprimanded for being conservative and not understanding education through games. Small children are bombarded with such ideologically saturated games as How Broad My Native Land, The October Revolution, and War Heroes. The more intelligent educators try to explain that children find most ideas boring and complicated. Children should first be taught basic morality, logic, and esthetics. Only then can they study history and discuss ideas. But such recommendations are taken by the authorities to be, at best, a sign of ideological immaturity.

The necessity for lying leads many people to think about escaping to the woods, out of the country, or to God, away from this realm of lies, fear, and idiocy. Yuliy Daniel's story "Atonement" expresses the Soviet intellectual's dream:

If only I could forget the past—go away, follow the gipsy caravan. . . . It's a dream dear to my heart. A Soviet intellectual longs to get away from it all like that—kicking up the dust on the road with polished shoes as creased as an accordion. Ah, all those lovely gipsy girls! . . . Come on, Mishka, cheer us up!

> I answer the gipsy girls: In my heart
> The free and open roads are barred.
> I cannot move, I cannot jump or break away.
> My ties are strong. Look, I cannot leave.

Mishka was nearly in tears over the guitar. Everybody smiled with embarrassment. Of course it would be nice—but how can you really get away? Union officials, party bosses, endless queues—they're everywhere.[1]

My escape was into science and philosophy. After the research on acupuncture, I was assigned to study changes in blood sugar. Our biologists assembled hypotheses about the functioning of the liver, pancreas, kidneys, and other organs connected with the regulation of blood sugar. They developed a model they translated into mathematical equations. We mathematicians had to determine whether these equations reflected the actual functioning of an organism. The biologists "sucked blood," as they put it, from rabbits, and projected curves. Then the mathematicians used an analog machine to represent their equations. By manipulating various circuits they obtained on the oscillograph curves resembling those obtained by the biologists. This was called "modeling." At first I took this for real science, but the more I saw, the more disillusioned I became. I realized that as long as the proper parameters are established the machine can be used to verify contradictory hypotheses. We were merely reproducing the biologists' theories. If these were valid, then our formulas might also be valid; if they were invalid, then our models were unacceptable. Lenin wrote about "mathematical idealism," in which matter disappears behind formulas. Soviet biocybernetics is permeated with this "mathematical idealism." Cybernetics is increasingly becoming mere verbiage, and offshoots are proliferating. The philosopher Kopnin quipped, "All we need now is portmanteauology." [2] The pervasive ideological falsehood turns science into a "cyberniad."

71

Many people convert their longing for God into a primitive mathematico-physico-technocratic mythology, a belief in the magic wand of cybernetic machines and formulaic incantations.

The passion for yoga and parapsychology is only one expression of the longing for scientific mysticism. With some delay—the Soviet Union is always behind in fashions—ufologists appeared in Moscow and Kiev. I met some of the more prominent ones. How strange that even intelligent people can long for miracles so badly that they lose their scientific skepticism and concern for facts and logic. Ufology has had a particularly strong influence on mathematicians, physicists, and astronomers, people who are supposedly accustomed to precise scientific thinking.

A physicist who was also a parapsychologist and ufologist said to me, "We have a chance to establish telepathic contact with a flying saucer. They've been observing Earth for a long time and apparently don't want to interfere in our history. You understand politics. We'll put you in touch with them and have you speak on behalf of Earth."

"Let's ask them to finish off the guards in the camps and prisons with their magnetic rays," I replied with a straight face.

"That's a splendid idea!" the physicist exclaimed. "But you know, they're probably very humane and won't agree to it."

"All right, perhaps we can just ask them to put the guards to sleep."

When you realize that even learned cyberneticists think this way, you see that it isn't at all funny. Victor Glushkov, for example, is advocating a single automated control system for the entire Soviet Union.[3] The concealed meaning in his project is that machines will replace the stupid government. Beyond that lies the idea that he, Victor Glushkov, will control the cybernetic state. We've had enough of such foolish leaders. Glushkov considers himself a Marxist (sincerely, I believe), but he fails to understand that there are economic and historical laws and classes and social groups with their particular interests and ideologies. The development of society will be determined by its own basis and superstructure and not by the cyberneticists. Automated control systems will be subject to the passions of the cyberneticists, as well as to their intellects. The systems will have no regard for people, and the latter will deceive them and perhaps rebel against them when the cybernetic-socialist paradise becomes too hellish.

The cybernetic myth is increasingly replacing the myth of a socialist paradise in the Soviet Union. Can this be deemed progress? At first men worshiped rocks, then animals, ancestors, Aphrodite, Zeus, and finally Christ. Then they concluded that they need not worship gods and instead began to worship progress, the working class, and the leaders. Today they worship machines and formulas. At first there was an ascending line toward Christ. Then came a descending line toward magic and paganism. It is no accident that the worship of formulas is frequently intertwined with a traditional occultism based on ancient magic and cabala.

A case in point is Mykhaylo Klokov, a professor of botany with whom Tanya and I became friendly.[4] A fascinating old man with a paradoxical cast of mind, he called Marxism a mystic teaching but had quite a positive attitude toward other forms of mysticism. He proposed that dialectics be replaced by "polyalectics," but when I asked him what he meant by this he replied only in metaphors. At that time the existence of genetics as an independent science was being threatened by the quackery of Trofim Lysenko, and I asked Klokov what he as a botanist thought of the Lysenko school.

"I'm not a psychiatrist, and I don't understand these mental diseases," Klokov explained. "A botanist was recently defending his dissertation at the Academy of Sciences. I explained to those present that I had studied magic, white and black. In my opinion, the doctoral candidate had made a very significant contribution, but to magic and not botany."

When we first met Klokov, Tanya and I were just beginning to learn about the history of Soviet science, and the professor's paradoxes were amusing. He loved to tell stories about Lysenko and to criticize Einstein from a theosophical point of view. Klokov knew Ukrainian history and literature well, and through him we met other theosophists in Kiev. Several of them were intelligent people who gave me insights into problems I had not known about. Yet I was also repelled by the way most theosophists took reality as a steppingstone toward the theosophical paradise. In response to my tirades against the persecution of Ukrainian culture, Klokov's wife told me a parable.

"The Devil saw peasants tilling their soil. Envious of their solidarity in labor, he scattered rocks in the fields. But at the suggestion of the angel who appeared to them, the peasants piled the rocks together and built a shrine to God. That is how people can turn satanic evil into good."

"You've forgotten the rest of the story," I said with an angry smile. Twenty Ukrainians had just been sentenced to labor camps, and I had lost some of my optimism. "Having built the shrine, the peasants went in to sing praise to the Lord. In the midst of their singing they heard the angel's mocking laughter. He was Satan. The peasants rushed at him with raised fists, but the door was locked. Their shrine had become a prison."

"How can you live with such apocalyptic pessimism?" Klokov's wife asked me. She had revealed the secret of her theosophy: one must hide from the abominations of our age behind ideological hallucinations. People use Christianity, theosophy, Marxism, cybernetics, or other achievements of the human mind as rose-colored glasses, and they plug their ears with filters and transformers that turn the screams of their fellow men into the "music of the spheres."

But it was not Klokov's treacly philosophy that finally alienated Tanya and me from him. One day he gave us his poetry to read. We discovered that he had been publishing poetry in Ukrainian for many years under the pseudonym Dolengo. His poems were a surrealistic mixture of socialist realism and theosophical bathos. Even worse than the literary falseness was the fact that Dolengo had been a hangman of Ukrainian culture in the 1920's and 1930's. He, Ivan Mykytenko, and Volodymyr Koryak had been particularly active in persecuting Ukrainian writers.[5] Mykytenko died at his battle post: he committed suicide when he sensed that his turn would be next.* Koryak disappeared in 1937, probably deported to a Siberian labor camp. Dolengo proved to be the most perspicacious. Realizing that it was dangerous to be even a "tag-along," he began a new career as the botanist Klokov. But his new profession also proved suspect. When Lysenko renewed his attacks on the geneticists after the war, Klokov had to save himself by moving away from the "hot spots" of science. Today he can think whatever he pleases, albeit in a narrow circle of friends. Polyalectics spares him the need to think about his fellow men (he was a close friend of Yevhen Sverstyuk's) or to feel pangs of conscience over his crimes against the Ukrainian people.

I write about this because few people want to remember the past, especially in the Soviet Union. "A country must know its informers," Solzhenitsyn wrote. And its hangmen, too, I might add. Almost no one knows about Professor Klokov, and those who do know him respect him for his anti-Marxist views. The young people are not at fault here: they have not been permitted to learn their own history. But many of the "martyrs" they admire were fools, and others were hangmen. Suffering is not a merit; it is no guarantee of intelligence, honesty, or courage.

---

* Mykytenko had the misfortune to fight in the Spanish Civil War. Almost all the Soviet participants in that war, including Mikhail Koltsov, who had finished off the Spanish Trotskyists, proved to be "enemies of the people."

In May 1962, an evening in honor of Anatol Petrytsky, the most prominent artist of the Ukrainian renascence of the 1920's, was held in Kiev. The hall was jammed with young people who applauded every hint at the abominations of Stalinism. I would have applauded, too, if I hadn't been sitting with a man who had taken part in the renascence and was able to comment on the speeches for me.

Almost all the speakers, who now claimed to have been Petrytsky's friends, had either helped his persecutors or watched indifferently as he was hounded. Petrytsky's wife sat beside them, crying because her husband's contribution to Ukrainian culture had been recognized posthumously. I remembered Ivan Karamazov's words about the mother who forgave the murderer of her child. Murderers should not be forgiven, at least here on earth. By forgiving them we condone their complicity in the "first circle" and make it easier for them to commit new crimes.

Almost no writers—"engineers of the soul," as they were called—have publicly confessed to complicity in Stalinism. I can remember only the Avar poet Rasul Gamzatov, who repented in *My Daghestan* for having taken part in the vilification of Shamil, the leader of the native resistance to the Russian occupation of the Caucasus.[6] Volodymyr Sosyura repudiated his verses in praise of Stalin by reading in public excerpts from his poem *Mazepa*.[7] People do not want to repent because of pangs of conscience, yet only such repentance frees a man from the burden of his guilt and from dependence on what others think. Otherwise repentance is replaced by alcoholism or suicide.

Just when our despair at the indifference we saw all around us was becoming almost completely intolerable, a speech by Ivan Dzyuba suddenly appeared in *samizdat*. Dzyuba had spoken at an evening in honor of Vasyl Symonenko, a leading poet of the Ukrainian revival of the 1960's who had died at an early age.[8] Tanya and I discovered that three blocks away from us there lived a man who was openly speaking his mind. Society has a habit of ignoring or persecuting gifted people while they are alive and making them into icons once they are dead. On behalf of Vasyl Symonenko's true friends and admirers Dzyuba told the authorities, "Vasyl is not yours and you will not be able to kill him with your love." I went to visit Dzyuba and met an intelligent and modest man who by inclination was indifferent to politics. This disturbed me. We needed "politicians," people who would disseminate *samizdat* and deliberately spread information.

Reading about the crimes of Stalin and his henchmen is one thing, but the psychological influence of an eyewitness is quite another. One such eyewitness who gave me the incentive to join the fight was Karl Shalme, a Latvian who had run away from home during the Civil War, fought in the Red Army, and then joined the secret police. He claimed never to have killed innocent people. In 1937 his friends and co-workers began to be taken away.

"What's going on?" Shalme's wife asked him one evening. "Ivan Ivanovich was arrested yesterday. Isn't he a genuine Bolshevik?"

"If the authorities are taking him away, they must have a reason," Shalme replied. "They'll determine whether he's innocent." He hadn't finished answering when a knock came at the door and three men walked in. "On what basis?" Shalme asked.

The agents answered by hitting him in the face. "That's our basis!" They turned the apartment upside down, broke dishes, tore pillows apart, stole all the money, and took Shalme away. His prison cell was so jammed that everyone had to stand.

"Why have you been arrested?" he was immediately asked.

"I don't know. I'm innocent."

"Surname, name, and patronymic?"

"Shalme, Karl Ivanovich."

"Fascist spy! Ten years of labor camp."

Shalme decided that he was in the hands of the regime's sworn enemies and vowed to remain silent because they would kill him if they discovered that he was a Chekist. He remained silent in the camps for twenty years. His wife lived in abject poverty because no one would give her a job, and their two children were always hungry. When the Germans came, neighbors advised Shalme's wife to report that her husband had been taken away by the Bolsheviks. She refused and lived in even greater poverty. The Germans deported the children to work in Germany. After the war she searched for her children and waited for her husband. Now the couple were here with Tanya and me. Shalme passionately loved the violin and claimed that he owned a Stradivarius; we didn't believe in the Stradivarius, but we did believe that suffering had purified him. No wonder he loved music.

Shalme asked me to bring him Schopenhauer, and I lent him *Counsels and Maxims.* When I came to take the book back, Shalme ecstatically read out all the misogynist and misopedist aphorisms. I attempted to rebut them, but Shalme cited hundreds of examples of human vileness in the camps. I tried to justify Shalme by saying to myself that he had lived through a lot. Each time that Tanya and I visited Shalme, he would interrupt our intellectual discussions to run out on his balcony and shout at neighbors for shaking dust onto it, or at children for making noise. We began to realize that Shalme's love for his missing children had been distorted into a hatred of other people's children.

A juvenile gang appeared in Shalme's neighborhood. The boys would get drunk, insult and beat up passers-by, and break into apartments. They even climbed through the balcony into the apartment of a paralyzed man and made indecent advances to his wife while he watched helplessly. Shalme tried to persuade his neighbors to file complaints against the rowdies, but they were all afraid. The militia could not do anything without witnesses. After one of our discussions Shalme, Tanya, and I saw a group of boys and girls, obviously drunk, having a good time. Shalme grumbled about dissolute young people. I defended them by saying that they weren't hurting anyone.

Suddenly one of the youngsters walked up to Shalme. "Why are you out here, old man? Nothing to do?"

I asked the boy to be more polite to his elders.

"Shut up, you shit, I'm not talking to you!"

"That's no way for you to talk. There's a woman here."

The boy swung back and hit me. It doesn't take much to knock me down. When I got up, a crowd had gathered. I rushed at the rowdy, beside myself with rage. Shalme put his arms around me. "Calm down," he whispered. "The militia will take care of him."

The boy's elderly mother ran up and begged him to behave himself. He cursed her soundly. Finally everyone calmed down and went his own way.

The next day Shalme urged me to file a complaint. After my experiences in the Light Cavalry I had no sympathy for the militia and refused. Then Shalme insisted that this was the only way to intimidate the rowdies and keep them from terrorizing the neighbors. I agreed to write a complaint.

The investigator called Tanya and me to testify. He was so amiable that I forgot he worked for the police. Then came the confrontation with the rowdy. He had a pitiful, ingratiating smile and a hangdog look. I repeated my testimony, but in a slightly milder version. The boy confirmed everything except that he had cursed his mother. "I love her, I'm her only son," he whimpered.

The militiamen gave us the record to sign. I signed it without looking at it. They wouldn't lie, would they? The boy hesitated and then began to read the record. "Enough, everything's clear now," the investigator said, urging him on.

When he had finished reading, the boy said reproachfully, "But I said that I didn't curse my mother!" The investigator reluctantly added his words to the record.

When I saw Shalme again, he insisted that I had given the investigator incorrect evidence. I should have testified that there was group hooliganism. What was the point of filing a complaint against the one boy? He'd be put away, but the others would remain at large. Besides, a KGB major who lived in the same building had seen the whole incident and had heard the ring of metal. He thought that someone had had brass knuckles. I calmly explained that there had been no group hooliganism and that the KGB major's story was unconvincing.

At the trial several weeks later Tanya and I repeated our testimony. Shalme elaborated his theory of group hooliganism and brass knuckles. It became clear that the boy could be given a long sentence. Tanya and I began to mitigate our testimony and to deny that brass knuckles or group hooliganism had been involved. The defense counsel realized what we were doing and tried to make us admit that we had invented almost everything. The woman judge, who had been shouting only at the accused, now began to shout at us: "You ought to be more polite!" I shouted back at her, "I'm not on trial yet." It worked.

The prosecutor began his speech for the summation by citing the latest party resolutions. Then he established a direct link between hooliganism and political crime. He concluded by demanding a sentence of seven years' imprisonment. Tanya and I shuddered. Shalme beamed. In her speech for the defense the lawyer argued that there had been no crime, simply an unpleasant misunderstanding, and asked for an acquittal. When the court retired to chambers, the boy burst into tears. His mother came up to us and apologized for his behavior. We, too, were close to tears. It was our fault that the boy would get seven years.

The court returned with a one-year suspended sentence. Twenty percent of the boy's wages would be docked, and if he was convicted again during the next year, a year in a labor camp would be added to the new sentence. Tanya and I sighed with relief. Leaving the courthouse, we were too ashamed to look at each other. The investigator, the judge, the prosecutor, and Shalme were all bandits. The hooligan was a lamb by comparison with them. We had sided with the bandits against the lamb. We realized that the falsified trials of the past could very easily be repeated. Several scoundrels come to an understanding, and an undesirable person is locked away. Had we confirmed that there were brass knuckles and group hooliganism, the boy would have received a long sentence.

I met Shalme again after 1968, when the danger of prison was looming before me. He reproached me for not coming to see him. I explained that I didn't want to see people who helped the authorities trump up trials.

"You mean that criminals should go on misbehaving and even committing murder?" he asked with astonishment.

"No, it's the fault of the authorities, of those who tortured you and your wife. First we have to deal with the cause of hooliganism— the KGB and the militia—and only then with the hooligans."

Six months later I learned that Shalme had been committed to a psychiatric hospital. The diagnosis was paranoia.

The story of the Jewish writer N. had an even more powerful effect on Tanya and me. Before the war she had been friends with Vera Gedroyts, who had been a student of the famous Dr. Roux in Switzerland.[9] Roux urged her to stay with him, but she returned to Russia and was put in charge of the Tsar's hospital. She was friendly with the last Empress and later always spoke of her with respect and love. During the Civil War Gedroyts was taken out to be shot simply because she was an aristocrat, but she was saved by a Cheka officer who remembered that she had hidden him from the tsarist secret police.

Vera Gedroyts was acquainted with many Russian writers and revolutionaries. Under the pseudonym Sergey Gedroyts she published three small volumes of memoirs. Then Konstantin Fedin turned to her with a request: he had contracted pulmonary tuberculosis and wanted to go to Switzerland for treatment.[10] Gedroyts wrote to her Swiss friends, and Fedin was admitted to a sanatorium. The treatment was successful, and he returned to Russia. The fourth volume of Gedroyts's memoirs was being prepared for publication. Fedin read the manuscript, was displeased, and banned it.

Several years later Gedroyts was invited to become the director of Roux's hospital. The letter said that she was the best surgeon in the world and could do a great deal for the development of science if she lived in Switzerland. But Gedroyts did not want to leave her homeland, even such as it was at the time. On her deathbed she asked her friend N. to preserve the letter. "The day will come when love for Russia will not be reprehensible. This letter will serve as proof of the achievements of Russian science. Give me your word that you will save the letter."

When the secret police came to N. in 1938, they found Gedroyts's letter. N.'s husband was arrested and accused of being an "international spy" because he had a letter from Switzerland. Twenty-four witnesses were interrogated. Only one of them, a janitor, gave unfavorable testimony. He had been shoveling snow when N.'s husband walked by and said, "What hard work you have!" The janitor interpreted these words to the NKVD as anti-Soviet propaganda. N.'s husband was very brave at the interrogations and did not confess to anything. His cellmates called him "the Saint." They all advised him to confess: it was foolish to remain silent under torture. Even the interrogators began to call him "the Saint." They were drunk when they questioned him and amused themselves by throwing wine and vodka bottles at his head. In the end they let him go: there was only one witness, and the suspect hadn't confessed. They cautioned him to keep quiet.

N.'s husband returned home trembling and emaciated. When his wife asked what had happened to him, he pointed to the walls, doors, and ceiling and remained silent. At night they pulled a blanket over their heads in bed, and he told her what had happened. A week later N. reminded her husband about their promise to Vera Gedroyts. He begged her to forget it. She forced him to telephone the NKVD because they had promised to return his papers when they let him go. "You motherfucking saint!" the interrogator interrupted in mid-sentence. "Do you want to pay us another visit?" N. realized her cruelty. It took ten years for her husband's fractured skull to kill him.

Tanya and I met many, many such families. It seemed that almost every family had a member who had served in the secret police and another who had been imprisoned. People such as Shalme combined the two roles. At first we hated the secret police for having destroyed the Revolution. But then our hatred became deeper and turned into an anger at all the hangmen who had murdered millions of nonrevolutionaries. Why did these millions of people have to perish? Because they wanted to live a little better, or because they didn't want to march off to paradise, or because they wanted a different paradise, or because they didn't want anything at all from their benefactors?

8

REPRESSION AND ALIENATION

In 1965 I went to Moscow to meet Victor Krasin.[1] Tanya, to her great joy, had been given by him Pasternak's *Doctor Zhivago*.[2] In return we sent him a *samizdat* edition of Saint-Exupéry's *The Citadel*. Krasin had been a university student during the Stalin years. His father, a professor at Kiev University, was executed in 1937. Victor formed a group with several friends to study Gandhi's philosophy. They were arrested for this and sentenced to labor camps.

Krasin told me that two writers, Sinyavsky and Daniel, had been arrested after they published their works abroad under pseudonyms.[3] I asked my friends in Moscow to get the two men's books for me. One friend—he had studied with Sinyavsky—immediately picked up the telephone. "Bring me something by Sinyavsky."

I was stunned by his boldness. "Whom did you call?"

"The provincial party committee. I have a friend who works there."

Back in Kiev reports were spreading about arrests of Ukrainian intellectuals. On September 4, 1965, Sergo Paradzhanov's film *Shadows of Forgotten Ancestors* premiered at the Ukrayina Cinema.[4] Ivan Dzyuba addressed the film makers on behalf of the population of Kiev.[5] After the initial congratulation Dzyuba turned to the spectators and announced that twenty intellectuals had been arrested. The purges of 1937 were drawing near, he declared. The theater manager tried to tear the microphone away. Paradzhanov came to Dzyuba's assistance: "Let him speak!" When the microphone went dead, young people in the audience spoke in support of Dzyuba.

Foreign radio stations reported that Dzyuba had been arrested. I went to see him. People had been calling him all day to verify the news. "They must have mixed me up with Ivan Svitlychny," Dzyuba laughed.

On March 23, 1966, I learned from a friend connected with the militia that Alexander Martynenko, Ivan Rusyn, and Yevheniya Kuznetsova would go on trial in two days. I told Dzyuba, but he refused to believe me, because none of the relatives or witnesses in the case had been summoned to court yet. It took me a long time to convince him that my information was reliable.

On the morning of the twenty-fifth, about fifteen of us gathered at the courthouse. Our group included Yevhen Sverstyuk, Ivan Drach, Lina Kostenko, Lyubov Zabashta, Oles Berdnyk, and the wife of Ivan Svitlychny, who had also been arrested in 1965 but for some reason had not been brought to trial.[6] Militiamen at the door prevented us from entering. An argument broke out. Why were they not letting anyone in when the law said that the trial should be open to the public? The militiamen cited a court order.

Five or six of us went to the Prosecutor's Office. The reception room was jammed. Dzyuba explained to the secretary that we were from the Writers' Union and had to attend the trial of a colleague. The secretary effusively invited us to come into her office out of turn. After all, we were writers, engineers of souls. "Is it a murder trial?" She smiled solicitously.

"No," Dzyuba replied.

"Raping a minor?" She continued to smile.

"Article 62 of the Criminal Code."[7]

The secretary looked up the article. Her smile was replaced by icy wrath. "Anti-Soviet agitation and propaganda?"

We explained that the charges had been trumped up in the manner of the trials of the 1930's. According to the law, trials of this kind could not be held *in camera*, and we had the right to attend. The secretary asked us to leave the room; she would telephone her superiors.

While we were standing at the door, Lyubov Zabashta began to reproach me for speaking Russian. I patiently explained that I had lived in Kirghizia and Odessa, where Ukrainian is almost never heard, and so found it difficult to speak the language.

"But aren't you Ukrainian?" she asked.

"Yes, I am."

"Then you should speak your own language!"

"But that's not important. The important thing is fighting for freedom of thought!"

The prosecutor's secretary interrupted the argument by calling us in. The trial was being held *in camera* legally, she announced, and the prosecutor was too busy to see us. Lina Kostenko sarcastically reminded us of Kafka's *The Trial*.

At the courthouse militiamen were guarding only the doors leading to courtrooms. We darted up the stairs leading to the District Prosecutor's Office. Two militiamen ran after us. "Where are you going, citizens? That's a restricted area!"

Dzyuba told the militiamen that we had been told that the Prosecutor's Office was always open to the public. The militiamen hesitated and then, pointing for some reason at me, announced that they would throw us out. "We have orders not to let you in."

"Do you have a photograph of me in your orders?" I asked. "How do you know that I am not allowed to enter?"

"We've been told not to let any of you in!"

Nevertheless, we managed to get through to the prosecutor. "Why is there an order not to admit us to the Prosecutor's Office?" Dzyuba asked.

"What do you mean, you're not admitted? Why are you lying?" the prosecutor asked. "Anyone can enter."

Just then one of the militiamen opened the door. "There's the man who told us about the order," Dzyuba said. "Isn't that so?"

The militiaman nodded assent.

"It must be an order from another department. What do you want?"

"We aren't being admitted to a trial under Article 62. Why is the trial being held *in camera*?"

"By law."

"But the law says that trials can be held *in camera* in only three cases: if there is a danger of revealing a state secret, if the accused is a minor, or if the case involves sexual depravity. Why was this trial closed to the public?"

"The law stipulates that the court decides whether to hold the trial *in camera*."

"But only in the three instances the law provides for. On what basis have you closed the trial?"

"On the basis of the law."

"But the law says . . ."

"On the basis of the court's ruling."

And so the circle went around and around.

Suddenly Zabashta gave a hysterical cry. "Why are you speaking to us in Russian?"

"Because I'm a Russian."

"But you're in Ukraine. Lenin said . . ."

"These are the fools one has to deal with all the time," Dzyuba whispered to me. I nodded in agreement. Zabashta was concerned about the language in which this farce was taking place, while we were concerned about people. A heated argument about the Ukrainianization of the administrative apparatus broke out.

In the end, forced to leave, we gathered at the main entrance. Dzyuba and several others continued to demand that we be allowed to attend the trial, but the militiamen replied that the courtroom was small and all the seats had been taken. Finally four people were admitted. Lina Kostenko commenced to write down the proceedings, but militiamen confiscated her notebook. Without hesitating, she threw a bouquet of flowers to the accused. The court officials and militiamen dropped to the floor as if it were a bomb.

Later we learned the details of the trial, which was described in the verdict as "open." Alexander Martynenko was sentenced to three years, Rusyn to a year, and Kuznetsova to four years. I asked Dzyuba why some defendants recanted or even betrayed their friends, why those who had behaved courageously at this and other trials could be counted on one's fingers, whereas the rest incriminated their friends and tried to shield themselves. Dzyuba replied that the people who had behaved badly had been protesting for emotional reasons and did not have a firm basis for their convictions. I had to agree.

After the trial my contacts with the Ukrainian patriots became more frequent, and I managed to read several letters of protest against the illegal arrests. One of the letters was signed by the famous aircraft designer Oleg Antonov.[8] I decided to write a similar letter and to obtain signatures from Russian and Jewish intellectuals. When I showed my letter to two scientists, they approved it but advised me to get the signatures of Academician Glushkov and Professor Amosov.[9] "That way it will be easy to get signatures from many less prominent scientists," they advised.

Glushkov was an hour late for the appointment. "What is your business?" he asked dryly when he saw me.

"People are again being put on trial for their convictions. I want you to sign this letter of protest."

"Yes, you're right," Glushkov said when he had read the letter. "The trial of Sinyavsky and Daniel damaged the country's reputation. But I've already mentioned this to the Central Committee. Those two should have been tried on criminal charges. I've heard that they were involved in currency speculation. What trials in Kiev are you writing about?"

"Ukrainian patriots were on trial a week ago."

"Oh, the ones who were carrying on like hooligans at the cinema? Some fellow named Dzyuba spoke there, and his henchmen wouldn't let the people who were scared leave. They attacked the cowards with their fists. It's bad to be a coward, but what sort of freedom fighters are these people if they deny others the freedom to be afraid?"

"I know Dzyuba's 'henchmen,' " I replied. "They're frail little intellectuals, and they wouldn't fight even if they knew how."

"Were you there?" Glushkov asked.

"No."

"What sort of mathematician are you if you don't base yourself on the facts?"

"Were you there?" I countered.

"No, but I heard about it from a member of the Presidium who witnessed everything."

"And I heard about it from a dozen people, including some who hate or are afraid of the Ukrainian patriots. You're a party member and should understand that one's social class can distort one's perception of the facts. My facts are more reliable, because I have more witnesses, and some of those witnesses are opposed to the Ukrainian patriots."

"Neither of us was there, so there's no point in continuing this argument. Do you know what OUN means?" *

"The Organization of Ukrainian Nationalists."

"Yes, the Banderites. They and the fascists murdered thousands of Russians and Jews."

"Not all of them fought with the fascists. Most Ukrainian peasants were opposed to Stalin because they remembered the famine. When they saw what Hitler was like, they rose up against the fascists, too."

"Either you don't know history or you're juggling with the facts. I'm from the Don region, and I know there was famine there as well as in the Kuban region and in Siberia. The famine was the fault of the kulaks."

"But troops were stationed at the borders of Ukraine to keep starving people from going to Russia. I heard about that from people who were involved in the collectivization campaign."

"I have no time left. I will get all the details about the Ukrainian trials and will call you if I need to."

After Glushkov, I showed the letter to Amosov's co-workers. "Don't

* See note 8 on p. 388.—TRANS.

go to him because he'll telephone the KGB immediately," they cautioned. "He's a member of the Supreme Soviet."

"What if I come with Lina Kostenko?"

"Then perhaps he'll sign the letter. He's very eager for recognition by intellectuals and professionals."

"Will any of you sign it?" I asked.

They exchanged glances, and the bravest one said, "We'll all sign it if Amosov does. Otherwise we're afraid."

The response of Amosov's favorites convinced me that seeing him wasn't worth the risk. I returned to the two scientists who had advised me to obtain the bosses' signatures.

"Scoundrels!" one of them exclaimed when they had heard me out. "Aren't we worth something, too? We'll sign it without the others."

In the end I obtained seven signatures on my letter. The next day one of the seven confessed to me that his wife had raised a stink because he had signed. "But I'll leave my signature on," he added with a guilty expression. I saw that he was deathly afraid: his wife was on one side and his conscience on the other.

"All right," I said, "I'll burn the letter, because there aren't enough signatures." He welcomed my decision with a sigh of relief.

When I told Dzyuba about my adventures with the letter, he was very sorry that he hadn't been present at the talk with Glushkov so that he could ask about the "henchmen." He did not agree with me that there hadn't been enough signatures. It was not a question of quantity, he said. The KGB must be shown that not everyone will remain silent.

People from Moscow brought us excerpts from the record of Sinyavsky and Daniel's trial. Our sense of Kafkaesque absurdity grew stronger. Kafka himself was becoming very popular with young people at this time. Several of his stories were published in magazines, and a volume that included *The Trial* was published in an edition of nine thousand copies of which six thousand were exported. I was struck by Kafka's profound understanding of absurdity. It was very funny to see Soviet critics writing about him as a "singer of alienation in decaying feudal-capitalist Austro-Hungary." What sort of socialist society were we living in if we recognized our own alienation in his?

In philosophy, treatises on alienation were sprouting like mushrooms after rain. At first the philosophers argued that they were studying the early Marx, before he became a Marxist. Later they claimed that according to bourgeois philosophers the young Marx was a humanist and the later Marx was an antihumanist. Passages in

Capital were found that clearly indicated that Marx thought about alienation in his later years as well, but in a more mature way. A philosopher I knew told me that previous translations of *Capital* were unsatisfactory because they did not include the passages on the theory of alienation. Now a new translation was being prepared. My acquaintance also told me that Marx had written many drafts in preparing *Capital*. He wrote the philosophical part first, the scaffolding for his theory, but in the finished book he eliminated almost all the philosophy and left only the scientific part. My acquaintance was in raptures about the deleted passages. "For contemporary philosophy," he said, "the part that was left out of *Capital* is even more important than *Capital* itself." Where is it now, that scaffolding for *Capital*?

I began to see the link between the theory of alienation and contemporary Western literature. When Ionesco's *Rhinoceros* and Beckett's *Waiting for Godot* were published in translation, all my friends and I were fascinated by the theater of the absurd. This was genuine realism; the absurdity of the twentieth century cannot be conveyed by critical realism. Then Sartre's autobiography, *The Words*, and his plays were published. My friends did not like the plays, but I thought that some of them were splendid. Camus, who was also published in the Soviet Union at this time, had an even greater influence on me.

When I had had my fill of the new literary trends, I began to notice negative phenomena both in my own consciousness and predilections and in those of the people around me. Pessimism, skepticism, and cynicism were on the increase. I was developing a kind of masochism. The works I found most satisfying were those in which the hero mocks himself and his ideals, in which ideals change into their opposites and sacred words conceal a loathsome reality, and in which the hero dies without any heroics, or only absurd ones. My favorite word in philosophy became "crap," the Soviet equivalent of Biblical vanity.

The songs of Vladimir Vysotsky and Alexander Galich came to the rescue.[10] Of Vysotsky's songs I liked several that depicted the moral corruption of society, but I was repelled by his descent into the criminal world and his use of criminal argot for its own sake. What attracted me to Galich was that on first impression he seems to be writing about the pessimism of the Soviet intelligentsia; but as I listened to his songs day after day, masochistically relishing the tragedy of our revolution and the mockery of sacred values, I rediscovered a faith in the simple things of life that I had admired so much in Remarque and Heinrich Böll: a piece of bread, faith in man, love, nature, and art.

When Galich uses argot and themes from criminal songs, he reflects the fact that the Soviet Union is riddled with labor camps and prisons. The entire country is under police surveillance, and every citizen is in relation to the militia and the KGB in a way similar to the thief's relationship with the militia. But when you look beneath this superficial level in Galich's songs, you see the philosophical significance of underworld motifs. A criminal in a labor camp or prison, if he is not simply a scum, reflects on elementary values on which refined culture and spirituality are built: freedom, respect for oneself and one's comrades, and women. The criminal in the camp is beyond the law, but by the same token he is beyond the official lies. In the camps everything is stripped bare: here are the oppressors, here are the oppressed, and here are the informers. I do not want to exaggerate the merits of labor-camp life, with its slave labor and lies, but it is easier here to avoid the social falsehoods and to find friends who will not betray you. If you are a man, all your merits are emphasized. Your human features manifest themselves in even the slightest actions.

My growing skepticism and despair turned my love for the Gospels into a love for Ecclesiastes and the Revelations of Saint John. My interest in the latter did not last long, however: I found something pathological in it. I escaped being overwhelmed by an apocalyptic vision of the world only by finally finding a subject that brought together my mathematical and philosophical interests. At one of the seminars at the Institute of Cybernetics my boss, Antomonov, analyzed criteria for self-organization proposed by an American cyberneticist. During the discussion I spoke up about the excessive schematism and formalism of these criteria. I was required to define organization and propose my own program for its study. I took as my point of departure the thesis that philosophy will have the right to exist only if it can be developed to the level of a science. Failing that, it will be mere scholasticism.

My discussions with Antomonov went on for about a month. Gradually I formulated my basic theses about organization and information. The major weakness of many cybernetic theories appears to be that they have inverted the relationship between the mathematical apparatus and the contents of the theory. The natural sciences proceed from a description of a given phenomenon to the development of a theory. Formalization and mathematization are introduced only when the theory has been sufficiently developed. The mathematical theory of information was based on feedback systems, and it deals for the most part with quantitative aspects of informational processes. I do not know of a single fruitful application of information theory to the study of living systems.

Basing my research on the theory of reflection, which Diderot had hinted at and Lenin had developed somewhat, and then on the writings of the philosophical cyberneticists, I managed to establish a link between information and organization and to look at informational processes from a different point of view. The philosophical debates with Antomonov enabled me to formalize and mathematicize some of my notions about organization and information. I was able to develop a new formula for the quantity of information, which radically differed from the classic theory. Using this formula, I was able to mathematicize a number of models of organization and informational processes.

Antomonov took a great interest in my work, and we agreed to write a semiphilosophical and semimathematical study of the theory of organization and information (the two theories had become one for us). By chance I came across a critique of the philosopher Alexander Bogdanov, against whom Lenin had fulminated in *Materialism and Empirio-criticism*.[11] Bogdanov had written a book entitled *Tectology: A Universal Organization Science*. When I obtained the book, after a year of effort, I discovered that its philosophical aspects were too mechanistic to appeal to me. But I also saw that Bogdanov had anticipated certain cybernetic postulates and that some of his ideas might be useful in my work. Reading Bogdanov led me to a conclusion that was very important for me: if a philosopher is intelligent and original, one can always find something that will stimulate one's own work, no matter how remote his philosophy may be.

At first my research went smoothly. There were discussions with Antomonov, lectures, and articles. Then I had a misunderstanding with Antomonov. Without asking me, he invited a journalist who proposed to write about me and my work in a magazine column on young scientists. I flared up and said sharply that popular scientific magazines profane science. The journalist was dismayed; I had to apologize and then explain calmly that my work was not finished and so could not be written about yet. When the journalist had left, Antomonov told me that no subject could ever be finished, and my honesty would only result in my not writing anything at all. His second argument was the good of the laboratory: articles in popular magazines help win influence in society, because only specialists read the scientific journals. I sarcastically reminded him of Amosov, who despised journalists but continually lured them in. When a journalist was expected in the biocybernetic department, the fanciest and most complicated machinery was rolled into the room where he was to conduct his interview, to impress him with the superiority of biocybernetics over ordinary biology. Antomonov laughed but assured me that he had a more honest approach toward newspapermen.

A controversy broke out in the press at this time between "telepaths" and "antitelepaths." The arguments on both sides were scholastic, based on precedents and analogies. Both factions naturally leaned on dialectical materialism. The absence of scientific thinking was obvious: one faction wanted a miracle, and the other did not want one. The same was true of the controversy about life on Mars and alien visitors to Earth. The followers of Academician Tikhov argued that life exists on Mars and Jupiter.[12] The followers of Academician Fesenkov found the idea of life on other planets so blasphemous that they defined life as "protein forms" and tried to prove that these exist only on Earth.[13] Tikhov displayed a form of hylozoism (the doctrine, usually associated with the theories of the early Greek philosophers, that all matter is sentient), while Fesenkov's views were anthropocentric. These controversies convinced me that sound skepticism is lacking even in the natural sciences. It has been replaced by faith.

People in the Soviet Union like to say that dialectical thinking is the basis for our scientific achievements. But since the 1930's the Soviet Union has not created a single new trend in science that can be compared to cybernetics or structural analysis. Vladimir Propp developed his ideas in the 1920's, long before Western structuralism appeared.[14] In the 1930's we had the work of Lev Vygotsky and Dmitriy Uznadze in psychology, and Nikolay Vavilov and Nikolay Koltsov in genetics.[15] This is also true of art and literary scholarship. The 1920's gave us the philosopher and literary scholar Mikhail Bakhtin and the avant-garde literary group Oberiu, which included Alexander Vvedensky and Daniil Kharms.[16] The victory of dialectical materialism led to the mechanistic and voluntaristic Lamarckianism of Lysenko, the mechanistic dialectics of Stalin, and the shallowly rationalistic theory of socialist realism. If we exclude those philosophers who use Marxist phraseology only as a cover and the Young Marxists, who appeared after the Twentieth Party Congress, we must conclude that in philosophy there has not been a single fresh idea in three or four decades.

Then how does one explain Soviet success in space research, physics, and mathematics, areas where Soviet science does not lag behind the West? There are many explanations. Lomonosov lived in a backward and barbaric country.[17] He would obviously not have become a distinguished scientist if he had not studied with Western scientists. The most prominent Soviet physicists studied under pre-revolutionary or Western physicists. Mendeleyev, Butlerov, and Lo-bachevsky were able to accomplish their work before the Revolution, without recourse to any dialectics.[18] Soviet achievements in space are based on the prerevolutionary work of the mystically inclined Tsiol-kovsky.[19] The technical aspects of the Soviet space program can be explained by the advantages of government ownership of property, which permits the economy to be focused in one direction. Even un-der Stalin's "wise leadership" the Soviet military industry managed to catch up with the Nazis in only a few years. Peter the Great was able to turn a barbaric country into a powerful state through concen-tration of forces and government involvement in the economy.

Another reason for Soviet achievements in theoretical physics and mathematics is that mathematics is based on formal logic, and dialec-tics comes into it only in a formalized manner. Who introduced dialectics into mathematics? Bourgeois thinkers—Newton, Leibniz, Kantor, Lobachevsky, and Russell. What dialectical contribution have Marxist mathematicians made to mathematics? Some of them ridiculed mathematical logic, which tried to go beyond Aristotelian logic. Theoretical physics is closer to nature than mathematics and hence must be more dialectical, but the basis of theoretical physics is mathematics or formal logic. The dialectical relationship between ex-periment and theory was developed by Western physicists. The the-ory of relativity and the quantum theory are achievements of West-ern bourgeois physicists.

The almost complete involvement of my scientific and philosophi-cal interests in my research at the institute in 1966 and 1967 made me very happy. But in the middle of 1967 I began to encounter dif-ficulties: no matter how I tried, I could not prove a theorem that was essential to my dissertation. I struggled with it for about six months; Antomonov nervously urged me to publish my results, but I thought it unconscientious to publish mere notes, and my relations with him deteriorated. Nevertheless, I prepared to defend my dissertation and passed a candidate's examination in philosophy. When the philoso-pher who examined me read my paper, he suggested that I write a dissertation on philosophy. I told him about my intention of study-ing the meaning of life, using the theory of reflection and certain cybernetic concepts as a point of departure. My examiner was a phys-icist by training and did not consider himself competent to evaluate my views on ethics. There were progressive young philosophers at the Institute of Philosophy concerning themselves with similar problems, he said, and he gave me the names of three I should see. I had known one of them previously, from his involvement in *samizdat*.

It was to these philosophers that I read my theses. They were interested but announced that my work was philosophy and not science. "Why don't you have any references to Freud?" they asked.

I replied that I did not consider Freud a serious scientist.

"Then what about Pavlov, whom you do quote?"

"There's no doubt he caused a lot of harm in psychology," I replied. "But his achievements in neurophysiology are beyond question."

"You have very many references to Engels. Isn't there anything newer, Wittgenstein, for example? Have you read him?"

"Yes, but the problems he studies and his approach to philosophy don't interest me."

The young logical positivists began to argue that Marxism is a mystical teaching. I demurred, of course, but at the same time laughed to myself: a *samizdatchik* was proving the validity of Marxism to official Soviet philosophers. Such are the paradoxes of a decaying ideology, reminiscent of the days when the popes were atheists.

Although in my professional work I also met official philosophers who were secretly Sartreans or theosophists, I encountered logical positivists most frequently. Their movement has been given impetus by the growing importance of science, particularly mathematics. Philosophers who disagree with official tenets have a very simple way of concealing themselves. If they want to develop a particular thought by Sartre, for example, they pay their respects to the founding fathers (one quotation will suffice) and then fulminate against Sartre. In doing so they need not play the hypocrite: any sensible follower will disagree with his teacher on some points. Ostensibly they write about these differences of opinion but at the same time develop other ideas by Sartre. On the surface this development of Sartre's thinking appears to be a resounding refutation.

Another kind of philosophical Aesopian language involves the use of cryptic terms understandable only to a few specialists. But experience shows that Aesopian language does not always work: although they cannot detect "sedition" in the contents because of their inability to think independently, party philosophers can sense deviations in the manner of exposition and the language. I met a prominent Soviet philosopher who questioned me about *samizdat*, the Democratic Movement, and my attitude toward Marxism. "How strange that some young people are still Marxists!" he exclaimed when I had expounded my views. He had always considered himself a neo-Kantian, but because Marxism shares some features with Kantianism he could write "Marxist" treatises almost without going against his conscience. The more intelligent party philosophers suspected him of heresy but could not prove anything. "They're not interested in the meaning," the philosopher explained. "They're satisfied if there are quotations from Marx, Engels, and Lenin."

A positivist in Kiev with whom I talked after 1968 described the current state of Soviet philosophy by saying, "We now have almost every philosophical movement, from religious to Marxist. There is also a small group of party philosophers who are less philosophers than quotation mongers and who merely follow the latest directives. Almost everyone despises them, but no one is afraid of them because they don't understand anything. Only the Young Marxists are attacked by the authorities. It serves you right. Perhaps you'll understand now. You Young Marxists are attacked because yours is the only revolutionary philosophy. Other philosophers can rebel, too, but their rebellion is not a consequence of their philosophy."

9

ZONES OF SILENCE

In the Soviet Union, the social sciences, liberal arts, and many areas of life contain zones of silence and taboo subjects.

Sexual relations have been taboo for many years and are discussed only in terms of romantic love, friendship, the equality of men and women, motherhood, child rearing, and men's support of women. Society finds it awkward to admit that not only the bourgeoisie is concerned with sinful sex. Sexual hypocrisy is an extension of the ideological hypocrisy. The total ideologization of society has led to the ideologization of sex as well, and people toss about between sexual depravity and neurotic purity. The two extremes complement each other, and one can turn into the other.

When I practiced hypnosis, I asked a well-known sexologist in Kiev to propose to those of his patients who were somnambulists that they take part in my experiments. One patient, who was interested in telepathy, took part in the experiments for about a year. When we got to know each other better, he confided to me what he and the sexologist were involved in. Most of the patients were hysterical women and neurotic girls suffering because of their forced chastity. "You worry about the proletarians and peasants, and we'll take care of the broads," the fellow proudly explained to me. "We give them what society cannot." His philanthropy amused me. It was not prompted by humanitarian motives, of course, but what could I say? Tolstoy is wrong in part because he fails to see that evil can lead to good, not a very great good or a pure one, but a good nevertheless.

A woman friend once confessed to me that she had been suffering for five years because her husband could not . . . She was too embarrassed to go on. When I cautiously questioned her, I discovered that she didn't even know about intercourse. Once she had finally understood her family drama, I advised her to make her husband get treatment, to be unfaithful to him, or to get a divorce. "But he's so intelligent and honest!" she cried. "He'll think that I'm horribly dirty."

"No, he's not so intelligent and pure if he hasn't thought about you and at least read the proper books," I replied. (But such books were almost impossible to obtain. At the time only platonic love was written about.) "You're a normal woman with normal needs. We're both scientists and could discuss the problem with your husband scientifically."

The tragedy of the failed revolution has left deep marks on society, and almost every family I met had a drama involving sex, conflicts between the generations, professional problems, crime, or drinking. Many people, particularly girls, confided to me intimate tragedies that they would have been ashamed to tell their closest friends. God, how many hysterical, neurasthenic, or downright giddy women there were! The men were even worse. Petit-bourgeois women are merely fools, but their men are falser in their pursuit of the good life and lie more, both to themselves and to others. In the typical family the husband secretly curses the Soviet regime but explains that he has a wife and children to support. His wife despises him for being a coward and dreams of a Prince Valiant. In Soviet society Eve is more often dissatisfied with Adam and with her life, whether it be affluent or impoverished. When she falls, she falls lower than Adam, and her sex life is more abandoned and more refined by comparison with his more vulgar and superficial corruption. But when a woman realizes that she is a human being, she liberates herself more quickly from the illusions, pride, and falsehoods of her surroundings.

For some reason that it took me a long time to understand, family dramas always grew out of or grew into sexual dramas. My eyes were opened when I met Boris. He was an alcoholic and was deathly afraid of women. He introduced me to Freud and Okudzhava.[1] Boris and I spent so many evenings drinking in smoke-filled rooms that both Freud and Okudzhava became intolerable to me. Okudzhava's lovely sorrow began to sound like spiritual corruption and Soviet decadence. Even tape recorders became repugnant to me.

I read Freud in an attempt to comprehend Boris's drama but he did not understand much. In childhood Boris had discovered that he was physically incapable of having sex. His schoolmates found out and began to mock him. He had to change schools and conceal his deficiency from his family and friends. But the mockery continued to haunt him. He began to drink more and more. As is usually the case, the drinking merely reinforced the primary problem, and a closed chain was established in which cause and effect joined as a single whole. I tried to break the chain by finding what I thought was the weakest link. I persuaded Boris to go to a sanatorium to be treated for alcoholism. There he encountered boorishness from the doctors and taunts from the patients. He fled, developing toward me mixed feelings of hatred, fear, and hope, all of which became new links in the chain. A woman friend tried to break the chain in another place by showing Boris that women needed him. Things turned out even worse.

Another zone of silence is the nationalities problem. The party committee once summoned me to report on the seminar I was conducting at the Institute of Cybernetics. I was asked why I did not follow the official plan. I replied that I didn't want to lose the students by repeating the same subjects every year. We had all studied the standard subjects at the university and in the seminars of the previous years. Hence I selected subjects in ethics and esthetics that had not been studied but would be of interest to scientists. "After all, we're striving for the all-around development of people," I explained. This demagogic phrase satisfied the party ideology supervisors, and they proposed that I speak at a conference of propagandists at the Academy of Sciences about my principles and methods in propaganda work. I thought out my speech carefully, not wanting either to lie or to risk losing the seminar.

At the conference, one speaker after another discussed attendance rates, increases in the ideological awareness of scientists after political-education meetings, and other nonsense. I began my speech by saying that after the unmasking of the cult and the boring lectures on philosophy at the institutes, young scientists had become scornful of philosophy and politics. (The people in the audience nodded in agreement.) Our propaganda work had to be changed. I based my own work on the following assumptions. One, attendance must be voluntary. At first it may decrease, but later it will increase if the seminar is interesting. Two, scientists cannot be given the same political-education program as people with primary or secondary schooling. Three, new subjects have to be found. Four, we need discussions and not lectures. And five, a subject such as "What Is the Essence of Art?" is bound to fail because it is only for professionals. It can be presented as the question "Do the Martians Have Art?" The same subject formulated concisely will evoke discussion and permit us to look into the crux of the problem.

Having said this, I glanced at the chairman of the conference, who was beaming with pleasure at my innovative ideas. I picked up courage and threw in a bit of sedition. "Unfortunately, all propagandists encounter 'zones of silence,' subjects that may not be mentioned or may be mentioned only in generalities. The nationalities problem is an example." Here I sensed with my skin how horrified the audience was. The chairman even jumped up: everyone was expecting another speech like Dzyuba's. But I had no such intention. Whom could I propagandize here for Ukraine? Three or four people might silently agree with me. I had to save the seminar.

"In the nationalities problem," I continued, "Lenin's words are merely repeated. We know that Lenin spoke about the need to Ukrainianize Ukraine. But the times have changed. Should we criticize Lenin or try to develop his ideas? We propagandists are frequently faced with such questions." The tension in the audience grew. "I think that we need special seminars on the nationalities problem for propagandists. We have to break down the zones of silence." (One of my reasons for intruding into this forbidden zone was the hope of obtaining information about the true purposes of the Central Committee of the Ukrainian party in the nationalities problem. More truth is spoken at such seminars than in public, and I might discover new facts for *samizdat* about the party's great-power chauvinism.)

The chairman smiled again. The danger of a seditious speech had passed. The speaker was obviously naïve but dedicated to the party. Afterward the chairman warmly thanked me for my "brave and fresh speech" and suggested that I write an article about "new methods of propaganda work." I agreed.

A week or two later the party committee telephoned and asked me to send over a curriculum vitae for the Central Committee. I was confidentially informed that the Central Committee wanted to give me a certificate of honor and to display my photograph on the municipal honor board as the best propagandist in Kiev. Dzyuba and other "unreliables" roared with laughter when I told them the story. Tanya and I imagined how the KGB would come to search us and we would point to the certificate of honor from the Central Committee. "Do you know whom you're searching?" we'd ask. We underestimated the KGB. It told the Central Committee who I was, and I never heard about the certificate again.

Although I was derisive of the "legalists," I made other attempts to legalize sedition because I thought then that the legal sedition of *Novy mir* was more useful for the development of thought in the USSR than all *samizdat* put together. Events proved that my hopes for Aesopian literature and legal opposition were unfounded. The authorities desperately wanted to reanimate their dead ideology, but they cannot do so because they are dead men themselves. They are afraid to revive the ideology with the help of young people lest a deviation develop, and in any case they do not have the young people on their side. Official Soviet Marxism is extremely cowardly and is not even an ideology so much as a phraseology.

As a propagandist I often dealt with party and Komsomol activists. The first interesting one I met was a member of the party committee at the Institute of Cybernetics. Before the Cultural Revolution in China he preached Maoism to me. Much of what he said was fascinating and supported the Chinese Communist Party. When the Cultural Revolution broke out, I asked him what it meant, but he wasn't able to explain it for lack of information. Kuo Mo-jo's letter of repentance convinced him that the Chinese party was oppressing culture in a Stalinist fashion,[2] and he admitted to me that he had been wrong.

At a Komsomol meeting I quarreled with another party activist from the institute, accusing him of demagoguery and even calling him a provocateur. He suggested that we meet for a discussion, the first of many meetings. His principal thesis was: "The October Revolution was conducted by boors. We have to get rid of the dimwits in the leadership. The technical intelligentsia must come to power. We've had enough of cooks' children." I reminded him of Merezhkovsky's words about the "coming boor."[3]

"Well, what of it?" he rejoined. "Merezhkovsky's prediction was correct."

"But then Merezhkovsky threw himself into the embrace of the boors Mussolini and Hitler!"

The party activist replied that this did not negate the validity of his observation about the workers' and peasants' revolution.

Several weeks later he told me that he had spoken about me with the party bigwigs at the academy and suggested that I join the party. "You know how to blather in their language, and you know all the dogmas," he said. "We can make a career for you. People like you are needed to put an end to the bureaucrats. There's a possibility that we shall gradually be able to seize power from the Central Committee, throw out the idiots, and replace them with intelligent people."

Our discussions dragged on for months. I argued that the rule of the technocrats would be no better than the present bureaucratic rule. It was foolish to think that an honest man could join the party and not become a scoundrel. I gave my acquaintance all the *samizdat* that I had for him to read. He finally gave in. "All right, what am I to do?" he asked.

"Independent thinking is a principle of democracy. Find an activity in *samizdat* that will suit you."

He got bored and gave up both his party work and his connections with me. Such people are terribly reluctant to think for themselves. They desperately want leaders and *Führer*s, even "democratic" ones.

Another party boss I met at this time was in charge of cultural and educational activities for young people. After the dispersal of the Club for Creative Youth, from which most of the leaders of the patriotic opposition in Kiev emerged,[4] he withdrew to his institute and organized interesting activities from there. I used his connections in party and Komsomol circles to improve the cultural work at my institute. The man was very interested in Dzyuba, Svitlychny, and other activists in the Ukrainian movement. I gave him *samizdat,* and he brought me rare books.

Then we lost sight of each other for several years, and met again only in 1969, after I had been thrown out of my job. He was very drunk but recognized me and immediately set about scolding me. "Ukraine needs people like you, Dzyuba, and Svitlychny. The Central Committee of the Ukrainian party is protecting Dzyuba and Svitlychny from arrest, while you're swimming against the tide. I can introduce you to Ovcharenko.[5] He's my friend. If you promise not to make trouble, he'll get you a good job."

"Ovcharenko is a scoundrel," I replied. "And besides, I have absolutely no intention of changing my views."

The party boss ridiculed what he called my Marxist illusions. "I'm in charge of three hundred Communists. They're sheep; they need a strong hand and a whip. Mathematicians, physicists, and technicians should be running the government. Only in this manner will Ukraine become independent."

"The whip and the strong hand are a Nazi notion," I objected.

"Well, what of it? Not everything Hitler said was stupid."

The argument became senseless.

"All right, good-bye, my utopian friend," the party man said. "Remember, we only want to help you." He was the first nationalist-technocratic party member I met. Later I heard about a similar party functionary with a Maoist deviation.

In 1967 Antomonov assembled the staff of the laboratory and announced that the directors of the institute had decided that our research was not topical (they had a point) and were thinking of shutting down the laboratory. There was a way out, however. The Presidium of the Academy of Sciences of the Ukrainian Republic had been assigned a project involving research in space medicine, biology, and psychology and had offered it to our institute. Glushkov didn't want to become involved in it and was trying to limit the institute's involvement to one laboratory. Antomonov read the proposed research plan. It was enough to keep an entire institute busy and included problems that were unsolvable within the present state of science. "We have to invite Stanisław Lem," I joked. "He is a man full of ideas."

Antomonov proposed another solution: we could transfer the laboratory to the Institute of Physiology. The choice was between psychology here and physiology there. Psychology won by a small majority.

Our research turned out to be classified. Applications were made to the personnel department for security clearances. Antomonov gave me a flattering reference, but I was not issued clearance. He then proposed that I work as a "Negro": study a particular problem without knowing what it actually involved. A period of reorganization began while we studied the literature on the psychology of perception, memory, emotion, attention, and volition. I suggested that we hire a psychologist. "You're aware that psychologists don't know anything," Antomonov rebutted. "You're quite capable of handling the psychologist's job. After all, you're a mathematician."

Our first assignment was to write a manual on psychology as it applies to engineering. The chapters were divided among the staff members. I was assigned perception, memory, and volition. The deadline was far off, but we did not study the problems until a week before the work was due. Not being specialists in psychology and not knowing what was important for astronautics, we selected material from the mountains of research to suit our own interests.

When we turned in the assignment, we received a new one, almost identical, but with the requirement that we mathematicize our previous work. We proceeded in the same manner—by copying from books and by inventing hypotheses and passing them off as theories. I was reluctant to mathematicize and had a heated discussion with Antomonov. He admitted that our research wasn't very serious but argued that we had to save the laboratory. I replied that I could not pluck formulas from the air. Each new formula had to be the result of minute psychological research. Antomonov advised me to incorporate my formula for information. The falsehood made me sick, but the argument that this was for the good of the laboratory won out, and I included my formula. Our bosses were satisfied.

Our next assignment was to study the complexity of a particular job for an operator, such as a driver, pilot, or astronaut. I tried to use my previous work on information, and a friend constructed a special apparatus at my request for use in the experiments on complexity. I came up with a formula that was suitable only for a limited range of actions by an operator. Almost all of us at the laboratory understood that we were helping our bosses deceive the Academy of Sciences, which was deceiving the Central Committee, which in turn was deceiving the population.

Through our laboratory's connections with the Space Center we learned details of the Soviet space program. Our laboratory, for example, was assigned to come up with a biological or psychological task that would require a computer on board the spacecraft, just so that the first computer in space would be a Soviet one. We also discovered that the government was responsible for the death of three cosmonauts: it insisted that the spacecraft be launched before the reliability of all the systems had been verified. Scientists objected, but Soviet science, as they say, is party-minded and therefore must serve as a means for publicity and demagoguery.

Having learned many such examples of cosmic absurdity, I tried to convince Antomonov that we were accomplices in a deception and were assisting in the preparation of further catastrophes. Antomonov's rebuttals were weak; he knew even more than I did: he had a security clearance, whereas I was only marginally informed.

At a conference of leaders in space research the Soviet lag in astronautics came under discussion. One scientist pointed to the lag in electronics and other technical areas. We couldn't overtake the Americans in one area when we were behind in others. A concentration of efforts in one sector would give only temporary results if other sectors remained underdeveloped. Another scientist blamed the lag on the interference of people who knew nothing about astronautics. (Everyone realized that he had the Central Committee in mind.) A shorthand report of the conference was sent to the Central Committee, but to no avail.

On one occasion inspectors arrived from the Space Center to check our work and discuss our problems. The other staff members were absent on assignment at the time, so the inspectors had only me to speak to. I warned them that I did not have security clearance. They asked why.

"Political unreliability."

The inspectors questioned me, expressed their sympathy, and scolded me for being naïve. They leaked stories about their experiments, one of which profoundly shook me. Volunteers for space experiments are paid huge sums and are therefore in endless supply.

One woman sat in a chamber for seventy days. On the sixty-eighth or sixty-ninth day she saw the ceiling coming down on her. Naturally she took fright. Her reactions were recorded by electroencephalographs, electrocardiographs, and other instruments.

"What's the point of such an experiment?" I asked.

"What do you mean, what's the point? To study reactions to danger. Leonov and Belyayev were scared stiff when they carried out their experiment in space."

"But before such an experiment, a number of alternative working hypotheses are proposed. After the experiment some of them can be excluded. Did you have any such hypotheses? What were you determining?"

"Nothing. We were simply studying the reaction."

"But the woman could have had a heart attack or developed a neurosis because of her fright."

"We checked her heart. Besides, there can't be any scientific progress without victims."

Then we discussed how to control emotions. All the cosmonauts experienced great fear, which some of them openly admitted. Fear interfered with the control of the spacecraft. I said that Western psychology, as far as I knew, had not solved the problem yet, but raja-yoga has methods for controlling the unconscious, and I recommended books. Yoga goes hand in hand with telepathy. The inspectors told me that an American astronaut had conducted a successful experiment in telepathic communication. Then they asked, "Would it be possible for our rocket to connect with an American rocket, attach an explosive device, and get away without the Americans noticing anything?"

I was repelled by the scientists' stupid fantasy. However, as to telepathy, I explained that even if telepathic communication were possible, the necessary level would be achieved only in hundreds of years. They promised to try to set up a secret telepathic laboratory. Finally I couldn't help myself and reproached them for working in behalf of war.

"The Americans will overtake us if we don't increase our power!" they rebutted.

"But the American scientists think the same way. The arms race will continue, and you know that sooner or later arms have to be used."

"But we can't give in to them!"

"We have to do everything possible to achieve mutual disarmament. There are so many arms now that both sides will be destroyed if war breaks out, and as for neutrals—only the Papuans will survive."

The inspectors reproached me for being utopian.

"But some scientists in the West boycott military research," I replied. "Why can't ours do the same? Because we are for peace?"

Several months later a friend and I were invited to set up a parapsychological laboratory for the Navy Department. Realizing that the choice was between interesting research and our consciences, we turned down the offer.

During a discussion of telepathy at one institute I stated that I had studied the subject for many years and had concluded that telepathic phenomena do not exist. The telepathists of Kiev accused me of treachery, but later they understood my point and stopped their experiments. Subsequently the laboratories in Leningrad, Moscow, and Novosibirsk were shut down.

My disappointment in not finding honest and creative work in telepathy or biocybernetics nudged me toward further reflections about the nature of the Soviet state. *Samizdat* literature gave me historical material and revealed the psychology of the society. I vividly remember the great esthetic satisfaction I derived from reading Solzhenitsyn's *Cancer Ward*.[6] The first pages were difficult, and I had to put the book away. I tried to figure out why *Cancer Ward* was so difficult to read and decided that it was because of the language. I found it somehow un-Russian. Yet when I resumed reading, my sense of bad Russian disappeared, and only life was left. I did not understand my first response until I was approaching the end of the book. We have been satiated with fiction whose smooth, correct words and phrases slip into the mind and just as easily slip out, like water filtering through sand. The rough language in *Cancer Ward* grates on the mind and forces the reader to pay attention to every word. We find a similar roughness in Dostoyevsky. His awkward sentences are even harder to grasp, but they serve to concentrate the reader's attention, and when he has overcome this difficulty, Dostoyevsky sucks him into his terrible world. Dostoyevsky casts such a strong spell that language and ideas disappear, to reappear later as one's own, and only the heroes' lives remain.

The literary craftsmanship of *Cancer Ward* at first concealed Solzhenitsyn's thoughts from me. Russian literature had finally reattained the heights of Gogol, Dostoyevsky, and Tolstoy. Until I read Solzhenitsyn, I had thought that naturalism was unartistic, and in some cases even pathological, because it broke ground for its anti-pode—decadence. Now came this different naturalism, which was allegorical because all our history is a huge allegory.

Later I met a man who knew the hospital described by Solzhenitsyn. He told me that Solzhenitsyn's portrayal was so accurate that even the doctors were recognizable. The conclusion he drew from this was negative: *Cancer Ward* was mere photography. It was a stupid conclusion, of course. I, too, had thought that way before I read the book. But Solzhenitsyn's unnaturalistic and, to my mind, unsuccessful play, *Candle in the Wind*,[7] shows that he has a special vision of the world: he does not give free rein to his artistic imagination but, rather, penetrates through the phenomena of the real world to its spiritual content and creates an allegory or parable. This is confirmed by Solzhenitsyn's other failures: Stalin in *The First Circle* and Lenin in *Lenin in Zurich*.[8] There is, however, another reason for the artistic failure in these books: hatred. A genuine artist must be capable of feeling hatred, as any other powerful emotion, but the hatred must not cloud his vision. If the artist does not artistically transform the emotion, it will produce only a grotesque or a cry of despair. Grotesques may be artistic, but they are not appropriate to Solzhenitsyn's genius.

In my circle of friends there were many arguments about the women in *Cancer Ward*, particularly Vega. It seemed to me then that Solzhenitsyn's genius had failed him here, but now I no longer think so. Yes, she is not a fully developed, rounded character. In prison, however, men are haunted by a double image of woman: she is beautiful and unattainable, connected with everything sacred, and at the same time a broad, a female devoid of all features except one. It is no accident that Vega is the name of a star with a special, secret melody to it. Vega is the incarnation of the prisoner's dream, and Solzhenitsyn has masterfully expressed this.

A significant role in my intellectual development was played by Shulubin's idea: ". . . for Russia in particular, with our repentances, confessions and revolts, our Dostoevsky, Tolstoy and Kropotkin, there's only one true socialism, and that's ethical socialism."[9] Torn out of context, the idea immediately loses its luster, but in the novel it is a continuation of what the early Tolstoy had given me. One reason for the defeat of the October Revolution was an ethical one. The contempt for ethical values that resulted from the absolutization of class led to an ethical relativism in theory and a barbarity in practice. This chapter in *Cancer Ward* is as important for me as Ivan and

Alyosha's argument in the tavern in Dostoyevsky's *The Brothers Karamazov*.[10]

Months after I read *Cancer Ward* Shulubin's remarks about Bacon's doctrine of idols suddenly came to my mind. I had understood the significance of myths in Soviet society even before I read Solzhenitsyn, but now my thoughts were propelled still further in this direction. I began to look more closely at the role myths play in history. Myths about the party, its leaders, the best system in the world, the fascist Trotsky, the Gestapo agent Tito, "nation-traitors," progressive tsars, Yermolov, the suppressor of the Caucasus, as almost a Decembrist,[11] the traitors Mazepa and Shamil—all these and thousands of other major and minor myths and idols have caused immeasurable harm.

"The idols of the theatre are the authoritative opinions of others which a man likes to accept as a guide when interpreting something he hasn't experienced himself," Shulubin says. One idol after another comes to mind. Marr, who reduced linguistics to Marrism;[12] Stalin, who destroyed all linguistics, including that of the Marrists; Lysenko, Pavlov, the classics of Marxism-Leninism-Stalinism; Mayakovsky, Pushkin, and Shevchenko as police truncheons in literature are all idols. We cannot blame those who became idols. Yermilov, who hounded Mayakovsky to an early grave, used Mayakovsky as an idol, a filter for his thoughts.[13] The brilliant Pavlov, Shevchenko, and Marr and the paltry Lysenko were all turned into idols when orders were issued to worship them. Dialectics was turned into verbal tight-rope-walking, and a revolutionary party turned into a policeman because it tried to monopolize power and destroy the dialectics of society. It is incorrect to call Soviet society an ideocracy, because the idea is dead and the corpse of the idea, the idol, contains concepts far removed from the original meaning. The idea is dead because its development was coercively halted and all other ideas were banned.

Tolstoy studied how the church bureaucracy struggled with religious teachers. All the teacher's ideas are declared absolutely correct and beyond criticism. Then the teacher's mistakes or secondary ideas are advanced to first place and the primary ideas are ignored. Specialists in interpreting the sacred texts are interposed between the teacher and the flock. Theologians, propagandists, philosophers, and secretaries in charge of ideology manipulate the sacred texts and effortlessly prove that love of one's fellow man requires that he be burned at the stake; the "union of workers and peasants" requires that the latter be forcibly turned into serfs; freedom of conscience requires that Uniates and Baptists be persecuted; [14] and internationalism requires that Jews be hounded and entire nations be deported.

Reading what Solzhenitsyn has written about idols, one realizes that myths have dimmed man's vision and distorted his experience since the beginning of history. "The truth must be concrete," Marxism teaches. With the aid of metaphysical "dialectics" this dogma has been turned into scholasticism. Today it means that all the principles of Marxism must be renounced ("Reality has changed," the ideologists intone). Tomorrow it will mean ignoring facts that contradict the party's general line. The omnipresent falseness makes use of truth and lies, the absolute and the relative, the genius of Marx and the paltriness of Khrushchev, the sincerity of youth and the cupidity of the bourgeoisie. And over all this loom great, ominous clouds of fear. The Soviet state is a logical consequence of the Mongol yoke, the paranoia of Ivan the Terrible and Peter the Great, the state-dominated church, the autocracy, and the secret police.

10

BAPTISTS, JEWS, AND NATIONALISTS

Upon finishing *Cancer Ward*, I turned to "The Easter Procession" and the prose poems and discovered a new aspect of Solzhenitsyn's thought—his Christianity.[1] It revealed itself even in the choice of words and the construction of sentences. Solzhenitsyn overcame the falseness of language by employing words and turns of speech that had, one would think, long been archaic, and he resorted to parables even more deliberately than in his previous work. Tanya and I watched a procession to the Cathedral of Saint Volodymyr in Kiev shortly before we read "The Easter Procession" and witnessed the vile mockery of believers by young rowdies. When we read Solzhenitsyn's description of atheist hooligans—"The truth is that one day they will turn and trample on us all"—we knew how precise and realistic he was.

Before that I had attended a prayer meeting of Baptists, probably disciples of Prokofyev.[2] A colleague at the laboratory told me about a new friend who was a Baptist. She unexpectedly quoted a Marx he had never heard about. "She keeps talking to me about the young Marx," my colleague said to me. "Do you think her quotations are genuine?" I confirmed that they were. In the Soviet Union even opponents of Marx cannot get by without quotations from the gospel.

The Baptist woman invited my colleague to a prayer meeting on the outskirts of Kiev. I decided to go. I had thought that sectarians were more ignorant and downtrodden than the faithful of the official Orthodox Church, and here a sectarian was quoting the young Marx, with whom not even all the official philosophers were acquainted. More surprisingly, she apparently understood this Marx, who is particularly difficult because of his Hegelian and Feuerbachian language.

Getting off the suburban train and walking into the woods, I saw

107

militiamen lurking in the bushes. The meeting had to be close by. I heard singing and, walking toward it, came upon a crowd that included simple peasants with infants in their arms. There was no sign of the religious zeal or dejected expressions I had expected. On the trees were posters with religious slogans. I was surprised that the melodies were those of secular songs; some were even from familiar Soviet songs. The lyrics, in no way remarkable, dealt with the familiar Christian ideas of love, brotherhood, and mercy.

A little way off stood a group of young people who were laughing and smoking. I walked over to them, because Baptists don't smoke and I wanted a cigarette. I listened to the conversation. Someone swore casually. There were girls in the group, and I winced involuntarily, but the girls didn't seem to notice the foul language. One member of the group had gray hair and a sensitive, intelligent face. I began to realize that this was a group of students with their teacher, sent by the party committee, no doubt.

"They don't smoke or drink," the teacher said jokingly. "Now there are some sects where they say their prayers, pair off, and head for the bushes. That's the kind of sect I want to join!"

The boys laughed loudly, and the girls tittered. At first I listened to them with sympathy. They seemed to be normal, cheerful boys and girls. The others were strange and alien. How barbaric to believe in God, to make the sign of the cross, or to mutter prayers in the second half of the twentieth century. I was disturbed only by the foul language and the cynicism, but I had emancipated myself in matters of sex long ago and now ridiculed the vestiges of my moralism.

The leader of the atheists approached the Baptists. His congregation followed him. They joked about the Baptists' pompous trivialities. Even this good-natured jesting offended the Baptists. "Why are you bothering us?" they asked. "Don't smoke here. The woods are big. Go somewhere else. We're not bothering you." The jokes turned into gibes, and the crowd broke up into quarreling groups. Neither side heeded the arguments of the other. But the believers were hurt and pitied the atheists, whereas the atheists expressed no feelings.

Seeing that I had stopped smoking (now I was ashamed to be associated with the atheists), a girl from the Baptist group approached me. She had delicate, animated features. She asked me who I was, why I was here, and whether I was a believer. I explained. In return she told me about herself. She was a student at a technical college. A year before, shaken by her mother's agonizing death, she had fallen ill. Everyone abandoned her. Then Baptists came to help her in the house and give her comfort.

"They do everything harmoniously and beautifully," she said. "They all take care of one another. I sing in the choir and draw posters."

"But you must be bored. This is all so primitive and out of date."

"Yes, sometimes I'm bored. But that's my fault. We have many interesting books, and there are a lot of young people in the choir."

"Why are your melodies secular? I think the ancient church melodies are closer to the spirit of religion and more beautiful."

"I like these better. And the words are so pretty. My friend composes the music and the words."

Then the Baptists formed a semicircle, and a young man addressed them in a nervous, excited voice. Many of the Baptist brethren were in prison. They had appealed to the government, which promised that they would be released if they were not guilty of any crimes. The speaker's angry words verged on an accusation against the government. But it was difficult to find fault with what he said: the accusation was in the tone and the implications.

A second speaker stepped forward. "The school year will be starting soon. Our younger brothers and sisters will go to school. They will be greeted by taunts and insults. Let us pray to God that He may grant them strength and endurance."

I had never heard about religious persecution, and the Baptists' speeches were revelations.

A discussion broke out again. The atheists let themselves go even more. An elderly woman approached their leader and gently explained that the Baptists were not doing anything bad. On the contrary, they were struggling against drinking and debauchery. She read her verses, which were simple but touching. I do not like sentimentality, but by comparison with the atheists' arguments the verses were very appealing. The atheist leader replied with primitive verses in the style of Mayakovsky's propaganda verses.

"Who are you?" I asked the leader, unable to take any more.

"I am Vladimir Stal, a Russian poet."

My hatred of the self-satisfied pig burst forth, and I punned, stuttering and stumbling over the words, "I can see that you're a Stalinist. I am a Russian mathematician, and I say to you that you are all boors and scoundrels. What are you doing here?"

Stal was disconcerted. I was ashamed of my pathos, my stuttering, and my bad pun. The believers looked at their new champion fearfully. They had tried not to provoke the enemy, and I was causing a scandal. I quickly left for the railway station.

When I told my colleague about the incident, she related her own experiences. She had been sent by the party committee to preach atheism to a different group of sectarians, having been told stories about the sect's bigotry and fanaticism. She witnessed a scene very similar to the one I had witnessed. When she tried to agitate the believers, she encountered calm certainty and simple convictions. Her scientific arguments were powerless in the face of the beliefs held by these naïve and credulous people. She began to attend their meetings. Seeing that she was tolerant toward them, the sectarians invited her home for tea. She grew to love several of them. When one family was hounded, she helped find jobs for them and looked after the children. I asked her to introduce me to the family, but nothing ever came of it. She must have been afraid that I would be tracked by the KGB.

Solzhenitsyn's prose poems revealed to me yet another aspect of his genius. I was brought up in a spirit of class hatred and shall probably never be rid of it. Thus I was particularly touched by "Lake Segden." Everything in the story is so familiar, and yet how profoundly Solzhenitsyn speaks about the "servants of the people": "An evil prince, a squint-eyed villain, has claimed the lake for his own: there is his house, there is his bathing-place. His evil brood goes fishing here, shoots duck from his boat." But the thought is incomplete without the final words of the story: "Beloved, deserted lake. My native land . . ." [3]

The terrible history of the country rises before you, and you see the similarity of the evil khans, princes, tsars, and present-day rulers. How strange that everything is being blamed on ideology today! The Tatar and Mongol khans, the Orthodox autocrats, and the Bolshevik pastors of the people had different ideologies, but in essence they were alike. When you read the history of the Russian state, the "re-unification" of Ukraine with Russia, and the *samizdat* from the labor camps, you cry in despair.

Solzhenitsyn looks at people doing morning exercises. They are concentrating so hard and their movements are so ritualized that they seem to be praying. They are worshiping the body. But why not the spirit? This perception of the chief failing of our civilization—its bourgeois nature—had been festering in my mind for a long time, but now I found it expressed succinctly and pellucidly. Solzhenitsyn would hardly agree with such an interpretation, yet a genius is a genius precisely because he depicts life much more broadly and deeply than his consciousness and ideology would normally permit. Every reader sees in great books what he sees in life itself, and each age understands the Bible, Goethe's *Faust*, or Shevchenko's *Kobzar* in its own manner.

In political terms Dostoyevsky was, in Lenin's phrasing, an "archreactionary": anti-Semitic and anti-Polish, a supporter of the Slavophile seizure of new territories. But it is not this political aspect that is most important about him. As an artist he showed Russia on the brink of a precipice. In his lampoon of the Russian revolutionaries of the 1860's, *The Possessed*, he foresaw the "diabolism" of the Stalin era.[4] And this was only one small insight. Even his most reactionary ideas contained grains of humanism. Only the superficiality of their artistic perceptions and their party-minded eyeglasses kept the revolutionary democrats and their successors from perceiving these truths.

In "The Story of My Experience" Boris Dyakov described his stay in the Stalinist labor camps, presenting new information about the sadism of the camp authorities.[5] Yet there was something appalling in the approach Dyakov, a sincere Communist, took to the labor-camp theme. His main thesis was that the dedicated, rock-hard Communists in the labor camps were surrounded by enemies—Banderites, White Guards, and Vlasovites.[6] The camps had to be strict, and the guards' sadism was justified. When a campaign to buy government bonds was conducted among the prisoners, the enemies naturally refused to support it, but the sincere Communists rejoiced at this proof that they were still trusted and considered to be Soviet people. One Communist was in anguish because he didn't have the money to buy a bond. A White Guard officer commented that the Communists were like fish in a frying pan, jumping with joy at being fried. I was horrified to realize how myths can distort human feelings, not to mention ideologies. The Communists saw their enemies being tortured and justified the authorities' brutality. Although they were victims, too, they felt closer to their torturers than to their fellow victims because they shared party allegiance with the former.

A similar unbending faith in the party line and mythology is described in Eugenia Ginzburg's *samizdat* account *Journey into the Whirlwind*.[7] Ginzburg, a Stalinist, was arrested in 1937 and sent off by train to a labor camp. During the trip the Communists quarreled with the anti-Communist prisoners. The Communists could not tolerate the anti-Soviet propaganda and drowned it out by singing "How Broad My Native Land," which contains the words "I know no other land where people breathe so freely." They were being transported to slave labor, and yet they rejoiced in their freedom like fish in a pan. "You could make nails from such people," the poet Tikhonov said.[8] There it is: these people were made of iron, not flesh and blood. Above stood the "iron" Dzerzhinsky and Yezhov.[9] Below them were the "rock-hard, unbending screws." The words in quotation marks are not mine; they are the words the Communists applied to themselves, accurately defining their inhumanity. Supermen they all were, from top to bottom.

For such true believers being human meant "abstract bourgeois humanism," intellectual rot, and bourgeois prejudices. The intellectuals wavered, doubted, pitied, indulged in introspection, and—O holy Stalin!—were even capable of loving a woman from a different class. The "screws," as Stalin called them, disregarded all obstacles and marched in proletarian stride ("Who's stepping with his right? Left! Left!" Mayakovsky exhorted) toward the radiant heights of labor camps, prisons, and *psikhushkas*, where they could despise the bespectacled intellectuals to their hearts' content.

Only one thing is strange in all this. The true believers wailed ferociously as they were tortured by their party comrades not because they felt pain or hatred for their torturers, but because they despised themselves and their fellow prisoners. They bemoaned their imaginary crimes against Joseph Vissarionovich and the wise party; they wept at having betrayed the Revolution and the people. The men of iron proved to be soft-skinned and tearful. They spat on themselves and betrayed everything they had fought for. On the other hand, the "rotten, petit-bourgeois, abstract-humanist little Jew poet" Osip Mandelstam struck his drunken torturer in the face, wrote a poem savagely deriding Stalin, and died in a labor camp reading Petrarch.[10]

How many such confrontations between the myth of iron and the human spirit there were! Take the introspective Ukrainian intellectual Les Kurbas, who supported the Revolution as long as it brought liberation to Ukraine and the workers. But when the Revolution became a counterrevolution, those who had stood like rocks slavishly followed the party's general line. The brilliant Tychyna, who wrote odes to Stalin and exalted the tempering of steel (to be used against the enemy, of course), turned first into a fellow traveler and then into a political scum and a poetic nonentity. Meanwhile Kurbas, soft intellectual that he supposedly was, suddenly became rebellious and inflexible and perished without betraying his fellow men or his ideals. Kurbas's example opened my eyes to Ukraine and to the significance of introspection, doubt, and culture for strength of spirit. I began gradually to think of myself as a Ukrainian.

During my third year at the university, in 1959, the party had had one of its periodic outbursts of Ukrainophilism. The professors were urged to deliver their lectures in Ukrainian, but they were all "internationalists" and stubbornly continued speaking what Mayakovsky called "the language that Lenin spoke." Only a party organizer named Libman spoke a mangled Ukrainian. I got up and mockingly asked him not to murder the beautiful Ukrainian language. I didn't give a damn about my native language, but my "internationalism" would not tolerate a Jew's teaching me Ukrainian, which was becoming extinct—quite properly, I thought—under pressure from the language of the Communist future. As a cosmopolitan I believed that national problems had been invented by narrow-minded nationalists. The world should as soon as possible have only one language and one culture—Russian or English, it didn't really matter which. Yet even in those anti-Semitic and internationalist years something Ukrainian flickered inside me. I loved Shevchenko's *Kobzar* and Lesya Ukrayinka's *The Forest Song*, and Ukrainian songs brought tears to my eyes. But it was a tiny flicker, growing dimmer with every year.

In Kiev I learned about the young Tychyna, with whose primitive later verse I had been tormented in school. I discovered something very profound in Ukrainian culture—a mysterious optimism, an unsentimental tenderness, and a deep religious strain. Ukraine, I discovered, had two poetic peaks, Shevchenko and Tychyna, who converged in their depths and summits. Tychyna reached his peak in *Solar Clarinets*, which he published in 1918. After that he descended, first to a not-always-successful formal refinement and word play, then to an esthetic and political self-negation, and finally to a minus-Tychyna in the anticulture of socialist realism.

What were the psychological and social reasons for the degradation of Tychyna's genius or the talent of hundreds of other writers? The Ukrainian poet and critic Vasyl Stus wrote a brilliant essay entitled "A Phenomenon of the Age," examining Tychyna's fall stage by stage and discussing the psychological and social reasons. Stus writes that Tychyna's "glory as a genius, forced to be a pygmy, a jester at the court of a bloody-handed king, was banned. His glory as a pygmy, a parasite on the genius's body, was ensured by a huge propaganda apparatus. . . . The poet's genius turned against him and became an enemy with whom he had to wage constant warfare lest his 'sin' against the age be revealed." [11] But a complete psychological study of the problem remains to be done.

Tychyna, Kulish, and the Ukrainian artists of the 1920's wedged open for me the door to the potential riches of Ukrainian culture, but I continued by inertia to think of myself as a Russian. Shortly after the trials of 1966, however, Ivan Dzyuba's *Internationalism or Russification?* began to circulate clandestinely in Ukraine.[12] Until we read it, Tanya and I had believed that except for fostering anti-

Semitism and deporting small nations the party was conducting a correct policy toward the nationalities. Now we learned that Lenin had spoken about "Ukrainianizing the Ukrainian cities." Not only was self-determination permitted in Leninist theory, but the development of Ukrainian culture was actually required. We realized that what is preached in the Soviet Union is not Marxism or Leninism. Dzyuba proved that the Leninist nationalities policy of the 1920's had nothing in common with what is happening today. He explained how the "Ukrainianizers" in the Ukrainian party of the 1920's were liquidated and cited dozens of cases of conscious and unconscious Russian chauvinism. Many of the examples staggered us. Dzyuba wrote, for instance, that "recently . . . even the 450th anniversary of the 'voluntary annexation' of Kazan' was celebrated, that same Kazan' which Ivan the Terrible butchered to a man." [13]

Other facts cited by Dzyuba seemed to us at first to be exaggerated, for example, his claim that a person who speaks Ukrainian will be told to speak "human"—that is, Russian. But then, under the influence of Dzyuba's book, I began to speak my native language. At first it was difficult, because my active vocabulary was limited and everyone around me was speaking Russian. One day in a shop I asked a young man, in Ukrainian, to hand me a book. "Can't you speak human?" he snarled. The blood rushed to my head, and right then I became a Ukrainian once and for all, the way Soviet Jews fully realize that they are Jews when they are barraged with "anticosmopolitan" or "anti-Zionist" propaganda. Still later such remarks ceased to offend me, because by then I had developed a national pride.

When my wife, Tanya, who is half Jewish and half Russian, read Dzyuba, she realized that she would remain a Jew as long as there is anti-Semitism, even though she knew no Hebrew or Yiddish and her knowledge of Jewish culture was limited to Sholem Aleichem and Perets Markish.[14] But she loved Aleichem and other Jewish writers as much as I did and as much as she loved Russian, French, or English writers.

In one Ukrainian town a history teacher, a Jew, bravely told her pupils about what was happening in the country—the trials, the falseness of socialist realism, the degradation of society, and so forth. Yet when her pupils asked her about the nationalities problem, she sent them off to official reference books. Several months later she read Dzyuba. At her next class she apologized to the pupils. "I didn't understand anything about the nationalities problem," she explained and proceeded to summarize Dzyuba.

On September 29, 1966, I was invited to attend a mass meeting at

Babyn Yar.[15] Tanya and I barely found a place to stand. Some four or five hundred people had gathered, and more were arriving by taxi. All around were piles of refuse and ashes. Someone remarked that these were the ashes of the Nazis' victims. I was astounded by his stupidity, but then I did see a hint of the tragedy at Babyn Yar in those piles of ashes. Militiamen stood around the crowd and calmly watched.

The people broke up into smaller groups. An old woman was crying that her children had been murdered here. One of the groups began to grow in size. Victor Nekrasov was making a speech about the regime's refusal to erect a monument to the victims of Babyn Yar. Later on, Dzyuba spoke at another spot. The crowd around him was so large that I caught only scattered phrases. His main points were a protest against anti-Semitism and the regime's attempt to sow discord between Ukrainians and Jews, and a call to all nationalities to fight jointly for their national rights.[16]

An old man became agitated when he heard Dzyuba's Ukrainian: Ukrainian spoken at Babyn Yar meant that an anti-Semite was speaking.

"What is he saying? Who is he? What right does he have to speak?" the old man asked.

"He's talking about a monument," I replied, barely restraining myself.

"Oh! Can you tell me why there's no monument?" the old man asked with surprise.

"An anti-Semitic government cannot erect monuments to Jews," I snapped back. The old man backed away. "That's another reason why there's no monument," I called after him, "because you're afraid!"

When Dzyuba had finished, the writer Borys Antonenko-Davydovych told the audience how a group of Ukrainian writers persuaded the government to ban Trofym Kichko's anti-Semitic book, *Judaism Without Embellishment*.[17] "Khrushchev wanted to use Ukrainian hands to persecute Jews," Antonenko-Davydovych explained. He added sadly that despite the formal ban, Kichko's book was still on sale.

An old woman ran up to Dzyuba. "They shot me here!" she cried. "I lay under the corpses for two days before I came out. My apartment is near here—I can see Babyn Yar from my window. I can't live here, I'm afraid! I've been writing to the authorities for years, trying to get a new apartment! Please help me!" She explained that she was one of the few witnesses to survive the killings. She had gone to the Writers' Union to ask that her testimony be written down but was refused. "You write it down and send it in," she begged Dzyuba. He and the old woman embraced, and she wrote down his address. Later I asked Dzyuba whether she had come to see him. No, she hadn't.

A Jewish boy jumped up on a mound. Anti-Semitism is a form of "antihumanism," he announced. Since the persecution of man often begins with a persecution of Jews, Jews must lead the struggle for humanism and not think only about themselves. As an example of genuine humanism he cited a "fairy tale from the land of Hans Christian Andersen." When the Nazis ordered Jews in occupied Denmark to wear the Magen David, the King and Queen and the entire populace put on the yellow stars. The Nazis were taken aback by this turn of events, and the Jews were rescued from Denmark. This was the first time I heard the story; later it became widely known.

As I became more involved with Ukrainian activists I saw that the Ukrainian national movement can be described in terms of three currents: patriots, nationalists, and chauvinists. The patriots love their nation and their culture but at the same time care about other nations, because they understand that the fate of every nation depends upon the fate of mankind as a whole. The patriots support all the political and human-rights demands of the Soviet Democratic Movement as a whole but also point to specific national problems of which the democrats are not aware. The nationalists are concerned only with the national question and national freedom and pay no attention to social, political, or religious problems. The chauvinists, who are not a current but only a few scattered individuals, are motivated by their hatred of other nationalities, particularly Russians and Jews.

The Ukrainian movement, in its cultural aspects, can also be divided into "culturists" and "dumpling eaters" or "villagers." [18] The culturists collect folklore, set up choirs, and revive ancient rituals. An example is the sculptor Ivan Honchar, who put together a large private museum of folk art, utensils, embroideries, paintings, icons, Easter eggs, and weapons. His apartment is small, and he has room to display only part of his collection. When guests come, he plays recordings of Ukrainian folk songs and ballads. He has three volumes of guest books filled with entries by Ukrainians, Germans, Japanese, Russians, Jews, and Crimean Tatars. Many of Honchar's items cannot be found in official museums and make a splendid impression.

The surgeon Erast Binyashevsky collected several thousand *py-sankas*—intricately decorated Easter eggs. The custom has its roots in pre-Christian mythology. At one time every province and even every village had its own traditional designs. But today *pysanka*s are made less and less in Eastern Ukraine, and the designs are becoming vulgar and socialist-realist. The art is also being lost in Western Ukraine, but beautiful *pysanka*s with ancient ornaments can occasionally be found. Binyashevsky managed with great difficulty to publish an album of Ukrainian Easter eggs.[19] Most of the copies were exported: the government needs foreign currency and propaganda about the flourishing of Ukrainian art under Soviet rule. Binyashevsky longs to publish a second album of additional designs, but the KGB has opened a campaign against the culturists and he is hardly likely to succeed.

The "villagers" are interested only in reviving ancient customs and rituals. There is a similar movement in Russia whose best known representative is Vladimir Soloukhin.[20] The villagers manifest their patriotism by wearing the Ukrainian uniform—Cossack mustaches and embroidered shirts—and singing Ukrainian songs. They are afraid of people like Yevhen Sverstyuk and Valentyn Moroz. Why irritate the authorities, why bring down Moscow's wrath on Ukraine? Many of them hate other peoples because of their own inferiority complexes and fear.

Iryna Steshenko was a villager whose lineage went back almost to the first princes of Kiev, and for many people she was a symbol of old Ukraine.[21] Shortly after the trials of 1966 Steshenko told me a touching story. She, Oksana Ivanenko,[22] and several other writers were invited to see the Minister of Commerce of the Ukrainian Republic, who delivered a revolutionary speech.

"Comrades! A foreigner arrives in Tbilisi and eats Georgian shashlik. In Armenia he drinks the local brandy. But in Kiev he eats and drinks exactly the same things as in Moscow. And yet we have our Ukrainian cuisine. Let me hear your proposals for what we can do in this respect."

Steshenko was asked to teach her Ukrainian recipes to the chef at a leading restaurant. She beamed with joy at finally having won a concession from the authorities. I looked at her and wondered, at what price? Twenty people were sent to camps and prisons that year. To satisfy the patriots the authorities threw them a bone—partial Ukrainianization of restaurants. And they were satisfied with their victory!

When I first met Steshenko, she was very friendly toward me. But when I began to speak Ukrainian, she suddenly turned against me. I also noticed that some of the patriots I respected were avoiding me. Later I learned that Steshenko was spreading rumors that I was a

KGB agent and was trying to win the confidence of Ukrainians. "On top of that his wife is Jewish!" she said.

It is no coincidence that the villagers and chauvinists betray their friends to the KGB more often than anyone else. Such people are characterized by stupidity and various complexes, and the KGB knows how to make use of these traits. Liberalism, cowardly thinking, apathy, and fickleness are one reason for political conformism and betrayal, but another reason is doubt and pessimism. My awareness of this began with a reading of Dostoyevsky, particularly *The Possessed*. Until I was twenty-six I could not read Dostoyevsky, with his tangled plots, emotional confusion, and sentimentality. Kafka, Ionesco, and the surrealists prepared the way for my understanding of him, and my love for him came suddenly and all at once. I read his books like an addict.

My closest friends also developed a passion for him. At first our discussions were limited to exchanges of raptures and analyses of particular ideas. Then we focused on the possessed revolutionaries and counterrevolutionaries. If God does not exist, then everything is permitted. If I have to forgive hangmen, if I must come to the kingdom of heaven past the suffering of a thousand people, then I renounce heaven. If the crystal palace of the future must be constructed on the tears of even one small child, then I reject this future. At first glance such ideas are humane, if utopian. But when I read Dostoyevsky's *Diary of a Writer*, I became aware of the reactionary views Lenin had pointed out. They are present in the fictional works as well, but concealed from view by Dostoyevsky's genius as an artist and his compassion for the insulted and the injured.[23] In *The Possessed* all the blame is heaped on the Verkhovenskys, the Yids, the Polacks, liberalism, and the International—in other words, foreigners. Elsewhere Dostoyevsky blames Catholicism, which leads to materialism and socialism. All this is contrasted with the Russian man, God's elect, who is also Everyman. (Soviet chauvinists are fond of the notion that Russian nationalism is really internationalism.)

When I pointed out such reactionary ideas in Dostoyevsky to my friends, they indignantly accused me of a vulgar perception of art and a Marxist inability to think things through. I retorted that a writer's ideology must be distinguished from his artistic vision. I love Dostoyevsky as a profound thinker and artist, but not as a politician. His political views contradicted his own Christianity. How, one immediately wonders, did Dostoyevsky's humanistic principles and compassion for the oppressed lead to his anti-Semitism, his support for the tsars' hypocritically Slavophile policies, and his friendship with such bastions of the system that gave rise to oppression and hunger as Katkov, Meshchersky, and Pobedonostsev? [24] Dostoyevsky himself answers this question when he analyzes Shigalev: [25] a demand for unlimited freedom leads to unlimited despotism.

This is also true of Dostoyevsky's own system of political views. Like his antipode Shigalev, Dostoyevsky is an ethical maximalist, although their basic moral values differ. But Dostoyevsky also comes to adopt views that contradict the ones he started out with. The struggle for a better society must not cause any suffering, yet it is impossible for any activity not to affect the interests of others and not to bring about suffering. When we adopt a stance of ethical maximalism, we either condemn ourselves to sterility and indifference ("Thou art neither cold nor hot: I would thou wert cold or hot," *Revelations* says of the indifferent) or lend our support to some inhuman ideology.

My friends objected that I was foisting my own ideology on others. When I asked them to propose an alternative, they offered Tolstoyism and a renunciation of all ideology. I raised the argument that we find in Tolstoy not love for one's fellow man—that is, an active goodness and an attempt to help people—but only goodness, which amounts to not committing evil and thus being indifferent. (Tolstoy himself was superior to Tolstoyism and actively campaigned against the death sentence and the inhumanity of science, technology, and industry.)

Dostoyevsky has refuted attempts to renounce all ideology: "If God does not exist, then everything is permitted." My circle of friends understood God to mean the spiritual basis of life and morality. If life has no meaning, then everything is permitted and all human actions are senseless. During the next year or two my principal opponent concluded that "everything was, is, and always will be crap." He was a man of unusual spiritual strength, but few people can be complete pessimists without descending to an ideology of despair and supporting various inhuman positions. Our arguments grew more heated every day. My friend predicted that I would move toward "diabolism"; I predicted that he would betray his ideals. Every argument would end late at night with exchanges of quotations from Dostoyevsky. "If God does not exist . . ." I would call out in parting.

This idea struck me as important both for theoretical reasons and for its consequences in daily life. The Soviet crime rate was growing every year. The press at first ignored it and then began to write about crime in the West. Some of the books and articles about crime in the United States contained fascinating facts and analyses. Truman

Capote's *In Cold Blood* made a strong impression on me by showing that there was a qualitative similarity between the growing crime rates of the United States and the Soviet Union. Even some details were similar. In the United States, for example, two soldiers stopped a passing motorist and shot him dead. A similar event occurred near Kiev. In both cases the motive was boredom. "It's a rotten world," Capote's Latham said. And his accomplice, York, added, "Anybody you kill, you're doing them a favor." [26] That is a pure and simple popular expression of the Dostoyevskian thought.

Such absence of emotions and apparent motives is a new quality typical of our times. Man's actions are less a product of the creative urge than an attempt to escape from boredom. In Kiev two schoolboys tied up a classmate, spread newspapers around her, and set her on fire. Calmly smoking their cigarettes, they waited for her to die, then left without concealing their traces. I questioned people who had read psychiatric reports on the two boys. They had been diagnosed as mentally normal.

Intending to write an article about crime and its causes, I talked to a woman doctor who was a prominent specialist in female crime. She let me read the records of interrogations of teen-age prostitutes. One of these cases clearly illustrated the nature of the modern growth of crime. A village girl who had just arrived in town to study at a technical college was asked by a classmate to sleep with him. She refused. A week later she got drunk and went to bed with him. The following day he brought a friend, and the two of them slept with her. Then five, six, or seven men a day would visit her. Her "endurance" was talked about throughout the school and the town. Soon she was receiving twelve to fifteen men a day. On one occasion she entertained an entire visiting soccer team. Eventually her sexual organs became diseased. One day a group of ten or twelve boys seized her in the woods. "Don't, I'm ill!" she begged. "What's the matter, too weak?" the boys asked. A second, smaller group came to her rescue and drove off the first group. She offered to satisfy them in other ways. After that she never refused anyone. She developed a nervous disability, and her genitals became more inflamed. When she went to a hospital, the doctors called in the militia. The investigator asked her whether she had enjoyed her promiscuity. "No, not very much," the girl replied.

The woman doctor explained to me that the girl was not a nymphomaniac. She was promiscuous because she was bored and wanted to set some sort of record. Who can spit farther, who can eat more, who can have sexual intercourse more often? This widespread pursuit of records also comes from spiritual emptiness.

When I asked the doctor about the reasons for the growth of crime in the Soviet Union, she replied, "We don't have any statistics or scientific analyses of crime. Even I as a specialist don't have them. But according to my observations it is girls without a father or a mother who resort to promiscuity most frequently."

"That's not a convincing explanation," I objected. "The absence of a parent can explain only a small percentage of crimes. There must be more general reasons. You're a Marxist and should look for the social reasons, taking into account the qualitative similarities in the growth of crime in the United States and the Soviet Union."

"No," she replied, "the Americans have different reasons. I don't think that social factors explain Soviet crime."

Half a year later *Novy mir* published an article that discussed various Western theories of crime.[27] Each section began with an appropriate quotation from Dostoyevsky's *Crime and Punishment*. The author brilliantly demonstrated that each theory was capable of explaining only individual cases and not the over-all increase in the crime rate. I was surprised that the author did not quote Dostoyevsky's most important thought: "If God does not exist, then everything is permitted." I believe that this is the primary reason for the growth of crime throughout the world. Nietzsche said that God had died. The news reached only a handful of intellectuals in his time, but today it has penetrated into the masses. God is dead, and nothing equal to him has been created.

In the Soviet Union the "construction of Communism" replaced God in the popular mind for a time. Now people either reject that faith or hold on to it only by habit, ignoring the contradictions between its tenets and their thoroughly unsocialist lives. There are other reasons, of course: the hypocrisy of the regime's moral appeals, the inequality in the distribution of consumer goods, the petit-bourgeois psychology, and the boorishness and lack of education. The masses envy the ruling class and blindly protest against the oppression, the senseless, slavelike labor, and the lack of worthwhile entertainment. The growth of alcoholism, narcotics addiction, and mental disease are still another factor. But all of them have as their underlying reason the lack of a basis for moral taboos.

I often argued with young people about what is and what is not permitted. Proving that a particular taboo made sense was almost impossible. Some people were helped by the moral training they were given in early childhood. But the semieducation prevalent in the society allows the intellect to disregard moral intuition and taboos. For most people morality is based on a fear of punishment: God is a policeman. However, such fear is not enough to prevent the growth of crime. A young man sent to the labor camps for a petty crime usually comes out a professional criminal. The labor camps and prisons are schools of crime, addiction, and perversion, and the number of repeat offenders is growing.

The growth of crime was my main point both when I insisted that it was necessary to have a clear-cut political position and to participate actively in *samizdat*, and when I argued with apologists for the existing system. In my disputes with the latter I emphasized the parallelism in the growth of crime in the United States and the Soviet Union, which testified to the underlying unity of the Soviet and capitalist systems and proved that they are two varieties of one societal form.

My disillusionment with the state of affairs in the country made me decide to study history, particularly party history, and contemporary affairs, and to analyze the failure of the Revolution with the aim of working out an action program. These tasks called for establishing intimate links with Ukrainian and Russian *samizdat* circles and for typing and exchanging manuscripts. I had no desire whatever to fall into the hands of the KGB quickly, and I thought that clandestine work in *samizdat* would be more productive than public protests.

In May 1967 my friends and I received from Moscow Solzhenitsyn's Letter to the Fourth Congress of Soviet Writers.[28] His emotional force and irrefutable logic penetrated the thick curtain of party phrase-mongering like a blinding light. Some intellectuals were more impressed by the letter than by any of Solzhenitsyn's fictional works. Responses soon appeared. Eighty-four writers addressed a collective letter to the Congress supporting Solzhenitsyn, and Georgiy Vladimov wrote a remarkable personal letter to the Congress.[29] It was now possible to hope that the intellectuals, at least those in the humanities, had awakened and would not continue to be silent. This hope was not dashed by the Congress, for it was clear that the authorities were afraid to have Solzhenitsyn's letter discussed.

In November, on the fiftieth anniversary of the October Revolution, we learned that workers had rebelled in Pryluka, a factory town with a population of sixty-thousand about seventy kilometers from Kiev. A short while later I met a woman who had been in the town at the time and whose brother worked at a factory there. From her I learned all the details of the insurrection.

A young man who had just completed military service was working in a factory in Pryluka. Good-natured and bright, he was liked by everyone who knew him. One evening he went to a dance and found a gang of drunken teen-agers pestering the girls. The boy spoke up for the girls. He was strong and well built and, though unarmed, forced the ruffians to put away their knives. When the militia appeared on the scene, the teen-agers quickly disappeared. The militiamen tied up the boy's hands, dragged him into their car, and drove him to the station. There they beat him so savagely that they fractured his skull. By morning he was dead. The militia doctor reported the cause of death as a heart attack. No one believed the story, because the body was found to be disfigured with blows when it was released to the relatives.

The entire factory turned out for the funeral. The mourners moved past the militia station where the murder had been committed. To his misfortune, the militia captain stepped out just then. His appearance triggered an explosion. "Down with the Soviet SS!" a woman cried. Other women supported her. The mob rushed to the station, smashed everything that came to hand, and beat up the militiamen. Workers from other factories joined the rebels. The authorities sent in a small garrison that was stationed in the town. Fire engines were brought in to hose down the rebels, and five people were arrested; the workers set fire to the engines.

All the factories were on strike for three days. The authorities fled. The workers tried to seize the prison where the five arrested men were being held but were afraid to storm it. They sent a letter to the party's Central Committee demanding that the murderers be turned over to them, that the arrested men be released, and that all the party and government employees in the town be dismissed. The rebels threatened to blow up the gas pipeline that passed through the town if the government sent in troops. The workers reminded Brezhnev of their pride in having driven the Nazis from Pryluka with their bare hands and promised that the town would rise up again if their demands were met in a purely verbal way. An army general flew in from Moscow in response to the letter. He addressed the town populace, tore off the insignia on the militia captain's uniform, and trampled them underfoot. (What marvelous actors these servants of the people are!) The general then ordered that the arrested men be released and dismissed the town authorities, but he refused to hand over the murderers on the grounds that this would be lynch law. We had severe laws against murder, he announced, and the guilty party would be punished in accordance with the law. Later several party leaders related the same story to me, although not in such detail.

Toward the end of November 1967 my friends and I learned from the *samizdat* grapevine that Solzhenitsyn would be celebrating his fiftieth birthday on December 12. All my friends set about composing telegrams and letters of congratulation, agonizing over their texts, struggling to find the right words to express their love for a writer who had restored Russian literature to its previous high place, a man of great conscience who had bravely and honestly brought up the problems besetting the country. One of my friends received a very warm response from Solzhenitsyn with a postscript thanking everyone who had sent him greetings. His reply immensely pleased us. We were happy in the thought that our culture existed again and hopeful that it would not be destroyed once more.

III

OUTLAWED

We are doomed to remember everything
and to tell others.

Yuliy Daniel, *Prison Poems*

11

PRAGUE SPRING AND
MOSCOW SUMMER

Nineteen sixty-eight began happily. My friends and I listened to the leaders address the country and cheerfully poked fun at them. They were standing on shaky ground, and the smell of spring was coming from Czechoslovakia.* A visiting Pole told us that young people and intellectuals in Poland had begun to put forth demands for democratization. Władysław Gomułka, the Secretary of the Polish party, resorted to the tried and true method of spreading anti-Semitic propaganda. His campaign was partly successful in isolating the Jewish and "Jew-loving" intellectuals.

In Czechoslovakia, under pressure from Czech intellectuals and Slovak patriots, some party leaders spoke out against Antonín Novotný's dictatorship and replaced him as First Secretary with Alexander Dubček, although Novotný remained President. (In the "socialist" countries, party leaders, who represent part of the population, have more power than presidents or prime ministers, who formally represent the entire population. This undemocratic practice actually helped to start democratization in Czechoslovakia in 1968.) Novotný also resorted to anti-Semitism, but the workers did not respond to the bait, and he only hurt his own cause. Then General Jan Šejna attempted a putsch against the party's Central Committee. Failing to obtain the support of the officers and soldiers, he fled to the United States. (He realized that Brezhnev would not be interested in a man whose game was up and might turn him over to Dubček.)

* Instead of using all the material about events in Czechoslovakia that I have now, I am relating only what we learned in Kiev at that time. People in Moscow knew considerably more than we did, but even they were limited to fragmentary reports. Soviet citizens have few opportunities to verify news, and imprecise information often has a strong influence on them.

Every morning at the laboratory I would relate the latest developments in the Prague Spring. My colleagues listened with great interest. "Šejna has driven a stake into Novotný's grave," I announced the morning I learned about Šejna's flight. "He's proved that Stalinists sell out Communism at every step. Novotný will not be President for long." Further events confirmed my view. General Janko, a deputy minister of defense connected with Šejna, shot himself. Novotný was stripped of his powers.

Our joy over the Prague Spring was clouded, however, by rumors of an impending trial against Alexander Ginzburg, Yuriy Galanskov, Vera Lashkova, and Aleksey Dobrovolsky. We obtained a letter by Larisa Bogoraz and Pavel Litvinov, addressed to "world public opinion," in which they described the illegal methods and trumped-up charges in the case.[1] At the same time we heard reports that Pavel Radziyevsky, one of our old friends from Kiev, had turned out to be a provocateur. Since I knew him well and didn't believe the stories, I decided to see Victor Krasin in Moscow to learn more about Radziyevsky and the trial.

Krasin was disturbed by the events in Czechoslovakia and the trial. He gave me several Czechoslovak newspapers that discussed doing away with preliminary censorship and strengthening the role of trade unions and workers' councils. Krasin, who could barely tolerate even my Marxism, thoughtfully commented on the articles. "It looks as if Dubček will succeed in proving that Communism can exist in practice...."

Krasin also gave me several *samizdat* articles and books, including Sinyavsky's *Fantastic Stories*, Daniel's "Atonement," and *The Confession of Victor Velsky*.[2] When I had read my fill, I asked Krasin to tell me about Radziyevsky. He explained that when Radziyevsky was released, after three months in Lefortovo Prison, he praised the KGB and lashed out at his companions. Dobrovolsky and later Ginzburg, Galanskov, and Lashkova were arrested because of him. Although Krasin cited some of Radziyevsky's testimony against his friends, I was still not convinced that he was a provocateur: there were too many rationalized arguments and two few facts.

I went to see Radziyevsky and, pretending complete ignorance, asked him about his investigation. He told me in detail how he had been caught, how he had behaved at the interrogations, and how Pyotr Yakir had accused him of being an informer.[3] Dobrovolsky had brought several *samizdat* articles to Radziyevsky, in a folder labeled "Dobrovolsky," and had asked that he have them retyped at work.

"Is there anything dangerous here?" Radziyevsky asked. "I can't vouch for the typists."

"No, these are minutes of meetings of Old Bolsheviks."

Radziyevsky glanced through the articles on his way to work. He removed one that seemed dangerous and had the others retyped. A week later the KGB came to him, found the folder with Dobrovolsky's name, and arrested both men. Radziyevsky expressed a suspicion that Dobrovolsky had been a provocateur. "But perhaps he's simply mad," Radziyevsky added. "His head isn't quite right."

From what Radziyevsky told me about his interrogation I realized that he had made several small slips. But all people under investigation, even those experienced in KGB confrontations, make mistakes. Dobrovolsky, for example, gave Galanskov a message asking him to accept responsibility because he, Dobrovolsky, could not go to prison now. Galanskov, known as the Prince Myshkin of the Democratic Movement, accepted responsibility for Dobrovolsky's ties with the NTS [4] and thus helped the KGB concoct the case. He withdrew his testimony at the trial, but it was too late: he was sentenced to seven years in labor camps. Ginzburg was sentenced to five years, Dobrovolsky to two, and Lashkova to one.

When Radziyevsky was released, he told all his friends about the investigation and his impression of the investigators: "They're polite and they smile while they're questioning you. Only once did a guard shout at me. They've changed since Stalin's days." Radziyevsky was naïve in this respect, but that was hardly reason to accuse him of treachery.

I asked Radziyevsky to introduce me to Pyotr Yakir. We visited several people. Some didn't want to see us; others said they didn't know Yakir. I had decided to turn to Krasin when Yakir telephoned and arranged a meeting. At first he suspected me of playing a nasty game, but toward the end of our conversation he dropped his suspicion that I worked for the KGB. "Whom do you know in Moscow?" he asked me.

"Krasin."

"Aha, the Christians. Are you one of them, too?"

"No, I'm a Marxist."

"Party member?"

"No."

"Well, I'm a bit of a Marxist, too."

When I visited Krasin again in February, I found Pavel Litvinov with him.[5] I was pleased to see that the offspring of the Old Bolsheviks, as well as some of the Old Bolsheviks themselves, were on our side. Litvinov showed us the many replies he and Larisa Bogoraz had received to their appeal to world public opinion; only one letter castigated them.

When I came home from Moscow, I turned to my friends for advice. I wanted both to write for *samizdat* and to remain unnoticed. It did not seem expedient to support the protests, and yet it was impossible to remain silent while Stalinism was being resurrected. Finally, my emotions won out over my friends' admonishments. On March 8 I wrote a letter to *Komsomolskaya pravda* in reply to one of the many slanderous articles about the Ginzburg trial.[6] Having illusions about courtroom procedure, I based my arguments on facts that could be verified easily if the authorities put me on trial. I showed the letter to Tanya before sending it off: my actions would determine what happened to her and the children, and there was no doubt that prison lay at the end of the road I had chosen. Tanya thought that such letters were futile but told me that I must follow my conscience.

In the middle of May we obtained the first issue of the *Chronicle of Current Events*, a typewritten journal that reported arrests, searches, and other persecution of dissidents.[7] This first issue was devoted to the trial of Galanskov, Ginzburg, and Lashkova and to the persecution of people who had signed letters in their defense. The *Chronicle* immediately became a valuable source of information about events in the country, the methods used by the KGB, the various oppositional currents, and an avenue of approach to people whose views were close to ours.

We also received from Moscow Anatoliy Marchenko's *My Testimony*, in which he described the post-Stalinist labor camps.[8] We learned that they had begun to fill up with political prisoners not after the trial of Sinyavsky and Daniel, but as early as 1956, and that the camp authorities were utterly ruthless. Even *One Day in the Life of Ivan Denisovich* paled by comparison with the horrors Marchenko described. I bought a typewriter and spent a month retyping his account.

On May 20 I was summoned to the party committee at the Institute of Cybernetics. There I found Kirill Ivanov-Muromsky, a biologist and assistant secretary of the party organization, whom I had met in 1961, when we rented adjoining rooms in an apartment. He had become an alcoholic at sixteen, because of the suffering and baseness he had witnessed as a boy at the front: he drank to forget. He was wasting a tremendous talent: he had lectured on physiology to medical students while still a schoolboy and had been involved in perfecting some sort of weapon at the outbreak of the war. Later he worked as the secretary of a district party committee in the Odessa Province and conducted research on electric sleep. He had joined the Institute of Cybernetics immediately after it was set up. Amosov thought highly of him at first but then became disillusioned and threw him out. Ivanov-Muromsky and I had formerly spent much time together, drinking and discussing politics. He always made fun of my "Communist illusions."

"I respect your patriotic feelings," Ivanov-Muromsky began now at the party headquarters, "but I advise you not to go to the Shevchenko Monument on May 22."

The transfer of Taras Shevchenko's remains from Saint Petersburg to Kaniv, where he was buried, by way of Kiev had been commemorated on May 22 since the turn of the century. During the 1960's citizens of Kiev, particularly students, gathered at the Shevchenko Monument on this day to sing Ukrainian songs and read Shevchenko's poetry and their own. In 1967 the militia arrested four or five people who had made speeches at the monument, whereupon the crowd marched on the Central Committee headquarters. There firemen hosed down the demonstrators, but to no avail. Finally a member of the Central Committee came out and urged the crowd to go home. An old woman announced that everyone had come to the monument to honor Shevchenko; why had some people been arrested? The demonstrators demanded that those arrested be released.

"All right, I shall telephone the militia, and if the people detained haven't committed any crimes, they will be released," the Central Committee man promised. "Now break it up and go home!"

"No, not until they're released!" the crowd called out and proceeded to march to the militia station. Those who had been detained were released.

I myself had never attended the May 22 meetings and was surprised by Ivanov-Muromsky's advice. "Why shouldn't I go?" I asked.

"There will be an anti-Soviet demonstration there. Leaflets with anti-Soviet slogans have been distributed throughout the city. If you show up, your action will be interpreted as anti-Soviet."

"If that's the case, the KGB itself must be distributing the leaflets. I don't believe that the patriots did this."

"I myself read a leaflet found in Holosiiv Park. It said, 'Brethren! Let us assemble at the Shevchenko Monument on May 22 and announce: Muscovites and Jews, get out of Ukraine!' "

"I know the Ukrainian patriots and haven't met any who think this way. This is a provocation."

"Nevertheless I advise you not to go. You'll lose your job."

"I'll complain to the Central Committee."

Ivanov-Muromsky smiled sardonically. I flew into a rage. "If that doesn't help, I'll complain to the UN about discrimination against Ukrainians!"

"I advise you to think twice about it. You have a wife and children."

"Very well, I'll check out the demonstration today. I won't go if it's going to be chauvinistic. I have no desire to see my wife and children booted out of Ukraine."

At Yevhen Sverstyuk's I learned that many people had been cautioned not to attend the meeting. In some institutions everyone was forbidden to go, in others only certain people. In still others—the Institute of Education, for example—everyone was required to go. Leaflets had been distributed, and there had been two or three Russophobe graffiti at the university. "But there are asses everywhere," Sverstyuk commented. At the university announcements were posted inviting students to a Festival of the Friendship of Peoples to be held on May 22 at the Shevchenko Monument.

Ivanov-Muromsky telephoned me on the twenty-first, having telephoned my wife first to tell her that she shouldn't let me go: "His attendance will be interpreted as anti-Soviet propaganda." My wife replied that she saw no reason for me not to go.

"Well, have you decided?" he asked me now.

I told him about the officially sponsored festival.

"You'll be sorry if you go."

"Your statement is blackmail and discrimination against my rights."

"As you wish."

On the morning of the twenty-second I was called in to see Victor Glushkov. He was not in his office when I arrived, and his deputy, Academician Pukhov, spoke with me instead.[9] I had behaved impertinently at the party headquarters, he told me, and was planning to attend an anti-Soviet demonstration. We got into a heated discussion, and Pukhov played his trump card. "Your boss came to see me today. He said that you're a bad employee and haven't accomplished anything in cybernetics. He asked that you be dismissed."

"I've recently received a prize for excellence," I replied. "Antomonov hasn't once criticized me for bad work. Call him in and have him say this to my face."

"I'm too busy for that. You've been working here for six years and are still an ordinary engineer."

"I have somewhat different ideas about science and a career."

"A person who doesn't dream of a career is a bad employee. You're not growing. We don't need you. I advise you to submit a voluntary resignation."

"I will complain."

"Go right ahead, even to the UN."

I immediately went to Ivanov-Muromsky and in the presence of his subordinates told him that he was a scoundrel for having reported what I had said confidentially about the UN.

Antomonov was waiting for me when I returned to the laboratory. He told me that he had been ordered to dismiss me on any pretext and advised me to "resign voluntarily." If I didn't, I would still be dismissed, but with a blot on my record.

"I have no intention of helping them persecute me," I replied.

My colleagues sympathized with me, but some of them said that the laboratory would be disbanded because of me. Later I learned that many of the people who had signed petitions had "resigned voluntarily" precisely because of this argument. My own view was that if my colleagues cared more for their hides than for conscience, I had the moral right to disregard their hides for the sake of not collaborating with the KGB in its crackdown on freedom of thought.

My case quieted down for a time. Meetings were held throughout the Soviet Union at which people who had signed protests were censured, dismissed from the party, and fired from their jobs. Some signatories saved themselves by repudiating their views. One scientist announced that he had signed a petition while drunk. Another said that the letter he had signed had been brought by a pretty girl. "How could I refuse her?" The phrase became a byword in Kiev.

Pyotr Yakir, his daughter, Ira, and her husband, Yuliy Kim, arrived in Kiev.[10] Yakir, Kim, and the poet Ilya Gabay had written one of the best letters of protest.[11] Yakir told us about the letters received by Larisa Bogoraz and Pavel Litvinov—that "Yid breed," as they were called in the letters. There was no doubt that the campaign against cosmopolitanism of the late 1940's and early 1950's was being resurrected as a campaign against Zionism. At first the "Yids" had been usurers and bloodsucking capitalists; later they were socialists, Bolsheviks, and Chekists, then cosmopolitans, and now they were Zionists. And they were always poor patriots of Russia. But the Russian government was always just and magnanimous and rewarded the good Jews who served their native land.

The day after Yakir's arrival friends telephoned him to announce the death of Valeriy Pavlinchuk, a physicist from Obninsk who had signed the "Letter of the 224" and had run into many difficulties with the party.[12] Yakir had loved and respected Pavlinchuk so much that he was almost beside himself. We immediately drove to the airport but couldn't get tickets and had to turn back. Yakir pointed to a car behind us: "They're following us." He likes to play cops-and-robbers, I thought to myself. How does he know that it's *their* car? Later, when cars started to follow me, too, I discovered that KGB cars can be readily identified. I also understood Yakir's response: the first time you're followed you have a sporting interest in taunting the KGB or playing hide-and-seek. Later you lose interest or become frightened.

As we were passing a forest, Yakir suggested that we stop to pick mushrooms. I agreed. The car behind us immediately turned off into the forest.

"Shall we go meet them?" Yakir asked with a smile.

"Let's."

A young man with a criminal physiognomy ran out from the woods. (Later I learned to recognize KGB detectives by their darting eyes and vicious expressions.) As soon as he noticed us, the young man began to hum a song and bent down to pick a flower, then casually turned back to his car. We walked into the forest. There were no mushrooms, and we couldn't hear the detective. After wandering about a bit, we saw a bus headed toward the highway, but not in the direction we had come from. "Let's lose our tail!" Yakir exclaimed.

When the bus came out of the forest about a kilometer from where we had left the detective, we saw the same car. "Aha, he must have had a walkie-talkie," Yakir explained. The car did not follow us, but five or six kilometers later another car caught up with us and accompanied us all the way home.

A few weeks later my family and I went on a holiday to Odessa. I hinted to my mother that I might lose my job. She had dreamed all her life that her children would live well, and the news was a severe blow. She urged Tanya and me to drop our political involvements. "It's all useless," my mother said. "Think about yourselves, the children, and me." I calmed her down only by promising to try to keep my job and to limit myself to scientific matters.

My mother told me how she had seen Trotsky during his exile in Central Asia and how the working-class people had sympathized with him. "Even he wasn't able to do anything," she noted sadly. I told her in turn about the persecution of Lenin's wife, Nadezhda Krupskaya, his brother Dmitriy, and other relatives and friends. My mother wasn't convinced. "How do you know all this?" she asked. When I criticized Khrushchev, she defended him. "He gave you a pass to a sanatorium!"

On July 6 I went to Moscow and attended a birthday party for Pavel Litvinov. Of the many guests I knew only Krasin and Litvinov, but I had heard of most of the others. No sooner had I dropped a Ukrainian word than Petro Grigorenko and Vladimir Dremlyuga introduced themselves.[13] I also briefly talked with Larisa Bogoraz.[14] I became particularly close with Grigoriy Podyapolsky and his wife, Masha.[15] We laughed at the revelers and, like all intellectuals in the Soviet Union, gossiped about the leaders and exchanged anecdotes about meetings called to censure people who had signed protests.

Yuriy Eichenwald and his wife, Valeriya Gerlin, related the angry speeches delivered by the teachers at the school where Valeriya taught.[16] We all roared with laughter when she quoted a phrase about Larisa Bogoraz, "the wife of Sinyavsky and Daniel." In turn I told them about the courtly scientist who had not been able to refuse the pretty girl. It was on this occasion, when everyone had left, that Dremlyuga and I began the age-old conversation of Ivan and Alyosha Karamazov that I mentioned at the beginning of the book.

I spent about a week in Moscow, visiting one protester after another. I managed to spend a whole day with Grigorenko. He told me about his life and how he had arrived at the resolution to struggle for "socialism with a human face." His first steps were making a speech at a Moscow party conference, for which he was dismissed from the Frunze Military Academy, and setting up the underground Union of Struggle for the Revival of Leninism, for which he was interned in a psychiatric prison from 1964 to 1965.

In Kiev I had read about the Crimean Tatars and their struggle to return to their native land. The most powerful document was an article by Aleksey Kosterin. Grigorenko showed me the speech he had given on March 17, 1968, for Kosterin's seventy-second birthday. "What is granted by law is not asked for but demanded," was the core of his argument, and he called on the Tatars to demand the restoration of the Crimean Autonomous Republic. Grigorenko also set forth what he and Kosterin thought were the most effective means: making use of freedom of speech, press, and meetings, establishing contacts with people of all nationalities in the Soviet Union, and appealing to the world public and to such organizations as the United Nations and the International Tribunal. The banquet ended with toasts to the Crimean Republic and the Internationale. I realized then that Grigorenko was the most energetic, courageous, and politically intelligent man I had met.

Grigorenko and Kosterin's letter to the Budapest Conference of Communist and Workers' Parties offered a profound analysis of Stalinism, the Twentieth Party Congress, the continuation of Stalinism and anti-Semitism after the Congress, and the measures Communists must take against them.[17] Unfortunately, the letter was given little attention in *samizdat* and was not answered by a single Communist party. The smothering of Czechoslovakia was just around the corner, and those who remained silent were accomplices to the Czechoslovak tragedy.

I told Grigorenko that troops had been stationed on the border with Czechoslovakia and that rumors were being spread in the border areas that the Czechs were systematically sending small armed groups into the Soviet Union. Similar rumors had been spread before the invasions of Finland and Poland in 1939. No one in Moscow or Kiev had any doubt that Brezhnev and company would come to the assistance of their fifth colony and suffocate the Czechs and Slovaks in their fraternal embrace the way they had suffocated the East Germans in 1953 and the Hungarians in 1956.

Grigorenko showed me the letter Ivan Yakhimovich had written to the Central Committee.[18] Speaking as a party member, Yakhimovich told the Central Committee that the trials of Sinyavsky, Daniel, Ginzburg, Galanskov, and Lashkova were harming socialism, de-Stalinization, and the reputation of the country. Yakhimovich's letter was written in the language of classical Marxism, and many readers felt that its arguments and emotional tone were the most powerful they had ever encountered.

A philologist by education, Yakhimovich had chosen to work as the chairman of a backward collective farm in Latvia. He made the farm into one of the most advanced by improving the peasants' standard of living. He was one of the first in the country to pay peasants for their labor with money, and the Soviet press wrote a great deal about his accomplishments. When his farm increased its output, the district party committee ordered it to turn over to the state much more produce than it was required to. Believing that only the peasants' personal interest would increase the productivity of labor, Yakhimovich refused. The peasants loved him because he was one of the few honest Communists who cared about people.

In Moscow I also met an old party member who sympathized with the Left Opposition, although he had not belonged to it.[19] In talking about the purges of the Bolsheviks, he continually emphasized that the liquidated Trotskyists must not be identified with Stalinism. In his large Marxist library I first read Trotsky's *Lessons of October,*

Lenin's *Political Testament*, Bukharin's *The ABC of Communism*, and collections of articles by Stalin, Zinovyev, Kamenev, and Krupskaya. Both Bukharin and Trotsky, I found, took from Lenin's testament only what corresponded to their own views. I preferred Bukharin to Trotsky because of his concern for the peasants and his demand for gradual rather than abrupt collectivization; but he never mentioned democracy, and he succumbed to the Lenin cult. Trotsky was much less enthralled by this cult.

As we parted, the party member burst into tears and begged me not to renounce the October Revolution. "Yes, we were defeated, but one must study the reasons for this and not simply blame the October Revolution for all our problems, as young people do. You are the first young man I've met who knows even a little about the party's history and who tries to analyze it."

I gave him the address of another old party member in contact with us and asked that he send me books by oppositionists of the 1920's and 1930's through him. "Our generation is so broken that I advise you to be very careful in your dealings with old party members," he cautioned me. That other party member was indeed later unmasked as an agent through whom the KGB was trying to direct the Democratic Movement.

On my return to Kiev, a co-worker at the laboratory told me that I had been fired on the grounds that the institute was overstaffed. "We must reduce our staff by one person," Antomonov had announced at a trade-union meeting. "Plyushch will be fired no matter what. If we fire someone else, we lose two staff members; if we fire Plyushch, we lose only one."

Although the arithmetic was convincing, no one wanted to vote in favor of firing me. Antomonov then proposed voting by "American ballot": a list of staff members was distributed, and everyone put a cross beside one name. Most of the staff members put crosses beside their own names, but a few must not have, and the two or three crosses beside my name automatically gave me the most votes. Only the man who came to warn me had spoken up at the meeting to say that it would be better to fire everyone than to be involved in this dirty business.

Looking through the Labor Code, I found five or six reasons why I could not be fired. I went to the laboratory, pointed out the labor legislation, and demanded that another trade-union meeting be held because the first one did not have the right to "reduce" me in my absence, and there wasn't even a record of that meeting. Finally I explained that it did make a difference to me whether I was dismissed by my co-workers or by the administration: if I was dismissed by the former, I would have difficulty in bringing a suit against the latter.

The second trade-union meeting resolved that the previous meeting had been illegal and that I was needed in the laboratory. The question then was whom to fire. This placed me in an awkward situation: I was forcing someone to become a victim. I explained to my co-workers that the trade union had the right to block any staff reduction. This decision was approved and entered into the minutes of the meeting. Afterward there was another discussion about the "immorality" of exposing the laboratory to attack and the "morality" of silently watching people being persecuted for their views. Some of my co-workers tried to convince me that things weren't all bad and that I was exaggerating the danger of renewed Stalinism.

I took the minutes of the meeting to the personnel department. The manager told me that I would be dismissed in two weeks. I replied that I could not be fired, because I was supporting two children.

"It isn't our fault that you didn't report the birth of another child to the personnel department," the manager replied.

"That's not true," I rebutted. "You must have a record of this because I am issued gifts for both children on holidays." By tradition children are given bags of candy on holidays.

"And I tell you that the second child is not recorded!"

I walked over to the card file to look for my file. The manager ran after me, shouting and trying to stop me. I pulled out my file and showed her that both my children were recorded. The manager screamed that I was a rowdy and a smart aleck. People peered into the room, wondering if someone were trying to rape her. For a moment I thought that I had behaved despicably toward this gray-haired woman, but my feeling of guilt quickly vanished when I remembered who was violating whose rights.

I also took the minutes of the second meeting to the trade-union committee. The officials there told me that I didn't know the law. Staff reductions are decided by the trade-union committee and not at meetings. "Then why did you order a meeting held?" I asked. "Under the law you have no right to fire me." I proceeded to list all the points in my favor and showed the excellent reference Antomonov had given me several months before.

An outsider from the district trade-union committee intervened in the discussion. "It's too late now to resolve anything at the local level," he said. "You have ten days to file a suit against the administration."

I set about looking for an attorney, because I wanted to make the trial political. In Moscow it would have been difficult but nonetheless possible to find one willing to discuss the political reasons behind my dismissal. In Kiev I spent ten days trying to find someone suitable; on the twelfth day a legal expert explained to me that I should have filed a suit within ten days and then looked for an attorney. But August 1968 was approaching, and our personal fates were dwindling in importance.

When I met a visiting Czech, I questioned him about the evidence of an antisocialist revolution in Czechoslovakia which Soviet newspapers were citing. The Czech persuasively refuted all the Soviet arguments. He also revealed the truth behind the famous letter signed by ninety automobile workers who warned of the threat of counterrevolution and asked the Soviet government for "fraternal assistance": almost all of them were bureaucrats or security staff at the factory.[20] Talk about West Germany's aggressive intentions only amused the Czech. West Germany was so afraid of the USSR, he explained, that it would never dream of aggression against Czechoslovakia, even if it had a fifth column in the country. Besides, the Czechs and Slovaks remembered only too well the centuries of experience they had had with Germans. "The Czechs and Slovaks will never turn away from Russia," he concluded.

"But the USSR is planning to attack you," I replied.

"That's impossible. We're fraternal peoples, and Czechoslovakia is a socialist country."

"You know your brothers very poorly. Brezhnev won't give a second thought to socialism or centuries of friendship. Just remember Slánský's trial.[21] For the Soviet leaders, socialism is simply a screen for assuming power, and you're weakening their grasp."

"Perhaps. But Soviet soldiers won't attack Communists and Slavs!"

"What about Hungary? Why are the Soviet leaders slandering the Czechoslovak party without letup if they're not preparing the army and the populace for an attack against the 'counterrevolutionaries'? And why are Soviet tanks standing at the border?"

"I saw them when I was crossing the border. They're meant to intimidate Dubček and make him more compliant."

The argument was useless. The Czech placed too much reliance on "friendship" and "internationalism." I didn't believe a single word the Soviet leaders said. And the people? What do they know? They are fed lies every day. They believe that the Czechs, Slovaks, Poles, and Bulgarians were saved by the Soviet Union during World War II and yet have the temerity to be ungrateful. At the same time the people do not believe that those who say this are honest. Even at the institute I heard people who knew Soviet foreign affairs say, "Why did we sacrifice our blood? So that they can turn their country over to the Germans?"

Ludvík Vaculík's speech at the Czechoslovak writers' congress, "Two Thousand Words," the Action Program of the Czechoslovak Communist Party, and other translations from the Czechoslovak press, particularly *Literární listy*, appeared in Soviet *samizdat*.[22] *Dukla*, the journal of the Ukrainian minority in eastern Slovakia, was in great demand. Its pages were so full of the joy inspired by the Prague Spring that one didn't need to know other Czechoslovak newspapers and magazines to see that spring had really come.

The democracy, humanism, and sincerity of the Action Program, more than anything else, convinced us that the Czechoslovak party had begun to construct "socialism with a human face." The Soviet press responded by stepping up its attacks on Czechoslovakia. *Pravda* published an article in which anonymous leaders of the Czechoslovak party asked for assistance. The fifth column went into action. We were all expecting war and wondering whether Czechoslovakia's friends, Rumania and Yugoslavia, would come to its aid. There were rumors that they had promised Dubček military assistance in case of invasion and that Yugoslavia had begun to arm its population. We knew, however, that the Czechoslovak troops were stationed on the West German border and that their cannon were aimed at the West. Dubček was not prepared to repel Soviet aggression. West Germany, on the other hand, afraid of provoking the Warsaw Pact countries, had moved its military maneuvers away from the Czechoslovak border.

The ugliest aspect of the whole matter was the way Soviet newspapers reported articles about Czechoslovakia by Western journalists. Conjectures by the New York *Times*, Washington *Post*, *Daily Mail*, and *Il Tempo* were passed off as self-exposure by the imperialists. The freedom to fantasize and lie which Western journalists enjoy was exploited by the enslaved press of the Soviet Union. Once again freedom helped antifreedom. The immoral mendacity of Western journalists is always convenient for Soviet falsifiers. The reverse is also true, and the Western press has frequently used Soviet falsehoods to attack socialism.

Then, on August 21, came the news that Warsaw Pact troops had invaded Czechoslovakia. The following days were one long nightmare of shame and despair. We sat up every night, listening to broadcasts from Prague. Ludvík Svoboda wept because the Nazi occupation of 1938 had been repeated, drawing parallels between 1938 and 1968.[23] We all wept with him, powerless to oppose our leaders' violence with anything except tears and impotent hatred. We felt an excruciating shame at being Soviet citizens and Marxists. We were afraid for Czechoslovakia, the Soviet Union, and the whole world. A long, harsh winter of Stalinist fascism was setting in.

Living in this loathsome country became intolerable, because we could see no effective ways to struggle against the bandits in power. What could a pathetically small group of Soviet oppositionists accomplish, if even an organized, politically developed country, with its own government and army, unanimous in its resolution to follow its independent path, was powerless? People I barely knew would walk up to me on the street and cry out with anger and hatred, "Why are the Americans silent? If only the Chinese would start a war! Propaganda and *samizdat* aren't worth beans. We have to throw bombs!" The angriest and most desperate statements were uttered by the most moderate and liberal people. I tried to calm them and urged them not to indulge in adventurism, but I myself was inclined to take my chances.

I decided to go to the Czechoslovak consulate to apply for citizenship. Several Kievites had anticipated me. The consul was in Moscow, and his assistants thanked us for our moral support but advised us not to speak out, lest the consulate be accused of incitement. They knew as little as we did about events in their country. They said that the Czechoslovak ambassador to Moscow had been suborned by the invaders.

Someone proposed that we organize a demonstration, but after long discussions we decided against it: there were so few of us in Kiev that the arrest of demonstrators would paralyze *samizdat*. Instead we would support the Czechs and Slovaks by distributing the documents of the Prague Spring as widely as we could.

Tanya and I were going home in a taxi on the night of the twenty-first or twenty-second. The taxi stopped at the Paton Bridge across the Dnieper: an endless column of artillery units was crossing. "They're going to crush the Rumanians!" the taxi driver snapped. Our hearts stopped beating for a moment. The Rumanians would resist, and war would break out. Many young men were inducted into the army at that time and indoctrinated with lies about the counterrevolutionary aims of the Rumanian government. Soviet troops stood at the Rumanian border. Some Kievites thought of joining the army so that they could go over to the Rumanians if war broke out. But the idea was naïve: who would have believed such enthusiasm?

Andrey Sakharov's *Progress, Coexistence, and Intellectual Freedom* finally arrived in Kiev.[24] Although Sakharov brilliantly defined the problems facing the world and fearlessly exposed the pro-Stalinist policies within the Soviet Union, many of us found his proposals for reforming domestic and foreign policies impractical. No significant reforms seemed possible after Czechoslovakia had been occupied. I was particularly skeptical about his ideas on the rapprochement of the USSR and the leading capitalist countries. Yes, convergence is possible, but of what sort? Existing tendencies indicate a convergence that will lead the world to catastrophe. There is a growing tendency in the Soviet Union to renounce even the word "socialism" and to move toward state capitalism in its most inhuman form. If the West does converge with the Soviet Union, it will do so by becoming less democratic, increasing the concentration of capital, and merging monopolies with the state. Sakharov is aware of this danger and says in his essay that convergence must not become a collusion of governments.

Sakharov's essay was widely read and discussed by scientists and writers. I, at the time, was absorbed by another matter: Yakir telephoned on August 26 to say that Larisa Bogoraz, Victor Feinberg, Pavel Litvinov, Natalya Gorbanevskaya, Konstantin Babitsky, Vladimir Dremlyuga, and Vadim Delone had come to Red Square the previous day and unfurled banners protesting against the occupation of Czechoslovakia. They had been arrested immediately and would now be charged with conducting "anti-Soviet propaganda," "slandering the regime," or disturbing the functioning of street traffic and government offices. We were pleased by this show that not everyone in the Soviet Union supported the regime's aggression, but many of us were sorry that Litvinov had gone out to Red Square, because he was so important for *samizdat*. Yet we all understood that now speaking out was more important than common sense.

Meetings were held to drum up support for the "fraternal assistance" being rendered to Czechoslovakia. Some people stayed away from the meetings, others refrained from speaking, and still others protested. Those who disagreed with the government's policy were punished.

At the Institute of Cybernetics Glushkov gave a speech supporting the invasion and condemning the Czechoslovak opportunists and counterrevolutionaries. A colleague had invited a journalist. When

Glushkov saw the flare of the flashbulb, he turned pale and stopped talking. Even this unprincipled man did not want the world to know that he was supporting aggression. Afterward he passed a message to Victor Bodnarchuk, who had been dismissed from the institute for writing *samizdat*, that he had been forced to make his speech for the sake of the institute and science.

Toward the end of September, Rollan Kadiyev and Zampira Asanova visited Kiev on behalf of the Crimean Tatars.* [25] They had mandates from their people that clearly defined the positions they were to take. The Crimean Tatars had collected money for their representatives to travel to Moscow and Kiev, and Rollan and Zampira had come with a letter to the Ukrainian government. We learned from them that the KGB was spreading rumors that "Ukrainian nationalists" were preventing the Tatars from returning to the Crimea. We all broke into laughter. "What nationalists?" we asked. "Shelest, or Dzyuba, whom Shelest is persecuting for nationalism?" [26] The KGB was also spreading rumors in the Crimea that the Tatars wanted to deprive the Ukrainian and Russian settlers of their homes.

We went to see Victor Nekrasov. Zampira thanked him on behalf of the Tatars for supporting their struggle. Nekrasov told a funny story. While staying at a hotel in the Crimea, he had joked to a writer friend, "Let's make a revolution here. We'll follow the usual plan. First the railway station, the telegraph office, and the bank. Then we'll expel the Russians and Ukrainians and proclaim an independent Crimean republic. We'll ask the Tatars for political refuge and thus be able to live in a free country." The writer was later interrogated about his refusal to speak out against Nekrasov. "Do you think we don't know how you and Nekrasov wanted to start a revolution in the Crimea?"

We decided to introduce Rollan and Zampira to the Ukrainian patriots to draw their attention to the plight of the Crimean Tatars. The less official the writer was, the more sincerely he responded to our plea. Dzyuba and Zinoviya Franko [27] promised to gather signatures from Ukrainian intellectuals on a letter demanding that the Tatars be permitted to return to their homeland.

* The Crimean Tatars (who are distinct from the Kazan Tatars) were forcibly deported from the Crimea to Central Asia in 1944 because of alleged pro-Nazi sympathies. Almost half the Tatars perished of cold and hunger during and immediately after the deportation. In 1967 the Tatars were officially cleared of the charge of treason but were not permitted to return to the Crimea. Since then they have mounted a persistent and highly organized movement which has won the sympathy and support of many dissidents.—TRANS.

When we visited Andriy Malyshko,[28] we were met by his wife, Lyubov Zabashta, who had reprimanded me in 1966 for speaking Russian. Rollan explained that Crimean Tatar monuments were being destroyed and asked Zabashta to intercede with the Society for the Preservation of Monuments.

"I've often vacationed in the Crimea and haven't seen any destruction," she replied.

Rollan showed her a photograph.

"All right, I'll take a look when I'm at the sanatorium next year."

Malyshko walked in. His wife ran to him and whispered in his ear, and he disappeared into the bedroom. Zabashta explained that he could not talk to us because he had had a heart attack the previous night. "But he sympathizes with your people, of course."

On the whole, however, Rollan and Zampira left with an excellent impression of the Ukrainian intelligentsia, particularly of Dzyuba. Afterward they sent us their bulletins about the struggles and police persecution of the Tatars. On April 21, Tatars had assembled at Chirchik in Uzbekistan to celebrate Lenin's birthday. Militiamen and troops broke up the gathering with truncheons, belts, and alkaline water from hoses. They spared neither women nor old people, and Uzbeks and even Russians were beaten as well. Over three hundred people were arrested. A Russian captain who witnessed the carnage called out, "How dare you hit people? You're not SS men! I'll write to the Central Committee!" He was beaten so badly that he was taken off to the hospital, and the Tatars never were able to learn what happened to him.

In May eight hundred Tatars arrived in Moscow; on the sixteenth and seventeenth they were all arrested, loaded into sealed railway cars, and shipped off to Tashkent. Those who resisted arrest were beaten. By mistake a Turkish citizen was beaten with the rest. When he complained to his ambassador, the Soviet authorities apologized. The Turkish ambassador was satisfied: Moslems were being beaten, but they were not his own. The Tatars had placed high hopes on Moslems in Turkey and the Middle East. Their hopes were in vain.

I now set about looking for a job. Bodnarchuk, who knew many mathematicians, suggested two institutes in need of a scientist capable of developing mathematical models of various processes. I went to the personnel office. There someone looked at my work book, saw the entry "Dismissed at his own request," and immediately asked, "Why?" I lied halfheartedly about wanting to work on the subject matter of the particular institute. "All right, come back in a week," I was told. When I did, I discovered that there were no vacancies.

Bodnarchuk taught me how to make my "voluntary dismissal" seem more convincing. I tried to lie but found it repugnant. Besides, I didn't believe that the KGB had let me out of its sight.

At other institutes, it was always the same story. In some the department head would immediately say, "A signatory? I'll try to fix it up." But nothing could be fixed up. At the Institute of Psychology the administrator said, "We barely saved our own signatories, and you're asking us to take on another?"

At a biological institute I met an old friend who was a professor. He questioned me about politics and expressed sympathy for my plight. "If I give you a recommendation, they'll be sure to turn you down," he said. "I had better do this through intermediaries. Please excuse me; I'm in a hurry to get to a meeting. I'm reading a paper about new forms of bourgeois anti-Soviet propaganda." We laughed at the irony of it, but my laughter was not quite sincere.

I lied convincingly when I spoke with the director of the biological institute. My previous work partly overlapped with the institute's research, and he took an interest in me. The following day, however, he told me that there were no vacancies.

I went to the editorial office of Vyshcha Shkola [Higher School], a textbook publishing house, to apply for a job in the mathematics department. People who have a knowledge of both Ukrainian and mathematics are rare, and such "encyclopedists" are highly prized. I was turned down there, too.

A friend telephoned Radyanska Shkola [Soviet School], which publishes high-school textbooks. The people there needed an editor in the mathematics department so badly that they did not bother to check why I had been dismissed. They gave me two chapters from a book on methods of teaching mathematics and asked me to edit them and write a review. At home I looked through the two chapters and found significant mistakes in the style, the definitions, and even the answers to questions. I wrote a review and showed my work to Sverstyuk as a specialist in Ukrainian. Everything was fine.

On the way to the editorial office I noticed that a man and woman were tailing me.

"It's very good for a first try," the editor told me. "I'll telephone you tomorrow after I speak to the editor-in-chief."

Coming out of the office, I saw that my tails were hiding in the doorway of the adjacent building. I walked straight toward them. They darted into the building, but when I got on a trolley I saw the woman again. Nothing would come of my efforts, I realized.

The next day I was told that the editor-in-chief had turned me

145

down. "You wrote your application in Russian. That means you don't know Ukrainian."

"How can you say that? I wrote the review and did the editing in Ukrainian!"

"He didn't pay any attention to that."

Then a proofreader at Naukova Dumka [Scientific Thought] told me that an editor of mathematical and technical literature was needed. When I applied for the job, however, the response was "Come back tomorrow."

I went to see Borys Paton, the President of the Academy of Sciences of the Ukrainian Republic.[29] He was away. I then went to the academy's party committee and explained precisely why I had been dismissed. The party bureaucrats and I got into a political discussion. I brought up the danger of re-Stalinization; they spoke about bourgeois propaganda. Finally I said that I could not get a job with an entry about staff reduction in my work book and pointed out that the party committee was obliged to find a job for me, because there had been no legal grounds for my dismissal.

"All right, do you have anything in mind?"

"Yes," I replied. "There's a job opening at Naukova Dumka."

"Come back tomorrow."

The following day I was told that someone had already been hired for the job. But when I asked around, I discovered that the vacancy had not been filled. I wrote a complaint to the trade-union committee of the Academy of Sciences. An amiable chap interviewed me.

"Why did you explain everything in your complaint? You ought to have written it differently."

"But I've already tried a different approach. Those who need to know find out anyway."

"Yes, you're right. But what can we do? I'll try to find a job for you, but I can't promise anything. You know what politics are."

In desperation I went to the trade-union Central Committee. There I was told that the trade unions were unable to help and was advised to recant. I decided to give up looking for a full-time job and to turn to tutoring. At the university I was given a promise that I would be recommended to failing students, but not a single one was sent to me. Friends told me about a schoolgirl who wanted to be tutored for university entrance exams. She came for two lessons and then disappeared; she had been cautioned that meeting with me would keep her out of the university. She was Jewish to begin with, and ties with an "unreliable" would have guaranteed her rejection.

The only course left, I concluded reluctantly, was to become a professional oppositionist. This sort of work does not provide an income and leads only to prison. It was difficult to give up science, become dependent on my wife, and involve myself in the seamy underside of political life. Politics struck me as vanity, an overcoming of obstacles rather than an unfolding of one's abilities. Yet forgetting, moving away, shutting my eyes and ears, and remaining silent were also impossible. Above all, as an oppositionist I would not need to lie or to play the double role of "building the brilliant future" and opposing the dismal present.

The political struggle was growing in intensity. On September 5 Professor Daniil Lunts conducted a forensic-psychiatric assessment of Natalya Gorbanevskaya at the Serbsky Institute and pronounced her of unsound mind.[30] The Prosecutor's Office closed its case against Gorbanevskaya and entrusted her to the care of her mother. On October 7 Yakir telephoned to report that the people who had demonstrated in Red Square would go on trial in two days. I visited all my friends and collected a little money for the Muscovites. One woman refused to contribute at first: "Is this for the nationalists? I don't want to." I refused to take her money for the Muscovites, too. The Ukrainian patriots collected what they could, but many of them had already lost their jobs.

Natalya Gorbanevskaya has done a very good job of describing the trial in *Red Square at Noon*, and I shall therefore limit myself to details that are absent from her book but convey the atmosphere in which dissidents are persecuted in the Soviet Union.[31]

On the morning of October 9, the day the trial opened, we encountered a Komsomol detachment led by a man who was obviously an informer but tried to make himself look like an intellectual by wearing a little black beard and affecting educated speech. At first he willingly answered our questions. His name was Alexandrov, he said, and he was an engineer and Komsomol activist. He tried to speak from class positions about class loyalty and the importance of labor.

"Why aren't you working?" one of my companions asked him. "I've seen you at the courthouse during every trial in Moscow."

The engineer grinned derisively. "I've seen you at the courthouse, too."

On the first day of the trial KGB provocateurs tried to start a fight with Petro Grigorenko and Genrikh Altunyan,[32] and on the second day Zinaida Grigorenko and other friends would not let me attend, because the incident had shown that visitors from other cities could be subjected to provocations. I spent the time talking to Altunyan.

He was a party member, a major, and a specialist in radio technology who taught at the military academy in Kharkiv. In August the KGB had begun an investigation of the Kharkiv signatories and searched Altunyan and nine of his friends because of his meetings with Grigorenko and Yakir and his involvement in *samizdat*. Altunyan and I agreed to establish regular ties between Kiev and Kharkiv: there weren't many of our people there, and they had difficulty in obtaining *samizdat*. Since most of Altunyan's friends were Marxists, the liaison promised to be of particular interest to me.

When Ivan Yakhimovich, the one-time collective farmer, came to Moscow, he greatly impressed me with his purposefulness, energy, and optimism—the latter a rarity. He related how he had been expelled from the collective farm and the party. At a party meeting at the collective farm, a member of the district party committee explained to the assembled Communists that Yakhimovich had slandered the Soviet regime in his letter to the Central Committee, and demanded that Yakhimovich be expelled from the party. Nobody voted for the resolution. A second meeting was held, but only the collective farm's party organizer voted to expel Yakhimovich. Nonetheless, Yakhimovich was dismissed from the chairmanship of the collective farm without consultation with the farmers, an action that caused the party organizer's wife to leave him. The peasants continued to bring Yakhimovich produce.

Seeing the drinking bouts that were so common in Moscow, Yakhimovich forcefully spoke out against them as harmful to the cause. "We can see right away that you're a Marxist," we all teased him. Because of his strictness with his friends, some people called Yakhimovich a Trotskyist, even though their knowledge of Trotsky was limited to legends and rumors.

I returned to Kiev with a great deal of literature, including speeches by Ginzburg's and Galanskov's attorneys, Gorbanevskaya's account of her stay in a psychiatric hospital, "Free Medical Aid," and a letter by Grigorenko to KGB Chairman Andropov in which he discussed repressions, interrogations, and other similarly unpleasant things.[33]

From the *Chronicle of Current Events*, which had begun to include an invaluable survey of *samizdat*, I learned about Milovan Djilas's *The New Class* and Abdurakhman Avtorkhanov's *The Technology of Power*.[34] I managed to obtain both books, Djilas in typescript and Avtorkhanov on film. Retyping them was quite difficult and time-consuming. Although Djilas had a wider distribution in Kiev than Avtorkhanov, he made a less profound impression on me:

I had long since arrived at similar conclusions, and only his facts about Yugoslav and Soviet history were valuable for me.

I do not share Djilas's major thesis that a new exploitative class has appeared in the Soviet Union. To my mind, the bureaucrats who run the country have not become a completely independent class yet. After all, corporate managers in capitalist countries are not a separate class. Like the police and the army, they are the "servants" of the capitalists. The capitalists merely share part of their profits with them and win them over to their side against the working class. The Soviet state, which is an abstract capitalist, wins over Brezhnev, Kosygin, Andropov, and other "servants of the people" in a similar fashion. The case of Khrushchev is exemplary. He appeared to be the richest and most powerful representative of the "new class," yet what was he left with once he was overthrown? An apartment, a dacha, and a small pension.

A class is defined by its relation to the production and distribution of goods. The function of the Soviet oligarchy in production is limited to the management of labor. Like everyone else, the oligarchs receive salaries. They are high, to be sure, but no higher than the salary a director of a Western corporation receives. The privileges the Soviet oligarchs enjoy in addition to their salaries are on the whole illegal. The oligarchs *steal* part of the national product. Such theft has no legal basis; therefore, the oligarchs are no more an economically distinct class than ordinary thieves. They possess power as kings for a day. Stalin managed to become the sole master of the country, but the bureaucrats under him were mere cogs in the machinery of autocracy, uncertain even of the coming day. Since then a tendency has developed to reject the slogans of the socialist revolution and to institutionalize the bureaucrats' power and privileges, but it is limited largely to party technocrats and so far is only a tendency.

Yakir described to me his meetings with Khrushchev at his dacha after the latter had been overthrown. After a few drinks Khrushchev began to complain about his lot. "Nobody writes or comes to see me. Mishka [Sholokhov]! I made a man of him, and he never even telephones." Then Khrushchev pulled out a *samizdat* edition of Pasternak's *Doctor Zhivago*. "What a remarkable book! Everyone in the country should have been able to read it. Suslov and the other members of the Central Committee showed me quotations from it, and I believed them." Yakir almost slapped him in the face. First Khrushchev hounded the poet to his grave, then he praised him.

Nevertheless, Yakir decided to go to Khrushchev's funeral, because he had done so much for political prisoners. On the way, Yakir was detained on a pretext by the militia until the funeral had ended. Many Muscovites wanted to visit Khrushchev's grave on the following day, but the authorities declared a sanitation day at the graveyard for fear of speeches and expressions of sympathy. There you have the "new class."

Avtorkhanov's *The Technology of Power* discusses Stalin's struggle for absolute power and his methods of doing away with all potential opponents. The analysis is subtle and buttressed by valuable data. The one thing I did not like was the "artistic generalization"—the merging of several historical figures into one, which diminishes the reader's faith in the remaining facts. Despite its deficiencies, *The Technology of Power* served many readers as a handbook of party history, and one of my friends knew it almost by heart. Both *The New Class* and *The Technology of Power* were found during KGB searches in Leningrad. We knew that stiff sentences would be meted out to anyone caught reading them and gave them only to people we thoroughly trusted.

In October Tanya and I became acquainted with Klara Gildman, who had been a student in the department of mathematical linguistics at Gorky University. Klara was from Kiev, but because hardly any Jews were accepted into universities in Ukraine at that time (this is now true of the entire Soviet Union), she went to study in the Russian Republic. Five students in the department of history at Gorky University wrote a book entitled *Socialism and the State*, in which they criticized Soviet reality on the basis of Lenin's *The State and Revolution*. A Komsomol meeting was summoned, and the students were expelled from the Komsomol and the university for being "hypocrites": they had written an anti-Soviet work while serving as members of the Komsomol. (Some of them were later arrested and sentenced.) The next day Klara went to the Komsomol office.

"Yesterday you expelled those students because, as you said, they were hypocrites. Will you expel me, too, if I turn in my Komsomol membership card?"

She was told to leave the room. "We'll discuss it." When she was called back, they said to her, "No, you won't be expelled, because you honestly stated your disagreement with the party line."

A telegram from Kiev notified Klara that her mother had been taken to a hospital and was dying. Klara sat at her bedside for a month. While she was in Kiev, a friend informed her that she had been expelled from the university. Klara returned to Gorky to complain to the provincial party committee, which showed her a ruling from the dean's office: she had been expelled for not attending lectures and for taking part in a drunken student orgy. Though Klara explained that she had been in Kiev at that time and provided a certificate from the hospital, no one paid attention—the decision had come from above. When she took the matter before the Ministry of Higher Education in Moscow, Klara was told that she was too late. The official order was a further insult: she was expelled for "behavior unbecoming to a Soviet student." Willingly or not, Klara became involved with the dissidents. By cracking down on all protests, the KGB either intimidates people or turns them into active oppositionists.

12

FRIENDS IN UMAN

At the end of December I was told that Yekaterina Olitskaya, a former Social Revolutionary * who had written a book of memoirs,[1]
was living in Uman, a town about two hundred kilometers from
Kiev. Arming myself with a letter of introduction, I went to see her
with a Crimean Tatar friend. Olitskaya knew about us from *samizdat,* and the letter proved to be unnecessary. I spent several days in
Uman, talking with Olitskaya and her sister-in-law, Nadya Surovtseva,† about recent trials, the Crimean Tatar national movement,
and new items in *samizdat.* In return the women told us about their
lives.

Olitskaya had been arrested by the Cheka in 1923. Then came the
usual journey: labor camps and exile in Siberia and the Far North.
She spent a total of thirty years getting to know the avenging sword
of the "unabstract humanists." It is interesting to compare Olitskaya's memoirs with Eugenia Ginzburg's *Journey into the Whirlwind.* Olitskaya met Ginzburg in transit between prisons and describes some of the same incidents, including the quarrel between
the Stalinist women prisoners and the normal prisoners, whose heads
had been half shaven.[2] Ginzburg and Olitskaya were both struck by
the degree to which the Stalinists had been indoctrinated. But
Olitskaya's book shows the gulf between a person brought up in a
prerevolutionary humanist spirit and a fanatic whose mind had
been warped by the revolutionary myth, which distorts reality and
cripples the personality. For all her amazement at her party comrades' barbarity, one senses in Ginzburg an affinity and understand-

* The Social Revolutionary Party was established in 1901. It had a populist orientation
toward the peasantry and was regarded as a bitter rival by the Bolsheviks, who suppressed it immediately after coming to power in 1918.—TRANS.
† Solzhenitsyn mentions Olitskaya's brother Dmitriy Olitsky in *Cancer Ward* and discusses his wife, Surovtseva, in *The Gulag Archipelago,* Volume 3 of which contains a
photograph of her.

ing for them. When Olitskaya looked at her ideological foes, she felt
—as Zinaida Tulub, who traveled in the same railway car, put it—
like a prehistoric dinosaur.[3]

Olitskaya was indignant at Ginzburg's story about the Social Revolutionary Derkovskaya, who asked her party leader in prison
whether she could accept a cigarette from a Communist. "I knew
Derkovskaya. We were not fanatics," Olitskaya said. "They were the
fanatics! Although she passed through the whirlwind of prisons and
labor camps, Ginzburg did not learn from the destruction of her
party. She repeats her torturers' slander about other parties; she repeats the myth that the Social Revolutionaries were fanatics and
hysterics. She retained all her party intolerance."

I remembered Olitskaya's words when I read *Love of Electricity*,
a story by Ginzburg's son, the "Marxist oppositionist" Vasiliy Aksyonov.[4] Not bothering to reflect on Bolshevik history, Aksyonov trots
out the hackneyed images of the Social Revolutionaries as hysterics,
adventurers, and demagogues. He does not see a single positive figure
among the Bolsheviks' opponents. But then who in the Soviet Union
would be permitted to depict an honest and intelligent Social Revolutionary devoted to the workers' cause? Still, if Aksyonov has conscience and pride but lacks the courage to write the truth, he ought
to have remained silent about the Revolution. Does Aksyonov perhaps sincerely believe that all Social Revolutionaries were "servants
of the bourgeoisie"? In that case it is difficult to say what is preferable: an honest Aksyonov who has a mythological consciousness or a
dishonest Aksyonov who sees the truth but keeps it to himself.

In *Journey into the Whirlwind* Ginzburg depicts two kinds of
torturers: sincere fanatics and sensible scoundrels. Having experienced both the sadism of a Soviet Ilse Koch and the authority of
mercenary jailers, she unhesitatingly prefers the latter.[5] They can be
bribed, and their weaknesses can be exploited. I saw both types
among my doctors in Dnipropetrovsk, and I also think that sincere
fanatics are more frightening than rapacious hypocrites, who like to
live well and allow others to live a little, too.

In their jokes and stories about themselves, their comrades, their
persecutors, and fellow party members, Olitskaya and Surovtseva
displayed a remarkable similarity, which highlighted their striking
psychological differences. Listening to them, I was reminded of
Democritus and Epicurus, both of whom considered themselves ma-
terialists. Legend has it that Democritus gouged his eyes out because
eyes see only phenomena and conceal reality. In reply to the assertion
that the sun is a huge flaming ball Epicurus maintained that he was

interested in the sun only as he saw it—small, gentle, and life-giving. Like Democritus, Olitskaya loved the truth and spent her life looking for it. For her the labor camps were a testing, a struggle between good and evil, the spirit and the fist. Surovtseva loves life. Like Epicurus, she has always been concerned with art, language, laughter, and the happiness of people.

Brought up in an intelligent and progressive family of Ukrainian patriots, Surovtseva is an aristocrat in the best sense of the word: a noble, cultivated person. Such people are always essentially democratic. Surovtseva's Ukrainian is a synthesis of high culture, the popular language of songs, proverbs, and jokes, and the criminal slang of the Soviet camps, without which the labor-camp period of socialism cannot be properly described. In her memoirs of the camps she writes about how beautiful nature was in Siberia and Kolyma, which she loves despite the suffering, cold, and hunger she experienced there. Through her eyes one sees the nightmare of twenty-eight years in camps and prisons as a tragicomedy in which human beings transcend inhuman conditions through laughter and a healthy love of life.

Olitskaya loved Surovtseva's laughter but was strict with herself, other people, and ideas. For her the labor camps represented mockery, man's fall to the level of informer and torturer, and his rise to courage, compassion, and wisdom. She saw the struggle between good and evil and the victory over evil through virtue and love. I was struck to see that Olitskaya had Teilhard de Chardin's *The Phenomenon of Man*.[6] After thirty years in the camps, to which she was sent as a young and uneducated girl, she avidly read books on philosophy and literary criticism. She asked me informed questions about cybernetics and the philosophy of mathematics. She loved Dostoyevsky, Bulgakov, and Kafka; she advised me to read Mikhaylovsky and Chernov, and she was amazed by my dated interest in Freud.[7] "Isn't there anything newer?" she asked. "We lived through this passion God knows how long ago." I was struck, too, by Olitskaya's freedom from ideological and moral narrowness. At seventy she had tolerance and a logical, lucid, and wide-ranging mind, and was searching unflaggingly for truth and beauty, without a trace of self-importance.

Olitskaya was extraordinarily pure in her intentions and actions. One of her friends, a very honest and principled woman, told us that the director of a museum in Uman had been caught stealing. He was allowed to keep his job. Olitskaya asked what sort of relations her friend had with him now. "As usual," the friend replied. "We smile and say hello to each other." Olitskaya could not understand this. In turn, the new principled revolutionaries could not completely understand her. Why not go on greeting the scoundrel? Why expose oneself to attack over such a trifle instead of saving oneself for more important battles? Olitskaya was just as principled when she encountered the regime's lies, immorality, and corruption. In 1972, when she was interrogated in my case, she refused to give testimony or to have anything to do with the KGB.

Olitskaya and Surovtseva had a friend, Zora Andreyeva, the wife of a Russian anarchist. Completely different in character from Olitskaya and Surovtseva, Andreyeva possessed a similar strength of spirit and had shared the same fate. She introduced me to a woman who had been a Bolshevik for many years and to the children of a Bolshevik leader. I asked Andreyeva how she could be on friendly terms with members of the party that had destroyed her friends. "It's ridiculous to talk about those parties," she replied. "The times have changed, and the problems are different. People from all parties have survived, decent people who stayed alive in the labor camps and prisons. All of us made many mistakes. The people I introduced you to were not scoundrels, and so we are friends."

During the Civil War Andreyeva worked in the underground in Sevastopol and ran a palmistry shop frequented by White officers. She liked to frighten them with the prospect of death and learned military secrets from those whose tongues were loose, then passed on her information to Makhno and other anarchist detachments.[8] When the Civil War ended, Andreyeva read the palms of Bolsheviks, Mensheviks, anarchists, and Social Revolutionaries, but the lines of death were visible in so many hands that she dropped palmistry. Although there is probably no rational explanation for palmistry, Andreyeva's story conveys the import of what was happening: the death of the Revolution and of almost all the honest revolutionaries. A party of vampires survived, dead men who held sway over the living, killing with their breath all the living ideas of the Revolution.

Sara Yakir, the wife of the Red Army commander Iona Yakir, also hid in the underground during the Civil War. She had the same assignment as Andreyeva: gathering information from White officers who frequented her barber shop (Bolsheviks were concealed behind the wall). Sara Yakir suffered a great deal when she heard her son, Pyotr, and his friends mock the October Revolution and curse the old leaders. I had once argued about this with a friend, and when I visited the Yakirs, I repeated his words about the Bolsheviks' stupidity, purposely exaggerated, to point up the superficiality of such attacks. Sara Yakir interrupted me. "Lyonya, do you, too, think that

October was an adventure and that all the Bolsheviks were scoun-drels? How can you say that?"

I found it very difficult to reply to this old, sick, half-blind woman who had witnessed the destruction of the Revolution, her family, and her native country and who daily saw those she loved spitting on what was most sacred to her. Each time I set out to go home to Kiev, she would say to me, "Lyonya, don't take any *samizdat* with you. They'll arrest you. They follow everyone who visits us."

She and her family—her son, Pyotr, her daughter-in-law, Valya, her granddaughter, Ira, and Ira's husband, Yuliy Kim—were all very good to me. I always stayed with them despite the unnatural nervous tension, my concern for my safety, and my serious disagreements with Pyotr. The tragedy of the Yakirs, beginning with Iona's, was my tragedy as well. Our love for one another outweighed all our in-tellectual, political, and even ethical disagreements.

Sara Yakir almost never involved herself in our business and our arguments, and I had few opportunities to speak to her, although I wanted to ask her about her husband, the Civil War, and the 1920's and 1930's. "Have you been reinstated in the party?" I once asked her.

"No, and I don't want to be," she replied. "You think that I was expelled after my husband was arrested? No. It was when our troops were advancing toward Warsaw, in 1921. I was friendly with one of the commanding officers. He fell in love with a woman who rejected him, and he shot himself on the eve of the attack. The following day, after the battle, we discussed the suicide. 'He shot himself for a broad!' one of the comrades said. 'He couldn't give his life in battle with the enemy. A dog's death for a dog.' "

That night Sara Yakir and the wife of Yakir's adjutant, Dubov, buried the suicide. In the morning they told Yakir what they had done. A party meeting was summoned, and Sara Yakir and Dubov's wife were expelled from the party on Iona Yakir's proposal.

"And you haven't returned to the party since then?" I asked.

"No. Iona never mentioned it, and I didn't want to join. And I didn't regret what I had done."

Pyotr Yakir later told me that there were many detectives at his mother's funeral. "They were afraid that I'd make a political demon-stration. The shits . . . they don't understand that I don't exploit my family name."

Why do I mention Sara Yakir when I write about Olitskaya? I have always compared the honest Old Bolsheviks to Olitskaya,

Surovtseva, and Andreyeva. Almost all the Old Bolsheviks were to some extent broken, and not because they were weaker than their opponents. The Bolsheviks were defeated first morally and then politically. Olitskaya, Surovtseva, and Andreyeva were politically defeated and tortured, but their moral victory is indisputable. It is easier to resist an enemy than fellow party members, particularly when they have the party leadership and the "people" behind them. When Sara and Iona Yakir were interrogated and tortured, they had only themselves to rely on: the ideal for which they had fought had been defeated, and their entire struggle before, during, and after the October Revolution was in question. How much spiritual strength is needed to avoid giving in to one's torturers! People found succor either in fanaticism or in an unusual strength of mind which permitted them to re-examine their lives, to find the mistakes they, their comrades, and their leaders had committed, and to uphold the ideas that survived this merciless criticism.

With the exception of Petro Grigorenko I did not meet people of this latter type. But re-evaluation was much easier for him than for those who had started the Revolution, fought against the Whites, and carried out the collectivization and industrialization campaigns. Grigorenko's conscience is clean because he was not even an indirect accomplice to his party's crimes. His only regret is that he remained silent, did not understand, believed the torturers, and made mistakes when he struggled against their lawlessness.

Surovtseva also found re-evaluation difficult. She, too, had belonged to a Communist party, although in her case it was the Austrian. Surovtseva studied at Saint Petersburg University, where Mykhaylo Hrushevsky was working at the time.[9] When she asked him immediately after the February Revolution what young Ukrainians should do, he replied that they must go to Ukraine and fight for their country's rights. After the October Revolution Surovtseva traveled throughout the countryside, agitating the peasants to support the Central Rada.* Although she did not understand agrarian problems or politics, she sincerely promised the peasants everything they wanted. (A year later she was told what the peasants were saying about her: "If we could get our hands on that young lady who promised us land, we'd stuff her cunt with dirt.") Then Surovtseva worked in the Ministry of Foreign Affairs of the Central Rada and the

* Established in Kiev in 1917, with Mykhaylo Hrushevsky as its head, the Central Rada (Council) at first sought Ukrainian autonomy and then proclaimed an independent Ukrainian National Republic, which fell to Bolshevik forces in 1919.—TRANS.

Skoropadsky regime,* passing on information to those who were opposed to Skoropadsky and the German occupants. When Skoropadsky and the Germans were driven out, Surovtseva traveled with the Ukrainian delegation to the Congress of Versailles and then to Vienna. Settling in Vienna as a poor émigrée, she managed to acquire a doctorate in philosophy from Vienna University. She was active in the international women's movement and the pacifist movement, and she campaigned against anti-Semitism, worked with an anarchist group, and wrote articles. During the famine of the early 1920's in Ukraine, she was Hrushevsky's deputy in a relief organization.

When Yuriy Kotsyubynsky arrived in Vienna,[10] Surovtseva became acquainted with the flowering of Ukrainian culture that occurred after the Bolshevik victory. Instead of trying to persuade her, Yuriy gave her paintings and books by contemporary Ukrainian artists. Surovtseva began to agitate for the Soviet regime. In 1923 reports reached the West that prisoners on the Solovetsky Islands had been executed at the whim of the camp administration.[11] The right-wing press raised a stink. Surovtseva rushed to Kotsyubynsky for an explanation. He, too, was disturbed, but in a little while he received literature about the islands that discussed "re-education of criminals through labor" and quoted testimony by prisoners about how well they were treated. With the enthusiasm of a convert, Surovtseva attacked the mendacious bourgeois press. Joining the Austrian Communist Party, she became friends with Franz Koritschoner, its founder, and met Clara Zetkin, Bertrand Russell, and American socialist millionaires.[12]

The Soviet government valued Surovtseva and proposed that she carry on propaganda among Ukrainian émigrés in the United States and Canada. She requested permission to see Ukraine's flowering with her own eyes: living details would help her to defend the Soviet regime and propagate Communism more effectively. In Ukraine Surovtseva threw herself into the turbulent literary life and worked for the People's Commissariat of External Affairs. She was friends with many leaders of the Ukrainian renascence. She didn't know how the peasants were getting along, but she saw with her own eyes the artistic and literary explosion. Many émigrés believed the government's promises and returned from exile. In 1924, even Hrushevsky returned to resume his scholarly work.

The following year Surovtseva was summoned by the security organs. The young officer who interviewed her asked her to report on

---

* A conservative regime in 1918 headed by General Pavlo Skoropadsky and supported by the German and Austro-Hungarian forces of occupation.—TRANS.

the "Trotskyist" Yuriy Kotsyubynsky. "How dare you suggest that?" Surovtseva shouted at him. "Kotsyubynsky is a devoted Communist and a Red Army commander. Who are you? A child!"

"As you wish," the officer replied. "We are obliged to verify all the information we receive. But I warn you—don't mention our conversation to anyone!"

A year later Surovtseva was arrested on a charge of connections with Austrian intelligence (she had danced with the ambassador several times). Surovtseva denied everything, but the investigator showed her an obituary in an émigré newspaper announcing that the Bolsheviks had shot her when she returned to Ukraine to carry on nationalist underground work.

In 1931 or 1932, when she was already serving her sentence, Surovtseva was interrogated about the counterrevolutionary activities of Hrushevsky and other members of the "nationalist underground," but she refused to testify. In 1934 she learned that Hrushevsky had died in mysterious circumstances, and then, in 1936, that Yuriy Kotsyubynsky, the chairman of the State Plan and deputy chairman of the Council of People's Commissars of Ukraine, had been executed without trial as the leader of a "Ukrainian Trotskyist bloc" that was aligned with a "Ukrainian Military Alliance." While in exile Surovtseva married Dmitriy Olitsky, who soon disappeared in Siberia. After the unmasking of the Stalin cult Surovtseva settled down in Uman. Today she reads a great deal and tutors French and English.

What saved Surovtseva from cracking up? The psychoideological basis of her courage alone could not have saved her. Ukrainian culture, for the most part, is characterized by an absence of decadence and emotional excess. In this respect Surovtseva is a true Ukrainian intellectual. Resisting the pressure of interrogators and camp guards is very difficult if one's mind is confused and one bears traces of the corruption against which one is speaking out. Surovtseva has a precise, sober mind, no evident complexes, and no repressed feelings of guilt toward other people. Yes, she made mistakes. She praised and fought for the "new Ukraine," thus helping her torturers. But she is not excessively penitent. She understands the tragedy of Ukraine and the Revolution and her own involuntary guilt. Excessive penitence is insincere; it involves pride and vanity. I saw a provocateur who had repented but continued to work for the KGB.

Olitskaya and Surovtseva had an extraordinary moral influence on all their acquaintances. The happiest event in the *psikhushka* for me was receiving postcards from them. The saddest event, after the capitulation of Dzyuba, Yakir, and Krasin,[13] was the news that Olit-skaya had died. I thought a great deal about the stories Olitskaya and Surovtseva had related and fondly remembered such trifles as sleep-ing under Surovtseva's labor-camp pea jacket.

As I was leaving Uman I asked the two women to give me their memoirs for *samizdat*. Olitskaya at first refused, claiming hers had no literary merit. Only when I reminded her that, although memoirs by Bolsheviks and Mensheviks were circulating underground, there were none by Social Revolutionaries did she agree. In Kiev I imme-diately set about disseminating her memoirs. All my friends in Moscow and Kiev were excited by the book, and it sooned reached the West. Many readers wanted to visit Uman, but I asked them to refrain: Olitskaya and Surovtseva were under surveillance and had to be spared trouble.

Sadly, Olitskaya and Surovtseva were searched when I was arrested in 1972, and both volumes of Surovtseva's memoirs were confiscated. We lost a valuable literary work and historical document about the Revolution and Civil War in Ukraine, the emigration, and the Ukrainian renascence of the 1920's. The second volume was devoted to the labor camps and prisons of Sibera and, although it had less historical value than the first volume, gave a new description of the Stalinist terror.*

Olitskaya, Surovtseva, and Andreyeva are examples of a human spirit that has overcome animal fear (they still had a human fear) and surmounted the absurdity and vulgarity of its surroundings.

In Uman I also became close with two young friends of Olitskaya and Surovtseva, Victor Nekipelov and his wife, Nina Komarova. Victor was a poet—he had degrees in both pharmaceutics and liter-ature—and seemed to have little interest in politics, but honest people in the Soviet Union find it difficult not to protest or to be-come involved in *samizdat*. Victor worked as a pharmaceutical en-gineer at a vitamin factory until he was hounded from his job for discussing the political events of 1968. He and Nina resettled in the Moscow region, found jobs in a pharmacy, and became acquainted with the Moscow oppositionists.

In July 1973 Victor was arrested for "defaming the Soviet state and social system": he had supposedly written "slanderous" poems about Brezhnev, drafted the outline of a "slanderous" book that the inves-

* I ask anyone who knew Surovtseva or read her writings in the 1920's to send me in-formation about her. Perhaps Austrian Communists, anarchists, members of the pacifist or women's movements, or Ukrainian émigrés remember her?

tigators entitled *The Book of Wrath*, and—according to one witness whose testimony was not confirmed in court—passed on a copy of the *Chronicle of Current Events*. Realizing that they did not have enough evidence to convict Victor, the investigators provoked "anti-Soviet discussions" between him and his cellmates and then sent him to the Serbsky Institute for Forensic Psychiatry.[14] After spending two months there, he was ruled to be sane, placed on trial, and sentenced to two years in a labor camp. My wife was searched in connection with the case.

Today Victor and Nina live in a small working-class town near Vladimir. They are abysmally poor, because Victor cannot get a job even as an unskilled laborer. He has renounced Soviet citizenship and applied for his family to emigrate but continues to be turned down. His daughter was not admitted to kindergarten. They are anti-Soviets unto the seventh generation.

13

NATIONALITIES PROBLEMS

Back in Kiev, moral problems cropped up constantly in everyday life. Rumor had it that Svitlychny was a provocateur because he had been released from prison without being put on trial. Dzyuba was a provocateur because he wasn't being "taken away." So-and-so was a KGB agent because he had made a drastic proposal. Someone else was an agent because he had praised Trotsky in a large circle of friends. What were we to do? Provocateurs did exist, but we would not accomplish anything if we suspected everyone. We developed the tactic of discussing a particular job only with the person who was to carry it out and of never mentioning who had brought in an item or was retyping it. But this was difficult.

An army lieutenant visited me on one occasion, a party member who lived in a small town. He mentioned that he had heard about me from Radio Liberty.[1] Having spent his life battling with officials who drove him from jobs and played dirty tricks on him, he had now been accused of being anti-Soviet and had come to me because he wanted to distribute *samizdat* and take part in the Democratic Movement. "I will write a book about my life—dispossession of the kulaks, service in the Mongolian Army, the stealing and the lies of the higher officers—and you can disseminate it."

I explained that all I could do was to slip a book into *samizdat*. Censorship was not practiced, and people retyped only what they found interesting.

"All right, pass the book to the West," the lieutenant replied.

"But I don't know who passes things to the West. And why do you need that? Aren't you writing for our people?"

"Yes, but I don't have any money. Ask the Herzen Foundation— I heard about it on the radio—to pay me."[2]

This made me suspect the lieutenant as a provocateur. "How can

162

you, a party member, accept money from an unknown organization?"
I asked. "What if it's an espionage service? Besides, I don't know
whether it pays. And I don't have and don't want to have any ties
with the West."

As he left, the lieutenant asked me for *samizdat* items he could distribute in his town. I gave him several innocuous articles and advised him not to make any anti-Soviet statements in his book.
"You're not a politician, philosopher, or sociologist," I explained.
"Write only the facts. Our people are educated and will draw their
own conclusions. You can get a stiff sentence for sharp remarks."

The lieutenant brought me his book several months later. Although it contained very interesting facts that I had not known before, I found it of questionable reliability. If it was a deliberate falsehood, it could be used in court. And it contained numerous spiteful,
frequently senseless attacks against the regime. The lieutenant telephoned me after I had read the book. "Well, have you passed my
book to *samizdat* in Moscow?"

I suggested that he see me to discuss the book. Fearing that he
might come with KGB men, I left comments in the margins: "Bad.
Doubtful. Not serious. Really?" I wanted to add "anti-Soviet" but
realized that if he were sincere, my remark could be used against
him. When the lieutenant arrived, I gave him the manuscript and
said, "You're behaving like a provocateur. You talk about *samizdat*
on the telephone, you mention payment, and you write needlessly
spiteful things. Perhaps you're not an agent, but simply stupid. In
either case you are dangerous for my friends."

The lieutenant cried and tried to prove that he was honest. I felt
sorry for him and was ashamed of my words, but what could I do?
I emphasized that I had said all this only because of his proposals.
Besides, there was no reason for him to go to prison because of indiscretion. The lieutenant left in tears.

Suspicion is immoral, but so is lack of caution. One must find a
tactic to avoid injuring people by labeling them provocateurs and
yet also to avoid being caught by the KGB. The tactic must be moral,
and the morality must be intelligent, tactful, and flexible. Yet in-
extricable tangles occur when one has to slash through the knot of
contradictions and inflict pain on everyone concerned.

Moral problems presented themselves in the nationalities question
as well. The conditions in which Soviet nationalities live have led to
deep-seated dissension and misunderstanding. In such circumstances
I found it very difficult to rebuff a scoundrel who was a Jew or a Tatar. He had behind him the sufferings of his people, and I had my

formal allegiance to the oppressors. If I were publicly to tell a Jew that he was a scoundrel, some of his fellow nationals would interpret my words as "You Kike bastard!" Dealing with a Russian scoundrel was much easier, because then I could speak out as a member of an oppressed nation.

The man in the street easily recognizes the leaders' anti-Semitism in the official anti-Zionist propaganda. Yet anti-Semitism is not merely a product of history, a blind national and social protest, or a scapegoat; it is also a specific attitude toward others. One of my friends was a Jewish intellectual who once explained to me how he felt about workers: they are dirty, mercenary, and thievish. When I tried to refute him, he produced "facts." He was only telling me what he had observed, but he saw the facts through a special filter, from a particular point of view. Although he was a Jew himself, in his vision, his logic, and his attitude toward others, my friend was little better than an anti-Semite. The only difference was that for him the scapegoat was the workers.

Another example was a talented and educated poet who was a monarchist. It was very strange to see a live monarchist in the Soviet Union, and a young one at that. After many discussions he became a democrat. He met some Crimean Tatars and felt very sympathetic toward them. Then he went to work in Uzbekistan. When he returned to Kiev, he told me that Uzbeks are "dirty animals," that "we Russians brought them culture, and they're ungrateful to us," and that I was naïve about the Tatars. He had been sympathetic toward them only because he had met several educated, Russified Tatars. But most Tatars oppress Uzbeks—"animals," I corrected him—and seize all the best jobs for themselves. I called him an anti-Semite, which offended him. "But you haven't noticed how you've ascribed to the Tatars all the features anti-Semites ascribe to Jews. Why aren't the Tatars permitted to return to the Crimea? If they're oppressing someone in Uzbekistan, they won't oppress anyone in their native Crimea."

My friend Alexander Feldman translated Sartre's *Réflexions sur la question juive* from a Polish version.[3] We all admired the profundity of the essay, but I thought that it did not devote sufficient attention to the social roots of anti-Semitism and that, in exposing the anti-Semitic myth of the Jew, Sartre created a myth about the anti-Semite as Satan. I met many anti-Semites. They were ordinary people with various virtues and vices, and none of them were devils. Some were capable of playing all sorts of dirty tricks on Jews without pathologically hating them. If there are devils in the USSR, it is not they who determine the policy of persecuting Jews.

Sartre noted an interesting aspect of unconscious anti-Semitism. Some people, even democrats, characterize scoundrels as Jews. One frequently hears, "Ivanov stole three kilos of meat. He's a Jew." Or "Ivanov is an honest man. His mother is Jewish." Thus the Jewish aspect is emphasized in both positive and negative statements. In the first case a generalization is made. In the second, an exception to the rule is presented. A democrat who made such a statement would be offended if his remark were interpreted in this way, but for some reason he will never mention that the thief Ivanov is a Russian or a Ukrainian. A Russian's nationality is mentioned in official propaganda only when he is being praised. A Ukrainian's is mentioned only when he is a Banderite or has spoken in favor of friendship with the Russian people. Only rarely will you hear a Russophobe nationalist say about a scoundrel, "He's a Russian," or "He's a decent man even though he's a Russian."

I caught myself several times adding "Jew" when I was praising someone. On the conscious level this was through a desire to emphasize that Jews are good people, an attempt to overcome the myths about Jews. But if there is an attempt to overcome a myth, then that myth must exist in the unconscious. Some of my Jewish friends were offended when I praised them as Jews and not as individuals. The Jew senses in such compliments an amazement that he is decent, disinterested, or courageous. This may be a morbid sensitivity, but the situation of the Jews is morbid, and it unavoidably produces morbid responses to gentile friends.

When blacks appeared on the street in the larger cities, people had several responses: curiosity ("Look, there's a real live Negro!"), compassion ("How the Americans humiliate these poor fellows!"), and malice ("Look, there goes a black ass!").* The blacks did not like any of these responses. "It's harder for us here than in America," one black student said. "There they don't gawk at us like rare animals." The curiosity and compassion soon disappeared, but the malice increased: "Those bastards are going around with our sluts" (any white girl seen with a black man was called a slut). Dirty stories were told about the blacks' sexuality, boorishness, and contempt for Russians.

Similar complaints were made about Arabs. Anti-Semitism turned

---

* Note that American racists remark about the color of the skin, whereas Soviet racists talk about asses. To each his own, I suppose.

into anti-Arabism but with this addition: "We feed them and go to war for them, but they can't fight and only ruin our weapons." Koreans and Vietnamese were treated somewhat better, though some of the hatred for the Chinese was transferred to them. Feelings about whites from Western Europeans were ambiguous. On the one hand there was envy: "Look at the way those swine gorge themselves!" On the other hand: "We'll show them! They ran from the Germans, but now they're advancing on us."

Such attitudes are not typical of the population as a whole but are displayed for the most part by the lower-middle class, with all its boorishness and petit-bourgeois psychology, and by party and government bureaucrats, who differ from the previous category of chauvinists only in their greater hypocrisy and cynicism. A party member will rarely say "Yid" or "Banderite." Instead he will call a Jew a "Zionist," a "profiteer," or a "tradesman," and a Ukrainian a "bourgeois nationalist" or even a "Zionist."

I had long been familiar with Jewish mistrust of Ukrainians but first met Zionists when I became involved in Boris Kochubievsky's case in 1969. When I offered Kochubievsky's wife and friends to find an attorney for him in Moscow, they replied that they would find one themselves. Later I learned that they were investigating who I was and why I, a Ukrainian, was interested in the case. Their investigation stretched out, and I proposed an attorney in Kiev. He agreed to take the case, but then refused and suggested someone else. We decided to trust the attorney and settle for his choice because time was running short. At Kochubievsky's trial the new attorney made no objections to the prosecution's case. It turned out later that the first attorney had a small offense on his record, and the KGB had blackmailed him into suggesting to us its own attorney.

Kochubievsky's troubles had begun in 1967, when he stated at a lecture on international affairs that Israel had not been the aggressor in the Six Day War. In May 1968 he was forced from his job. The following August he applied to emigrate to Israel. His wife, Larisa, was expelled from the Komsomol and from teachers' college for "Zionism," although she was half Ukrainian and her father worked for the KGB. The associate dean at the college said to her, "I know a girl who's married to a Jew, and she says all Jews stink. You love him —that's nothing; where you're going, the whole country will stink."

At a Komsomol meeting, Yevgraf Duluman (a former theology student who is now a specialist in atheism) asked Larisa why she was going to Israel.[4]

"I love my husband and will go anywhere with him," she answered.

"That's not love. That's merely sexual attraction," Duluman insisted. "I could easily hypnotize you and evoke the same response toward myself."

On September 29, 1968, an official meeting was held at Babyn Yar. Until then people had gathered at the site spontaneously, but this year the authorities decided to defuse the meeting by turning it into an official demagogic assembly, just as they had tried to defuse the meetings at the Shevchenko Monument on May 22. Most of the speeches at the official meeting were about Israeli aggression. When Kochubievsky heard from a philistine that the Nazis had killed very few Jews at Babyn Yar (only seventy-five thousand), he wrote a protest against anti-Semitism and the persecution of Jews who wanted to emigrate.

On May 13, 1969, several young Jews gathered at the courthouse where Kochubievsky's trial was beginning. Soldiers guarded the doors, and plainclothesmen filled the sidewalk and the courtroom. Yuriy Nikiforov, my old friend from my university and institute days, was in command. The soldiers told us that we could not go in because the courtroom was full.

The crux of the prosecution's argument was that Kochubievsky had wittingly made false statements about anti-Semitism. Kochubievsky rebutted that even if his assertions were wrong, he was not guilty of slander, because he had been convinced that he was right.

"You've had higher education and passed your graduate exams in philosophy," the prosecutor replied. "You know the Constitution of the USSR and therefore must have realized that the things you mentioned cannot happen in our country."

"You lousy Yid!" the Jews who had assembled at the courthouse joked. "You know the Constitution says there's no anti-Semitism in this country."

Boris's brother came out and told us that one of the plainclothesmen had kept whispering to him, "You Yid! You lousy Yid!" He must have hoped to provoke Boris's brother to an anti-Soviet outburst and in fact almost succeeded. I asked that the plainclothes internationalist be pointed out to me. It was Nikiforov.

The court's anti-Semitism was revealed most clearly when the associate dean at the teachers' college testified. She denied having said to Larisa Kochubievsky that Jews stink and insisted that she had only put this as a question. The court ruled that the question was entirely proper. Boris Kochubievsky was found guilty of anti-Soviet slander and sentenced to three years in a labor camp. I collected what information I could about the trial and passed it on to the *Chronicle of Current Events*.[5]

When I visited Moscow again in April 1969, General Grigorenko told me about the KGB's new provocations against him. Stories were spread among soldiers and workers that he was a Jew and had falsely claimed to be a Ukrainian when he joined the party. The charge was ridiculous in light of the law and party statutes, but it stopped being funny when one realized that the authorities were playing on the base instincts of the masses. The KGB also disseminated an anonymous letter, supposedly written by Crimean Tatars, asserting that Grigorenko was both insane and anti-Soviet.

Grigorenko once pointed out some sort of apparatus in the windows of a neighboring building: the KGB was flaunting its surveillance of him in an attempt to scare away visitors. When a Western journalist visited him and asked him about harassment, Grigorenko motioned to an object hanging down to the window from a tree. "They're bugging me. From every side and in every room!" The next day the microphone was gone.

On April 17 a stranger telephoned Grigorenko and suggested a meeting. Grigorenko agreed without hesitation. In Soviet conditions one doesn't ask why, because the telephone is usually tapped. The stranger refused to come to Grigorenko and suggested meeting in two days at a commission shop across the street. "I'll be carrying a newspaper," the conspirator explained. Grigorenko's wife, Zinaida, laughed when she heard that. "The KGB's donkey ears are showing again." *

A friend warned Grigorenko that the meeting was a well-prepared major provocation, and on the nineteenth a number of Grigorenko's friends assembled at the commission shop. The donkey ears had already arrived—old acquaintances from trials, searches, and surveillance. A KGB general sat in an official car parked nearby. Grigorenko's friends stood around, pretending not to know one another. So did the agents. When the man with the newspaper appeared, a KGB agent ran up and whispered in his ear. The man left, and the

---

* These donkey ears are almost always visible. One can understand why factories, institutes, collective farms, and even the Central Committee and Politburo perform poorly; but the KGB, which alone has access to correct information and can afford not to lie, also functions inefficiently. We were so embarrassed by our guardians that we would often make jokes about offering them our services to teach them how to do a clean job.

two groups broke up. Ours, as always, was laughing. Grigorenko wrote to KGB Chairman Andropov, protesting against all the incidents of blackmail, provocation, and harassment. He did not receive a reply.

Grigorenko believed that the Democratic Movement must develop new tactics. *Samizdat* had taught young people and intellectuals that there is such a thing as freedom of the press. The demonstrations in Pushkin Square and Red Square brought up the question of constitutional rights to demonstrate.[6] Grigorenko argued that the public had to be made aware of the freedom of meetings, organizations, and trade unions. He notified the Moscow City Executive Committee that a group of people intended to organize a public meeting about constitutional rights. The committee was required by law to supply suitable premises for the meeting, but it replied that all the auditoriums were booked for a Komsomol celebration and postponed the decision until Grigorenko was arrested.

An American who introduced himself as an associate of Dr. Benjamin Spock, the active campaigner against the war in Vietnam, once visited Grigorenko and proposed that democratic organizations in the United States and the USSR join forces. "Do you have such an organization?" the American asked. To his credit, however, he added an understanding smile.

When the general explained that freedom of organization exists only on paper in the Soviet Union, the American countered, "Then why don't you demand official permission for a democratic organization?" The proposal coincided with Grigorenko's own plans, and he urged his friends to establish an organization that would defend human rights and explain their rights to people. Unfortunately, most of the Moscow activists argued that Grigorenko's idea was utopian. At first I agreed with them, but later I realized that developing an awareness of legal rights was more important than any possible practical results. I tried to find support for the general's plan, but few people were willing to go along with us.

On one of my visits to Moscow I met Alexander Ginzburg's mother, Lyudmila Ilyinichna.[7] My talks with her helped to prepare me psychologically for prison and the *psikhushka*. I was struck by her laughter and *joie de vivre*. Although she was suffering for her son, she related the most horrible episodes from their life with a sense of humor. "How can you survive all this if you don't laugh?" she commented.

Lyudmila Ilyinichna spoke a great deal about Alexander. She did not overrate him, but she did love him as a splendid young man whom she had borne and raised and who believed in the rightness of his actions.

Alexander's fiancée, Irina Zholkovskaya, was waging a drawn-out battle to register their marriage. They had submitted the papers shortly before Alexander was arrested, but were told that as long as he was being held at Lefortovo, the KGB's special prison for political cases, a marriage could not be registered. (There is no mention of this in the relevant regulations!) They were promised that it would be registered once he was at a labor camp. At the camp, however, a sign was prominently displayed stating that no marriages could be registered there, which meant that Irina could not visit him.

I met Irina only once. She told me of her expulsion from Moscow University, where she had taught Russian to foreigners. Her connections with the "NTS supporter" Ginzburg were discussed at a public meeting. "How can you love him?" a teacher asked Irina. "He wants to establish fascism in our country." Then with a tremor in her voice, she added, "Just imagine what would happen if he came to power. He'd come home in the evening all covered with the blood of Communists, our blood, your colleagues' blood, and you'd embrace him!"

I had no sooner returned to Kiev than I learned that Grigorenko had been arrested. On May 2 someone had called him from Tashkent, supposedly at the request of Mustafa Dzhemilyov, and asked him to come to Dzhemilyov's trial.[8] Arriving in Tashkent, Grigorenko discovered that he had been tricked: the date of Dzhemilyov's trial had not been set yet. The Uzbek KGB arrested Grigorenko on May 7, and searches and interrogations in his case were begun. The questions the investigators asked made it clear that he would be sent to a psychiatric prison, and an open letter in Grigorenko's defense was distributed.

In May workers at the Kiev Hydroelectric Power Station assembled to protest their poor living conditions. The meeting was conducted by Ivan Hryshchuk, a retired major who had worked as a tutor at the workers' dormitory until he was fired for helping workers obtain residence permits. The KGB tried to drive a wedge between workers and intellectuals—one of its favorite tactics—by pointing out that Hryshchuk enjoyed a good pension, but Hryshchuk produced a receipt showing that he had been donating his pension to a children's home. Unlike the KGB men, he was earning his living by honest labor.

The KGB suffered a defeat also at an official meeting the next day. The party organizer at the power station imprudently commented, "We must all think about the welfare of the workers' state and not listen to non-worker elements." Angry women rushed to the stage and listed all the mistresses for whom the organizer had arranged living quarters while working-class families with small children huddled in barracks and listened to the same promises year after year.

A world conference of Communist parties was being planned for June 1969, and I decided to go to Moscow to obtain *samizdat*, deliver Ukrainian items, and propose an appeal to the conference. I believed that a letter to Western Communists must not only be based on legal grounds, but must also unmask the anti-Communist nature of the Soviet regime. If Grigorenko had not been arrested, he would have written such a letter himself. My position was not supported by others. I had placed hopes on Leonid Petrovsky, but he preferred to use a mild, purely legal approach and to speak only about the threat of reviving Stalinism.[9] After many arguments, I ended up signing a toned-down version. Ten people signed it.[10] Many others refused to dirty their hands. Why appeal to those scoundrels? they wondered. We never did receive an answer to our letter. Yet Western Communists are astonished at how "right-wing" the Soviet opposition is!

In Moscow I managed to obtain an anonymous essay, "The Transformation of Bolshevism." A criticism of the Soviet system from the viewpoint of Bolshevik theoretical and programmatic works, this analysis was typical of oppositionist Marxists. But it also contained something new—an attempt to analyze the reasons for the failure of the Revolution.

The author was a fair polemicist and theoretician, but his isolation from the Moscow dissidents hurt him, since Moscow is the link between scattered groups throughout the Russian Republic. The allergy many Muscovites had developed quite understandably for Marxist terminology severely restricted the circulation of such writings in *samizdat*. This is why "The Transformation of Bolshevism," Dzyuba's *Internationalism or Russification?*, my *Letters to a Friend*, and many other works were not widely read in Moscow. For this same reason I could not obtain *The Decline of Capitalism*, a programmatic essay by Marxists in the Volga region. I explained this to the author of "The Transformation of Bolshevism," but he could not do without the Marxist quotations or terminology. "They express the essence," he insisted.

"But they also distort it," I replied, "because the USSR is a new type of exploitative society, and we must find more appropriate terms. Besides, a renewal of style will have a fruitful influence on thought, and vice versa."

Peculiarly Soviet conditions are responsible for the drama of such Marxists: the anti-Marxists refuse to listen to the Marxist opposition, and Marxists such as the author of "The Transformation of Bolshevism" display a certain dogmatism and mental inertia. Both attitudes are consequences of the official propaganda. One good friend, an erudite and thoughtful girl, mentioned that she had obtained a Western edition of Trotsky's autobiography. "Give it to me," I said, "you won't read it anyway." It turned out that she had thrown out the "Marxist drivel." Although psychologically understandable, this phenomenon leads to adverse ideological consequences. Such concepts as class, masses, workers, reaction, and militarism have been debased in the Soviet Union, but they do have a meaning. In discarding the words, people frequently ignore the phenomena they represent. Without these concepts ideology inevitably becomes eclectic, illogical, and inadequate to the problems.

A surprise was awaiting me when I returned to Kiev. As in previous years, young people assembled at the Shevchenko Monument on May 22 to sing songs and discuss the anti-Ukrainian repressions, but this time the most active "slanderers" were photographed and tape-recorded. Komsomol leaders at the university were called into the dean's office to identify the voices. Most of the Komsomol leaders failed to do so, but some were so zealous that they identified people who had not attended the meeting. A system of denunciations always leads to personally motivated slander.

Yakir telephoned on May 18 or 19. "Will you sign a letter to the UN Commission on Human Rights? It's about violations of rights, illegal trials, and psychiatric prisons."

"Of course," I replied. "But from what point of view are you evaluating events?"

"From a legal point of view. Violations of the law. We're setting up an Initiative Group for the Defense of Human Rights in the USSR.[11] Will you join?"

I naturally agreed.

In June Tanya went on a business trip to Kharkiv. She telephoned home in excitement. "You must come immediately. There are remarkable people here. They're very close to you intellectually and politically."

When I arrived, I met some wonderful people with whom I spent several days in continual discussions. My talks with Arkadiy Levin were particularly lengthy.[12] Our views of the Soviet system generally coincided: it was an ideocracy and an instance of state capitalism. We had introduced the term "ideocracy" independently of each other and of Berdyayev, who had used it in *The Origins of Russian Communism*.[13] We had also independently come to use the term "state capitalism." The Kharkiv dissidents had started with an analysis of Lenin, whereas I had started with the young Marx: his *Economic and Philosophic Manuscripts of 1844* give a more profound understanding of such a society, although he does use the unfortunate term "vulgar Communism."

Mostly I talked about such ethical problems as the meaning of life and the relationship between means and end. The differences in our criticism of the regime were similar to my differences with the author of "The Transformation of Bolshevism," although the people in Kharkiv were interested in a wider circle of problems and did not rush to draw conclusions.

I took Dzyuba's *Internationalism or Russification?* to Kharkiv. The city is so Russified that Ukrainian can be heard only from the farmers who come to the market. When the Kharkiv philistine hears Ukrainian, he responds with "profiteer," "Banderite," or "fascist." He is not concerned that the peasant has to bargain because he cannot survive on his wages. He sees a man with a different language and different clothes, an illiterate boor who dares haggle over prices with him. With its chauvinism, its gray, faceless people, and its ugly socialist-realist architecture, the city became a symbol of vileness for me. It has its merits, no doubt, but all I saw there was a handful of splendid people, the police station, and the monstrous courthouse. I came home with mixed feelings: I had made friends, but they were on the point of being arrested.

Several Crimean Tatar friends, among them Zampira Asanova, visited me in Kiev. On June 6, the second day of the conference of Communist parties, Zampira had taken part in a demonstration in Mayakovsky Square, the slogans of which were "Long live the Leninist nationalities policy!," "Communists, return the Crimea to the Crimean Tatars!," and "Freedom for General Grigorenko!" Plainclothesmen beat up the demonstrators and shouted chauvinistic phrases. The only benefit the Tatars derived from this conference was that instead of being arrested they were sent back to Uzbekistan. There disturbances had broken out in May, when the umpire at a soccer match favored the Russian team and the Uzbeks started fist-fights. Several people were arrested, unrest broke out, and whites were beaten and killed in several towns.

When I asked the Tatars to explain the hatred of the whites, they replied with examples. A Russian bus conductress who saw an Uzbek woman wearing a yashmak tried to make her take it off. The woman refused, and her husband hit the insolent "civilizer" in the face. Uzbek militiamen explained that a party regulation forbade the wearing of yashmaks in Tashkent. Although they were obliged to side with the conductress, in practice they limited themselves to reprimanding the "hooligans."

Nor does the gradual disappearance of the Uzbek language from the capital of Uzbekistan earn favor for the "elder brothers." After the earthquake in Tashkent many Russians came to make easy money at the construction sites. The newspapers praised this as yet another manifestation of "fraternal assistance," but the Uzbeks were upset that newcomers were flooding their city and increasing drunkenness, prostitution, and national disproportions. The example of what had happened to the Crimean Tatars also strengthened the Uzbeks' hatred of the whites.

Because the Crimean Tatars traveled throughout the Soviet Union, we learned more and more about the national movements in the various republics. In Grozny Chechens blew up a statue of General Yermolov, the tsarist conqueror of the Caucasus. All the nationalities, including Ukrainians, were pleased to see such an answer to the theory of progressive colonizers, executioners, and gendarmes.

Ukrainian intellectuals were heatedly discussing Oles Honchar's novel *The Cathedral* at this time.[14] I considered Honchar an ordinary socialist realist and at first refused to read the book, but gave in when the controversy about it persisted. Artistically the novel was worthless. Its language was primitive, its style a combination of realism and sentimentality. But the Soviet vocabulary did not save Honchar. The protagonist of Honchar's novel was a worker who had been promoted to a party post. Vashchenko, the secretary of the party committee in the Dnipropetrovsk Province, recognized himself in the unflattering portrait and, being a relative or a friend of Brezhnev, felt that he had the party behind him and could attack the novel. But his target was not so much Honchar as those who dared to praise the novel in defiance of the party's general line. Numerous journalists, teachers, and writers lost their jobs and were expelled from the party.

On June 17, 1969, the poet Ivan Sokulsky was arrested. Copies of Moroz's "Report from the Beria Reserve," Dzyuba's speech at the evening in honor of Vasyl Symonenko, and a "Letter from the Creative Youth of Dnipropetrovsk" were found in his home.[15] The latter particularly irritated the authorities, because it described Vashchenko's purge and the Ukrainophobia and moral corruption of the bureaucrats. In January 1970 Sokulsky was found guilty of anti-Soviet propaganda and sentenced to four and a half years in a labor camp.

Why such persecution of everything connected with *The Cathedral*? Honchar had expressed a minimal measure of truth about the destruction of Ukrainian historical monuments and the official contempt for the Ukrainian language and culture. To be able to get away with it, he had constantly looked over his shoulder and glorified the authorities, yet even such a cowardly and wretched book evoked the displeasure of the party and the praise of the patriots. *The Cathedral* was even translated into Russian for Moscow *samizdat*.

Yevhen Sverstyuk wrote "A Cathedral in Scaffolding," in which he took Honchar's scattered images and built a true cathedral, a profound essay that transcends Saint-Exupéry's *The Citadel* and analyzes the spiritual impoverishment of the masses in modern times.[16] After reading the essay I told Sverstyuk that I had the sensation that he had walked past a pile of manure, tossed a pearl from his pocket into it, then pulled the pearl out, cleaned it off, and made a gift of it to Honchar. Sverstyuk merely smiled.

Significant works were being created in other fields as well. Yuriy Ilyenko's film *Saint John's Eve* was a milestone in the development of my understanding of the Ukrainian question and dislodged the remnants of my feckless internationalism.[17] Based on the story by Nikolay Gogol, the film contains a historical allusion in almost every scene. In one episode, for example, Cossacks are pursued by Tatars to the strains of a tsarist military march. This anachronism conveys the tragedy of Ukraine, caught between Turks and Tatars on the one hand and the tsars on the other.

The heroine of the film, a young mother, breast-feeds her baby. An ax appears, and blood flows. One sees the Cossack regiments driven by Peter the Great to build Petersburg, the new center of the rapacious empire, where thousands of them died from hunger and unceasing labor, and the Ukrainian peasants who starved to death by the millions in 1933, when Moscow shipped away their grain and then let it rot.

175

A boat sails down a river in the film. On board are Catherine, her favorite, Potyomkin, and Gogol's character Basavryuk, who represents satanic evil. A hawser appears on the screen and divides in half. Tanya and I laughed: the censors had cut a segment but overlooked the hawser, making the film even more poignant for those who knew what had been cut. Ilyenko's intention had been to show his heroes, Petro and Pidorka, being towed on a raft by the boat, and Petro finally cutting the connection.

Tanya and I were almost in hysterics when we left the theater. We did not want to think or talk. I could only blurt out what was most important for me: "We must break with that boat and its progressive helmsmen!"

An equally significant milestone in my thinking was Mykhaylo Braychevsky's monograph *Annexation or Reunification?* [18] It was the first truly Marxist book in *samizdat* to analyze the role of Bohdan Khmelnytsky and his treaty with the Russian Tsar in 1654. Braychevsky rejected both the prewar conception of Khmelnytsky as a traitor to Ukraine and the postwar Russophile interpretation, which makes him a hero who found the best way out of his situation by turning to Russia. Braychevsky also brilliantly proved Shevchenko's thesis that union with Muscovy had placed Ukrainians in an even more terrible situation than had rule by Poland. A country that had been culturally developed and almost completely literate, on the threshold of a bourgeois farming and manufacturing system, Ukraine fell into darkness and bondage.

Most important in Braychevsky's study was his analysis of Khmelnytsky's class positions. Khmelnytsky asked the Tsar for assistance only because he was afraid to base himself on the Cossacks and the peasants. He loved his country but saw it through the eyes of the upper class, which aspired to become master of the enfranchised peasantry, and never even thought of enlisting the support of the masses. Yet when Khmelnytsky saw the first fruits of the union with the Tsar, he entered into secret negotiations with Sweden; only death prevented him from realizing this intelligent plan. The Swedes were far away, and Ukraine could have remained autonomous while gaining strength to win full independence. Ivan Mazepa tried to carry out this plan during the reign of Peter the Great, but his lack of faith in the strength and intelligence of the people led to defeat and, ultimately, the enslavement of Ukraine by Russia. *Annexation or Reunification?* proved that Marxist methodology has not exhausted itself and can provide a profound analysis of history if it is applied objectively, with full consideration of the facts.

At the end of June Major Hryshchuk was arrested in Moscow. The workers at the Kiev power station had sent him to the Central Committee with a complaint about their housing problem. A newspaper article hurled abuse at Hryshchuk without a word about the workers or their demonstration; in this version of the incident, Hryshchuk had promised gullible people apartments and then gone off to Moscow to drink away the money he had collected from them. Doubts were cast on his role in World War II and his behavior in a Nazi concentration camp. I tried to locate Hryshchuk's family and friends to learn about his trial, but he had vanished, and his fate is a mystery even now. Criminals told me that they had seen him in transit to the Dnipropetrovsk *psikhushka*, but he was not there when I arrived.

In July Genrikh Altunyan was arrested. He had applied for reinstatement in the party at the Central Committee but was told that he would be arrested if he did not keep quiet. Altunyan then made available for *samizdat* a record of the interview.[19] Altunyan is an Armenian, but his friends include Ukrainians, Russians, and Jews. By place of residence it would have to be Ukrainian nationalism, but since there were references to Jews, was it perhaps Zionism?

That summer Tanya and I visited Western Ukraine and the Carpathian Mountains. As we traveled west, we caught glimpses of peasant cottages. In Eastern Ukraine the cottages are frequently thatched with straw, and the peasants' faces are dour and worn. In the West the cottages are neater; fewer are thatched; the doors and windows are decorated with carvings, and the people's faces show sparks of thought. In the Carpathians I was impressed by the Hutsuls, an ancient Ukrainian tribe with its own dialect and customs. The Hutsuls' gait is harmonious, and their faces manifest pride.

We stopped one night at a Hutsul's cottage. He refused to take our money and at first was wary of Tanya's Russian speech and our city clothes, as if expecting only propaganda and denunciations from people like us. But he relaxed and became talkative when he saw that we were familiar with Ukrainian history and culture. He praised Austrian times—there had been cattle, grain, and wildlife—but spoke less favorably of Polish times: the battues organized by the aristocracy killed off the game, young people were corrupted, and the gendarmes were highhanded. About Soviet times he mentioned only that the border guards had completely destroyed the wildlife and that there was no hay or cattle. "Then things became worse under the Poles and even worse under the Russians?" I asked.

"In 1916, when I served in the Austrian Army, I was taken prisoner by the Russians. At that time the Russians had grain but no harvesters. Now they have harvesters but . . ." The peasant smiled craftily and said no more.

In Eastern Ukrainian villages one occasionally hears discussions about foreign affairs, but they are always regurgitations of newspaper phrases or completely improbable rumors. The Hutsul peasant had his own views. He obviously read the newspapers and pondered them. Our talk reminded me of a conversation that some friends from Moscow had had with another Ukrainian highlander. Counting off on his fingers, the old man had said, "I did time under the Czechs. I did time under the Germans. I did time under the Russians." The phrase "did time" put Germans and Slavs in the same category and expressed a point of view that is rarely met with in Eastern Ukraine: the Russians are invaders just as much as the Germans were. With the exception of elderly people, peasants in Eastern Ukraine approach the occupiers from class and not national positions.

I cautiously questioned everyone I met about the Ukrainian Insurgent Army.[20] But who would admit to having fought on its side? People who had been neutral, however, often spoke with anger. The ceaseless guerrilla warfare against the Germans and Russians had exhausted the population. Toward the end of their struggle against the Russians, the guerrillas had become thoroughly embittered and frequently robbed and killed both civilians and one another.

In Lviv we visited friends. The husband, a gifted Jewish actor, censured my "Ukrainian nationalism." He was constantly being persecuted as a Jew, primarily by Ukrainian bureaucrats. He told us that someone was breaking off the noses on statues of Pushkin and Gorky. "That's nationalism for you." I replied that at a Kiev cemetery reserved for high officials, someone was systematically breaking off the nose on the monument to the wife of a Ukrainian party leader. "It's a spontaneous protest against official propaganda," I explained. In addition to Ukrainians, Russians, Jews, and Poles, Lviv has a fifth nationality—KGB men, who comprise about ten percent of the population. For young people in Lviv, Pushkin and Gorky are poets of this nationality.

The actor's wife took my side and reminded us of the cold-blooded anti-Semitism of the KGB and the authorities. The actor related how with the tacit consent of the Soviet authorities, part of the population of Lviv slaughtered Poles immediately after Soviet troops entered the city. I reminded him that Lemkos, a branch of the Ukrainian people, were deported from regions ceded to Poland after

178

the war. The Soviets calmly watched as Ukrainians and Poles fought one another. In Ukraine Uniates were forced to convert to Russian Orthodoxy, while in Czechoslovakia they were converted to Roman Catholicism with the connivance of Moscow, in an effort to destroy the Ukrainian national church.

When I visited Lviv again in the autumn, I discussed the nationalities problem with a Ukrainian patriot. The trouble was the terrible tangle of historical grievances, recriminations, and subjectivity. Facts and more facts were cited from all sides, emotions barring their objective evaluation. Billboards in the Carpathians advertise for workers in the Crimea. Western Ukrainians are reluctant to go, despite their high unemployment, because they sympathize with the Crimean Tatars—entire Western Ukrainian villages were deported to Siberia. They're perplexed, too; geologists and road workers come here from Russia, and the area is rich in useful minerals. Western Ukrainians do not understand why retired army officers from Russia settle in Ukrainian cities and are given privileges when Ukrainian boys who have finished their army service are sent to Siberia and Kazakhstan.

An anonymous "Letter from a Great-Power Chauvinist" was circulating in *samizdat*.[21] The author, a professor from Ufa, discussed his encounters with nationalism in Central Asia, the Baltic States, the Caucasus, and Ukraine. He ended the letter with a phrase about the "hundred-headed hydra" of nationalism, which might destroy the achievements of the October Revolution. The facts cited by the professor were on the whole correct, but he did not mention any cases of Russian prejudice. This blind spot in his vision was the crux of the problem. I countered with a letter of severe criticism entitled "To Rossinant," borrowing the term from a poem by Galich.[22] He had punned on Cervantes's Rossinant and "Ross," or Russian, to describe Jews who serve the regime. Basing my letter on Lenin's observation that the nationalism of an oppressed nation is engendered by Great-Russian nationalism, I argued that Russian chauvinism, as espoused by the professor from Ufa, is the cause of all chauvinism in the Soviet Union.

The professor described an incident at a party committee office where the secretary spoke Tatar in his presence. " 'Perhaps I should leave?' I asked. 'No, no, study our language.' If that's not nationalism, then it's boorishness." The professor demonstrated so clearly that the talk about republics and federation is a fiction that all I had to do was to quote his words. Speaking Tatar in the presence of a Russian is boorishness!

The professor is angry that in Bashkiria there is a practice of accepting more Tatars and Bashkirs into universities than Russians. But if half the population of Bashkiria is Russian, as the professor says, how is the Republic to defend itself against Russification except by giving natives preferential treatment? Even Lenin argued that the practical inequality in favor of the Russians should be compensated. They have their own highly developed culture, their thousands of schools, and their publishing houses. Yet the professor insists that tact and good breeding require everyone to speak Russian in the presence of Russians. Since Russians are present everywhere, everyone must speak Russian at work, meetings, and conferences. The Russian man in the street succinctly phrases the essence of Soviet internationalism: "I understand only human language!" And yet when a Crimean Tatar or a Jew speaks "human language," he is reminded that he is not a Russian: the Tatars betrayed their motherland during World War II, and the Jews are betraying it now. It is deplorable—if understandable—when a Russian is beaten for being a Russian, but why do Russians not see that Jews, Crimean Tatars, Ukrainians, and Georgians are being beaten because of their nationality? Why do only the "renegades"—Kosterin, Sakharov, and Bukovsky—see this?

The professor's letter helped me to understand the logic of Russian nationalism and the morbid reaction of national minorities to the "friendship of peoples." I signed my article with the pseudonym that I used for all my articles on the nationalities problem: Maloross [Little Russian]. This is what the tsarist regime called Ukrainians.

Returning from Western Ukraine, I soon set out for Moscow to deliver Ukrainian *samizdat* and information for the *Chronicle*. Ilya Gabay's wife, Galya, arrived from Tashkent, where her husband's case was being investigated, and told us about the trial of ten Crimean Tatars. They once again showed us democrats the strength a movement gathers when it is supported by an entire people. Until then oppositionists on trial had softened their positions, for tactical reasons, or because of political indifference, or because they considered discussions with pseudo-judges pointless. All three positions make sense, but when you know that your entire nation is backing you, your personal views and tactics in court take second place.

The Tatars were the first political prisoners who conducted themselves at trials in the manner of prerevolutionary political prisoners. They missed no opportunity to unmask the court and express their hatred for their torturers. They demanded that the trial be discussed in the press and—since an entire nation was on trial and not simply ten people—that observers from the Central Committee and the government be present. At first only KGB men were permitted to enter the courtroom, but when the Tatars declared that they would not participate in the trial, the public was allowed to enter. Several people began to record the proceedings, but KGB men took away their notes. The Uzbek militiamen who were guarding the courthouse quietly expressed their sympathy for the Tatars and their hatred of the Russians.

My old friend Rollan Kadiyev was a typical intellectual (his working-class chums amicably poked fun at the way he, a fat man, had jumped through the window of a railway car when the Tatars were deported from Moscow to Tashkent); he went on a hunger strike to protest the authorities' refusal to let the defendants have legal and political literature. Galya told us that Kadiyev was now thin as a rake and could barely walk. Yet he conducted himself in a proud and dignified manner. Like the other defendants, he rejected the prosecutor, who was famous for his cynicism and stiff sentences, and the judge, who was a party member. One of the charges was that the Tatars had criticized the policies of the Communist Party, and this provided sufficient legal grounds to reject the judge as an interested party.[23]

When one of the defendants was asked whether he had been convicted previously, he replied, "Yes, in 1944, together with my entire people, on a charge of betraying the motherland!" Such utilization of Soviet laws was not new in the opposition movement, but the Tatars carried it to its logical conclusion and exploited every possible point of law. The judge and the KGB were furious and must have regretted that they had let the public enter the courtroom and that the defendants were being tried for slander, which allowed a maximum sentence of only three years. Venting their anger on Galya, the authorities told her to get out of Tashkent within twenty-four hours. The trial lasted a month. At the end, between five and seven hundred Crimean Tatars held a sit-down demonstration at party headquarters. The militia was called in to disperse them.

Disturbed by the trial, new documents about the crimes committed in 1944, and my discussions with the Crimean Tatars, I wrote a long article about their national problem.[24] The Tatars had been "rehabilitated" by a decree of the Supreme Soviet in 1967, which explained that a new generation had attained maturity, thus hinting that the previous generation, an entire people, consisted of criminals who had been justly convicted. The Crimean Tatars were referred to as Tatars who had previously resided in the Crimea and thereby were denied a separate nationality. Cynically it was stated that they had taken root in Central Asia: an entire people had taken root on someone else's land by decree. Finally, the Crimeans were graciously permitted to live anywhere in the USSR in accordance with the identity-card regulations. This was done to prevent their settling in Crimean villages, where identity cards were required. Now when a Crimean Tatar settles in the Crimea without prior permission, the militia can evict him in twenty-four hours. Such are the dialectics of politics in the USSR. Any aspect of the law can be used against the citizens. Equality of the sexes is used against women; class justice against workers, peasants, and the intelligentsia; identity cards against Crimean Tatars, workers, and dissidents; and the lack of identity cards against collective farmers. Every humane and intelligent idea is turned into a new method of exploitation.

What does the "rehabilitation" of a people mean? It is an admission that a nation can be criminal. Since this notion is latent in Soviet ideology (Ukrainian or Jewish nationalism is always bourgeois, but Indian nationalism is not always bourgeois), I tried in my article to analyze dispassionately the question of good and bad nations from the viewpoint of genetics. Does a national genotype exist? Apparently, yes. But it refers to a statistical description of a nation. Particular psychological features—introversion and extroversion, for example—are genetically dominant but are not subject to ethical evaluation. A biological or mental trait is socialized as a specifically historical feature. Thus in Jews the same statistically dominant features give rise to prophets, Christ, Einstein, Freud, and Kafka on the one hand, and the moneylender and bourgeois on the other. In any particular historical period one or another negative trait can statistically predominate under the influence of social conditions, popular mythology, and relations with other nations. But even if a given nation as a whole is committing evil at a given moment, it cannot be juridically judged and punished as a nation. Individuals and not nations are criminal. The criminals are those who judge and punish an individual for his allegiance to a particular nation, class, or religion. This is precisely what genocide amounts to.

Paradoxically, the study of racial differences was considered to be racist and fascist in the Soviet Union for many years. Since the theoretical denial of a fact is often compensated by a distorted recognition of the fact in practice, the Soviet denial of racial problems and differences goes hand in hand with a racist attitude and terminology.

Shortly before Stalin died an article was prepared for *Izvestia* with the title "I Renounce the Traitor People," for which signatures were gathered from the few "correct" Jews. This national racism is a logical development of the class and religious racism of the 1930's and goes back to the inquisitorial division of the world into God-chosen and infidel peoples. When, in the 1930's, people were punished for their family connections or their social backgrounds, and not because of any criminal activity, this amounted, legally and ethically, to ordinary racism.

I continued the article by trying to examine the situation of very small nationalities—the Chukchi, Kamchadal, Nentsi, and Yakut.[25] These have in common the fact that they are dying out. The people drink to excess; venereal disease is rampant, and the number of deformed babies is increasing. Thinking that children of Russian fathers are more fit for the harsh life in the Far North, the Yakut have developed a custom whereby a woman will ask a white man to impregnate her, with her husband's consent. The Ministry of Education of the Russian Republic investigated the case of a white teacher who had debauched an entire settlement of Nentsi. The teacher explained that the men had asked him to live in turn with each of their wives.

The white plunderers who swamped Yakutia's diamond mines and construction sites brought with them sexual corruption, syphilis, alcoholism, and knifings. A drunken white man will kill a Yakut without provocation; the Yakut is not human, and the militia won't bother with the case. The Soviet press reports that Yakut culture is flourishing and unions of writers and artists have been established. But as such unions in the European republics are largely concerned with hampering culture, it is doubtful whether they have a different function in Yakutia.

Petro Grigorenko told me about the Chukchi, with whom he lived out his term of exile after his speeches at the Frunze Military Academy. Until the Revolution the Chukchi had occasionally been given drink by an American trader in exchange for furs. After the Revolution full equality was established, and vodka became available at all times. Seeing that the Chukchi had stopped working, the authorities began to ration their vodka, but clerks continued to sell it under the counter for bribes of furs. Then it was discovered that the Chukchi children were dying off. A study determined that they were eating decaying whale meat. The practice was stopped, but even more children died. A second study determined that the nutrients in the whale meat were more important than the disease microbes. Now the children have been taken away from their parents and put in boarding schools. This will hardly have a happy outcome for the Chukchi.

American Indians and Australian aborigines no doubt have faced similar problems, but these have at least been recognized and studied. In the USSR, however, the problem is not recognized: all the nations have reached the socialist level of development with a progressive culture (national in form and socialist in content) and are merging into a single Soviet people with a transitional stage of two native languages. Anyone who raises the nationalities problem is sent for re-education to a labor camp, a prison, or a psychiatric hospital. This is why the nationalities problem is so acute.

I left my article in Moscow to be retyped for fear that I would be caught with the draft on the way home.

During this visit to Moscow I also learned about burgeoning Russian nationalism, in the unfavorable sense of the word. A club called The Motherland had been set up in Moscow, and rumor had it that the "Russites," as its members were known, longed for a truly Russian state, truly Russian leaders in the manner of Catherine II and Elizabeth Petrovna, and a truly Russian language. I was not able to meet any of these "true Russians," but a girl who was close to them told me that they were disturbed to see all sorts of Jews, Komi, and Mordovians considering themselves Russians and corrupting the Russian language with their accents and bad grammar.[26]

Yet what are the non-Russians to do? The Soviet regime wants to make them Russians, while the "true Russians" do not want them to speak Russian. The Russians move into their territories, hardly ever learn their language, and insist that internationalism requires everyone to speak Russian. The non-Russians can't even throw their elder brothers out on their ears: that would be nationalism and chauvinism. When I pointed this out, the girl replied that Ukrainians come to Russia and grab all the best jobs. There are four prisons in Moscow, and each one has a Ukrainian warden.

"Put into practice the slogan in that prerevolutionary novel by Vynnychenko," I suggested.[27] " 'Russian butchers, get out of our Ukrainian prisons!' Expel all the national minorities from the labor camps in Mordovia, and you won't have Ukrainians running your country."

The Russians' animosity toward the national minorities is completely unintelligible. When Ukrainian or Jewish chauvinism appears, it is the result of an inferiority complex, a lack of self-respect, and a hatred of the oppressors. I am ashamed when Ukrainians proudly say, "Sahaydachny burned down Moscow seven times," [28] and count the famous Russians who had Ukrainian blood. Are we so untalented that we must look for our great men among the Russians? But when Russians argue that they are good (what self-respecting man will say this about himself?), when they claim to have saved the world, one sees how sad and ludicrous they are.

This false pride is not the only symptom of the Russian inferiority complex. Another is the tossing about between worship of the West on the one hand and campaigns against "cosmopolitanism" and the counting up of Russian discoveries in science and technology on the other. Russians rename scientific laws and apparatuses (the Petri dishes used in microbiology are called Ivanov dishes); they claim that Euler was a Russian mathematician,[29] and they denounce the theory of relativity because it was developed by the Jew Einstein. This national inferiority complex reached the height of absurdity under Stalin: he declared Euler a Russian but at the same time threw many Jews out of the ranks of Russian science, and he drank his famous toast to the great Russian people in secret gratitude that it had not overthrown him and put him on trial at Nuremberg.

But let us not hasten to conclusions. Take one Ukrainian I knew who had a refined sense of humor, esthetic tastes, and solid erudition. He claimed that the Ukrainians are a nation of bandits who have never accomplished anything. When I inquired about him, I discovered that rumors that he was a Jew had been spread at Kiev University. He was persecuted and began to hate everything Ukrainian. Or take a Jew whose toes were trod on by Jews and Russians. He became a fervent Ukrainian nationalist who despised everything Jewish and Russian. All this is self-seeking ideology. Hit from the right, you turn to the left. Hit from both sides, you become a pessimist, a cynic, or a KGB man. (Hysterical ideologists who hate the regime often become KGB agents.)

Or take Ilya Glazunov, the leader of the Russites in Moscow.[30] Monarchy, Orthodoxy, truly Russian culture—Glazunov mixed together all the old slogans and rehashings of Rousseau. Back to Russia, he argued, back to peasants who wear bast shoes, light their cottages with torches, and respect the truncheon. I listened to my friends talk about Glazunov and wondered: Poor Russia, why do you need such patriots? Where are you headed, to Gogol's vision, to Dostoyevsky, to the Apocalypse? A year or two later a profile of Salvador Allende by Glazunov appeared in *Literaturnaya gazeta*. After leaving the USSR I read a report that Glazunov was traveling in the West, boasting of his assignment to paint a portrait of Brezhnev himself, the master of the Russian people and all progressive humanity. The circle had closed; Glazunov had reached a new rung in his career, and Holy Mother Russia entered a new age of self-enslavement. These sad and absurd scenes did not prevent me from seeing the "non-true Russians"—Bukovsky and Sakharov, for example—or from hoping that they would be victorious in Russia.

Almost immediately after the trip to Moscow I went to Lviv again. Tanya had visited the city while I was in Moscow and had come back as excited as after her trip to Kharkiv. She had met several Ukrainian patriots, including Vyacheslav Chornovil and Mykhaylo Osadchy, and found that they were close to me in their views and tactics. I took with me the *Chronicle of Current Events*, the letter from the professor in Ufa, and information about Genrikh Altunyan's case. In return I obtained Western Ukrainian documents and, because the national question was concerning me more and more, a copy of Rabindranath Tagore's *Nationalism*.

Chornovil was a journalist who had been sentenced in 1967 to two years in a labor camp for putting together *The Misfortune of Intellect*, a collection of documents on the arrests and trials of 1965–66 in Ukraine.[31] When I met him, I was struck by his thin, nervous face, intelligent and passionate eyes, and kind smile. His wife was deeply religious but refused to talk about religion. For her God was something intimate, not to be discussed with others. Vyacheslav, on the other hand, eagerly responded to comments on culture, history, nationalism, socialism, and the situation in Czechoslovakia. Unfortunately, he was often away, and I was left alone with his extensive collection of books.

I also met Mykhaylo Osadchy, one of those people who joined the opposition movement when they saw the privileges enjoyed by the "servants of the people." Osadchy had been a university lecturer in journalism and an instructor in the party committee and had seen the closed shops to which only the higher party ranks have access. As a sincere Marxist, he could not remain blind to such injustice, and his revulsion was reinforced by the party's anti-Ukrainian policies. He was sentenced to two years in a labor camp for anti-Sovietism and Ukrainian bourgeois nationalism. Afterward he wrote *Cataract*, a remarkable account of his arrest, trial, and imprisonment that has both political and literary value.[32] I wanted to arrange with Osadchy to translate *Cataract* into Russian but discovered that people in Moscow had anticipated me. In 1972 Osadchy was rearrested for having written *Cataract*, as well as some "nationalist" poetry, and sentenced to seven years in a labor camp.

My friends in Lviv got together one evening to celebrate the marriage of S., the son of a UPA leader. S. had recently completed a labor-camp sentence; his parents were still serving theirs. Although he did not give the impression of a sufferer or a hero, I was immediately struck by the labor-camp look in his eyes. He watched with a shy, astonished smile as his friends and beautiful young wife laughed and joked. I remembered S. when I met Yuriy Larin, Bukharin's son.[33] These are people from the *Gulag* world, who have known persecution all their lives.

That evening, when folk songs were sung in honor of the newlyweds, I discovered something profoundly Ukrainian in the Ukrainian songs. A Ukrainian may call himself a Russian, not know the language, and despise the people, but if he spent his childhood in Ukraine, he becomes a Ukrainian again in song. In Eastern Ukraine folk songs have been turned into propaganda by the radio, and no new ones are being written. In Lviv, however, I heard both religious songs and new folk songs. And my friends did not sing them in loud, drunken voices, as Eastern Ukrainian peasants do.

I sensed in these songs an extremely tender and respectful attitude toward women. The feminism expressed in them sharply distinguishes Ukrainians from Russians: Ukrainian songs show no sign of the contempt or the exaggerated courtly respect in which Russians hold women, or of that pathological deification of the flesh which is mixed with a sense of woman's sinfulness and corruption. Ukrainian culture does not share the Russians' hysterical condemnation of women. The Ukrainian peasant woman may appear obedient in the presence of guests, but she will tell her husband exactly what she thinks when they are alone. She is the mistress of her house.

The feminism inherent in Ukrainian culture explains why Ukrainian women did not mount a hysterical campaign for emancipation but, rather, struggled jointly with men for human rights, and why the contemporary intelligentsia has given women a large role in the patriotic movement. Ihor Kalynets and Iryna Stasiv-Kalynets, for example, are both poets, and thus I expected them to be neurotically competitive.[34] But I discovered nothing of the sort when I met them at that party in Lviv. Both are extremely gifted and have made valuable contributions to literature, but their poetic visions are entirely different.

The morning after the party Chornovil and I visited Valentyn

Moroz, who had recently come out of a labor camp. I knew Valentyn from "A Report from the Beria Reserve" and considered him to be the best and most original Ukrainian essayist. After four years of labor camps and hunger strikes, Valentyn was extremely emaciated. Later I frequently encountered the effects of imprisonment. Ex-prisoners show a certain aloofness and alienation from the world; in some of them this takes the form of a morbid reaction to noise, a coarseness in expression and behavior, and a heightened curiosity about "outsiders."

Valentyn did not talk about the labor camps, and we discussed Czechoslovakia. I accused Dubček of failing to organize passive resistance to the Soviet occupation on the model of Gandhi's resistance to the British in India. Valentyn reminded me of Martin Luther King's failure and argued that the Czechs and Slovaks would have been provoked to an outburst of anger, which would have been used to justify a bloody repression similar to the one in Hungary. Valentyn would at times retreat into himself and not listen to us. At other times he would get actively involved, and we would become aware of his tremendous spiritual energy and relentless mind. We did not stay long with him: he was weak and had to take medication. In parting he suggested that I read about the Borotbists, Ukrainian revolutionaries who had supported the Soviet regime in the 1920's and then been destroyed by the GPU.[35]

Western Ukrainians have the advantage of possessing Ukrainian books published in Poland and Germany before the war. From them I was able to learn about the nationalist movements in Western Ukraine in the 1930's. Soviet propaganda calls all of the nationalists fascists and Banderites, including those who had been opposed to the Banderites. It became clear to me that the populace took a hostile attitude toward the Soviet forces that occupied Western Ukraine in 1939. Some people joined with the Nazis but then turned against them when they had had a taste of fascism. The left wing of the national movement, including the Communist Party of Western Ukraine, was accused of espionage and liquidated by the NKVD.

A Western Ukrainian poet wrote a poem about the departure of Soviet troops from Lviv when the Nazis invaded. NKVD men had killed all the prisoners in the Lviv prison, and the Nazis found only blood-spattered cells when they broke in. The Nazis, not entirely stupid, informed the population about the Bolshevik crime. The poem shook me with its anger and passion and its new techniques and images. Not knowing whether the author was accused or not of writing the poem, I cannot name him.

I had already heard from Tanya that Soviet troops retreating from Kharkiv had thrown hand grenades into the cells at the prison. While I was at the *psikhushka* I heard from eyewitnesses about a similar massacre in Uman, where the Bolsheviks during the war murdered both political prisoners and common criminals. After the war, according to Khrushchev, Stalin longed to exile the entire Ukrainian nation to Siberia.

The Western Ukrainian patriots have a vital advantage over their Eastern compatriots: close links with the peasants, workers, and Uniates, who are struggling to have their own Ukrainian Catholic Church. These links give the oppositionists greater credibility and make them politically more active than the people in Kiev or Kharkiv. The excessive interest in language and literature and the political indifference that so vexed me in Kiev were much less prominent in Western Ukraine. The Eastern Ukrainian abstention from politics meant that we learned about repressions in Kiev via people in Lviv or even Moscow. When a search or an arrest took place in Moscow, we learned about it that same day or at most a few days later. But when a similar event occurred in Kiev, we often heard about it only months later—or never at all.

The crackdown of January 1972 shows that the KGB is playing a positive role in one sense. It has politicized an apolitical, cultural patriotism, and it has united Eastern and Western Ukrainians and then divided them according to a new criterion: their steadfastness and resistance to betrayal. The only question is whether the KGB will succeed in embittering the Ukrainian patriots to the extent that they will become chauvinists. The *samizdat* that has come out since 1972 reveals such a tendency. On the whole, however, the Ukrainian patriots have remained democrats while increasing their political activism.

My friends in Lviv carefully questioned me about the Moscow democrats and their attitude toward the national question. I was indignant that so little information about Ukrainian events reached *samizdat* and that all the national movements had weak links with the *Chronicle of Current Events*, but the discussions I had in Lviv showed me the reason why. The patriots suspected the democratic opposition in Moscow and cited examples of its chauvinism. One member of the Initiative Group had insisted to Chornovil that Russians, Ukrainians, and Byelorussians are a single people. Other Russians were perplexed when national oppression was mentioned to them. "How can you talk about oppression when your Ukrainians will soon have all the Central Committees in their hands?" they argued. The Ukrainian patriots also remembered the position taken by Russian parties at the turn of the century. Only the Bolsheviks gave support to the separatists, but once they had come to power they used armed force to return the newly independent republics to the fold of Holy Mother Russia. Bounced between Hitler and Stalin, Ukraine could find no way out of its tragic dilemma.

The discussions I had and the prewar books I read in Lviv strengthened my belief in Ukrainian independence. The sheer vastness of the territory ruled by the Soviet regime is conducive to bureaucratization, centralization, and cultural and linguistic leveling, and to centripetal militaristic forces that impede democratization. Secession would give an impetus to the struggle for genuine democracy and socialism in Ukraine. The question of Ukraine's future status—cultural autonomy, federal union with Russia, or complete independence—should be decided by the Ukrainian people themselves and not by foreign powers.

The development of Ukrainian political thought will be determined in some measure by the sincerity and clarity of the nationalities program put forth by the Russian opposition. If the Russian oppositionists hedge the issue or espouse unity within a single state or preach the divine mission of the Russian nation, all the other national movements will become more Russophobe, with a consequent danger of fratricide and a new antisocialist *Gulag*. The Russians may then succeed in establishing yet another empire but pay the price of being enslaved by it. Only when the Russian democrats state their position on the national question unambiguously and without reservations, only when they prove to the other nationalities that they have no intention of being their benefactors or guardians, will an alliance with them in the struggle for democracy be possible.

14

THE SCREW
TURNS TIGHTER

Back in Kiev I learned that two members of the Initiative Group, Mustafa Dzhemilyov and Anatoliy Levitin-Krasnov, had been arrested.[1] I found it strange that people were being arrested individually and not in groups. Levitin-Krasnov is a religious writer who has actively espoused freedom of conscience and written numerous *samizdat* articles, of which I had read only a passionate defense of Grigorenko entitled "A Light in the Window."[2] I met him just once. One morning I awoke at Grigorenko's house to find a gentle face smiling at me. In our brief discussion Levitin-Krasnov questioned me about Chornovil, whom he knew, and people in Kiev. He did not understand the Ukrainian problem, but he disliked Russian messianism.

Sensing that I would soon be arrested, I feverishly set about writing articles. Oppositionists were being sent to psychiatric prisons more frequently, and I began to write an outline of my intellectual evolution, having no doubt that the KGB would explore everything. I quit because the task was boring and returned to my essay "The Results and Lessons of Our Revolution." My friends were translating Sverstyuk's "A Cathedral in Scaffolding" into Russian, but none of us could work calmly.

A group of people were arrested in Kiev. They had been earning money by copying poetry, essays, and pornography on Eras, small Czechoslovak offset machines to which access is strictly limited. Soon after that my friend Oleg Bakhtiarov was arrested.[3] He had given the typists a political piece. I went to their trial but was not permitted to enter. One of the witnesses talked about Bakhtiarov. I sensed that an amalgamation would be cooked up: pornography, Bakhtiarov, and myself. I decided that I would defend myself by talking at the trial about amalgamations, sexual defamation, and the hypocrisy of Soviet

191

education. For contrast I would cite amusing sexual incidents in the lives of Marx and Engels, which showed them to be men with healthy minds and a critical attitude toward hypocrisy. My trial would be a mockery of the police and the court.

On September 29 Tanya and I went to Babyn Yar. We arrived late and immediately found ourselves in a surrealistic setting of plainclothesmen and young, inspired Jewish faces. The plainclothesmen were of two types. One group was well fed and carefully groomed and had the self-satisfied look of pythons. The others resembled persecuted animals. The plainclothesmen tried to pick fights, asking people why they had come and why they were lighting candles. To honor the dead, was the answer. People gathered to place wreaths at a rock on which a promise to erect a monument had been inscribed. Two young men brought triangular wreaths of yellow flowers; when they placed one triangle on top of the other, a Star of David was formed. The plainclothesmen raised a hullabaloo, shouting that Communists as well as Jews were buried there. "Nobody is forbidding you to come here with a cross," a demonstrator replied. "You can even bring a five-pointed star."

An elderly Jew joined the chorus of KGB men and argued that Jews had been forced to wear the yellow star by their enemies. When the young Jews reminded him that at one time Bolsheviks had had the five-pointed star cut out on their backs and explained the history of the Star of David, the old man brought out his final argument: "They'll close down our last synagogue." I felt sorry for him, but the young Jews finished him off. "Why do we need a synagogue that has renounced Jewish history and the Star of David?"

I went home and immediately sat down to write an article, "There Is No Monument at Babyn Yar." The surrealism of what I had seen was especially poignant because the offspring and the heirs of the Red commissars had faced one another at Babyn Yar. The offspring had rebelled again, and the heirs continued to apply the methods of the tsarist secret police. Only now they called their victims Zionists instead of "Jew Masons," "Jew Cadets," or "Jew Communists." I read my article to many friends because I wanted to add to the facts I had mentioned and to improve the style. For this reason the article ended up in the KGB archives instead of in *samizdat*. You can imagine my surprise when I read a garbled version of it in *Vestnik Iskhoda* [*Herald of the Exodus*], the journal of the Jewish emigration movement.[4] Even more surprisingly, an acquaintance confidentially informed me that he had written the article. He had forgotten that he had heard me read it and had even suggested changes.

One evening I attended an auction with my sister. Ada had spent almost her entire life in a Russian-speaking milieu and considered herself a Russian, but she had heard from me about the cultural movement in Kiev and had visited Ivan Honchar's museum. Sculptures of Shevchenko and Franko, poems by Lina Kostenko, a painting by Lyudmyla Semykina, and ceramic and wooden amulets were being auctioned off that evening, and many young people were present.[5] My sister studied them and repeatedly whispered to me that she had never seen such people. Indeed, there was warmth and love and no posing or violent expression of emotion. We drank a bit and, as always in Ukraine, sang songs.

Ada could not take her eyes off Alla Horska, an original painter in the monumental style.[6] Alla combined masculine strength with spirituality, artistic taste, and irony. She joked ceaselessly and soon overcame my sister's shyness. I remembered Alla's jesting reply when I had once asked her about her views: "I am a sexual democrat." I had never encountered such concentrated vital force in a woman. Friends told how when Alla saw that someone lacked money for food after being fired, she rounded up a car and brought potatoes from a farm, all the while poking fun at the hungry person.

When the auction began, I set myself the goal of securing the poems of Lina Kostenko, whom I considered to be the best poet in Ukraine. Ada hoped to get the painting by Lyudmyla Semykina. The bidding for it was heated, and finally only Alla and I were left. Ada begged me to raise my bid, but I was unemployed and could not keep up. Just as Ada was giving me a sad look, Alla approached us and made her a gift of the painting. She did this with so much tact and humor that my sister could not refuse.

Later Ada and I visited Lyudmyla Semykina's studio. After she was expelled from the Artists' Union, Lyudmyla supported herself by sewing clothes. Instead of following fashions, she studied the clothing worn in Kievan Rus' and designed new clothes that were both modern and national in spirit. Her clothes were so special that a person who put them on immediately straightened up and was transformed. Lyudmyla also took an active part in the revival of Ukrainian customs and designed costumes and masks for holidays. At first her fashions were ordered only by prosperous Ukrainian liberal women, of whom there were not many, but soon her designs became fashionable and led to imitations.

I was surprised by Lyudmyla's attitude toward her work. When she got carried away, she would talk in great detail about her views, her creative searches, and her philosophy of clothing. She was not a smooth and polished talker and her grammar was faulty, but I could listen to her for hours. When she described the numerous dirty tricks the bureaucrats in the art world played on her, she would get very excited and carry on about their immorality and stupidity, in sharp contrast to her close friend Alla Horska, who never lost her sarcastic calm.

Both in her clothes and in her painting Lyudmyla looked for sources and thus was close to the Kiev ceramicists, particularly Halyna Sevruk, whose ceramic sculptures depicted various historical scenes.[7] These ceramicists had created a cycle titled "The Signs of the Zodiac" and a fascinating series of Gogolian devils. I loved to escort people from Moscow or Novosibirsk around the museums and studios of Kiev to show them the real Ukraine.

In the meantime friends had finally found a job for me in the printing shop of a factory that manufactured machinery for sugar refining. I was hired as a temporary substitute for a woman on leave. The job consisted of cutting printed sheets into pages, putting the pages in proper sequence, and stapling them. Several times a week I had to take the finished pamphlets to the Office of Technical Literature. A dozen pamphlets would be sent to the ministries, the Central Committee, the journals, and the infamous *Glavlit*, or Soviet censorship. What they were censoring was not very clear to me. A new method of manufacturing sugar? A new screw in a sugar-refining machine?

"You won't hold out very long here," my new boss warned me. "Only women work here, and they're constantly replaced. The wages are low, and men don't want to slave away for nothing."

But I quickly mastered the skills involved in stacking the pages (everything else was done by machine) and soon managed to disconnect my consciousness from the work. By speeding up the job I could finish in four or five hours and then go about my own business. This wasn't permitted and annoyed the boss, but he himself was often away and only asked me to have a solid excuse for my absences. We didn't have a telephone, and the only danger was that our supervisors might stop by. This happened twice; once I got away with it, and once I did not.

When I was first applying for the job, I realized that the place was very tempting for both me and the KGB. I could resist the temptation to make use of the printing facilities, but the KGB was weak-willed. After several days my boss said to me, "I often copy dissertations and rare books on the side. Do any of your friends need poetry printed or something? I won't charge much."

"I have a philosopher friend who can't get hold of an article by Marx for himself and his friends," I replied, having in mind the rare *Economic and Philosophic Manuscripts of 1844*. My boss forgot that he was supposed to care only about the money and told me that he wouldn't be able to do the job that month. The following day he was photocopying a dissertation, and a week later I was told that I had to leave. The fish hadn't taken the bait.

I asked that no entry be made in my work book: an employer who saw "engineer" followed by "stitcher" would realize that I wasn't employable. But the entry was made, and again I became a parasite. When Ira Yakir visited us in October, I played to the hilt the part of renegade, and we spent several days arguing about philosophy and politics and slandering the system in our decadent intellectual way. A knock came at the door the morning after Ira left. I had barely reached the door when two men with courageous expressions on their faces burst in. For some reason KGB men always conduct searches with the expressions of men going off to battle.

"What do you want?" I asked them sternly.

"We have come to make a search, Leonid Ivanovych!"

"I can see that, but where are your search warrant and your witnesses?" (The Code of Criminal Procedure requires witnesses to be present during a search or seizure. The persons who are being searched and the witnesses must be informed of their right to be present at all actions of the investigator and to make statements for the record about such actions.) My voice was nervous and uneven. Although I had expected the visit, my feelings were a mixture of hatred and confusion.

"We have a warrant, of course, and we shall go get the witnesses."

"What case is the search connected with?"

"The case of your friend Oleg Bakhtiarov."

"And what are the charges?"

"That is none of your business. We shall search here for slanderous literature."

I calmed down a bit, for conviction would mean a sentence of no more than three years. Besides, there was only the small amount of literature that I hadn't put away when Ira Yakir had left.

The witnesses were led in: a retired army officer bursting with pride at having been asked to help catch a spy (who else could I be if the KGB was involved?) and a nurse from a kindergarten. She begged the KGB men to let her go home to do her laundry, and they promised not to keep her long. I was surprised that the woman immediately sided with me without even asking about the charges and did not shudder when I uttered the magic phrase "KGB man." She examined the rock and plant collections with curiosity and asked about a drawing that hung on the wall. To pass the time I told her the story of the drawing.

My older son, Dima, had taken drawing lessons at the Pioneer Palace when he was seven. Three of his drawings were picked for an exhibition of children's art. The day before the opening, Udovychenko, the Minister of Education, visited the exhibition. The party has its policy for the development of children's art, and the minister is responsible for seeing that it is carried out without deviations. Udovychenko stopped in front of a drawing entitled "The Fox" and said indignantly, "Look at the tail! That's not a fox! That's a dog! And what about those trees? This is formalism. Remove it!" When the minister moved on, a friend of ours who was in his retinue walked up to read the name. The young deviationist was Dima Plyushch.

In the next room the minister spotted another deviation from the party's policy. "That's called 'The Ship'? The shape is all wrong! And the clouds are unrealistic! This is abstract art!"

The artist who had mounted the exhibition spoke up for the young offender: "This is a child's vision of the world. Many children of this age see the world in colors and not forms."

"Well, if an artist thinks that it's childlike, then let it stay," the minister replied.

Our friend read the name on the tag. It was Dima again. She looked up above "The Ship" and saw Dima's third drawing, "The Swan," where the real sedition was: the colors were no good, and the bend in the swan's neck was all wrong.

Like many uneducated people, the nurse had a profound respect for artists. Delighted to see that a seven-year-old could draw so well, she showed so much compassion for me that the KGB captain who was conducting the search told her several times to stop talking to me. To annoy him, I added a detail in my story about the drawing. When Tanya learned that "The Fox" had been banned, she asked that it be returned. The artist in charge of the exhibition said to her earnestly, "Your son must have talent if the minister paid such attention to him."

The search was under way at full speed. Several drafts of the article entitled "There Is No Monument at Babyn Yar" were lying on the table. But Captain Chunikhin, the senior of the two KGB men, promptly dropped the article when he discovered the draft of "The Results and Lessons of Our Revolution." The beginning was heavily marked up and written in the form of paradoxes, so the captain was out of his depth. "What revolution do you mean?" he asked.

"The February-October Revolution," I explained.

"Why is it yours?"

"I consider myself a Communist."

The retired officer interjected that I was against the party and the Revolution, that I disliked everything about the country, and that my son drew badly. The talk with the woman witness had calmed me down, but now I foolishly got angry. The KGB men supported the officer. I shouted that they had crushed the people, slaughtered the Bolsheviks, and calumniated Trotsky and Bukharin. The officer perked up when he heard me mention Trotsky: I had revealed myself as a Trotskyite hireling of fascism, Zionism, and imperialism. He reminded me with gusto of all the cock-and-bull stories about Trotsky while I shouted about Trotsky's role in establishing and commanding the Red Army.

I understood how stupid and degrading the argument was, but my hatred (mixed with unconscious fear, apparently) was carrying me away. I was saved by the woman witness. When I saw her fright and sympathy for me (I had been talking about the peasants and workers), I stopped arguing. The army officer tried to go on, but I told Chunikhin that they had not come here to discuss party history. The KGB captain asked the army officer to keep quiet: "You can see that Leonid Ivanovych is nervous." My sense of humor came back to me, and I remembered Ostap Vyshnya's observation that Ukrainians have a fatalistic saying, "Things will turn out somehow." [8]

Chunikhin got to the *samizdat* poetry. "Who is this Maximilian Voloshin?" [9]

"An apolitical poet from the turn of the century."

"Aha, he wrote about revolution."

"Yes, and he was for it. Just look at these lines."

"Why does he talk about God?"

"Even atheist poets like to write about God."

The captain handed the poems to his companion. He read them but decided they were not political when he saw the philosophical murk and the incomprehensible expressions. Chunikhin then pulled out several pages from a typewritten collection of poems. I was sorry to lose them, because they were the prison poems of Yuliy Daniel.[10] Fortunately the typist hadn't listened to me and had left out the biographical note I had written about Daniel. The captain looked through the poems and seized on the ones about Russia. When I realized the danger, I quickly made up a story about how poets love to confess their sins. "Who is the author?" the captain asked.

"Anonymous."

"Why?"

"I don't know. Perhaps the person who retyped them forgot to include the name. Besides, even Pushkin wrote anonymous poems that were not political."

"But perhaps you do know the author's name?"

"I'd tell you if I did. There's no sedition here."

The captain passed the Daniel poems to his assistant, who leafed through them with a bored expression until he saw the word "homeland." What was the author's attitude toward his homeland, he asked. I replied honestly that the anonymous author loved it. Obviously doubting me, the KGB man looked through the poems once more. The anonymous author was not particularly enthusiastic in his patriotism, but he did not slander. "Come now, who is the author?" the captain asked. "We'll take the poems away if you don't tell us."

"You don't have the right. You're supposed to be looking for slander."

"We'll send them to a literary expert for an opinion."

"Take them away, but be sure to give them back. I like these poems."

Captain Chunikhin obviously wanted to avoid quarreling about poems for fear that I would become uncooperative. It is very important for the KGB to come to terms with witnesses on many details of the questioning. Besides, he already had a fair catch: Zionism, slander against the KGB and the friendship of peoples, Ukrainian nationalism (a draft of a Russian translation of Sverstyuk's "A Cathedral in Scaffolding"), and slander against the Revolution. (My article began with the words "And so our revolution was defeated, just like the ideological counterrevolution. All parties suffered defeat." The KGB captain did not understand the idea, but the slander was evident, and he caught the hint that the Revolution must be continued.) In a letter the captain focused on the sentence "Until the Russian empire becomes a Union of Socialist Republics (each of these words must become a fact) dissension will continue to spread." He did not understand the parenthetical phrase, but he did see the slander in the assertion that the USSR is a continuation of the Russian empire. The search had also turned up articles from *Literární listy*, but these contained no slander, so no direct connections with the Czechoslovak counterrevolution could be established.

When my son came home from school, he looked at the KGB men, decided that they were bibliophiles and *samizdatchiks*, and ran outside to play.

Toward the end of the search the KGB captain found the statement to the trade-union Central Committee in which I had written about the violations of labor legislation in my case. He hesitated whether to take it and then left it behind. I realized only later that I should have hinted about slander in the letter. If it figured in the record of the search, I could demand that it be read in court.

When the search was finished, the KGB captain drew up a list of the items he was confiscating, including my typewriter. I read the list, and everything seemed in order, although a legal expert might have found something illegal about it. I refused to sign the record of the search, explaining that I considered the article under which it had been carried out to be unconstitutional. The captain argued with me and then suggested that I write down my refusal for the record.

I believe that a *samizdatchik* must determine his tactics toward the KGB in advance but should not follow an inflexible plan, because much depends on the situation. In this case my situation was advantageous: the few documents that had been confiscated could easily be turned against the KGB in court. Thus, after hesitating a bit, I agreed and wrote that I did not want to have even formal relations with the KGB because I considered it to be an anti-Communist and anti-Soviet, that is, unconstitutional, organization. The sentence came out awkwardly because I was trying to anticipate possible distortions and at the same time to express why I would refuse to testify in the future. I also intended to make this the main point in court and thus turn the trial of a political "criminal" into a trial of the police and the government.

Captain Chunikhin realized his mistake and urged me to cross out the sentence, but I refused. As he left, he asked, "Shall we send you the summons for interrogation tomorrow, or will you come without one?" I was surprised by his haste—time was needed to study the confiscated documents—but agreed to come without a summons. Forcing the KGB to observe all the formalities was boring, although it should be done: one principle of the Democratic Movement is that the guardians of the law must be forced to observe the law, and violations of the law must be dealt with through legal channels.

In the morning Tanya walked with me to the KGB office and said good-bye in case she was not to see me again. Captain Chunikhin smiled sweetly when he saw me at the entrance. He led me along endless corridors and up and down stairs. I had a sudden thought that this was arrest but then rejected it: they would want to talk to me first to see if I was going to be tractable. At his office Chunikhin, the smile still on his face, excused himself for a moment. Aha, I thought, he wants to confuse me about his intentions. I pulled out a book and began to read. Half an hour later Chunikhin returned, apologized for the delay, and began to praise the courage and profundity of my articles. Then in friendly tones he urged me to give up my involvement in *samizdat*. I pulled out an article about the interrogations of the young Lenin by the Okhranka, the secret-police department in tsarist Russia. "I am well acquainted with such methods of interrogation. Read how the Okhranka operated. The first step is flattery. The second is showing that the investigator is a friend who sympathizes with you and only wants to help."

Chunikhin declined to read the article. The friendly smile still on his face, he asked, "What, in your opinion, will I be asking you about?"

"The confiscated material."

"No, we haven't had the time to study it. The Kharkiv KGB has sent some questions for you about the Altunyan case. I shall write down your answers today."

"Read all of them at once. I must know what the specific charges against Altunyan are so that I don't unintentionally help the KGB convict him."

"Then you're acquainted with Altunyan?"

"You are beginning the interrogation, and I have told you to read all the questions."

Chunikhin was having a rough time with his role as a friendly investigator. Not wanting to make his relations with me still worse, he read the questions. Was I acquainted with Altunyan? Was he a member of the Initiative Group? What was the Initiative Group? What were its aims? And last, what other anti-Soviet actions by Altunyan did I know about?

As soon as Chunikhin read the last question I realized that he had lost the first round because of his stupidity. KGB men are incapable of taking the law into account and so can always be beaten with it. On the way to the office I had decided what tactics I would adopt: I would use the interrogation to illustrate my remarks about unconstitutional methods during the search. This time I would sign the record, but not without citing some illegal actions as a reason not to testify.

I therefore wrote that I was refusing to testify because I had been given a provocative question biased in favor of the prosecution. The law requires interrogations to be objective and forbids questions that suggest certain answers. Had I answered that I did not know of any other anti-Soviet actions by Altunyan, I would have indirectly confirmed that the Initiative Group was anti-Soviet. Since Chunikhin had established that I was a member of the group as well, I would have testified against myself and changed from a witness into one of the accused.

Chunikhin read my answer and realized that he had lost. He smiled sweetly again and asked me to add that those had been the questions of the Kharkiv KGB. Now it was my turn to smile. His second request was even more amusing. "Add that I read the questions to you after you told me that you would refuse to answer if I did not read all of them."

I did not have to agree. We were trading concessions, and in principle this could only hurt my cause. But I did not want to argue about trifles—I couldn't care less whether Chunikhin or the KGB men in Kharkiv got in trouble for making the mistake—and I added the words he requested. Chunikhin cheered up and insolently asked where I saw provocation and bias in favor of the prosecution. I explained. We began to argue about the meaning of the word "provocation." Seeing that I would not budge from my position, Chunikhin seized on the sentence about my participation in the Initiative Group. "Aren't you a member of the Initiative Group? Why don't you want to write about this directly?"

"Because I don't want to answer a single question even indirectly."

Chunikhin reread what I had written and pointed out a mistake. I agreed to have him correct it, thinking to myself that he was trying to exploit even my respect for grammar. Then Chunikhin proceeded very quickly to propose his own formulations, which at first glance seemed to be more precise than mine. When I rejected them, he would ask with surprise, "Why?" I pointed out that his formulations could be twisted in court.

When the interrogation had ended and Chunikhin had escorted me to the street, I asked him, "Why do you copy the Okhranka down to the last details?"

"What details?"

"You should know the history of your own organization! The Okhranka once dressed all its agents in identical pea jackets. All Russia laughed and pointed a finger at them."

"But our agents don't wear pea jackets!"

"No, they all wear identical raincoats, shoes with thick soles, and checked ties. Sometimes they all wear red scarves and imported jackets. The ones today looked like movie detectives—they all wore hats. My wife and I saw them on our way here."

"Leonid Ivanovych, you have a persecution complex."

"Does my wife have one, too?"

"I meant that you're exaggerating the surveillance. Why should we have followed you today?"

"That I don't know. Perhaps you were afraid that I'd skip the country."

From the interrogation I went straight to Tanya's office. We realized that I would be arrested. Then I went to see friends who had been called in to testify in Bakhtiarov's case. Coming home late that night, I looked around for a tail and finally spotted a young man who did not take his eyes off me. When I got off the bus, he stayed behind. I got on the next bus. The boy rejoined me at the next stop. I lost him in the subway but saw him again on the next bus, and he accompanied me all the way home. The KGB had taken into account my remark about pea jackets and used a less obvious, though equally stupid tail.

The boy did not have the typical criminal expression of a seasoned detective, because he was only nineteen or twenty and his profession had not left its mark on him yet. Without my suspicion I would perhaps not have spotted him. Actually I never did learn to recognize women agents. Tanya, however, did, and said that they came in two types: whores and Komsomol activists. Perhaps these professions have something in common?

The day of my second interrogation, Tanya again walked to the KGB office with me. Now our detectives had stopped pretending to be window-shopping, and again they were dressed identically. Chunikhin also no longer felt the need to put on an act. He still spoke as a well-wisher, but only because he hoped that I would again help him cover up his mistakes. But I was getting ready to be as tough as I could. The other witnesses in Bakhtiarov's case had told me about Chunikhin's intimidation, screams, solicitations to collaborate with him, and slanderous statements about the witnesses' friends, and I had my own taste of his intimidation technique. Until I met him I had believed that we intellectuals had the advantage of being mentally superior to the KGB men. Now I realized that Chunikhin, fool though he was, had experience on his side. He knew exactly what to expect from an intellectual.

The KGB usually begins an interrogation by choosing the most effective method of applying pressure. If the interrogator sees that the witness is ready to engage in a friendly discussion and is willing to overlook minor violations of the law, he immediately begins in a rapid tempo to supply his own answers to the questions. If the witness is tired, frightened, or confused, the interrogator tries to be human with him. Valentyn Moroz was quite right when he observed that if a person has admitted to A, the police put him under threefold pressure to admit to B, and then do not stop until he has reached Z.[11]

"Today we shall talk about Bakhtiarov's case," Chunikhin announced. "I expect that there will be no more misunderstandings and that you will help Bakhtiarov and yourself. He strikes me as an intelligent and honest man. You must corroborate this by honestly telling me everything you know about him."

He's placing his hopes on the Prince Myshkin in me, I thought. My God, what do their psychologists waste their time on? They've got my papers and the records of the 1964 interrogation. If they looked into them, they'd realize that I am not much of a Prince Myshkin. "Before I answer," I said, "tell me the charges against Bakhtiarov."

Chunikhin sensed a trick. "You're being evasive again!" he shouted. "You're not the person on trial, and the charges against Bakhtiarov should not interest you!"

"Then I will not answer. According to the search warrant, Bakhtiarov has been charged with slander. Investigations of cases on such charges are under the jurisdiction of the Prosecutor's Office and not the KGB. It's you who are violating the law."

"No, Bakhtiarov has been charged under Article 62, anti-Soviet propaganda."

"But the search warrant said 'slanderous documents'!"

"Leonid Ivanovych, why don't you believe me? Have I ever deceived you?" Chunikhin left the room. I started to read the Code of Criminal Procedure, which I had brought with me to upset him. KGB men cannot stand the book. "Why are you blathering about the law?" they shout to prisoners in labor camps. Chunikhin returned with a piece of paper. "Here's the warrant for Bakhtiarov's arrest. Read it. Article 62."

"How can I be certain that you didn't have this typed just now? Why were you away for so long?" But I had realized that there was no sense in insisting on my suspicion.

I had been saving my trump card for Bakhtiarov's trial. I did not want to use it now, but there seemed to be no choice. "Show me the record of the search at Bakhtiarov's house," I said. "I've heard that many breaches of the law were committed during the search."

"I didn't conduct it," Chunikhin replied, "but the lieutenant who did has legal experience. I don't think there was any violation of the law."

"You don't think so? You are in charge of the investigation and are responsible for the legality of the procedure and the lieutenant's actions as well. You have read the record and know, not just think, that it was drawn up in the most disgraceful manner."

"But what significance does the record of the search have? The important thing is what was found."

"Laws are made not for the sake of exercise in formalities, but to prevent investigators from acting arbitrarily. Remember what your organization did under Stalin."

"You keep mentioning 1937, but I wasn't working then," Chunikhin replied.

We started arguing about Stalin. Chunikhin brought up the victory over Hitler. I reminded him of Stalin's liquidation of the officers, his pact with Hitler, and the severe Soviet losses during the first years of the war. Chunikhin steered the conversation toward the goals of the Democratic Movement. "We shall smash the opposition without any difficulty," he announced.

I repeated to him what Pyotr Yakir had said to his investigator. "All the worse for you then. We're playing the role of the Cadets,* 'constitutional monarchists' who want the country to evolve toward democracy and are opposed to assassinations or a rebellion by a new Pugachov.[12] That Pugachov will smash the KGB and then set up a new paradise. When you're taken out to be executed, it is we who will demand that the verdict be rescinded. If the people, the majority, come to power, they will not be afraid of former KGB men. You may smash us, but then new Kalyayevs will come to shoot you.[13] Someone will talk about a 'different path,' and again there will be secret-police terror and violence, this time against the KGB."

"Thank you for the advice. Is Bakhtiarov's attitude toward us just as humane?"

"I don't know, but I do think that like all the democrats he is opposed to terror." I stopped arguing and asked for the record of the search.

Chunikhin argued a bit more but then went off to his superiors and came back with the record. The incriminating objects were "un-

---

* The Cadet (Constitutional Democratic) Party was formed in 1905 by liberals, including constitutional monarchists and republicans, and its main demand was for a freely and fairly elected constituent assembly that would sort out the empire's political problems. The party was suppressed by the Bolsheviks in 1918.—TRANS.

developed roll of film," "144 pages of typescript," and "fifty-page draft of article." I wrote down my reason for refusing to testify. The record had been compiled improperly, giving the investigator the opportunity to substitute anti-Soviet documents for the confiscated ones. The undeveloped roll of film containing the poems of Mandelstam, for example, could have been replaced with a film of *Mein Kampf* (although I saw no reason why Hitler could not be read).

Chunikhin leaped up with anger. "How can you suspect us of this?" He ran off to his superiors, then took me to a Colonel Borovik, who looked and acted like a Gestapo man in a bad film. I realized from his appearance that I, too, would have to change my tone and let an edge of iron into my voice.

Borovik announced that I would be prosecuted for the entry I had made in the record of the search. "We will not permit you to conduct anti-Soviet propaganda in a legal record!"

I began to answer in a cold, even voice but then lost my advantage as a law observer and revealed my fear by starting to shout about the famine of 1933, the purges of 1937, and the millions of labor-camp inmates. While I was shouting I made a slip of the tongue. "Your Lenin"—I had wanted to say Stalin—"destroyed more Western and Soviet Communists than all the fascists put together!"

If I hadn't corrected myself immediately, Borovik might not have noticed the mistake. Now he smiled maliciously. "Just a bit more and you'll start on that line."

Having won the round, Borovik calmed down. I settled down, too, and demanded that my comments on the record of Bakhtiarov's search and my reasons be entered into the record of the interrogation.

"We shall discipline the lieutenant for any mistakes in the record," Borovik replied. "If you're such a legal expert, you must obey the law yourself. According to the law you are required as a witness to testify. The Prosecutor's Office exists for the purpose of supervising the KGB. I shall call the provincial prosecutor, and he will explain your obligations to you. You can make your comments about the investigation to him. If you refuse and don't stop this pettifoggery, you will be prosecuted for refusing to testify."

I smiled and cheered up. Borovik was threatening me with a fine and compulsory labor, which would mean a deduction of twenty percent from my wages. Borovik understood my smile and added threateningly, "The prosecutor can immediately sign a warrant to arrest you under Article 62. Captain, call the prosecutor!"

Chunikhin left the room, and the colonel studied my face with a ferocious look. I returned it. We were like children trying to outstare each other. Chunikhin returned to report that the prosecutor was out of town.

"Very well, take him away!" Borovik barked. "There's nothing more to discuss with him." His tone made it clear that I would be detained until an arrest warrant had been obtained.

Chunikhin pointed to the door and led me through corridors in an unknown direction. The tension I had felt receded, and I began to consider what I would demand in the cell, but Chunikhin brought me to the exit and said, "We shall send you a summons." For some reason they were not ready to arrest me.

I went straight to Tanya from the KGB office. She thought that arrest was inevitable and urged me to slip up to Moscow to retain an attorney. We were worried about the entry I had made in the record. Would the KGB be able to exploit it in some purely legalistic fashion? I had no intention of discussing legal matters at the trial, which I wanted to make a political one, leaving the juridical niceties to the attorney. In Moscow I would settle various matters, say good-bye to my friends, and agree on the tactics the Initiative Group was to follow. It was clear that the campaign against the group was being stepped up and that attempts would be made to present all of us as anti-Soviets. The screw was turning tighter.

15

TRIALS IN KHARKIV AND KIEV

To get away from my tails—the KGB could arrest me at the airport or even in Moscow—I left through the window of Tanya's office, zigzagged around Kiev, and then dashed off to the airport. The attorney I met in Moscow advised me to change my tactics and adopt a purely legalistic position. Moscow lawyers had been rebuked so often for conducting "unpartylike" defenses (they frequently supported their clients' right to have their own convictions and demanded that legal procedures be observed) that the Moscow bar had prohibited its members from taking cases in other republics.

Moscow was not stinting in news and events. Anatoliy Marchenko had been given a trumped-up trial in the labor camp and sentenced to an additional two years. Mikhail Ryzhik had been sentenced to a year and a half of labor camp for refusing to serve in the army during the invasion of Czechoslovakia, although he had already done his military duty and twice been found innocent of the charges. Yuriy Maltsev, a member of the Initiative Group, had been sent for a psychiatric examination without a trial.[1] Natalya Gorbanevskaya, Tatyana Khodorovich, and Anatoliy Yakobson had been searched.[2] In Leningrad Vladimir Borisov had been committed to the violent ward of a psychiatric hospital for having made "slanderous" statements.[3] Pyotr Yakir received indignant letters from the "public." The authorities were obviously preparing to smash the Initiative Group by sending some members to psychiatric hospitals and others to labor camps. My friends and I agreed that we would refuse to testify and would turn our trials into indictments of the regime's lawlessness. I asked Yakir to continue signing my name to the Initiative Group's letters if I was arrested and not to believe any claims that I had testified against the group.

Stalin's ninetieth birthday was coming up in December. Jubilee articles were being prepared for the press, and posters with his picture were run off by printers. The authorities needed the Stalin they themselves had spat upon to stop the anti-Stalinist arguments of the opposition, to find an ideological justification for tightening the screws, and to help the dead man rise from the grave and tower over the country. It was a vampire regime, but without enough faith in its vampiric energy. God was dead; the entire country could smell the rotting, but the regime parodied the resurrection of God's successor. This Stalin was not a Nietzschean shadow of God, but a bronze horseman, a great corpse.[4] How could one help being reminded of Marx's observation about dead generations oppressing the living?

The daily reports about arrests and repressions in all parts of the country brought my friends in Moscow to the brink of nervous exhaustion. A typical example: I left Yakir's flat promising to return by eleven but did not come back until one in the morning. Pyotr was sitting up, angry and nervous. He shouted at me for my thoughtlessness in not calling. In addition to the general nervousness he had his own reason: everyone around him was being arrested, frequently for having ties with him, but he himself had not even been searched. If I had been arrested for visiting him, this would have been the last straw. He suffered for all of us and hence was often beside himself. I was disturbed by his undue sensitivity, and friends told me that he was behaving like a man possessed. I never saw any signs of it, but I was afraid that he would crack from nervous tension. I always said unpleasant things to my friends right between the eyes, but with Pyotr I hesitated for fear of causing a break in our friendship. I loved him very much—not for his views or his activities, but simply for himself.

I came home infected by the oppressive Moscow atmosphere. The tension was not as unremitting in Kiev, and I always slept a great deal for several days after returning from Moscow. Occasionally Muscovites would visit us to rest, discuss problems calmly, and chatter about nonpolitical matters.

In Kiev a letter from a Moscow physics professor named Rozin was awaiting me. Having participated in protests with Yakir and got to know him better, he wanted to warn everyone about Yakir's immoral behavior, including drinking bouts. Rozin's way of thinking was familiar to me. Noting a negative trait in a member of the Democratic Movement, liberals rush to attribute it to the entire movement and thus to discredit democratic strivings and to justify their silence.* The letter prompted me to write an article about the liberals' betrayal of the Democratic Movement, but before completing it I telephoned Pyotr to check what protests Rozin had taken part in. "He's from Kiev," Pyotr said with surprise. "Aren't you acquainted with him? I wanted to ask you about him because I've received a similar letter." We realized that the letter was KGB *samizdat*.

Soon afterward Zampira Asanova brought me another letter, full of dirty insinuations about the leaders of the Crimean Tatar movement. The letter claimed that Zampira used the people's money to travel around the Soviet Union, that she belonged to the harem of a Tatar leader, and that she had visited a Ukrainian hack writer and a Caucasian horseman. I readily recognized the former as a reference to myself and asked Zampira about the latter; it was the Avar poet Rasul Gamzatov.

Samizdat began to circulate transcripts of the meeting in 1933 at which Les Kurbas was hounded (the participants included the writers Leonid Pervomaysky and Ivan Mykytenko and several actors from Kurbas's theater) and of the writers' meeting in 1958 that denounced Pasternak (the participants included Vladimir Soloukhin, Vera Inber, and Boris Polevoy).[5] Although the trials had taken place in different decades, they were similar in that the "comradely criticism" laid the ground for administrative persecution. Kurbas perished on the Solovetsky Islands, and Pasternak was driven to his grave, but some of the intellectuals who persecuted them now pose as liberals. I understand that people like Pervomaysky and Soloukhin took part in the purges because of their youth, but they should at least admit in public to having been wrong. They refuse to do so. Pervomaysky remains silent, and Soloukhin is playing a "true Russian."

I got the idea of publishing an underground anthology, taking for the title a line from Galich's poem "To the Memory of Pasternak": "We'll remember by his name everyone who raised his hand." The first issue would be about Kurbas and would include biographies of him and his persecutors and the memoirs of an actor who had been

---

* There is another way to justify silence. At a gathering at Victor Nekrasov's one evening a woman guest had a few drinks and proceeded to tell me that I was a fearless Titan and that she envied my courage. I tried to explan that *samizdat* does not require all that much courage, but she stubbornly maintained that we were Titans. Then I understood that she wanted to respect herself. If I were a Titan, then she was a decent and honest person who understood and sympathized. Such a consolation is a cheap way of buying self-respect.

in the labor camps with him. The second issue would be about Pasternak, and the third about Alexander Grin, Marina Tsvetayeva, Osip Mandelstam, and Mikhail Bulgakov. For the fourth issue a fresh subject offered itself: Alexander Solzhenitsyn was expelled from the Writers' Union on November 4. But someone else put together the fourth issue, and events were now coming to a head so swiftly that there was no time for me to prepare the others.

We received a transcript of the meeting at which Solzhenitsyn was expelled and his letter to the Secretariat of the Writers' Union.[6] It raised our spirits. Several months later a collection of materials about the Solzhenitsyn case appeared in *samizdat*. Despite the voluminousness of the collection, many people volunteered to retype it. There were even persons who had never before dared to retype *samizdat* but undertook Solzhenitsyn because of the importance of the case. Most of November was devoted to retyping *samizdat*, looking for additional typists, buying a typewriter with type that would not be recognized, and changing the type on the typewriters we already had.

On November 25 I went to Kharkiv to attend Altunyan's trial. Ira Yakir and Vyacheslav Bakhmin arrived from Moscow, and in the evening we all got together to discuss how the witnesses should reply to the questioning in court.[7] The investigators had paid particular attention to a remark about religious persecution in a letter by the Initiative Group, because they realized that the people in Kharkiv had little *samizdat* and would be hard pressed to substantiate the claim. I told about the persecution of the Ukrainian Catholic Church and the Baptists. Someone remembered that a synagogue had been closed in Kharkiv. My friends had made many mistakes during the investigation, because they still believed in the KGB's humanity and thought that they would be able to avoid trial or at least to reduce their sentences if they supported the legality of their actions by citing facts.

In the morning, when we went to the courthouse, Altunyan's wife, Rimma, could barely hold herself together, but at the same time she had more illusions than anyone else. We visitors knew the verdict— the maximum three years under the article. The natives wondered how they could convince the court that there was no slander in the Initiative Group's letters, in Altunyan's statements, or in the *samizdat* that had been confiscated from him.

Strangely enough, we were all allowed to enter the courtroom. It was full of relatives and friends, plainclothesmen, and "representatives of the public"—party organizers from the institutions where Altunyan and his friends had worked. The room was stuffy. When Altunyan was led in, he smiled encouragingly at his wife and friends. Apparently he had no illusions left. A recess was called after the opening formalities, and afterward, when Ira Yakir and I started to go back in, a militiaman stopped us. "You may not come in. My superiors have told me to keep you out." We started to remonstrate with him, but an officer came up to us and said that there weren't enough seats. When we pointed to empty chairs, he replied that he did not intend to argue with us.

A painful wait in the corridor began. During the recesses the witnesses would come out to report on what was happening. Altunyan's defense counsel, a very intelligent attorney named Ariya, had advised him to adopt purely defensive tactics. Altunyan agreed, but because he was by nature a direct and emotional man, he could not follow the plan and repeatedly told the court about his political views.

The trial dragged on into the evening. We expected an adjournment to the next day, but at long last everyone was allowed to enter the courtroom for the reading of the verdict. The judges began by listing Altunyan's "merits"—a wife, two children, a stomach ulcer, thirteen years of irreproachable service in the army, four medals. "They'll find him innocent and even give him a fifth medal," I muttered. The list of merits ended with the phrase "but in view of the particular danger of Altunyan's actions . . ." Then came a list of his crimes: while leaving a bookstore in 1968 he had told so-and-so that the assistance rendered to Czechoslovakia was an act of aggression; he had spoken about government anti-Semitism at a party meeting; he had signed letters of protest and had compiled lists of repressions in Kharkiv, parts of which had been published in the West. I began to hope for a sentence of one or two years: why else first list all the mitigating circumstances? But the verdict was three years. "Serves him right!" a representative of the public said loudly. "Fascist!" I muttered at him through clenched teeth. Rimma Altunyan fainted in the corridor. We were all overwhelmed by hatred for the judges and pity for her: she was the only one who had to some extent believed in the authorities.

On November 27 we all gathered at Vladislav Nedobora's apartment.[8] A portrait of Lenin hung on the wall, and books on Marxism and history were scattered about. One of us worked on the transcripts of the trial. Others discussed recent events. The discussion was

211

carried out in writing, because we suspected that the flat was bugged. Someone told about a recently uncovered group of schoolboys who had a very simple plan: they would kidnap all the party leaders in the province, lock them into a bathroom, and finish them off with sulphuric acid. A resident of Kharkiv distributed leaflets with appeals to end Jewish domination of the party and government. The rebel welcomed the party's policy toward Jews but thought that it should be carried out with more energy. At the same time Altunyan was being tried to the accompaniment of rumors about his Zionist group.

Someone else related that a group of students in Moscow planned to distribute leaflets on Stalin's ninetieth birthday. I argued that this was pointless. Systematic retyping of *samizdat* would be more effective. We were so few, we could not afford to lose anyone to the KGB, although there were, of course, some situations when leaflets were necessary—after the invasion of Czechoslovakia, when prices were sharply increased, or when the government committed an act of particular villainy. In the end we agreed that someone should talk to the students.

Late in the evening we heard a cry from the street. Veronica Kalinovsky had been coming to join us when she spotted militiamen.[9] We rushed to hide the transcripts of the trial, but before we had finished about ten men burst in. Vasyl Hrytsenko, an investigator from the Prosecutor's Office, was in command. He was loud and rude and did not look like the good-natured Vasya I had heard about. Policemen guarded the doors and windows. Nedobora's son began to cry. We had to shout at the policemen to make them behave more decently. When they started searching for *samizdat*, they immediately found part of the transcript, but the remainder stayed hidden right under their noses.

At the end of the search Hrytsenko told Nedobora, Ira Yakir, Vyacheslav Bakhmin, and me to put our coats on. His manner made it clear that we were being arrested. As we were being led out, we encountered Arkadiy Levin, who had come running when he heard that a search was taking place. We said good-bye, got into a Black Maria, and were driven off. Nedobora guessed that we were being taken to the Cold Mountain Prison. But after we were interrogated, Ira Yakir, Bakhmin, and I were allowed to leave. I returned to Nedobora's apartment. The next day his wife went to Hrytsenko to learn what had happened to him. I stayed at the apartment, my spirits at a nadir.

The Muscovites soon left Kharkiv, but I stayed for Arkadiy Levin's birthday, December 1. We spent the time in animated discussions about the tactics of the struggle, political economy, ethics, and the reasons for the failure of the October Revolution.

Three days later Nedobora was let out. His feeling of relief was mixed with shame for not having been arrested: he was afraid that he had given Hrytsenko the idea that he was withdrawing from the struggle.

On the evening of the first we got together at the Levins' to drink and argue. It was clear that our people in Kharkiv would all be arrested: the court had ruled to instigate criminal proceedings against the witnesses. When everyone had left, Arkadiy and I continued our discussion of the theoretical aspects of neo-Marxism.

Ira Yakir telephoned from Moscow. Searches had been carried out in six places, including Ira's apartment. Many writings, including my own, had been confiscated from her. I could well imagine how much because I had seen the mountains of *samizdat* that she had. The search of her apartment meant that the attack on her father, Pyotr Yakir, was being stepped up. Olga Iofe and Irina Kaplun, students who were friends of Ira's, had been arrested.[10] Ira hinted that the arrests were connected with the student preparations for an anti-Stalinist demonstration.

At four in the morning Arkadiy went to bed, and I lay down to read Antonio Gramsci's *Prison Notebooks*.[11] At six the doorbell rang, loudly and insistently. I woke up Arkadiy, and he opened the door. Hrytsenko had arrived with his men. "Ah, you again!" he exclaimed when he saw me.

"And you're breaking into people's houses again!" I retorted. "You have no right to come for a search at six in the morning!"

"Blathering about the law again? Get dressed!"

I started arguing about night searches, but Hrytsenko merely waved his hand, as if to say it was all useless. Arkadiy's mother looked at me with compassion. Realizing that my arguing frightened her, I fell silent. "I'll get some clothes together for him," I heard her whisper to Tamara. Hrytsenko behaved in such a way that everyone understood that I was being arrested. He looked around the room carelessly, aware that there would be no *samizdat*. When he had finished glancing at the books and papers, Hrytsenko wrote out a record and took away Arkadiy, saying to me, "You'll come for an interrogation today." Arkadiy and I embraced—good-bye for three years, as we thought then.

I could not remain at the Levins', because Hrytsenko's taunting behavior toward me during the search made me seem responsible for Arkadiy's arrest. Everyone realized that this was not so, but I could not look Arkadiy's family in the eyes. I went to stay with Vladimir Ponomaryov.[12] He, too, had been searched, and was arrested three days later.

The trial in Kharkiv led me to ponder the reasons for the degeneration of revolutions, with the Christian, French, and October revolutions as examples. All three degenerations had something in common, and it was obvious that ideology was not the cause. In all three instances degeneration set in when the administrative structure, the "servants of the people," seized power, appeased the enemy, and invoked terror against dissidents. The three revolutions also have in common paganization, nationalization, and the mythologizing of ideology. (Both Christ's ethics and Marx's science were turned into mythology.) When I read several books on the Inquisition, I discovered so many parallels with Soviet history that I realized they could not be accidental.

But there was little time for analysis. On December 21 *Pravda* published a cautious article about Stalin: he had accomplished great things, but he had also made mistakes. To some extent this article represented a victory for those who had opposed Stalin's rehabilitation. Some people in high positions had wanted a total rehabilitation.

On December 22 Alexander Kalinovsky arrived in Kharkiv for Altunyan's appeal trial. We were not allowed to enter the courtroom: the proceedings would be held *in camera*. Sasha and I sat outside, listening to attorneys discuss their cases. A fat attorney came out of the courtroom glowing with victory. His client had raped a girl. The prosecutor had demanded eight years, but the attorney had succeeded in reducing the sentence to six. Then he showed that mistakes had been made during the investigation and got a second trial, at which he proved that the girl had not suffered a physical trauma ("Everything healed, and the judge was reprimanded on my advice") and got the court to take off another two years. Now, at the appeal trial, the attorney was arguing that there had been almost no violence and that the victim was confused in her testimony. The new sentence was two years. "Now I'll go higher and prove that she's happy to have been made a woman, and I'll even get my client a medal." All the other attorneys burst into laughter.

Finally Ariya came out. He had managed to have the reference to the particular danger of Altunyan's crime deleted from the verdict, but the sentence remained the same.

Back in Kiev, Bakhtiarov's trial began on February 24, 1970. I already knew who had given what testimony. One witness was a classmate of Oleg's with an inclination toward risky ventures. The militia caught him on something and pressured him to become an informer in homosexual circles. Eventually he was recruited by the KGB and testified for the prosecution at my trial, although I had last seen him ten years before. The other witness against Oleg was also a classmate, a psychologically confused young man who had become a Tolstoyan. The KGB wanted to prove that Oleg had made him religious. He was caught with a great deal of *samizdat*, including two books by Djilas, an excerpt from Avtorkhanov, Berdyayev's *The Origin of Russian Communism*, and Svetlanin's *The Far Eastern Conspiracy*.*

I managed to get into the courtroom, but a KGB man led me out, saying, "There are no seats." A woman friend of Oleg's pointed to an empty one. "You have no right!" the KGB man barked at her.

Oleg adopted a purely defensive position, but he maintained it brilliantly. He explained the confiscated books by saying that he thought it necessary to know everything from primary sources, for we couldn't defend the official ideology if we didn't know our enemy. Oleg had conducted political-information sessions for his classmates. The Komsomol organizer of the class testified that Oleg's speeches about current events were brilliant and never deviated from the official line.

"Then you're saying that you can't conduct political-information sessions without Bakhtiarov?" the prosecutor asked angrily.

"Not as well," the Komsomol organizer artlessly replied.

The most difficult question facing Oleg was about a program in his handwriting that a witness from Siberia had passed to the KGB. It included a paragraph about banning the Communist Party of the Soviet Union in the society of the future. Oleg explained that he had copied the program from a book and sent it to the Siberian, who was an intelligent party member, for a sound criticism.

* Svetlanin's *The Far Eastern Conspiracy* describes his participation in a conspiracy plotted by Vasiliy Blyukher, the legendary Civil War hero. Even without knowing the materials of the Twentieth and Twenty-second Party Congresses, one can see that the book was forged. Svetlanin's Blyukher speaks like a White officer. I had advised Oleg not to conceal the book. The KGB would be afraid to speak in public about its own forgery. What was my surprise when soon after I read in the émigré journal *Grani* [*Facets*, published by the NTS (Popular Labor Alliance) in Frankfurt] an article boasting about how widely NTS literature is distributed in the Soviet Union: a book by a former *Grani* editor had been confiscated from Bakhtiarov in Kiev. A stupid forgery, which could only help the KGB, was passed off as an accomplishment. When a man has been imprisoned for possessing its forgery, the NTS boasts about how active it is. I also read the NTS program, which is intended for idiots with rose-colored glasses. It was given to me by Krasin, who laughed at it but then became an NTS follower and betrayed his friends.

Friends told me that the witnesses had testified against me as well during the investigation, and that Oleg had been told, "Your boss Plyushch is in a hospital now." Hence he was very surprised to see me in court.

The witnesses unanimously praised Oleg. Even those who had testified against him during the investigation were ashamed to repeat their testimony when they were face to face with him. Oleg was also fortunate in his choice of a defense counsel. The attorney successfully demanded that the charge of propaganda be changed to slander. Oleg was sentenced to three years.

After the trial I hurried to Moscow again for *samizdat*. Grigorenko's prison notes had become available.[13] I was shaken by his account of beatings and the jailers' cynical statements that they wanted him to die. I was also finally able to read Roy Medvedev's *Let History Judge*.[14] Medvedev had assembled an enormous amount of material about Stalinism, but his desire to be objective and his deliberate refusal to take a position resulted in a Khrushchevian lack of objectivity. Unlike Khrushchev, Medvedev thinks honestly, but he does not think bravely. One senses in his book a desire not to see more profound reasons for Stalinism than the isolation of the country or the disruption of productive forces by the war. I concluded that Medvedev was yet another non-Marxist who considered himself a Marxist. After all, Marxists must be fearless in their analyses. If Medvedev had softened his analysis for fear of the KGB, that would be a different matter, but he was fearless in his actions and apparently thought this way sincerely. That is, he did not think things through to the end.

In the name of a group of Communists I wrote a letter to *Unità*, with copies to *Humanité, The Morning Star,* Cardinal Koenig, Louis Aragon, Bertrand Russell, Jean-Paul Sartre, Heinrich Böll, Dr. Spock, and Mrs. Martin Luther King. The letter rebuked Western Communists for not being sufficiently critical of the CPSU, described the situation in the country, and appealed to Communists to develop a scientific theory of contemporary society. I do not know whether the letter reached the West, but we would not have received an answer even if it had.[15] Our sad experiences had killed any hope that Western Communists had changed.

In Kiev the regime's campaign against Ivan Dzyuba was being intensified. *Literaturna Ukrayina* published an article by Dzyuba stigmatizing the bourgeois nationalism of Ukrainian émigrés. Tanya and I went to see him. He explained that he had been shown many articles in the émigré press in which he was highly praised and his

Marxism was interpreted as a convenient mask for Ukrainian nationalism and even fascism. We discussed the term "nationalist," which Ivan abhorred. I pointed out that the term is applied by the KGB to everyone who loves his native land instead of Russia. Hence Ivan's terminological confusion had become a political mistake. As he agreed with this criticism of his article, I advised him to clarify his position by speaking out against specific Ukrainian fascists, rather than abstract enemies, and to do so not in *Literaturna Ukrayina*, which would twist things around, but in *samizdat*. Finally I advised him to emphasize his positive position on the national question by restating the major theses of *Internationalism or Russification?* He agreed.

Ivan and I decided to publish an anthology entitled *Babyn Yar*, bringing together material about party anti-Semitism and also pre-revolutionary anti-Semitism. The introductory section was to present a number of historical events tying in with the ravine: human sacrifices in pagan times; the battles between Kiev and Chernihiv; the battle of the legendary hero Kozhemyaka with the dragon (Dragon Ravine is in the vicinity); and the Beilis case (the body of the boy whom Beilis was accused of murdering was found near the ravine [16]). I turned to friends who were applying to emigrate to Israel. "Anti-Semitism is your illness, and it is your duty to treat it," they replied and refused to help gather material. The project never got off the ground.

In March 1970 I flew to Kharkiv again: Vladislav Nedobora and Vladimir Ponomaryov were to be tried on the tenth. I had already passed information about Altunyan's arrest to the *Ukrainian Herald* and now needed new information for the *Chronicle* and *Herald*.[17] More importantly, the people in Kharkiv had become very dear to me. They had already worked out their own tactics in answering questions, and I would be of little use to them, but I had to go to the trial. It is extremely difficult to be an observer at such trials, and the thought that I myself would inevitably be taken away did not make it any easier. Nonetheless, I had to be with my friends. Three years later Altunyan came to my trial, after having served his own sentence. Tanya told me later how she cried when she learned that he might not come because he had just got out of the labor camp and had trouble with a job. Nevertheless he came and faced an empty courtroom and crude KGB threats that he would be arrested again.

When I appeared at the courthouse, one of Altunyan's relatives glared at me angrily. "He's come here only to create publicity for the trial. Now they'll be given stiff sentences."

Nedobora's mother told me about her conversations with Hrytsenko. He had said that her son was a good person but was friendly with Plyushch, an especially dangerous anti-Soviet. In that case, she countered, the KGB was guilty of imprisoning good people, but leaving "especially dangerous" criminals to serve as bait for catching good people. When asked why I had come to Kharkiv, she replied that she had invited me to her son's trial.

Nedobora himself had been traumatized by being held for three days and then released, after which Ponomaryov and Levin were arrested. He was extremely upset by the arrest of his friends and the suspicion this aroused against him. He thought that I despised him for being too soft with Hrytsenko, for being liberal, or for God knows what else, and he found it difficult to look the wives and children of his imprisoned friends in the eyes.

Creating suspicion and dissension was a standard KGB tactic. Many people in Kiev received letters supposedly written by friends in the labor camps. "We have endured all the pain and degradation that a labor camp imposes," the letters would begin, "but we are disturbed by something else. People on the outside seem to have forgotten the common cause, are exploiting our situation and actually profiting from our woe." This was followed by various personal attacks: Chornovil and Svitlychny were supposedly pocketing money collected to help the families of political prisoners; most despicably, they held back funds destined to assist Valentyn Moroz. But the KGB's "donkey ears," as Zinaida Grigorenko liked to say, showed up in the pseudo-Ukrainian emotionalism, the Russian turns of speech, the grammatical mistakes, and the Ukrainian typewriter for letters supposedly mailed from Mordovia. The letters were obviously being written by a KGB specialist in Ukrainian *samizdat* and letters from the labor camps. Yet even if a good Ukrainian writer were assigned to help the KGB, he, too, would show his donkey ears, because KGB *samizdat* is unmistakable.

I spent two days sitting in the corridor outside the courtroom. The first day Veronica Kalinovsky took pity on me and kept me company. The militiaman who had shooed me out of the courtroom came up and insisted that there was no point in our being here. When I told him rather rudely to go away, Veronica disapproved. "He wanted to understand us," she insisted, "to figure out why we're sitting around here."

I was choked by mixed feelings of respect and anger at her Myshkin-like goodness. "All right, when we come to power," I said, "we'll appoint you Minister of Justice. You can save the KGB men and torturers from the people's wrath."

I discovered that Veronica's compassion was even stronger for animals than for militiamen. I also like animals, and by talking about dormice, gophers, and marmots, we were able to forget the realm of absurd terrorism in which we had found ourselves.

Lebedev, the prosecutor at the trial, was senile and thought of the trial as a continuation of the good old days of the 1930's. He would make brilliant slips of the tongue. "Accused Ponomaryov, when did you last see Kirov?" [18] He meant Pyotr Yakir, of course, but he was confused by the syllable "kir" in both names and by the fact that Stalin had murdered both Kirov and Yakir.

Bored by Lebedev's stupid speeches, Monakhov, the defense counsel, read Saltykov-Shchedrin's *History of a Town*.[19] He had no need to divide his attention: the book beautifully described what he saw before him, and the judge's and prosecutor's remarks were extensions of passages that he read. Monakhov demonstrated to the entire courtroom the parallelism between Lebedev's speeches and the words in the book, and his enjoyment of it.

Nedobora and Ponomaryov kept calm; they knew what to expect. Their innate respect for words caused them pain, however, when they had to admit to a mistake in a public letter. Instead of "a policy of concealed chauvinism" they had written "a policy of unconcealed chauvinism"; the prosecutor used their admission as a confession of slander.

I managed to see Vladik and Volodya only twice, when they were led out to the toilet. I raised a clenched fist. Vladik responded in kind. Our fists established a link between us and prerevolutionary generations. They were fists not of revenge, but of unity and succession. In his final speech Nedobora quoted Chaadayev's words about true love for one's native land having open eyes.[20] Nedobora and Ponomaryov had been sentenced by enemies of the people, men who tortured their country and insisted that anyone who disagreed with them was a slanderer.

After the verdict was handed down, late in the evening of March 11, we left the building by a back entrance. Hrytsenko pompously strode past us. "Gestapo man!" one of the wives shouted after him. "When they come to hang you, I'll put the noose around your neck myself!"

We all calmed her down. "You'll need the rope in the household. He'll croak by himself."

I stayed with Sophia Nedobora for several days. She confided to me that she had deliberately got pregnant so that she wouldn't be fired from her job. The conscious decision concealed an even more important unconscious wish to keep part of Vladik with her. I know another woman who did the same thing. How much horror there is in that country, and how much innocent goodness and love among the victims of the regime! As if Leviathan would take pity on their children and would obey its own laws protecting mothers.

Who took pity on Nadya Svitlychny when her infant son was seized from her family? She was arrested, and her child was concealed in an orphanage, to be returned to the family only after resolute protests. Even then the child was given to an elderly grandmother in a village far from the city. A child of two had been forbidden to live in Kiev! Who took pity on the young daughter of Ihor and Iryna Kalynets when they were arrested merely for being gifted poets and writing about the sufferings of Ukraine? Listening to Sophia, I remembered the slogan of proletarian humanism invented by the professional humanist Maxim Gorky in the 1930's: "If the enemy does not give in, he is destroyed." [21]

Before we had recovered from the trial, Tamara Levin was fired from her job for her bravery at the trial and her defense of Solzhenitsyn at a public meeting. The Levins' friend Roman Kaplan came to the trial. He was not allowed to enter and left without argument. Nevertheless, he was asked to submit a "voluntary resignation" from his job. Other friends were molested by the KGB simply because they remained friends of the Levins.

Breaking up a single group of *samizdatchiks* and holding three trials had two purposes: to traumatize everyone, and to prove to the top brass that the Kharkiv KGB was not idle and had come up with three political cases in half a year. There may also have been the calculation that both witnesses and defendants would behave less courageously at future trials. The decision had the opposite effect, however: people lost whatever naïve faith in legality they may have had and became firmer.

All these events ran parallel to celebrations of Lenin's hundredth birthday. Afraid to revive the Stalin cult, the authorities reverted to Lenin. His face stared at us from every newspaper and magazine. He was shown waving to the people, pointing a hand toward the glorious future, or studying a map. No matter how one may have respected him, one felt disgust for his face and his speeches. The fact that he was being exalted by a police government inevitably linked him with its lies and terror. One night in Moscow a huge head of

Lenin was suspended over the city from a dirigible and illuminated with searchlights: the epiphany of Lenin, a resurrection from the dead, an ascension. People responded to this atheistic parody of the Gospel with a series of Lenin jokes mocking his speeches, his baldness, his guttural pronunciation, and the solemn stories about him as child and man. The anecdotes were so widespread that even KGB men retold them.

Pravda published a set of theses on Lenin's birthday. A theory by Otto Bauer which actually had been ridiculed by Lenin was attributed to him.[22] Radio Peking hastened to inform Soviet citizens about the mistake. Everyone roared with laughter at the way the Central Committee had parodied itself. The Central Committee could think of nothing better than publishing a brochure that threw out the reference to Bauer but still ascribed his conclusions to Lenin. No psychoanalysis is necessary here to understand the inner meaning of the Central Committee's "Leninism."

The mistakes Prosecutor Lebedev made at Arkadiy Levin's trial on April 24 were even funnier. The hullabaloo of the Lenin festivities had not died down yet, and the trial clearly demonstrated what the authorities understood by "Lenin": a wild outburst of lawlessness, terror, and lies. Levin was charged with writing a letter to the public and an appeal to the United Nations. When Tamara was not permitted to attend the trial, Arkadiy refused to participate in it. Monakhov demanded that Arkadiy be released for lack of a *corpus delicti*. I had asked Monakhov before the trial to pay attention to anecdotes, but I was astounded when he told me that the prosecutor had referred to Levin as "the accused, Lenin," several times. Everyone laughed at this slip of the tongue, and the judge turned red with anger, but she was so hypnotized by the mistake that she made it herself. The slip expressed the other aspect of the official attitude toward Lenin: he was a revolutionary, a rebel, and a kike bastard. (The prosecutor knew that Levin was a Marxist.) The regime had absolutely no use for this Lenin and would gladly wipe him from people's minds. Stalin or Brezhnev would be much more convenient.

The KGB men retaliated for our laughter by guffawing, making rude remarks, whistling, and interrupting Monakhov: "Who needs you?" Arkadiy refused to make a final plea, declining, as he said, to be involved in this farce.

The prosecution's chief argument in all three trials was that the defendants were guilty of slander because, being educated men, they must have known that they were writing and signing slanderous statements.

Despite the alarming rumors that the KGB spread in the city, many people sent their regards to the defendants, and some even contributed money to the support of their families. After the trials some friends of the defendants kept their distance, but new sympathizers appeared in their stead. Even some of the people who had been delegated by the authorities to attend as "representatives of the public" understood the illegality and privately supported the defendants. As I left Kharkiv, I thought about Arkadiy's parting remark to me: "Thank God, I shall finally be able to get enough sleep in the camp."

16

CIRCLES TRAVELED
BEFORE

Early in 1970 three essays by Valentyn Moroz reached Kiev almost simultaneously. In "Moses and Dathan" Moroz rebuked the Byelorussian poetess Jeŭdakija Łoś for betraying Byelorussia by treating its culture as secondary and fawning before everything Russian. In "A Chronicle of Resistance" he attacked the Soviet policy of obliterating Ukrainian cultural monuments and institutions, which led to "deculturization, alienation, dehumanization, and loss of roots." "In the Midst of the Snows" criticized Dzyuba for taking a first step toward appeasing the authorities by publishing an article in *Literaturna Ukrayina*. The emotional power of Moroz's essays and the logic of his facts and analyses, all expressed in brilliant style, had such an impact that even those who were fervent supporters of Dzyuba had to agree with him that no compromises with the authorities were possible.

My friends and I discussed at length Moroz's thesis that Ukraine needed "martyrs" and "apostles." I argued that Moroz was too harsh in his criticism of Dzyuba. Actually, the mistake Dzyuba had made would help dissipate the Dzyuba cult. I had been sickened when I was shown a photograph of Dzyuba, his wife, and his daughter with a reverence appropriate to the Holy Family. Many of Dzyuba's followers lay in hiding, surreptitiously worshiping their apostle. Ukraine needs masses of citizens capable of independent thinking, but hero worship will only produce flocks of sheep. Martyrs are useless: the authorities create them by the thousands.

One evening toward the end of May, several friends were assembled at my apartment when someone knocked at the door. It was Moroz. He did not look like the man I had seen in Lviv. He was calm and concentrated, he had gained weight, his gestures were less awkward, and his air of alienation had disappeared. He threw himself completely into the subjects we discussed—the persecution of the Ukrainian Catholic Church, the plundering of the national cultural heritage, and the ban on selling decorated Easter eggs. When he told us about the searches and surveillance he was being subjected to, it became clear that he would be arrested any day.

One of the people present was a girl who had heard only rumors about the patriotic movement and hence was even afraid of the word "nationalist." No matter how I argued to the contrary, she identified the national movement with Russophobia. Yet Moroz, a passionate patriot, enchanted her like everyone else. The immense strength of his spirit is manifested in his gestures, his facial expressions, and his voice. At one time such people were described as "magnetic." Even when you disagree with Valentyn, you are charmed by his personality.

We discussed the problems of the movement. When I defended Dzyuba, Valentyn, although speaking of him with great respect, argued that his article undermined his authority and gave such people as Ivan Drach a justification for their appeasement of the authorities.[1] Dzyuba himself had once accused Drach of appeasement. People like Drach, Pavlychko, and Yevtushenko go by the rule "Ninety percent of my poetry for the KGB and ten percent for the people." But the people won't need even that ten percent. One of these poets had said to me, "I apply the carrot and the stick to the Soviet authorities." In reality, it is the authorities who do the applying. Such poets are allowed to write liberal poems to demonstrate to the West that creative freedom exists. When they exceed the limits of permitted liberalism, they are whipped with the stick and made to return to the path of virtue. Each year the limits on thought become more restricted.

When Czechoslovakia was invaded, Yevtushenko in a burst of sincerity sent a protest to the Central Committee, but he regretted his rashness the very next day. A Western correspondent having asked him, "Is it true that you sent a letter to the Central Committee?" Yevtushenko replied, "No, I did not send a letter!" He was thrilled by his clever reply—he had sent a telegram—and boasted about it to everyone who would listen.

We all accompanied Valentyn to the subway. KGB men followed us, making no attempt to conceal themselves. Valentyn only smiled, although it was obvious that he did not want to be arrested. We walked in silence, aware that the KGB would not let this remarkable man out of its hands; it would not forgive him his fearlessness. We parted in silence as well. "Good-bye" would have sounded false, and we could not bring ourselves to wish him fortitude during his next sentence. Several days later, on June 1, Valentyn Moroz was arrested again, after exactly nine months of freedom.

In May Vladimir Borisov, the organizer of the Union of Independent Youth in the town of Vladimir, committed suicide at Butyrki Prison.[2] The Union had applied for registration to the municipal authorities, in accordance with Article 126 of the Constitution: "The basic aim of the Union of Independent Youth is to assist in the development of socialist democracy and social progress in our country with all the means at its disposal."

I had spent a night with Borisov at Pyotr Yakir's apartment, during which he had told us about his goal of winning legal recognition for the Union. His approach was similar to Grigorenko's—demanding at every step that the promises in the Constitution be kept, explaining to the population, particularly young people, that certain rights exist, and insisting that these rights be used and not simply serve as a smoke screen.

Borisov was ordered to a psychiatric hospital. Later, when I was in prison, I experienced fear of psychiatric hospitals, and I know the moments of despair that can lead to suicide. Psychiatrists and KGB men welcome such a solution: it proves that their prisoners are disturbed and have suicidal tendencies.

In May 1970 Julius Telesin, a mathematician who had been illegally fired from the Central Institute of Mathematical Economics, emigrated to Israel.[3] I had met him at Yakir's. Julius made good use of his knowledge of the law in his battles with the KGB. His friend Professor Boris Tsukerman published in *samizdat* a series of letters he had written to various government bodies.[4] Julius called them "juridical symphonies." Tsukerman pointed out the absence of legality in all spheres of life. He would note a particular violation of the law and write a complaint about it to a government body. He would either not receive a reply or one that demonstrated ignorance of the law. Tsukerman would then write to the next-higher body, explaining the illegality of the lower body's reply. He would proceed in this manner until he reached Roman Rudenko, the Prosecutor General of the Soviet Union.

Thus Tsukerman demonstrated the total illegality both horizontally (in all spheres of the law) and vertically (on all levels of government). His symphonies became legendary. Despite my dislike of the crude language of Soviet laws, I derived great pleasure from this new form of satire against the system. Tsukerman had a particularly splendid overture about an article in *Izvestia* that harshly attacked

Dubček's Foreign Minister, "Jiří Hájek Knocks About the World."[5] Citing a law that prohibits propaganda and slander against fraternal socialist countries, Tsukerman drew Rudenko's attention to *Izvestia*'s heinous violation of this law.

The KGB loathed Tsukerman and Telesin because of their insistence on legality, their meticulousness, and their concern for form. In December 1970 the KGB confiscated seventy books and *samizdat* documents from Julius. He responded with satirical complaints. When the KGB tried to pump information from him, he demanded that the investigators be punished for breaking the law. Because of the illegal way in which the search had been conducted, the documents that were of interest to the KGB could not be used as material evidence. Telesin was told bluntly to choose between prison and Israel. Naturally he chose Israel.

The almost daily reports of searches, arrests, and stepped-up psychiatric terror were so oppressive that Tanya and I decided to visit my mother and sister in Odessa for a rest. There we met Nina Strokata-Karavansky. Her husband, Svyatoslav Karavansky, had been sentenced in 1945 to twenty-five years for belonging to the Organization of Ukrainian Nationalists. In 1960, after a law was passed making fifteen years the maximum term in prison, Karavansky was amnestied. He settled in Odessa, married Nina, and set about working as a journalist, critic, and translator. In 1965, however, he was rearrested and sentenced without trial to complete his term because he had written essays criticizing language policies in Ukraine and had appealed to Polish and Czechoslovak party leaders on behalf of Ukrainian political prisoners. In the labor camps Karavansky continued to write trenchant letters and petitions about the illegality of his arrest, the lack of political and civil rights, Russification, discrimination against Jews, and the wholesale deportation of Lithuanians, Latvians, and Estonians to Siberia. In retaliation he was transferred to Vladimir Prison in 1967. There he supposedly tried to smuggle out more petitions, for which he was charged with "anti-Soviet agitation and propaganda." In April 1970 Karavansky was tried again and given a new sentence of five years in prison and three in a labor camp.

Tanya and I visited Nina at the height of events: the prison court had just ruled that she had smuggled out invisible writings by her husband. The case was very mysterious. There were many manuscripts, but how had Svyatoslav been able to write them when he was under constant surveillance in prison? And where had he obtained chemicals for invisible writing? No handwriting analysis had been performed. The defense counsel argued that no crime had been committed, but Svyatoslav was found guilty and Nina was being threatened with a trial. The local newspaper published an article about her connections with a spy, and a meeting was called at the medical institute where she worked to discuss her behavior.

One day Nina informed me that a cholera epidemic had broken out in several Black Sea ports. Being a bacteriologist, she was astounded that the infected towns had not been put in quarantine. Certain that cholera would appear in Odessa, Nina forgot about her own troubles and worried only about the danger of a country-wide epidemic and the prophylactic measures that we should take. Several days later she told me that the city would be closed on a certain date. My mother, who was working at a sanatorium, said that the doctors had advised the patients to leave Odessa as quickly as possible. Nina was indignant at the city authorities who were ignoring the danger and thought only about having to feed and board nonresidents. "They never think about other people, only about themselves," she commented angrily as she worked out plans to fight the epidemic.

Zampira Asanova, who was visiting with us, rushed to the railway station. People were waiting in long lines to buy tickets. Similar queues had formed at the airport and the bus terminal. We got in line for bus tickets. Zampira was afraid to stay in Odessa: the KGB might take the opportunity to arrange a provocation against her. Seeing that she wasn't going to get a ticket by standing in line, Zampira disappeared, then returned ten minutes later with a bus ticket. "Oh, you intellectuals! I gave the cleaning woman three rubles, and she got me a ticket." Zampira was an intellectual herself, but her frequent encounters with the militia and the KGB had helped her overcome her disdain for bribery.

Moroz's wife and son were trapped in Odessa by the epidemic. When I met Raisa, she was disturbed that she would be cut off from news about Valentyn. I asked her permission to reply to Valentyn's charges against Dzyuba. Such a discussion would emphasize that, though in prison, he was still with us and that his ideas were alive in the resistance movement. (It was Valentyn who had given this name to the Ukrainian movement.) Although Raisa consented, Ivan Svitlychny later persuaded me not to start a polemic. A pity. Time showed that Valentyn had accurately predicted Dzyuba's fall. Valentyn's followers introduced a fanaticism and hysteria that he himself does not possess. One student, for example, went to Dzyuba to slap him in the face for being a traitor.

After Odessa was cordoned off a quarantine was declared at the sanatoriums, and notices about "gastrointestinal diseases" were posted. Even here fear of the truth overcame medical concerns. The newspapers and the television discussed dysentery and typhoid fever but made almost no mention of cholera. In the absence of reliable information, the populace spread wild rumors. A neighbor asked me if I knew where the cholera had come from. I said that I didn't. "The Yids are spreading it!" she exclaimed. Another neighbor, a retired army colonel, had his own theory: "The Americans are sending over planes and dropping germs." Despite their traditional anti-Semitism, fishermen and sailors blamed the Arabs: "We gave them all the food and arms they wanted, and they've repaid us with cholera." Political experts said that all blacks, slant-eyes, and Arabs should be prohibited from entering the Soviet Union because they're dirty, crude, and ungrateful.

The city was obviously not prepared for emergencies, and calcium hypochlorite was in short supply. For a time sanitary conditions in the city deteriorated instead of improving. Television reports showed people who had been caught selling calcium hypochlorite on the black market. We were not allowed to leave the sanatorium where we were staying, but there was no food, so we had no choice but to go into the city. Guards were posted at the gates, but everyone slipped through holes in the wall.

Swimming in the Black Sea was prohibited, but no reason was given. The doctors had circulated a rumor that cholera germs had been found in the sea water. I did not believe this and allowed my son to go swimming, but Nina Karavansky later confirmed that germs had been discovered near the sites where waste was dumped into the water. Deaths occurred. A hospital was set up in a boarding school for everyone who came down with diarrhea. My sister was mobilized to work there as a nurse. I visited her, despite the ban on leaving the sanatorium.

Ada related that the public reports of deaths were first exaggerated and then understated. The police were called in to stop unhygienic practices, and several restaurant managers were taken to court for violations. Roadblocks kept people from leaving the city. A collective-farm chairman was shot when he tried to break through to his village. The buses that had left the city before it was closed were stopped on the road. Conditions there were very bad: no food or water, no place to sleep, and intense heat. People said that if we were so unprepared and war broke out, everyone would die for lack of supplies. Police measures could be partly successful in limiting an epidemic but could not solve the problem of food and water supplies.

228

Visiting friends wasn't worth the effort, because the guards punished everyone they caught off limits. I plunged into my writing, returning to an essay about the psychology of fascism and Stalinism entitled "The Heirs of Stalin" and to an article inspired by the research of the Georgian psychologist Dmitriy Uznadze and entitled "Moral Orientation." [6] Uznadze provided me with a scientific basis for my conclusion that "Love thy neighbor" has a profound psychological significance. The essay dealt with orientation in personal and social life, "diabolism" in mass movements, and ethics in politics.

Tanya was working at this time on a long article about games. The Department of Games and Toys, in which she worked, approved new games for production and developed a methodology for their use in schools. Tanya had been assigned to write a report on sensory education, and she took numerous books on preschool psychology and education with her to Odessa. The subject absorbed her, and she plunged into Professor Venger's research on sensory development in children. Because she was pressed for time, I came to her aid. I had some experience with games, having written free-lance reviews of games for her department under an assumed name. In reading the relevant sources, I saw that most of them were either compilations of fine-sounding phrases or narrow methodological instructions that lacked a scientific basis and had to be taken on faith. Some of them contradicted common sense and what I knew about psychology. Tanya and I decided to think up, on the basis of Venger's research, a system of games that would develop a child's perception. We were greatly helped in our work by the writings of Freud, Vygotsky, and Elkin.[7] My interest in the psychology of games led Academician Snezhnevsky to conclude, in his psychiatric report on me in 1972, that I had a "mania of inventiveness in the field of psychology."

The epidemic raged on as we worked. The militia finally succeeded in establishing order—detachments had been brought in all the way from Kiev—and it was impossible to leave the sanatorium until the quarantine was called off. We called this our Boldino summer, a joking reference to the time in 1830 when Pushkin was confined by a cholera epidemic to his family estate, Boldino, for several months; during this period he wrote some of his best poetry.

Back in Kiev Tanya was immediately drawn into the squabbles at work. She had begun to have trouble shortly before our trip to Odessa. The woman director of Tanya's department was not familiar with preschool education (she had got the job because she was the sister of an important party official), and she mistreated her subordinates, behaved dishonestly, promoted worthless games, and ordered unnecessary projects. Things worsened when she hired as her deputy a man who lacked the requisite qualifications and proved to be an adventurist and a criminal. He introduced threats and surveillance and thought up useless tasks for the employees, including the preparation of a huge map of Ukraine to show the locations of toy and game factories, on which much time and money were wasted. When the employees raised objections with the director and her deputy, they were reprimanded for coming to work late and given assignments to write reports on complicated questions of child psychology within a short time.

By the time we returned from Odessa, Tanya's co-workers had managed to oust the deputy director, but this only increased the director's fury. She set about getting rid of them one by one. Unexpected support for the employees came from a woman known to be a Stalinist and a schemer. She possessed a curious kind of honesty, however, and although she did not understand what the conflict was about, she did see how predatory the director was. This woman had nothing to be afraid of, because she had worked as an informer for many years. She proudly related to her younger co-workers how she had served in counterintelligence with a partisan detachment in Western Ukraine during the war. She did not have a secondary education, let alone a background in educational theory, but she was given a job in the Ministry of Education immediately after the war for her "service to the party." It was she who was assigned to report on Tanya. Once she left behind her notebook. It was opened inadvertently—all the employees were issued identical notebooks—and found to contain a list of Tanya's visitors, with the hour and minute of their arrival and departure.

Tanya and I roared with laughter when the woman informer would call me, as someone knowledgeable in politics, to seek advice for dealing with the director. The director had the upper hand (a brother in the Central Committee was an excellent support) until she made a serious mistake. She won a prize for a game that had already been paid for. She wanted the money for herself, but to keep her subordinates quiet she listed them as coauthors and sharers in the prize money. They asked her to cancel the application, but she was so certain that no one would refuse money that she submitted an invoice to the accounting department, which, however, had been alerted to the illegal deal by the woman informer. Hushing up the matter was impossible, because too many people knew about it.

Auditors were called in, and a meeting was held at which the staff explained how they had been terrorized. The director's brother pulled strings in the Central Committee to keep the matter from going to court, but the director was asked to submit an application for retirement.

In the autumn of 1970 I was called to the district Executive Committee. This meant that the authorities were planning to bring charges of parasitism against me.[8] They would offer me an unsuitable job; I would reject it and then be charged with refusing to work. I expected provocative questions about why I had lost my previous job, but when I saw the director of the Department of Employment I realized that this would be worse than the KGB. The intellectual level here was so low that arguments and discussion were impossible. My impression was confirmed by the interview the director was conducting with two girls in my presence. They were prostitutes who had previously worked in a factory. The director flirted with them and made scabrous jokes. Their answers were half contemptuous and half frightened. It was obvious that they didn't want to work but were looking for a compromise.

When the girls had left, the director said, "So you want to work? What can you do?"

"I have a degree in mathematics. I can work at a research institute or as a mathematician at a factory. I can teach mathematics. I can be an editor or a proofreader in Ukrainian or Russian. I'm even willing to work as a stoker."

"A stoker? I'll call up a boiler room."

The job proved to be at a military detachment quite some distance from the city. A woman greeted me when I arrived. "But you're lame!" she exclaimed. "This is hard work. The boiler is fired with coal, and you have to shovel it in. What's your education?" I stopped short. The woman looked at my identity card. "An engineer? Why do you want to work as a stoker?"

"It was recommended . . . by doctors. . . ."

"Hm, politics? Don't be afraid to say so. We can't take you anyway if you've got a degree."

I lost my patience. "But I was sent here by the district Executive Committee!"

"Yes, and then that idiot will scold me."

"Can't you tell him that, right now, on the telephone, so he won't bother me?" I asked.

The woman telephoned the man who had sent me out and called him an idiot. "You yourself decided that people with degrees can't be hired for manual labor!" As I was leaving, she said to me compassionately, "Did you say something you shouldn't have?" I nodded. "There you are! You have to be careful. A lot of people are ready to report you."

When I returned to the district Executive Committee, I asked the director, "Didn't you know I have a degree?"

"That's all right!" he exclaimed. "Look at the list of job vacancies."

There were several openings for stokers and two for counselors at factory dormitories for women. I knew the problem the authorities have here. Counselors are supposed to conduct discussions, supervise the morals of these young builders of Communism, and take them on outings to see plays or films. But the women are bored by such activities and quickly corrupt their counselors. I said that I could be a counselor, but the director paid no heed. One Major Hryshchuk was enough. The director asked me to come back in a week.

"Would you like to teach mathematics?" he asked when I returned. "There's an opening." He called up the district Department of Education. "All right, you can go."

At the Department of Education I discovered that the opening was for a teacher of Ukrainian. I raised a fuss and gave up on the district Executive Committee.

At this time Ivan Svitlychny was called in by the militia and ordered to account for his means of subsistence. Ivan showed translation contracts and receipts. "All right," the militia colonel said, "but I advise you to get a permanent job somewhere, even if it's only on paper." Sverstyuk was told at the Institute of Botany that he was not working in his specialty. It was clear that a campaign was being unfurled against us. Some of us would be persecuted for being employed and others for being unemployed.

In the Democratic Movement things began to escalate. We received the Medvedev brothers' *A Question of Madness*.[9] Zhores Medvedev had been thrown into a mental hospital on May 29 without benefit of a trial or an examination. Prominent geneticists and writers, including Solzhenitsyn, joined forces to fight for his release. I met a friend of Zhores who believed that Lysenko's followers were at the bottom of all this. They could not forgive Zhores his book about Lysenko and wanted to show him that the secret police can still be a powerful influence in the hands of scientists who side with the regime.[10] Zhores was finally released only because of energetic measures taken by his friends, including Sakharov, who made an appeal at a genetics conference.

The release was a preliminary to an even greater success: Solzhenitsyn was awarded the Nobel Prize. We sat glued to our radios as the case developed. When the prize was awarded to Sholokhov in 1965 we were derisive, but our attitude changed as the Soviet press now unleashed a campaign of abuse against the "reactionary" Swedish academy. At the time of the Sholokhov award, the official view commended the academy for its progressiveness, but now it was reminded of all its sins. Logically Sholokhov should have returned his prize to the Swedes, but money proved to be more important than politics for the great socialist realist.

In November 1970, the Human Rights Committee, popularly called the Sakharov Committee, was established by Andrey Sakharov, Valeriy Chalidze, and Andrey Tverdokhlebov.[11] I was in Moscow when the committee issued its first documents. All my friends ridiculed its legalism and formalism, particularly the committee's statement that it intended to "assist the organs of state authority in establishing and applying guarantees of human rights." Many of my friends were legalists, but the idea of assisting the lawless guardians of the law struck them as ridiculous. The law may be our instrument, but we should have no illusions about its application. One member of the Initiative Group commented, "Well, all right. Our physicist friends will freeze standing in the cold outside courthouses. They'll see the drunken face of the law and hear obscene interpretations of the Constitution. They'll get a few blows on the head"—which is what happened to Sakharov's wife, Yelena Bonner, at Dzhemilyov's trial in 1976—"and that will cure them of consulting the KGB about human rights."

Levitin-Krasnov voiced the general opinion of the Initiative Group when he wrote that the committee's declaration was an academic discussion by learned liberals and a step backward in the development of the Russian Democratic Movement. Nevertheless, the committee's publication of theoretical works showed that a certain benefit can be derived from strict legalism. In time the Sakharov Committee moved closer to the Democratic Movement. Unfortunately, many Muscovites adopted the committee's apolitical stance. I thought then, and still think now, that it is wrong to insist that a struggle for human rights is not political. Law is a part of the state structure. If we demand from a state that it observe its own laws, we are requiring it to change into a legal and democratic state. Such a demand is clearly political. Many members of the movement do share an aversion for the word "politics," but an unconscious political platform is inevitably weaker than one in which the politics are consciously kept in mind.

On November 17 and 18, 1970, Valentyn Moroz was brought to trial in Ivano-Frankivsk on a charge of having written four essays. Ivan Dzyuba, Borys Antonenko-Davydovych, and Vyacheslav Chornovil were called as witnesses. Like Moroz himself, they refused to testify on the ground that the trial was illegally closed to the public. The prosecution tried to exploit the fact that Moroz's essay "In the Midst of the Snows" criticized Dzyuba. But Dzyuba declared that the essay was a personal matter between him and Moroz and not anti-Soviet propaganda.

The prosecution also tried to get Sergo Paradzhanov to testify that Moroz had slandered him by accusing him of stealing an iconostasis and other historical relics from a Hutsul village. The court would then have easily generalized the slander of a person into a slander of the regime. But Paradzhanov had officially protested against the theft of the iconostasis after he borrowed it for the filming of *Shadows of Forgotten Ancestors*, and when the KGB asked him to testify, he explained that Moroz had made a mistake but had not slandered him. Such a witness would only have harmed the KGB's case by confirming that the iconostasis had been stolen by the authorities. The KGB did not forgive Paradzhanov his intractability: in 1973 he was convicted of homosexuality and sentenced to five years in labor camps.

Moroz himself was found guilty of anti-Soviet propaganda and sentenced to six years in prison, three years in special-regime labor camps (the most terrible kind), and five years in exile. Statements, protests, and poems dedicated to Moroz soon began to circulate in Ukraine.

The Moroz case had barely become known when the most terrible news of all came. I was at home one day early in December when a friend telephoned. "Alla Horska has been murdered. Come to her house. Everyone is getting together there." When I arrived, I found many people, and new ones kept arriving, some from as far as Lviv and Ivano-Frankivsk. Everyone was waiting for Alla's husband, Victor Zaretsky, to bring her body home. No one knew how or why she had been killed. The theory that she had been murdered by the KGB was born before my eyes, but I could not believe it. Alla had been a support for the patriots with her energy, strength, and common sense, and she had taken part in protests and made a vital contribution to Ukrainian culture, but this was hardly enough reason to have her murdered. Today, however, when the KGB has murdered several dissidents, my certainty that it was not involved in Alla's death has lessened.

The murder was discovered by accident. Disturbed by Alla's absence of several days, Yevhen Sverstyuk and Nadya Svitlychny went to her father-in-law's house in the town of Vasylkiv, thirty-six kilometers southwest of Kiev. When no one answered the door, Yevhen and Nadya got the militia to open it and found Alla's body in the cellar. The militia behaved stupidly, as it usually does, which gave grounds for thinking that the authorities were responsible. The militia has an obsession about pinning the blame on the first suspects it catches. These were Yevhen and Nadya, as well as Alla's husband, Victor. When Alla's father-in-law was found on railway tracks with his head cut off, the militia advanced the theory that he had killed Alla and then thrown himself under a train. Stories were spread that he had frequently quarreled with Alla and accused her of hindering his son's career with her anti-Soviet activities. The KGB had called the father-in-law in for several discussions. It often made use of mentally unbalanced people against the opposition, and Alla's father-in-law was known to have had periods of mental disturbance. Thus even if the militia's theory was correct, the KGB bore partial responsibility, all the more so since shortly after the murder a party lecturer declared in public that nationalists had held meetings at Horska's flat.

The militia deliberately withheld the body for the funeral until December 7, a Monday, hoping that few people would come that day. But the building where Alla and other artists had their studios was crowded with hundreds of people. An exhibit of Alla's paintings had been set up in her studio. Every visitor was given a sprig from a snowball tree, the symbol of free Ukraine, to wear in the lapel. The Homin Choir sang, and people studied Alla's paintings and meditated, virtually in silence.[12]

Buses arrived, and over a hundred people boarded them to go to the new graveyard at the edge of town. There we found an official funeral band waiting. A young boy was being buried in the grave next to Alla's, and the mother sobbed and tried to throw herself in the grave. The band, which had been invited by the Artists' Union, would strike up a dirge and then fall silent. The musicians were cold and bored.

235

An official from the Artists' Union delivered a eulogy. The dead woman, he said, had been educated by the Komsomol and had been devoted to its ideals. It was all an abominable lie delivered by a man who had himself hounded Alla. She had been expelled twice from the union. In 1964 she had been involved in designing a Shevchenko stained-glass window for Kiev University. The committee that reviewed the window concluded that Shevchenko appeared to be behind bars. The artists were accused of formalism and harmful ideological conceptions, and the stained glass was destroyed. In 1968 Alla was again expelled from the union for signing the "Appeal of the 139."

When the official had finished, he signaled to the band to begin playing. I remembered Alexander Galich's words about Pasternak:

> But above the coffin rise the looters
> In a ceremo-nial pa-trol! [13]

Alla's friends took turns speaking, in shaky and broken voices. The union official tried to end the ceremony, but no one paid attention to him. In his reply, Alexander Serhiyenko [14] took his cue from Ivan Dzyuba's address when he defended Vasyl Symonenko against these vile people: "Independent and proud, Alla respected people and enjoyed the love of her friends and acquaintances. But like anyone capable of love, she was also capable of hatred. She openly despised the self-satisfied bureaucrats and operators in art. They could not bear the firm, mocking gaze of her gray eyes and repaid her with an intense hatred. They hated her for the very things for which we loved her." The detectives who were standing to one side in a group shook with anger when they heard this outspoken declaration.

Yevhen Sverstyuk spoke of Alla as if she were alive. His voice and expression ruled out any thought of insincerity, artificiality, or rhetoric. He summarized her life: discovery of Ukrainian culture, participation in the Club of Creative Youth, discrimination as an artist, the Shevchenko stained-glass window, expulsion from the union, death, and the rumor that she had been posthumously reinstated in the union. Some of his reflections were of the conventional kind, but we responded to the truth in his words—that Alla would always be with us. She could not cease to be.

Ivan Hel, a metalworker who had served three years in labor camps, arrived from Lviv to discuss the mystery surrounding Alla's death and her continuing life among us.[15] He urged us to divest ourselves of everything petty, cowardly, and self-seeking.

I listened to the eulogies with mixed feelings. Alla had been so vital that it was impossible to grasp that she was gone. Just recently Tanya and I had accompanied her home from the Svitlychnys', joking about the regime's pervasive stupidity and fear. An immense party and police apparatus was afraid of a handful of people scattered throughout the Soviet Union. Lina Kostenko had thrown flowers to the defendants at the trials in 1966, and the militiamen had dropped to the floor as if they had seen a bomb. Terrorist acts were extremely rare, yet the comrades from the Central Committee came with bodyguards even to meetings with schoolchildren, and KGB agents carefully checked everyone out to make sure there were no "signatories" present. I had told Alla a great deal about Petro Grigorenko. She read his articles and, sensing an affinity, very much wanted to meet him. Both of them will always be associated in my mind with freedom, democracy, energy, and laughter.

But when these memories and feelings receded and I saw the mourners again, a sense of irreplaceable loss overwhelmed me. Friends were departing forever, some claimed by death, others by betrayal. And then there were the union official and the spies, their faces blue with cold and anger. They, too, were wearing sprigs of snowball flowers in their lapels. I had seen some of these spies at the Ukrainian patriots' trial in 1966 and at Oleg Bakhtiarov's trial in 1968. Choking with hatred, I hissed at one of them, "And what are KGB men doing here?" Frightened, he stammered that I had confused him with someone else.

At the very end Vasyl Stus read his poem, "In Memory of Alla Horska."

> Flame fire, soul, flame fire instead of wails.
> When a black chill shrouds our sun,
> Seek the snowball's scarlet shadow,
> Seek its shadow in black-watered vales.
> For we are few, a tiny handful
> Fit for hopes and prayers.[16]

After the funeral Alexander Serhiyenko was fired from his job. Ivan Hel was given a reprimand, and the prosecutor threatened to bring charges against him for spreading rumors that Alla had been murdered because of her convictions. Liberals who cowered in their burrows and gossiped about dissidents and the regime spread rumors that Alla had been murdered by Ukrainian nationalists for revealing their secrets to the KGB. Other people claimed that the case involved a sexual drama. Some of those who had voted to expel Alla from the union in 1968 hinted that she was Jewish and not Ukrainian. As if such a suspicion would have insulted her! She never paid attention to nationality and only distinguished fools from intelligent people, scoundrels from honest people, and those who tortured Ukraine from those who loved her.

The eulogies delivered at Alla's funeral were widely distributed in *samizdat*, as was the material on Moroz's trial.[17] By placing Moroz on trial the KGB demonstrated that he had been correct in his polemic with Dzyuba. The severity of Moroz's sentence showed that a new stage of repression had been reached, but the political wing of the Ukrainian movement was only strengthened by this. As people read about the trial and the murder, cowards were winnowed away and the number of oppositionists increased.

Angela Davis was being tried in the United States at this time, and Soviet newspapers choked with indignation. The *Ukrainian Herald* compared the "humanism" of Moroz's judges with the unprecedented "cruelty" of Davis's judges. She wrote letters from prison criticizing the system, and she gave interviews. Fantastic! Could one imagine a correspondent coming to see Moroz not to slander him but to inquire about his condition and his views? How touching were the reports that Angela's access to her attorney was limited and—this made our hair stand on end—that she was given cold coffee!

At the same time that Valentyn Moroz was being sentenced to fourteen years' imprisonment for nothing more than expressing his views in several essays, the Presidium of the Supreme Soviet pardoned Yemelyanov, a former Minister of Internal Affairs in Azerbaidzhan who had been convicted of cruelty in 1953. A sadistic KGB colonel named Monakhov lived unmolested near Leningrad. In the camps on the Solovetsky Islands he had commanded an extermination brigade that had used staves with lead ferrules to murder several hundred Comintern members. Monakhov was not even expelled from the party, because Tolstikov, the secretary of the Leningrad party committee, would not permit it. Western Communists visit Leningrad, shake hands with Tolstikov as if nothing had happened, and smile at this man who supports the murderer of their party comrades.

Toward the end of 1970 I went to Moscow again to pass on news about events in Ukraine and to obtain *samizdat*, as well as fascist literature (i.e., extreme right-wing *samizdat*, which also exists) for my essay "The Heirs of Stalin." My friends were heatedly discussing an article by the pseudonymous A. Mikhaylov, "Thoughts on the Liberal Campaign of 1968," which criticized the liberal opposition, including the Initiative Group, from a position of social-democratic Marxism.[18] Mikhaylov's observations were couched in a condescending and dogmatic tone. He did not appreciate the political significance of legalism and moralism at the present stage of the movement, and he showed a marked predilection for underground activity. These mistakes kept many people whose views were close to Mikhaylov's from grasping his valid points. People particularly resented his assertion that the demonstration in Red Square on August 25, 1968, had been frenzied and hysterical. To be insensitive to the significance of moral outrage means standing on a position of shallow rationalism and pragmatism.

Mikhaylov's lack of understanding weakened the impact of his thesis that many members of the Democratic Movement romanticize its social roots. These lie in the discrepancy between the productive potential and the bureaucratic system of management and distribution, and in the conflicts of interest between scientists and intellectuals on the one hand and specialists and bureaucrats on the other. In the presentation of the Democratic Movement as a purely moral protest devoid of class origins, its true origins are glossed over. Mikhaylov quite rightly pointed out that the struggle for general rights—freedom of speech and thought, for example—is based on a narrow class position, because it ignores demands for worker self-management and the right to strike and does not concern itself with the proper management of the economy, the army, and the culture of the country. Intellectuals cannot do without freedom of speech, press, and organizations. The country as a whole also needs these freedoms, but the intellectuals manifest their class blindness when they ignore other freedoms.

Because all my friends were outraged by Mikhaylov's criticism, I spoke up for him. If we put aside his snobbery as a Marxist theoretician and his inability to think concretely, we would see the rational points in his article. Why did we not publish information about strikes? Why did we not try to establish links with the rebels in Novocherkassk, Pryluka, and other cities? I myself had sent the *Chronicle* three reports about workers' demonstrations in Ukraine which were not published on the ground that they were political. In what way is the freedom to strike less significant than freedom of conscience? Because it depends on other rights and is thus secondary? But strikes are a regulator of relations between the workers and the state. They are a step toward self-management and a specifically working-class instrument for obtaining rights, which workers can easily understand. Abstract, ideal freedom will be powerless if it is not "contaminated" by material freedoms and the right of the masses to call their leaders to account.

The Democratic Movement pays insufficient attention to material freedoms. Pyotr Yakir's snobbish statement that he doesn't care whether the masses are following us or not expresses the individualism and anarchism of the democrats. The Ukrainian patriots, by contrast, worship the masses in the form of an almost abstract, mystical nation, but because of their narrow concern for culture and their indifference toward politics they are nonetheless alienated from the nation, the living people. The Russian democrats and the Ukrainian patriots have in common an abstract consciousness and mystification of political interests.

The "liberal Marxists," who are actually non-Marxists, also manifest this abstract consciousness. Despite his class, approach, Roy Medvedev, for example, is as distant from the workers and peasants as his opponents, the democrats and the Russian nationalists. His "objectivity" is revealed in his inability to think things through and in his reluctance to give up outdated dogmas and veer into Marxist heresy. Hence he sees the country and its history subjectively. His work is not so much an objective analysis as an expression of unconscious fear of losing the ground beneath his feet, or the blood that will be shed if the masses rebel. The democrats mock Medvedev's cowardly thinking and his liberal hopes that the regime will gradually soften and evolve, but they share his avoidance of political conceptions and programs (that is, his "objective historical analysis"), which is at the root of his illusions.

I myself was guilty of this intellectual original sin of abstraction, alienation from my surroundings, and belief in the power of personal protest, and hence apprehended both the strengths and the weaknesses of the opposition movement. The reverse aspect of this intellectual original sin was a romantic reaction to Soviet reality that took the form of monarchism, Slavophilism, and nationalism. The Russian nationalist *samizdat* articles "The Word of the Nation" and "Three Attitudes toward the Homeland," which appeared at this time, sounded like a voice from the Stone Age, a call to restore the three bastions of the tsarist regime—autocracy, official nationalism, and Orthodoxy.[19] In the good old days these bastions had been more or less decent, but now the voice of nationalist romanticism could be heard, with its talk of the white race, uncontrolled hybridization, and the call of the blood.

In Moscow I went to a party where Vladimir Bukovsky was present.[20] His personality strongly reminded me of Valentyn Moroz's. Both men possess a spiritual strength and magnetism that draws completely different people. Volodya had recently come out of a labor camp. I questioned him about the *psikhushka*s and clearly remember his description of their most terrifying aspect.

You make a friend in the *psikhushka* in whom you can confide. The two of you love and support each other. Suddenly your friend intimates to you that he is Stalin or Napoleon, although he has shown no sign of mania or delirium before this. What are you to do? The change in his personality is so frightening that you want to cut loose from him. Yet you are the only person he considers his friend, and he jealously watches as you move away from him and converse with others. He makes scenes, and for months on end you have to pretend that nothing has changed. Your fear that you, too, will crack up becomes almost overpowering.

A day or two after the party I was at Yakir's in the evening, writing an open letter to Petro Grigorenko. His wife had let me read his letters from the psychiatric hospital, and I was shaken by the humanity and beauty in his slips of the pen—Grigorenko was embarrassed to show his sincere love for people, but he revealed it inadvertently.[21] The telephone rang, and a Western reporter told me in broken Russian that Volodya had been beaten up by an agent and taken away. I woke up Pyotr, and we spent the rest of the night calling up everyone we could. Volodya showed up toward morning. Yes, an agent had tried to prevent him from seeing the journalist, but Volodya had not been frightened. He was collecting information about the *psikhushka*s, because he could not forget what he had witnessed.

During this visit I saw a lot of Grigoriy Podyapolsky and his wife, Masha. They were always referred to as "Grisha-Masha": an evening at Grisha-Masha's; Grisha-Masha said . . . Grisha was a physicist, a member of the Initiative Group, and a poet. Although he was an anti-Marxist, he made me a gift of his poems after a night of heated discussion.

Grisha introduced me to his friends, including Gabriel Superfin, who was a walking encyclopedia of party history, philology, philosophy, and the past and present *Gulag* world.[22] No matter what subject we discussed, Garik was able to supply dates, names, and titles. He knew details about Ukrainian political prisoners that I had never even suspected. Such a memory usually affects intellectual and creative abilities, but Garik was an interesting historian, philosopher, and psychologist.

At Grisha-Masha's I established a closer relationship with Victor

Nekipelov and Nina Komarova, who had moved from Uman to Moscow. Victor and I discussed at length nationalities problems, with which he, unlike the Muscovites, was well acquainted, and child rearing. Victor had a wary attitude toward Freud's pansexualism, and our discussions revolved for the most part around these problems of vulgarization of the subconscious. Politics was not in his line, but the impossibility of remaining silent in a country of lies and terror inevitably leads to *samizdat*, protest, and prison. Nevertheless, I was staggered when I heard in the *psikhushka* that Victor had been arrested.

Poets were being imprisoned again for candid words and sincere poetry. Pushkin had been killed in a duel.[23] Griboyedov had been forced to serve Russian imperialism and was killed during a rebellion in Persia.[24] Other poets died of tuberculosis, hunger, madness, or by their own hands. Grisha Podyapolsky died of the strain of fighting Soviet vileness. Garik Superfin went hungry in prison because of his talent and memory, which remembered the living and the dead. Volodya Bukovsky was starving himself in prison, and his mother shouted to the world to save her son and to stop the advance of *psikhushka*s and *Gulag*s. Vitya Nekipelov's talented poems lie unpublished: who in the West needs poetry? And Vitya himself is being threatened with a new sentence because after his first imprisonment he wrote a passionate protest against the USSR's mendacious peace campaign, which it uses to conceal its aggressive aims.[25]

As I write, I can see from my window the magnificent landscapes of Norway, a country of grave and good men. (The ferocious intrepidity of their ancestors, the Normans, Varangians, and Vikings, has been replaced by a phlegmatic, tranquil goodness.) I see a lake, stone terraces, and forests, which remind me of my native Carpathians. If my people could travel here and to Switzerland, France, or England and see the living people of these countries, so different in their national traits and yet so similar in their humanity, all the Andropovs and Brezhnevs, it seems, would vanish like a bad dream. My people would understand that the evils of the West have been exaggerated a thousandfold and the evils of the Soviet Union understated a thousandfold, and they would see that life can be as humane and decent as it is in Norway.

My host is a Ukrainian (my God, who would have thought that Shevchenko's comparison of Ukraine to Judea would prove to be a metaphor for the Ukrainian diaspora: two million Ukrainians in Germany, France, Australia, Canada, and the United States!), but already there is something Norwegian about him. He tells how a flood of lies, torture, and executions swept over the impoverished and oppressed Ukrainians in semifascist Poland when the "fraternal" Red Army came to "liberate" them in 1939, and how the Ukrainian guerrillas heroically fought against the invaders.

A brief case tightly packed with *samizdat* in one hand and eight volumes of Marx in the other (given to me by Ira Yakir, because she had no interest in Marx), I set off for Kiev. The airport was closed because of bad weather, and after sitting around for several hours beside a KGB major in a dress uniform, I went to the railway station. Long lines for tickets had formed. My head was splitting with pain from the flu, and I had stopped worrying whether I was being followed. When I spotted a Ukrainian patriot I knew by sight, I walked up to him and mentioned our mutual friends. He suggested that I join him in his compartment without a ticket. "We'll pay the conductor during the trip," he explained. I replied that I had *samizdat* with me and did not want to encounter militiamen and controllers. "I'll carry your brief case," he said as he got on the train. But I was kept off, and the train left, my *samizdat* in the hands of an almost complete stranger. I went back to Ira Yakir and told her about the adventure. She laughed at my conspiratorial finesse. "You criticize the Muscovites for being incautious, but I've never seen anyone behave the way you do."

I arrived in Kiev at five o'clock the following morning. I had just stepped off the train and walked ten paces when two policemen approached me. "Come with us! We received a telegram that you got drunk and were brawling on the train."

"But I'm not drunk. And how do you know that it was I who was brawling? Did they send you my photograph?"

"Your ticket?"

"I threw it away. Let's go back to the train and ask the conductor whether I was brawling."

"There's nothing to ask," the militiamen announced and led me to the militia office in the station.

The major was completely drunk, and the lieutenant with him was tipsy. "You don't have a ticket. We'll bring charges against the conductor for taking a bribe and letting you travel without a ticket. Search him!"

"What will you search me for? The ticket?"

After further arguments, in which I cited the law and the major replied with complete illogic, the militiamen looked through the eight volumes of Marx page by page. "Why do you need Marx? Can't you get his writings in Kiev?"

"I don't have the money to buy them," I replied.

The militiamen found strips of paper inserted in the books. "Put them together, lieutenant," the major ordered, but the lieutenant was too drunk to do so. Knowing that there was nothing important on them and being in a hurry to get home before my wife left for work, I helped the lieutenant.

" 'Holiday greetings. Kisses. Yuliy Kim. Have gone for the doctor [*vrach*],' " the major read. "Who is this enemy [*vrag*]?"

"Not *vrag* but *vrach*," I explained. "After a kiss you don't go for an enemy, but you might go for a doctor." The militiamen roared with laughter.

The major ran off, probably to report what the search had turned up. He came back angry not at me, but at his superiors. Apparently the KGB had told him that there was no code involved and that he was an idiot.

My friends reproached me for being careless. The man to whom the *samizdat* had been safely delivered said to me, "Whom did you entrust your brief case to? He's got a salary of three hundred rubles a month to protect. He crapped in his pants on the way home."

I justified myself by pointing out that I had had a splitting headache and that my indiscretion had turned out well.

When I was under investigation in 1972, a KGB man said to me, "Do you think that you tricked us that day at the railway station? We know that your man was traveling in the same train, with your brief case."

On May 22, 1971, the day young people assembled at the Taras Shevchenko Monument in Kiev, several friends and I commemorated the date by getting together to read and discuss our articles about Shevchenko. I mentioned the theories of the 1920's, according to which Shevchenko had been a homosexual; I denied this and argued that in itself the question had nothing to do with literature. My friends, however, were afraid that such discussions would cause indignation in both official and private circles.

After Andrey Sinyavsky wrote *Strolling with Pushkin*, he was attacked by many émigrés, particularly elderly ones. The sixty years since the Revolution have taught many of us that love and adoration are not synonymous, that genuine love looks for understanding. Because he has understood history's carnival, Sinyavsky calls Pushkin a vampire. Loving Pushkin, he makes his own discoveries, even though half of them may be wrong. Pushkin's defenders perceive him through the myth of the genius and echo nineteenth-century raptures. The old émigrés accuse us of being warped by the Soviet experience, and perhaps they are right. We, however, think that they live in a Russia of sixty years or even several centuries ago. Russia has become the Soviet Union, and this must be taken into account.

After the discussion Tanya, Klara Gildman, and I went to the Shevchenko Monument, where a small group of young people had gathered. Plainclothesmen enclosed them in a tight circle. We could tell that they were KGB agents by their drunken faces and their indifference to the proceedings. For them this was merely another assignment. Police cars were parked nearby. We had arrived just in time for the unofficial part of the program. A young girl got up on the dais and spoke in fractured Ukrainian but then switched to Russian. (I emphasize this detail because as a Ukrainian I was pleased to see that this unappealing person did not belong to Ukrainian patriotic circles.) First she read an article from *Literaturnaya gazeta* in which Israel was accused of using émigrés to pump gold from the Soviet Union, and followed up with a pantomime and a comment in verse on the article. The pantomime was an exercise in vulgar sexual gestures and pelvic gyrations. The verse proclaimed that the Israelis have produced a cross between a cow and a giraffe (she outlined a large stomach to indicate pregnancy): the head of the hybrid is in Kiev, and the udder in Tel Aviv. Her peroration ended with the words "You will be a stinking kike." The audience listened in silence. This made my blood boil, and I shouted, "Fascist!"

"Don't interfere with the girl's speech!" the plainclothesmen hissed at me.

When she had finished, the crowd of young people called out in unison, "Shame! Shame!"

Then a boy mounted the dais, introduced himself as a student at the university, and denounced the speech as scandalous. All peoples must be brothers. He concluded by reciting Shevchenko's poem "Cold Ravine," which predicts a revolt against those who keep in bondage their own unfortunate brethren.

The next speaker hinted that since we Ukrainians do not defame Russians, they should not say such things about Jews. At this point two stout women led the protesting girl away. We assumed that she was being arrested, but it turned out that they had calmly allowed her to go home. The fourth speaker was an attractive young girl who read a poem in which she spoke of the KGB men standing here and trying to wither us with angry looks, but that new Decembrists would certainly appear.

It was time for us to go home, and we left the monument. I want to emphasize that there had not been a single chauvinistic utterance by a Ukrainian (and not because the KGB was present—some of the poems were sharply outspoken). Later we learned that we had missed a dramatic appearance by Anatoliy Lupynis, who said in his poem that Ukraine has been gagged and raped.[26] He was subsequently arrested, and I met him at the Dnipropetrovsk *psikhushka*. The authorities arrested not the fascist provocateur (their aim was clear: to incite Ukrainian youth against Jews and then claim that Ukrainians are anti-Semites), but an intelligent and honest man who passionately loves his country.

My friends' woes racked my nerves. Zampira Asanova's brother Zekerya contracted cancer and came for treatment to a hospital in Kiev, where I often visited him. His strength was ebbing, but he insisted that his condition was not serious. KGB men had beaten him up, he said, and damaged something. Whenever he left his ward, a KGB man who had been planted as a patient would slip out after him. Zekerya and I would smile at the agent's subterfuges, but my laugh was not very cheerful, for I knew about the cancer, and the KGB man struck me as a social symbol for an individual disease. Two months after Zekerya returned to Tashkent I received from his sister a letter that was a cry of pain and horror: Zekerya's daughter had drowned in an irrigation canal. I could not complete a reply to Zampira until months later, in prison. There I found the right words, because in the face of death no consolation is possible. The cancer ward that is the Soviet Union is all the more terrible when its citizens contract real cancer. The physical, mental, and social maladies are inextricably intertwined and all the more difficult to cure.

Tanya and I had a close friend in Uman named Vitaliy Skuratovsky who worked as a laborer because he had not been able to get into the institute of his choice. Vitaliy read and reflected a great deal, and although he was a *samizdatchik*, I always sensed that he was preoccupied by more profound matters than politics. He took no part in our discussions; only with people he was close to did he open up, and then one saw what a remarkably sensitive mind this seemingly ordinary young man possessed. Vitaliy would occasionally visit Kiev to obtain rare books, and I would give him new *samizdat* and read my articles to him. He rarely criticized, and for the most part he simply asked questions and clarified ideas for himself. There was nothing specifically Ukrainian about his appearance or manner. He had absorbed Ukraine into his blood and did not isolate his patriotism into a separate category or classify people according to nationality. He could not comprehend distorted, excessive love for one's homeland with its attendant inferiority complexes and unjustified pride.

Vitaliy worked at a vitamin factory, the same one from which Nina Komarova and Victor Nekipelov had been hounded. There he contracted a disease. The doctors diagnosed it as pulmonary tuberculosis and treated him for two years without any success. Finally he went to a tuberculosis institute in Kiev. He managed to be admitted only through a friend, although Soviet legislation promises every worker free medical treatment. After two months there Vitaliy was discharged because he had used up his quota of medical assistance and was sent back to work in a laboratory with harmful acids.

In 1972, when searches were carried out in Uman, Vitaliy was found to have *samizdat*. Two young men were sentenced to three years apiece, and lectures at factories and institutions in Uman warned of a nationalist organization headed by Nadya Surovtseva. She was said to be infusing young people with a nationalist spirit, which in normal language means that she taught them to love their homeland. Surovtseva's and Olitskaya's homes were searched for a printing press because the KGB was trying to learn why Solzhenitsyn had visited Uman. Olitskaya refused to answer the KGB men. Surovtseva mocked them. She possessed enough wit and humor to manage the whole KGB.

Vitaliy's wife left him because of his "anti-Soviet connections," taking with her one of their children. How vile people look when they divide property and children! For a man as sensitive as Vitaliy it was particularly terrible to see a person who had been close to him turning into a philistine. Then Vitaliy's friend Nekipelov was arrested in Moscow. In 1974 Yekaterina Olitskaya died of cancer in Vitaliy's presence. When I was at the *psikhushka* in Dnipropetrovsk, Vitaliy would visit Tanya and offer his silent support. He knew that I was ceasing to look human, and he wanted to see me before I was turned into a madman, but whenever he and Tanya came to visit, he was barred from entering. Some of Vitaliy's friends in Uman behaved very badly when they were interrogated, and his physical pain was augmented by agony over his friends. Vitaliy loved to listen to his mother and Nadya Surovtseva sing. Ukrainian songs gave him some relief.

Now Tanya and I have learned that Vitaliy is dying of cancer. Had he been properly examined in the first place, an operation might have mitigated his suffering and put off death. Instead he was duped by talk about treatment for tuberculosis. In the end three-quarters of his lungs were removed, but it was too late. His friends wondered whether to tell him that he had cancer and finally decided against it. Vitaliy sent us a letter to Paris. The handwriting shows how difficult he found it to hold the pen, yet he summoned the strength to write a few kind words. Knowing how much I love the ancient Sophia Park in Uman, he sent me his last photographs of my favorite spots. Vitaliy's friends in Uman, Kiev, and Moscow are powerless to help him. They say that he read my postcard with difficulty and is in great pain but will not suffer much longer. Ideas are not worth a brass farthing compared to Vitaliy and his reticent humanity. Deeds are the measure of a man; words only distort them.

Seeing Tanya off when we were leaving the country, Vitaliy said that he would find life difficult without her. Now he has repeated it in his letter to us. Victor Nekipelov, in a poem entitled "To Nina," gives a sense of this feeling:

> How do we survive this terrible winter,
> This file of blizzardy nights?
> The circle of friends grows weaker,
> The circle of informers ever bolder.

Russia, blizzards, winter nights. A long winter after a brief thaw. Someone has said that the night is gloomiest just before dawn; let historians find consolation in such optimism. As she said good-bye, Tanya asked Vitaliy what she could send him from abroad. "A boat," he replied, "a boat." He had dreamed all his life of sailing in his own boat on the lakes around Uman. Neither Tanya nor I can put that boat out of mind. Sailing, sailing, like Shevchenko, along rivers and lakes, on the old trade route between Scandinavia and Byzantium . . .

In November 1971, that fateful time before the crackdown, Anatoliy Lupynis was brought to trial. He had been sent to the Serbsky Institute, diagnosed as schizophrenic, and ruled nonresponsible. I telephoned Yakir to tell him when the trial was starting. The evening before the trial Sakharov called to say that he and his wife, Yelena Bonner, had arrived in Kiev. On the way to the courthouse with them in the morning I briefly explained the case: Anatoliy was being tried for having read his poems at the Shevchenko Monument. We found Ivan Svitlychny, Semyon Gluzman, Alexander Feldman, and a few other friends waiting at the courthouse. Svitlychny introduced us to Anatoliy's father, a collective farmer who was embarrassed to be in the presence of "educated people." Anatoliy had already spent ten years in the labor camps and walked on crutches because his legs had become paralyzed after a prolonged hunger strike. Now he would be sent to a *psikhushka*. Later we learned that the investigator had persuaded Anatoliy's father to save his son from going to prison by stating that his behavior had been eccentric since adolescence. "It's a hospital and not a prison," Anatoliy's father reassured us. "He'll have a rest and will perk up a bit there. They'll let him have visitors, and I'll be able to send him parcels." What father who does not know the true nature of a *psikhushka* would turn down an opportunity to save his son from prison? If we had known on the day of the trial what the investigator had said, we would have explained to Anatoliy's father what sort of a hospital was in store for his son and what sort of doctors treat the "patients" there.

To my surprise, we were all permitted to enter the courtroom. I thanked Yelena Bonner: "You see how they reckon with you!" But then the secretary of the court announced that because of the chairman's illness the trial was being adjourned for an indefinite period. Once again the authorities showed that one should not have illusions about them.

I did not attend Anatoliy's trial, because I was certain that I was going to be arrested, although there were no visible signs, and went to Odessa to say good-bye to my mother and sister. This time the authorities did not notify any of the witnesses, and Anatoliy's father was brought in at the last moment. My promise to Sakharov to call him— he had said he would come for this trial at any time—remained unkept. In Odessa Nina Karavansky's case was being investigated. Her friends were being arrested, and even distant acquaintances were harassed.

I came back from Odessa with the flu and spent New Year's Eve with friends. Tamara Levin arrived from Kharkiv. She sat by my bedside, and we argued, like Alyosha and Ivan in the tavern, about Russia's age-old problems. In the evening, when friends had gathered at the apartment, carolers appeared at the door. In the old days boys and girls would go from house to house at Christmas, wearing masks, carrying figures, and singing carols. Now young people in Kiev had revived this beautiful custom. Their visit was so touching and unexpected that we were all moved to tears. I did not know the custom

but remembered from my village childhood that carolers were rewarded with sausage, fruit, gingerbread, or coins. Yet these were
"scholarly" carolers who had studied the traditional forms of the
custom and knew its symbolism. "What can I give as a gift?" I whispered to Lyuda Semykina, who was with the carolers. She advised me
to respond with whatever came to mind. I proposed Hutsul toasts:
"Let's be!" and "May they all drop dead!" The carolers burst into
laughter.

That visit from the carolers was my last connection with the
Ukrainian patriotic movement, and I often thought about it when I
was in prison. "They" did not "drop dead" but were sharpening
their knives and teeth in preparation for a Union-wide sweep of
arrests.

When Tamara left a day later, I said to her jokingly, "It's a pity I
can never find the time to go over you with Freud." Now she is sitting here, beside a fireplace in the mountains of Norway, reading
samizdat and telling me about the Bible. Abraham "played" with
Sarah, and she laughed when she learned she was with child. Hence
they called their son Isaac: "he who laughs." The circle closed. The
father of his people, the creator of its culture, played with life, and
life overcame suffering with laughter. Culture, game, laughter, and
suffering—such were the major themes of my prison life. When I
promised Tamara to go over Freud with her, neither of us knew that
we would meet in Norway and talk about the Old Testament. Or
that we would begin a new circle and that the same themes would
excite us: Abraham, Sarah, Judea, Ukraine, culture, game, laughter,
and suffering. As Galich wrote in "Kaddish":

> I'm so tired of repeating the same thing again and again,
> Falling, returning again to the circles I've traveled before,
> I do not know how to pray, O Lord my God, please forgive me,
> I do not know how to pray, forgive me and come to my aid. . . .[27]

IV

THE

EPICENTER

She came,
and thoughts of a madhouse
curtained my head in despair.

> Vladimir Mayakovsky,
> "The Cloud in Trousers"

17

ARREST

Ivan Rusyn telephoned on January 14, 1972.[1] "Svitlychny and Dzyuba have been arrested!" I immediately called Tanya and then went to see Yevhen Sverstyuk, who was our neighbor in Rusanivka, a district of Kiev surrounded by canals and the Dnieper and inhabited by Ukrainian patriots, Jewish activists, and Russian democrats. We often joked about our Kievan Venice: "The moats are full. Put up barbed wire, bring in guards, and the camp will be ready."

Sverstyuk was in bed ill. When I told him about the arrests, he replied that KGB men had visited him the previous day to look for anti-Soviet literature. They had apparently wanted to arrest him, because they had sent for their own doctor when they discovered he had a fever, but then they took the *samizdat* and left. Yevhen showed me the record of the search. A great deal of *samizdat* had been seized— he had made no effort to conceal it—but none of it was particularly dangerous.

"What is this *Program of the Ukrainian Communist Party?*" I asked Yevhen.

"I don't know. It was given to me quite recently, and I hadn't even opened the envelope."

"Why didn't you have them state in the record that the envelope was sealed? Then you'd find it easier to prove that you didn't know what was in it."

Like so many people I knew, Yevhen loathed the law. Why bother pretending that you were dealing with guardians of the law when the law itself was false? "What difference does it make?" he said. "They can convict me on any charge they choose."

When Tanya got home from work in the evening, we took a taxi to Dzyuba's, speaking in allusions because we could not be certain that the taxi was not a KGB car that had been waiting near our house. Later, when I was in prison, Tanya would often be sent a taxi, even late at night or in an outlying district where taxis were usually not available. We frequently joked about the services we received from the KGB. The Writers' Union had given Dzyuba an apartment in a building for KGB employees. "Why should I suffer when the people start smashing the windows in this building?" he would say with a laugh.

The door to Dzyuba's apartment was opened by a plainclothesman. "Come in, come in! Ah, Plyushch! What are you doing here?"

"The whole city knows that Dzyuba is being searched, and I want to see with my own eyes how you harass the Ukrainian intelligentsia." I realized that I sounded hysterical, but I was horrified by the thought that yet another devastation of Ukraine was in the making.

Dzyuba's exhausted wife and mother-in-law listened in fright to our altercation. His daughter poked her head out and was led away to bed. Dzyuba himself calmly observed the search, smiling and reassuring Tanya and me. My mind settled down when I saw the strength concealed in his composure and his apolitical attitude toward the KGB.

When I mentioned lawlessness, an agent shouted, "I am the prosecutor responsible for supervising the KGB![2] Stop trying to turn the law to your profit! The search is being conducted in full observance of the law. You don't know the law, Plyushch, and yet you always cite it!"

A pile of *samizdat* poetry towered in the middle of the room. "Kholodny . . . Symonenko . . . Why do you collect all this?" an agent asked Dzyuba.[3]

"I am a critic," Dzyuba explained. "Authors bring their writing to me for analysis."

The situation became tedious. Dzyuba was obstinately silent. I reached for a book.

"Don't touch it!" an agent shouted.

"You're not the masters here!" Tanya rebutted. "Dzyuba will decide. You've already searched this."

Women agents arrived and took Tanya into another room for a body search. Tanya returned furious. "The bitch slit my panties," she whispered. "She cut her finger and dirtied me with her blood." We realized that they wanted to degrade us and to goad us into a hysterical outburst.

It was almost midnight now. Tanya demanded that we be allowed to go home to our children. The agents stalled as they tried to decide whether to detain us. When we were finally permitted to leave, Dzyuba was sitting with a deathly tired, absent look on his face. I wanted to say good-bye to him, but he looked so cold and reserved that I merely nodded.

Immediately after leaving we telephoned Svitlychny's wife, Leonida. She listened to our account of Dzyuba's arrest and told us how her husband had been arrested. Dzyuba had arrived with *samizdat* while Svitlychny was being searched. The KGB men searched Dzyuba and took him with them to search his home. Then Svitlychny was hauled off to prison. The KGB had found a good deal of *samizdat*, none of it dangerous except "The Heirs of Stalin." The essay was signed with a pseudonym, and only Dzyuba knew that I was the author, but there was an epigraph in my handwriting, which could serve the KGB as a thread. As it turned out, Dzyuba gave the KGB more than a thread: he revealed the author's name.

Tanya and I rushed home to telephone Yakir and give him the list of people who had been searched or arrested. He promised to inform Sakharov and to call the next day to get further Ukrainian news for the *Chronicle*. Later we learned that Vasyl Stus, Mykola Plakhotnyuk, Alexander Serhiyenko, Zinoviy Antonyuk, Leonid Selezhenko, and Danylo Shumuk had been arrested in Kiev. In Western Ukraine close to a dozen people had been arrested, including Vyacheslav Chornovil, Mykhaylo Osadchy, Iryna Stasiv-Kalynets, and Stefania Shabatura.

What were we to do with our *samizdat*? I had made it a rule to keep at home only the *samizdat* I was working on, but a good deal had accumulated because of my illness. In addition there were my articles and notes and an early draft of the third part of "The Heirs of Stalin." Now my work on the articles had to be wrapped up and the papers concealed. But where? We were no doubt under surveillance, and I would put my friends in a spot if I took my *samizdat* to them. Hide it at home? Where? No, we had to burn it. But what if the KGB didn't come and all my labors at the typewriter went up in smoke? How could I burn the Western edition of the *Ukrainian Herald* that I had received only two days before and hadn't read yet? If the KGB paid me a visit, it would be to arrest me. They had enough evidence to convict me even if they didn't find anything new. In the end Tanya and I decided to destroy only material that might incriminate others. Burning all of it took a long time, and the apartment was full of smoke the whole night. We concealed the remaining papers wherever we could, and not all together, in the hope that the searchers might overlook something.

In the morning Tanya and I arranged that she would telephone during the day. We wondered whether she ought to take any *samiz-*

dat with her, since she could be stopped and searched on the way to work. She left with very little, which she regretted later because she had not been stopped. But if she had been searched, I would not have forgiven myself for giving material to her.

I fell into bed. An impatient, insolent ringing at the door awakened me. The agents rushed in like bandits with frightened expressions. Why were they always frightened? No one was throwing bombs at them yet. Were they pumping themselves up with courage for their dangerous work? As the search got under way, I made malicious comments about the lieutenant's actions in the bedroom. He replied with jokes. The agents searched the rooms carelessly, certain that they wouldn't find anything. They had never found anything before, and thick smoke hung in the air. "Have you burned everything?" they asked when they saw the pail in the lavatory.

"Yes, I did."

"Then you must have had something to burn."

"Yes, Rabindranath Tagore's books, for example."

The lieutenant feverishly leafed through my diary for 1957 and 1958 and read an entry aloud.

"Are you trying to ascribe megalomania to me and to lock me up in a *psikhushka?*" I asked.

"How can you say that, Leonid Ivanovych? We don't send people to mental institutions. Only psychiatrists do that. And you're perfectly normal."

I remembered that it was KGB men, not psychiatrists, who had diagnosed me as schizophrenic in 1969, when Oleg Bakhtiarov's case was under investigation.

"You dreamed of creating a revolution in mathematics and philosophy?" the lieutenant asked.

"Look at the date on the diary entry," I replied. "I was eighteen then."

"Yes, you're quite right. Everyone dreams of glory at that age."

The telephone rang again and again, but I was not permitted to answer. Tanya and friends from Moscow were probably calling. The KGB men whooped with joy from time to time when they found something. The witnesses had expected to see guns and were disappointed until they realized how much forbidden literature was being piled up. This proved that I was thoroughly anti-Soviet. One of them began to read the literature on the sly and gave me compassionate looks, but he frowned when he saw the Western edition of the *Ukrainian Herald*: it left no doubt that I was an enemy. For his benefit I started to wage "anti-Soviet propaganda" by arguing with the lieutenant about Stalin and 1937.

When my older son, Dima, came home from school, he looked at the men and pretended not to understand what was happening. I told him in a whisper to telephone his mother so that she could warn our friends. I hoped that she would drop work and rush home. If the KGB did not allow us to say good-bye, I should have to wait God knows how long for a meeting in prison.

The lieutenant realized that he would not find anything interesting in my study. It was full of books on fairy tales and games and folders marked "History of Games," "Psychology of Games," and "Myth and Games." But he did put aside a folder containing Mykhaylyna Kotsyubynsky's manuscript on Shevchenko. I urged him not to confiscate it. "The search warrant mentions anti-Soviet and slanderous literature. This is philology and has nothing to do with the Soviet regime."

"We shall look through it just in case and return it to Kotsyubynsky," the lieutenant replied.

"It'll be awkward for you. After all, she's related to Mykhaylo Kotsyubynsky and Yuriy Kotsyubynsky. The film *The Kotsyubynsky Family* was shown recently. What if the West learns that you're accusing the Kotsyubynskys of being anti-Soviet?"

"That's all right, Leonid Ivanovych. We're not afraid of the West."

And yet they were afraid when they blackmailed Tanya and then begged her not to inform the West when and how I would be released.

The lieutenant picked up a folder with notes on Shevchenko and, without looking through it, put it aside for confiscation.

"Why do you need notes on Shevchenko?" I asked.

He looked through them and with a laugh read aloud, " 'Even Tychnya, who sold out Ukraine and her culture, said on his seventy-fifth birthday about Peter the Great: "I wanted to shit on this jackbooted tyrant." ' Did he really say that?"

"Yes, when the Leningrad Writers' Union gave him the Leningrad medal, The Bronze Horseman. You'll have to agree that it wasn't a very pleasant award for a Ukrainian. After the Battle of Poltava, Peter the Great flooded the town of Baturyn with the blood of civilians and then built Petersburg-Leningrad on Ukrainian bones."

Suddenly Lieutenant Colonel Tolkach gave a cry. The other agents rushed to him, but I remained where I was. Well, so what if they had found something more? But Tolkach called me over, too, hoping to shock me with his discovery of my hiding place. I had made bookshelves with plywood and boards and had concealed *samizdat* in them. When I was leaving for Odessa, Tanya had cleaned the house, and one of the shelves had moved slightly. As luck would have it, it was the *samizdat* shelf.

Tolkach leafed through the papers with a malicious grin on his face. "Aha, an article about how to make a printing press! You wanted to set up a print shop?"

"No. I copied that from an article in *Khimiya i zhizn* [*Chemistry and Life*] about how printing was done in the underground before the Revolution. I wanted to write an article about the difficulties then."

"And what about these leaflets?"

"They're not anti-Soviet. One is an appeal to Shostakovich to support Soviet political prisoners. The other is an appeal to Kosygin about Grigorenko, Gabay, and Dzhemilyov."

"Who wrote these leaflets?"

"Two students were distributing them at the State Department Store in Moscow."

"And how did you get them?"

"I went in there to buy something."

Tolkach read the leaflets but could not find anything anti-Soviet in them. Nevertheless, he telephoned the KGB to send a photographer. Aha, I thought to myself, they're going to have a noisy campaign in the press. For the average reader a hiding place is the best possible proof of clever and malicious enemies. The KGB had photographed a wall decorated with original mosaics in Svitlychny's apartment as proof of his "Ukrainian bourgeois nationalism."

Tanya still hadn't come home. I was beside myself at the thought that she had been arrested and was being interrogated. Klara Gildman arrived and whispered to me that Tanya had telephoned her. I was both pleased and angry to see her. A woman agent was immediately summoned to search Klara. When Klara returned, she was trembling with anger and humiliation. I tried to calm her down and told her about Tanya's search. "They're only degrading themselves," I explained. "We're still human beings, but they're turning into beasts." Klara was infuriated by my Tolstoyan forbearance toward the KGB agents and the witnesses. I thought of Dzyuba and the way Tanya and I had shouted at the men who were searching him.

Ira Pievsky arrived in the evening, and finally Tanya came home, accompanied by Ira's husband, Serhiy Borshchevsky, and Volodymyr

Yuvchenko, a history teacher who had been dismissed the previous year for "propagating Tolstoyism and pacifism" and forbidden ever to work with children. Tanya explained that she had gone around to all our friends. When she visited Alexander Feldman, she walked into the middle of a search and barely got away. We said good-bye to our friends quickly: they were being led away for further searches at their own homes. Klara protested vehemently. Her mother had had several heart attacks, was partially paralyzed, and would not be able to withstand a search.

The search went on and on, and Tanya and I said our good-byes until six o'clock in the morning. Tolkach asked me to verify the entries in the search record, but I told him that I wanted to be with my wife. The witnesses goggled at us and the searchers. One witness recognized Tanya—they had taken part in fencing competitions together at school—and now he felt very awkward in the presence of such "anti-Soviets."

Tanya and I went over the last four years. Yes, they were worth going to prison for. If we had not joined the opposition movement, we should never have come to know Olitskaya, Surovtseva, Grigorenko, Svitlychny, Sverstyuk, Dzyuba, and dozens of other splendid people. We had been happy these four years; we had been able to respect ourselves. I was going to prison not for the sake of abstract ideas, but for the sake of respect toward myself and others.

It was time to go. The KGB men were polite and quiet, like beasts that had eaten their fill. The children were asleep. I tried to wake up Dima—he had asked to be awakened when I left—but he wished me *bon voyage* in his sleep. Half an hour before leaving I wrote Tanya a coded message of love and best wishes, understanding that this good-bye was for a long time. The KGB men studied the note and puzzled over the literary nonsense—Fox, Rose, Prince. "Who is this Prince?" one of them asked.

"The French writer Saint-Exupéry wrote a story called *The Little Prince.*"

"Ah, yes, I've heard of it. A good book."

When we arrived at the prison, I could not be admitted because the warden was absent. Tolkach left me in his office, assuring me that the prison was clean and the food good and that I was merely being detained, not arrested. I was indifferent to everything and only wanted my KGB well-wisher to let me sleep. I actually fell asleep on his desk, and when he tried to wake me up several times, jabbering something incomprehensible, I just stared at him.

Finally someone led me to another room, where my pen, watch, and notebook were taken away from me with the promise that they would be given to my wife. A jailer undressed me in a special cell called by the English word "box," felt all the seams in my clothing, and peered into my anus. Voltaire's pirates had looked for jewelry in women's private parts, but what was my jailer looking for—*samizdat*, explosives? For whereas Voltaire's pirates had searched for alienated labor in the form of gold and diamonds, my captors were looking for alienated words and ideas. I felt neither degradation nor pain and was only sorry for the boy who was searching me. Here was a human being with a soul who used it merely to engage in socialist piracy.

I was led into cell number 40 and fell on the bed without undressing. I had an idiotic dream: the searcher and the prison warden Lieutenant Colonel Sapozhnikov were trying to rape me. My subconscious was attempting to make sense of the search procedure. I woke up with Sapozhnikov's salacious smile in my mind, and from then on thought of my first dream in my first prison cell whenever I saw him.

When I awoke, I heard an old woman calling out that she had brought dinner. Still half asleep, I took from her a bowl of slops and a bowl of burned porridge with threadlike objects in it. I was horrified to think that I would have to eat it. Later I realized that it was just that the porridge had been burned and something had fallen into it by accident on that first day. I fell asleep again and was awakened by a shout: "Lights out! Go to bed!" I undressed and fell into a heavy, dreamless sleep, a world where there was no KGB, no wife, and no children.

18

INTERROGATION

My first conscious day was the second. The corridor was quiet, and I became lost in thoughts about my family and friends. Had anyone been arrested? Had someone been caught with evidence? By evening I realized that things would go badly for me if I didn't develop a psychological method for dealing with life in prison. My fear for my family and friends could become irrational. I had to think about the past instead. I also had to avoid thinking about the future. I had already decided that I would either be given the maximum sentence in a labor camp or be sent to a *psikhushka*. If I went to a camp, I would be able to study people (I was particularly interested in the social and psychological causes of criminal behavior) and to think and write about psychology. On the other hand, if I were sent to a *psikhushka*, I would be able to observe human behavior in its most extreme forms. Later I discovered that my ideas about the *psikhushka*s had been all wrong. The patients were not interesting psychologically, because their behavior was distorted by drugs, and the neuroleptics I was given prevented me from carrying out observations.

Having prepared myself for the very worst, I almost stopped thinking about it. But I could not make myself give up all thoughts about life outside, and they would appear in irrational forms. After about six months of imprisonment I noticed that I had a morbid fear for my wife and children: she would be arrested; one son would be hit by a car, and the other would drown. It took me more than a week to overcome these fears by applying a kind of rational psychotherapy: I decided that since anything could happen, there was no sense in suffering over imaginary misfortunes. It would be a different case if something did happen. The fear had been produced by the total lack of news about my family. When a guard said something about my older son, my fear completely disappeared.

I was not disturbed by the prospect of interrogation, for I had long since decided what my tactic would be: I would refuse to have

261

anything to do with the questioning. Hence I found it easy to laugh at my interrogators' tricks. I could look at everything with a condescending fatalism, because nothing worse than a *psikhushka* was in store for me.

From time to time a guard would peer into the judas. Marx explained that judases are keyholes used for spying. The primary function has disappeared, and the secondary function has lost its shamefulness and obtained the full respect of the state. Yes, Russia has enriched the world with several key words and ideas: Soviet, KGB, *seksot*, sputnik, *Gulag*, *psikhushka*, and judas. The alienation that rules in the *Gulag* is symbolized by more than the alienated keyholes through which men guards watch women sitting on the closestool and women guards watch men. (For a long time I could not use the closestool when women were on duty.) When I was led to the adjoining building for interrogation, the guard would clap his hands to warn other guards with prisoners that we were coming. Listening to those claps, I was reminded of a set phrase Soviet newspapers use in reporting speeches by the leaders: "applause growing into ovations." That's where this applause comes from—prison. The guards' claps can be heard in that applause.

The Soviet Union is the country of man's maximum alienation from all his products—the state, the economy, science, art, morality, ideology, the Church, and even himself. Thus the country is riddled with symbols—alienated gestures, words, and ideas—in even the smallest things. Alienation is most apparent in prison, because here man's relations with the state have been stripped bare. The guards in the "isolators" (the special prisons for political detainees) are more decent than the guards in the labor camps, but they, too, have lost much of their essential humanity. One of the guards was a young girl with a cold, impenetrable face and a look that bored right through one. She saw every newcomer as an enemy. I could never think of her as a woman, because her job required her to spy on men. My criminal cellmates thought she was pretty, and it is true that she was more humane with them and even smiled at their jokes.

With the exception of Anatoliy Marchenko's *My Testimony* and Mykhaylo Osadchy's *Cataract*, labor-camp literature rarely treats sex, and yet it is almost the only subject both men and women criminal prisoners talk about. The women are particularly unrestrained in their behavior. During the second night I heard a woman prisoner hoarsely shout obscenities at the guards. They mocked her with lewd proposals and relished her utter degradation, not stopping to think that her cynicism was produced by their own inhumanity. The men prisoners are frequently satisfied with obscenities and stories about their escapades. Women, on trains and in transit prisons, provoke the men to tell lewd jokes and stories but feign outrage at their vulgarity.

In transit prisons I was always placed in a cell between the men and the women (the guards assumed that I would not carry on because I was a political prisoner). A man would say something gentle and tender to a woman. "You're so handsome and nice," the woman would coo in reply; "write a pretty song for me." But then the woman would unexpectedly insult her suitor. He would reply by calling her dirty names, which she obviously liked. This was still sex of a sort, and the man was proving his manhood with his obscenities. The woman would either become indignant or reply with even lewder words. Women who lose control of themselves fall lower than men: where the men simply cursed profusely, women who had given up feigning modesty would make subtle sexual insinuations.

I sat up one night talking with such a woman. She had been sent to a juvenile labor colony at the age of sixteen for hooliganism and was there introduced to lesbianism. (She cursed the old lesbians for their violence.) She spoke intelligently and honestly and showed a strong aversion to all forms of evil. She was Lithuanian, and when she learned that I was Ukrainian, she asked me to sing Ukrainian songs for her. I asked her to sing in Lithuanian. "I don't know any Lithuanian songs," she replied, "but I'll sing for you in Russian." She proceeded to sing sentimental romances and criminal songs with such strong feeling that the obscenities stopped being offensive.

On my third day I asked for a catalogue of the books in the prison library. "There is no catalogue," the guard replied. "The librarian will bring books around tomorrow, and you can pick out something."

When I learned that five books a week were issued, I began to divide my time between reading and working on the theory of games. I bought paper and a pen at the prison shop and set about writing, first a reconstruction of what I could remember of Vygotsky, Elkin, Venger, and other psychologists, and then the work Tanya and I had done. The writing went quickly. I soon discovered that in the quiet and absence of distraction the "Hindu method" was the most suitable: during the daytime associations were kept in the harness of logic; after lights out, however, I would let the monkey off the chain and permit myself to dream about anything that came to mind. Reminiscences of friends and thoughts about mythology, art, history, mathematics, and philosophy would all surface as my mind proceeded from one subject to another through intricate associations. When a promising thought occurred to me, I would surreptitiously make a brief note. In the morning, when I read my notes, I would find that most of them were rubbish, but two or three would be worth thinking about seriously. This was the freedom Victor Nekipelov writes about: "But only there, only there is my freedom."

When Tolkach summoned me for my first interrogation, I was convinced that he wouldn't get what he wanted from me. Realizing quickly that he couldn't intimidate me, Tolkach began by praising my article on psychological methods during interrogations. "But why don't you follow your own advice?" he asked. "You balk at answering any of the investigator's questions."

"Why should I be a slave to someone's suggestions?" I replied. "My article advised having a plan for how to behave during the investigation, but it also suggested keeping in mind the possibility of having to change the plan in response to new circumstances."

Tolkach then tried to determine why I would not give evidence. I refused to reply and limited myself to making an entry in the record to the effect that the charge of "disseminating anti-Soviet literature in the city of Kiev" was illegally worded. The KGB could restate it more broadly as "in the USSR," and then the entire population would fall under suspicion. I also refused to give positive evidence about anyone, because I knew many trials where the judges falsified evidence and interpreted it in favor of the prosecution.

"Leonid Ivanovych, why do you hate me so?" Tolkach asked off the record. "I haven't done anything illegal. I joined the KGB after the Twentieth Congress."

"I don't hate you personally," I explained. "I hate your vile anti-Soviet organization. You're merely a small cog that serves this organization."

"I'd understand if you simply hated me. We are enemies. But you show a great deal of anger, and that's bad. Even now there's a rabid anger in your eyes."

"I respect myself enough not to stoop to anger," I replied with a smile.

Tolkach and I sparred in this manner at every interrogation. Eventually we both got bored and realized that we would not extract anything from each other. He especially liked to reproach me for being a Marxist dogmatist and an abstract humanist. I sensed that he had studied political theory and carefully read my articles, so that he knew how to approach me and where to apply pressure to make me doubt myself.

On January 19 I received a parcel from Tanya, and Tolkach gave me permission to write to her. "We're human, too. We understand that it's rough when you have no news from home."

They're trying to extract something from the letter, I thought. Or perhaps they want to make me homesick and upset my balance. The KGB is known to practice this method. Victor Nekipelov was "accidentally" permitted to see his wife in the prison corridor. There are cases where people give in because of longing to see their families.

In my letter to Tanya I mentioned only books and my work on games. I had to show her that I was keeping my promise and working on the same subjects as before. This was to serve as a hint that I was also keeping my promise not to give evidence. Tolkach looked through the letter and questioned words and people's names. I realized where the danger lay: he might accuse me of using a code. "Ask my wife about these names," I said to him. "She'll show you the textbooks we studied."

Inwardly I felt fine these first days. My sense of responsibility and my constant agitation over the arrests had receded, and politics stopped being important. In my daily encounters with the guards I was helped by the ridicule in which I secretly held them. They thought that I was their victim. This was partly correct: I was a victim of the regime. But they were victims to an even greater degree and yet were unaware of the full horror of their situation. Awareness of one's external lack of freedom helps bring about inner liberation.

I obtained from the library Shevchenko's stories, which unlike his poetry are written in Russian. The stories are autobiographical and afford a great deal of material for a study of his poetry. But how much less intense is Shevchenko when he writes in Russian! The images and symbols are the same as in his Ukrainian poetry, but the different language weakens their emotional texture.

Songs helped me, too. As I had no cellmates, I could sing under my breath without inhibition. The guards peered in curiously, but they were apparently used to hearing Ukrainians sing in prison. Because the silence and solitude were conducive to self-analysis, I soon realized that my choice of songs accurately reflected my mood. When I was absorbed in memories (usually under the influence of books I had read), I sang Ukrainian songs. If my mood was produced by the present—an interrogation, a newspaper article, or a run-in with the guards—I sang Russian songs. Thoughts about the future evoked Russian and Ukrainian songs in turn. Dreams of freedom led me to sing Ukrainian songs, but thoughts about the *psikhushka* led to Russian songs.

At first glance the reason for these subconscious choices seemed to be that Ukrainian had been the language of my childhood. Yet my fondest memories of adolescence in Odessa were associated with the Russian songs I sang then. Gradually I began to see differences between Russian and Ukrainian culture. In these differences the two cultures have both advantages and deficiencies. The feminine character of the Ukrainian language, and indeed of our entire culture, is reflected in the sentimentality, crudeness, and loyalty of Ukrainian gendarmes. The decadence and violence that we find in Russian culture have contributed greatly to our understanding of the human spirit.

Ukrainian democratism has produced in literature numerous stories about the hardships of village life. Yet when they deal with the peasant theme, Ukrainian writers feel no need to express their penitence to the masses, as Russian writers often do. The Ukrainian intelligentsia has never been separated from the masses, and it has never occurred to Ukrainian patriots that they are not part of the people. The basic images in Ukrainian folk songs are exile and the distant native land. For Russians the images are their own prisons and their own Siberia. Ukrainians feel less guilt about their enslavement than do Russians, which is perhaps why I met with almost no pessimism in the Ukrainian opposition movement. The intelligentsia of the ruling nation, curiously enough, is much more pessimistic and tragic in its outlook. Russian intellectuals cast about between national arrogance and self-abasement. But the most honest Ukrainians and Russians join in castigating the vices in the history of their nations. Anatoliy Lupynis reproaches Ukraine for lying in the arms of her hangman. Victor Nekipelov uses the same theme but applies different images and symbols, reflective of a different history.

No amount of books, game study, and historical reflections could completely distract me from worries about my family and friends. When I finally received a letter from Tanya, I began to write to her every day about the books I was reading and the games I was designing.

I had a new interrogator by then, a captain whose name I don't remember. He interrogated me without trying to be clever, but, rather, expressing interest and generously bestowing smiles. He was soon replaced by a Captain Fedosenko, who suffered from an intellectual inferiority complex. Fedosenko immediately set about intimidating me: I'd get a stiff sentence, my wife would go to prison, and all my friends would be arrested. Tolkach had agreed with me that *samizdat* could not be destroyed (although he argued that the most active *samizdatchik*s could easily be caught), but Fedosenko kept telling me that we were only a handful of people and that the KGB would find a way to put an end to *samizdat*.

I had already written several letters to Tanya and now asked Fedosenko why there was no reply to them. He accused Tanya of being too lazy to write. Then he demanded that I stop using foreign words and such expressions as "The blue sky is visible through the window." "This is a hint that you are in prison," he argued, "and your wife will send the letter to the West."

In return I demanded that Fedosenko indicate precisely what subjects were permitted so that he could not hold back letters on the pretext that they contained classified information. After I had written eight letters I asked that my wife's letters be released to me.

"You write in code, and we have been forced to hold back all your letters," Fedosenko replied. "When the investigation has been completed, they will be given to your wife."

I realized that the KGB was pulling the wool over my eyes to get me to write something. "Angela Davis's attorney visits her every day," I said. "She writes letters of protest and statements for the press, and she drinks coffee."

"But she's a progressive figure," Fedosenko answered.

I barely mustered a smile in reply to this irrefutable argument and reminded Fedosenko that Lenin had been given milk in prison. There was a story in books for children that he had written coded messages in milk.

"But Lenin was a progressive figure," Fedosenko said.

"It's strange to see what a pathological love reactionaries have for progressive figures," I rebutted.

Such exchanges soon made Fedosenko develop a personal hatred for me. Nina Strokata-Karavansky, who was questioned about my case, later told Tanya that the KGB men choked with hatred when they mentioned me. Fedosenko's hatred grew out of his sense of inferiority and my obvious contempt for him. Although I did not deliberately offend him, I apparently showed my feelings in some way. Toward the end of the investigation Fedosenko began to display his attitude by openly insulting and threatening me.

A great many photographs had been confiscated during the search at my apartment. Not wanting them to be used against my friends, I made a statement in the interrogation record that I would reply only to questions about my relatives and public figures. I particularly wanted Surovtseva and Olitskaya removed from the category of public figures and hoped that they would not be searched or interrogated because my photographs of them had been found. But my efforts did not help them. Smiling maliciously and relishing the blow he had prepared, Fedosenko asked during one interrogation, "Shall we bring the old ladies from Uman or shall we take you to them?"

"It would be better to have the confrontation take place in Uman. Perhaps you could conduct the interrogation in Sophia Park, where I first met Surovtseva?"

"All right, then, you'll go to Uman."

Fedosenko also questioned me about my photographs of Jan Palach and Janusz Korczak.[1] I wrote in the record that Palach was a prominent Czech hero who had committed suicide by setting himself on fire to protest the occupation of Czechoslovakia and that Korczak had been burned to death by the occupiers. Fedosenko was pleased that I had entered something into the record. After lunch, however, he called me out again and urged me to strike the reference to occupiers. His superiors had apparently explained to him that I was using the interrogation to make propaganda and was mocking his ignorance of history. When I refused to change my statement, Fedosenko tore up the record and did not mention Korczak again.

One of my interrogations took place in the evening. A prosecutor responsible for supervising the KGB and an investigator whom I did not know were sitting in the office. Victor B. was brought in. I was overjoyed to see a friend. Victor had a confused look on his face, and I tried to cheer him up with a smile. Then Victor's testimony was read. He had stated that I had given him *samizdat* and was connected with Yakir, Grigorenko, Svitlychny, and Strokata-Karavansky. He called Yakir and Grigorenko "leaders of the Democratic Movement."

Not wanting to give testimony or to take part in the confrontation, I presented my objections in the form of questions to Victor. "Surely the Democratic Movement doesn't have leaders? Surely *samizdat* is not an organization?"

Neither Victor nor the KGB men could understand what I was getting at. Hoping that Victor would give me a hint whether Yakir had been arrested, I said, "Yakir will be arrested, and then your statement will be used as evidence against him."

Victor agreed—and I demanded that this be entered into the record—that the movement was not an organization and did not have leaders. The KGB was using him to prove that I had taken part in writing political programs. I got him to retract his statement that I had given him some of the more dangerous articles. I never took my eyes off Victor and tried to show him that I was ready to give him moral support. I also hoped that he would later tell Tanya about my tactics. (What if the KGB was lying to her and saying that I was giving testimony?) When the KGB men realized what I was up to, they shouted that I was behaving insolently, posing leading questions, and applying pressure to the witness. "Why aren't you looking at us? You're hypnotizing the witness!"

I laughed at their notions of hypnosis. Victor was taken away. Later Fedosenko told me that Victor had again changed his testimony, this time in favor of the prosecution. About a month afterward, I overheard Victor saying good-bye to his investigator. I realized from his tone of voice that he had been broken by the KGB.*

In February I was transferred to another cell. It was dark and damp and reeked from the overflowing closestool. An old man was huddled on the bed. He appeared frightened and did not move when I walked in. I asked him who he was and why he had been arrested. His name, I learned, was Kuzma, and he had been sentenced to ten years for taking bribes. He was a plumber and had pocketed eighty rubles from several people for making repairs. The investigator had charged him with taking seven hundred rubles and, by using threats and promises to release him if he cooperated, got him to confirm this. In court Kuzma explained how the false confession had been extracted from him, but this did not help. He still could not under-

* The story of Victor B. is one of the saddest I know. Victor is not a stupid man, but he is of weak character. He had previously had dealings with the KGB, which quickly took his measure. Late in 1971 Victor moved to Armenia for reasons of health. On January 13, 1972, he was flown back to Kiev and held under arrest for five or six days at the KGB's hotel, opposite the prison. I accidentally met Victor six months later. Having had a good deal to drink, he told me the details of his involvement in the case.

Victor had been very frightened and was unaware that his friends had been arrested. He was interrogated every day, and two KGB investigators were with him in his hotel room at all times. He was allowed to see his wife and son, who were still living in Kiev, only after the confrontation, late at night, with a warning not to see anyone else or to mention the case. Threats were made that his wife, who had a weak heart, would be called in for questioning, his son would not get into the university, and the family would be evicted from its apartment. Victor gave in and signed everything against Lyonya [Plyushch], Svitlychny, Chornovil (Victor was taken to Lviv for this), and other friends. At Lyonya's trial Victor was the main witness for the prosecution.

Victor occasionally came to see me later. He wept that he had betrayed his friends and allowed the KGB to suborn him. His son had been accepted at the university, and the family kept its apartment, but Victor lost his job. These experiences exacerbated a brain disease that he had suffered from earlier. He spent time in a psychiatric hospital, then became an invalid with a small pension. Once Victor told me that he had given his testimony in a fit and could not remember exactly what he had said. He was horrified by the thought that he, a sick man, was on the outside, while Lyonya, who was mentally healthy, was in a psychiatric prison. Today Victor is completely broken, both by his disease and by his agony at having betrayed his friends. He is a victim of the KGB to a far greater degree than those people who have been condemned to physical suffering in the labor camps and prisons.—TATYANA PLYUSHCH

stand why witnesses had lied about him and why the investigator had broken his promise. After he was sent to a labor camp, inmates explained all his mistakes to him, and he wrote some twenty-five complaints about the investigator, the judge, and the prosecutor. He was then transferred to the KGB prison for writing these complaints. Although several months had passed, he still had not been presented with the charges or summoned for questioning.

I explained to Kuzma that the authorities were violating the law. He had not generalized his complaints about the legal authorities into an accusation against the regime as such; thus he was not guilty, as his camp commandant had insisted, of propaganda or slander against the Soviet system. "You should demand to be given the indictment and to be questioned," I advised him.

Kuzma could not bring himself to do this. He was so horrified by the idea that he would be given an additional ten years for anti-Soviet propaganda that for days on end he lay motionless on his bed, not even getting up to use the closestool. Eventually I managed to cheer him up, but then Kuzma was called out for questioning and charged with slander. I explained to him that this article of the Criminal Code was within the authority of the Prosecutor's Office, not the KGB. Kuzma still refused to protest, and I only managed to persuade him to demand that his wife be informed about his transfer.

Kuzma had been complaining that his wife would not wait ten years and would be unfaithful to him. The subject of infidelity runs through the talk of all the married zeks. Even libertines who have never shown any interest in their wives worry about imaginary infidelities. I tried to convince Kuzma that his wife would be a fool to remain faithful to him. He agreed with me and even promised to drop a hint in a letter. Now Kuzma received a parcel from his wife, but his joy quickly turned into fury. She had sent him a cake, although she knew he did not like pastry. "This means she's completely forgotten about me!" he cried.

I drew Kuzma's attention to the shape of the cake: it was in the form of a heart. "You old dolt!" I scolded him. "Women are always more intelligent than men. She couldn't express her love for you in writing, so she used a cake to let you know. Her only mistake was in misjudging your mental abilities."

For a week Kuzma was in raptures over his wife's intelligence and subtlety. He was a changed man, and now he laughed at my jokes and stories about the KGB's idiocy. He began to read books, and when he read Iryna Vilde's novel *The Richynsky Sisters*, he marveled at her accurate portrayal of the mental state of the hero. His wife sends him a towel with which she has wiped herself, in order to give him part of herself. Kuzma had long since lost interest in sex, but he still dreamed of a towel.

Soon afterward Kuzma and I were transferred to another cell, one with a window overlooking the exercise yard. One day I heard Yevhen Sverstyuk's laugh and then his voice. He, too, had been arrested.

When Zinoviya Franko's recantation appeared in the press, I made angry comments about it, but Kuzma tried to justify Zinoviya. The cell next to ours was occupied by a woman. "Perhaps it's Zinoviya," Kuzma would say. "We can understand her recanting if she's in prison." But I was certain that the KGB had not dared to imprison Zinoviya. After all, she was the granddaughter of Ivan Franko, who was so highly esteemed by the authorities and so severely censored in his collected works.

"Have you read Franko's letter?" Fedosenko asked me during an interrogation session as he handed the newspaper to me with a malicious grin. Later in the interrogation a KGB man brought Fedosenko some papers. The two giggled as they read them. "Oh, Leonid Ivanovych, if you knew what's in here, you'd write a letter like Franko's!"

I surmised that a close friend had betrayed me. But the KGB did not understand the essential thing. We were fighting not for an abstract cause, but for our self-respect. My position would not change even if everyone betrayed and repudiated me.

When it became clear to me that I was sure to be sent to a *psikhushka,* I tried to face the problem honestly. On the one hand there was the danger of losing my mind from the confinement with mental patients and the treatment. Going mad, losing my wife and children, was terrible. But what would happen if I betrayed my principles? I might gain my freedom at a relatively small price. I could even avoid testifying against my friends and simply write a letter of repentance to a newspaper, repudiating my views and accusing myself of hostility toward the people. And then what? I'd lose my wife's and my friends' respect. Even the loyal subjects of the regime would despise me. Only alcoholism or a bullet in the brain would be left. In the end I would lose more than if I went mad in a *psikhushka.* My fear of the consequences of betrayal far outweighed my fear of confinement in a psychiatric prison.

In April Kuzma was told that he was being sent to a labor camp because the charges against him had not been substantiated. After he left I spent half a month in solitude. My work on games moved ahead quickly, and the library was soon exhausted. I asked for Lenin's writings, in order to study his positions on various questions. Sapozhnikov countered that political prisoners could not be issued political literature. "You always distort Lenin and exploit him in your anti-Soviet aims!"

I then proposed to the warden that my wife contribute classical literature—Gogol, Lermontov, Pushkin, Lesya Ukrayinka, and Ivan Franko—to the prison library. Sapozhnikov agreed, but Fedosenko was furious. "Our state is not so poor that prisoners have to contribute their own books! Demand from the warden that he buy the books!"

In May a pickpocket named Victor Sharapov was placed in my cell. He had been sentenced to three years in a labor camp, where he began to accumulate additional sentences for his efforts in behalf of justice. He beat up informers and hooligans and took part in several knife fights—all because he objected to his fellow inmates' vile behavior. Victor was one of the last romantics in the criminal underground. He loathed the immorality of the present-day criminal world. We frequently argued about the criminal code of honor. It struck me as being thoroughly inhuman, but in the end I agreed with Victor that the code was better than no honesty or moral principles on the part of the hooligans.

Victor had seen sent to the prison to serve as a witness in the case of a friend who had escaped from a strict-regime labor camp. His friend had crossed a number of borders before he reached Yugoslavia, where he killed several border guards.

One day we heard cries in the exercise yard. "This is Radio Peking speaking! The Soviet revisionists have once again betrayed socialism. Long live the bright sun Mao Tse-tung!" Victor listened closely. "It's my friend. He's playing the fool to avoid execution."

Until he joined me Victor had been in a cell with Danylo Shumuk, who had fought in the Ukrainian guerrilla movement during the war.[2] Shumuk had done time under Stalin and was now serving an additional sentence for writing a book about his experiences. Victor had also spent time with a political prisoner who had fled to Turkey, then become homesick and returned to the Soviet Union. Now he was being charged with "betraying the motherland."

Victor and I spent only a week together, but we quickly became close friends. I told him about samizdat, and he told me about the brutality of the authorities in the labor camps. He had served sixteen years and had eight left, if he didn't pick up a new sentence. His dream was to settle down near Tanya and me in Kiev.

Nadya Svitlychny was being held in a cell on the floor above ours. She had tuberculosis and was continually coughing. Fired by what Shumuk and I told him about her, Victor fell in love with her sight unseen. He would respond to her coughs by calling out to her through the window. She had become his Vega.

We spent almost all the nights talking. Victor refused to believe that I would be sent to a *psikhushka*. "You're saner than anyone I've ever known!" he exclaimed. I laughed at his naïveté. Who cared about my mental health?

On two occasions I was summoned to the warden's office to talk to psychiatrists from the Pavlov Psychiatric Hospital in Kiev. "Leonid Ivanovych, we hear that you hate doctors and don't trust medicine," one of them announced.

"The investigator is lying," I replied. "I believe that doctors like Professor Lunts from the Serbsky Institute are inhuman, but I have never generalized that into a statement about all doctors."

On May 5 Victor was called out for a confrontation. He returned depressed. "My friend is sure to get the death sentence. His dream is to take at least one KGB man with him. He praises the Yugoslav political prisons and says you can get a really good meal there."

At my next questioning Fedosenko spitefully showed me orders to send me to the Serbsky Institute for a psychiatric examination. The document listed the people who had spoken about my "eccentricities." Among them was Eduard Nedoroslov. I remembered his moralistic criticism of Marxism and the Democratic Movement. I had told him a long time ago that his "moralizing pessimism" might lead him to become a traitor, to which he had replied that I would resort to "diabolism" and terrorism. Now my claim that his stand was immoral had been proved true.

I wrote a statement demanding to be examined in Kiev, since almost all the witnesses in my case were here. I also asked that my wife appoint a psychiatrist of her choice to the psychiatric panel, as the Code of Criminal Procedure permits. Fedosenko promised to consider my statement and sent me back to my cell.

Victor was shaken by the news. The day before he had heard about his friend, and now he was losing me. We had come to love each other during this brief time. Victor feverishly collected my belongings and made me gifts of a small bag and a slab of butter. He also told me how to avoid being beaten or robbed by the criminals on the train and in the transit prison. "The thieves won't touch you," Victor assured me. "They respect politicals. As for the hooligans, they're cowards, and if you show them that you won't back down, they'll leave you alone."

I left Victor a list of books that would interest him, and Tanya's address. Perhaps she'd be able to send some of them to him. Today all I have to remember Victor by is a flower carved from bone that he sent to Tanya from his labor camp. Zek Sharapov's bone flower in Paris! The carnival of the twentieth century!

At the end I coughed in Nadya Svitlychny's direction. She and her cellmate responded with coughs. Victor and I were saying good-bye and making arrangements to correspond when we heard a cry in the corridor. "I won't go to the *psikhushka!*" The voice was familiar. Could it have been Vasyl Stus's? I was led out with my belongings to the "box" and searched.

"Did you hear anything just now?" Sapozhnikov asked, walking in.

"Some sort of cry. I couldn't make it out," I lied.

"I believe you. You never try to deceive."

Fedosenko entered, his stony mask barely concealing his exultation. "Your requests have been refused. The Serbsky Institute is the supreme authority in forensic psychiatry. If the Serbsky gives you a diagnosis, it's sure to be correct. According to the law, you—and not your relatives—must propose your own expert. This is done to protect people from dishonest relatives. There have been cases where wives have committed husbands they wanted to get rid of."

"What a stupid law!" I exclaimed. "What if I don't have my own doctor? And what if I request that my wife choose the psychiatrist? And why didn't you tell me your interpretation of the law at the outset? I would have proposed a psychiatrist myself. Give me a piece of paper. I will write a statement."

"It's too late. You have to go. The escort guard has come to get you."

"You're a scoundrel! You don't just obey orders in this inhuman organization. You take the initiative yourself!"

"Come now, why be so nervous?" Fedosenko replied. "You'll take a trip to Moscow, and if you're found sane, you'll come back to us."

19

PSYCHIATRIC EVALUATION

The trip to Moscow began with a ride to the Lukyaniv Prison in a Black Maria. The "box" inside it was small and stuffy, and with my stiff leg I could neither sit nor stand comfortably. At the prison I sat in the Black Maria for over an hour until, unable to tolerate the box any more, I began to protest. Finally I was driven to the railway station, past the Lybid River, where my son and I had often strolled. Guards with police dogs patrolled the station. I was placed in a separate compartment with a barred door. Opposite it were curtained windows, and the compartment next to mine was jammed with women. The train resounded with the screams and cries of guards and prisoners. Zeks were being counted off and identified by the photographs in their dossiers. With me was a special guard from the prison.

During the trip the prisoners wrangled with the guards about water (our food was salted herring) and the toilet. "I need a drink!" Half an hour or an hour later the guards would bring water. "I have to piss!" My neighbor, an elderly woman who had been a party member and had been convicted of stealing government property, mumbled, "Soldier boy, tell the warden that I have a weak bladder."

"You shouldn't have drunk the water, Granny!" the guard replied.

Finally the prisoners were led out in groups to the toilet. The women peered into the cells along the way, and the men bellowed as they fought over the women. After the trip to the toilet the prisoners settled down contentedly to leisurely conversations, exchanging information about themselves, their sentences, and other prisoners they had met. Romances sprang up. The men asked the soldiers to give food to the women. The women passed along smokes.

"And what are you in for?" my neighbor asked. "Homosexuality?"

"No, politics," I replied, finding her question entirely understand-

275

able. Who else would be placed apart from everyone?

"What do you mean, politics? Are people still being imprisoned for politics the way they were under Stalin?"

"No, not quite as much."

The woman was embarrassed to tell me her own charges. She was a party member and yet had gone to prison for a petty crime. She explained that she had worked at a dairy. "You know how everyone takes produce home. I was caught with butter. The guards at the checkpoint were angry at me and caught me with it."

"You're lying!" other zeks shouted at the woman. "You stole by the carload. They wouldn't have put you away for a few kilos."

The woman was offended. How could they accuse her of being an embezzler, a profiteer? She had taken the butter for herself and not to resell. Her friends related how people steal and how much they receive on the black market. Although I knew the answer, I asked them, "If everyone steals, then who goes to prison?"

"Those who provoke their bosses or are too greedy."

The women then proceeded to discuss the romance of convict life. One woman convict told about her romance with an Afghan khan who had become a Communist and come to the land of victorious socialism. He was not understood there and was packed off to a labor camp. The khan would drop down a "horse"—a note on a string— from his cell to the woman. She received his declarations of love with satisfaction. The khan got bolder with every note, describing his passions and dreams. But when he became insolent enough to describe the way khans make love, the woman broke off the correspondence. We laughed at the Communist khan's carnival tragedy: his dreams of love went back thousands of years, but his fellow Communists were forcing him to live by the laws of *Gulag* romance.

Russia is undergoing the *étape* stage of her development. No wonder the French military term *étape*, designating a halting place for troops, has migrated from textbooks on historical materialism, party history, and political economy into labor-camp slang and there acquired a new meaning—the exile of convicts and the route they travel—just like the word "camp" and more recently—thanks to Solzhenitsyn—the phrase "archipelago of camps." But this most recent *étape* should not be pulled out of historical context. The Mongols sent Slavs on an *étape*. The Decembrists proudly went on an *étape* to the mines of Siberia. Dostoyevsky marched along an *étape*, and after the liberal reforms of Alexander II, rebellious Poles and Populists were deported by *étape*.

Finally Stolypin, the Chairman of the Council of Ministers under Nicholas II, mechanized the *étapes* by introducing railways from Western Europe, and convicts were sent off to Siberia in Stolypin cars.[1] Today only intellectuals remember Stolypin, but every worker or peasant has heard about Stolypin cars. Stolypin wanted to perpetuate autocratic Russia and prayed that he would be given twenty years to set up a bulwark for autocracy, but he succeeded only in immortalizing his name in a railway car for convicts.

I called a guard in the morning. "Give me something to read."

"Prisoners in transit aren't permitted."

"Then what am I to do?"

"Fuck the walls!" Nevertheless, he brought me some junk, which I read from boredom, about World War I, the Revolution, and the Civil War in Kharkiv. Suddenly I came across a reference to Zatonsky and his little daughter.[2] I knew the daughter. She was the mother of Ira Rapp, who was married to Volodya Ponomaryov. Zatonsky waged revolution and helped set up the Soviet regime in Ukraine, was declared an enemy of the people, and then was posthumously rehabilitated. His daughter suffered for her father, then for her daughter, who had been fired from her job, and her son-in-law, who was imprisoned in the same Kharkiv jail. Ira visited her husband in a labor camp and saw a portrait of her grandfather in the camp commandant's office. I looked for Volodya's writing on the wall of the exercise yard and was given a book about Zatonsky. What a remarkable, spiraling Ukrainian-Russian carnival!

On May 9, Victory Day, the guards had a few drinks and became friendlier. "*Etape* tomorrow," they announced. The next day there was a body search in the box and a line-up for the bath. A thief winked at me and victoriously pulled out a forbidden needle and razor blade. On his chest he had a tattoo of the Kremlin, Lenin, and a naked woman being pecked between the legs by an eagle. The psychoideology of the convict: myths of Lenin and Prometheus. This was the first time I had seen a chest tattoo of Lenin. At the *psikhushka* many prisoners had such tattoos.

"Why did you tattoo Lenin?" I asked one of them.

"He spent his whole life in prison, just like me."

"Nonsense," I replied. "He only spent a few months in prison, under investigation, and was sentenced to exile."

When we were led off to the Black Marias, I looked back at a sign I had grown to love: "The meaning of life is in selfless, honest labor for the people." The women prisoners in the Black Maria expressed

277

their sympathy for me and shouted at the guards that I should be placed in another box, because my stiff leg would not allow me to sit and the low ceiling would not allow me to stand.

In the Stolypin car I asked a Kazakh guard who stood beside my cell to open the curtains on the window.

"You want to see the greenery?" he asked, pulling the curtains back. Hills and fields swam past. I hummed Ukrainian songs. The guard listened for a while and then began to sing in Kazakh. Pointing to a hilly region, he said that at home the hills were just as green as these. He obviously knew that I was a political but never mentioned the subject.

The criminals hate Central Asians and say that they make the worse guards, but in my experience, Russians and Ukrainians were the vilest. The best of all were the Balts. The Central Asians were the most assiduous in carrying out orders but never acted against the zeks out of spite. My Kazakh guard was an example. When he was asked to pass on a note, he furtively looked around to see if any superiors were nearby and refused. But he did pass on tobacco and food —with just as fearful an expression. The criminals shouted "Animal!" and "Slant-eyes!" at him for his refusal to pass on the note, but he simply gave them a guilty smile and said, "The lieutenant will see."

During the night guards crowded around the women's cells and questioned the young ones about their adventures. The girls were happy to reply, and the guards became more and more impudent. A window had been opened, and since the women were very cold, they asked the guards to shut it and leave. But the guards lingered on. They were soldiers and rarely had the opportunity to be so close to women. Muffling myself in my coat, I could neither sleep nor think because of the cold and the guards' shouts.

When we arrived in Moscow in the morning, I was assigned decent guards. The women asked an officer to put me in a wider box, and I arrived in Lefortovo Prison like a king. There I was searched, given a bath and a medical examination, and sent to my cell. The prison was not as clean as the one in Kiev, and the walls were cracking and peeling. But the cell did have a lavatory pan and a washbasin, and there was ample toilet paper. After all, this was the capital of the first socialist state in the world.

In Kiev I had constantly quarreled with the guards over toilet paper. A guard would hand me a scrap of paper. "More!" I would say. He would give me another scrap. "More!"

"That's enough," the guard would argue. "Everyone except you has enough. I can't keep paper in stock for people like you."

I would return to my cell and demand to see the duty officer. "Why is everyone except you satisfied?" he would ask when he arrived half an hour later. "Do you think you're a gentleman?"

"Aren't you ashamed to argue with a prisoner over toilet paper? You're an officer and an educated man."

Opening his white, sheeplike eyes wide, the officer would shout, "Stop these discussions! You don't have to go to the toilet if you don't want to."

I would sit down to write a complaint, trying to phrase it humorously because it could be used by psychiatrists and because protesting about toilet paper was so degrading that I had to laugh at the guards and myself. In my complaint I would relate the argument with the officer and defend my position from a medical, philosophical, legal, and economic point of view. I would write about the legal but not physiological equality of men under socialism. If the officer complained that the country was short of paper, I would suggest that the authorities turn to my wife. She would supply the whole prison with paper, and of a higher quality at that. Quoting Herzen's *My Past and Thoughts*, I would write about the dignity of an officer's rank and the officers of the tsarist gendarmerie.[3] My cellmates would roar with laughter. Sapozhnikov would arrive and promise to settle the question, but a week later the scene would be repeated. Life in prison is reduced in many respects to a purely biological level.

When I had studied my cell at Lefortovo, I asked the guard for books. "The librarian isn't in," he replied. "Here, read this." He handed me a volume of Tolstoy's articles on education. I had not read them before and found a good many interesting ideas. I was particularly impressed by Tolstoy's observation that the most important thing in educating children was influence through the unconscious, which was very close to the position Tanya and I had taken.

The next day I was taken to the Serbsky Institute. In the reception room a young doctor took down my data. I was shaved, bathed, dressed in hospital clothes, and led into a three-room ward. Inmates immediately walked up to introduce themselves.

"I'm a Marxist. Mania of reformism and Marxism."

"Oh, you're Sevrukas, from the Baltic?[4] I've read about you in the *Chronicle*."

Another patient came up to me. "I'm a Zionist. Refused to be drafted. That fellow over there is also a Zionist. He's our theoretician. He has a medical degree. It's a pity you weren't brought here sooner. We were told that you'd be coming. Krasivsky from the Ukrainian National Front has already been here.[5] A remarkable lad."

Sevrukas pulled me off to the lavatory for a smoke. "Watch out for the matron. She spends the whole day playing dominoes with us and then reports everything she's heard."

"Are there any real psychos?" I asked.

"See for yourself. I don't want to say anything."

Sevrukas showed me Yuriy Belov's parodies of Chinese posters.[6] Count Belov, a Maoist, accuses the right-wing revisionist Brezhnev and his protégé Professor Lunts of persecuting real Communists.

A pile of books lay in the corner. The fellow with the medical degree silently studied me as I looked through the pile. I was pleased to see that it contained exactly what I wanted: Stendhal, Stefan Zweig, and some biographies.

Sevrukas was called out to see the nurse. He had declared a hunger strike in protest against the medical treatment. I advised him that there was no point in protesting during the psychiatric assessment.

A sumptuous lunch of porridge and stewed fruit was served. Afterward everyone sat down to play dominoes. I leafed through Sevrukas's mathematical books. Suddenly I was called out, dressed, and driven back to Lefortovo. I still don't know why I was taken to the Serbsky for two hours. Perhaps one hand did not know what the other was doing. Or perhaps new orders had come from above, canceling the investigator's order to send me there for an inpatient examination.

I spent the next few days alone, without any books. Then one evening a bunk was brought into my cell. Are they giving me a stoolie? I wondered. A lean boy was led in. His eyes and gestures showed that he was an experienced convict.

"An antique?" he asked me.

"What's that?"

"An anti-Communist?"

"Yes, Article 70, although I'm not an anti-Communist in fact. But how did you guess?"

"Your kind is easy to recognize. I'm in for currency. Transferred from Butyrki. I was serving time there for embezzlement. I'm a shop manager. Victor Mikhaylovich. I was just transferred away from one of yours. Ilya the poet."

"Ilya Gabay, from Moscow?"

"You know Ilya?"

"I've heard about him," I replied cautiously. The mention of Ilya had renewed my fear that Mikhaylovich might be a stoolie.

Mikhaylovich began to recite Gabay's poems. He liked them very much and remembered even long poems, some of which I had read in *samizdat*. My suspicions about Mikhaylovich began to dissipate. Would a stoolie have been specially trained in poetry? Hardly.

Mikhaylovich was also cautiously studying me. He perked up when he learned that I belonged to the Initiative Group. He knew the law and all the legal niceties by rote, and he explained that I would be given an outpatient assessment at the prison. "They don't want the labor camps and *psikhushkas* to know about you."

Mikhaylovich had no interest in politics, but he was familiar with literature and loved to talk about it. His father had been a French Communist and a specialist in political economy who came to the Soviet Union in the 1930's to help build socialism. He realized in time what was coming. Leaving his son with a party boss in Moscow, he moved to Central Asia and found work as a bookkeeper. In this manner he managed to avoid arrest and accusations of espionage and Trotskyism. Victor grew up accustomed to luxury. When his father came back, Victor returned to a poorer way of life, but his taste for the finer things stayed with him and brought about his first prison sentence. When he was released, he decided to steal legally. He graduated from a commercial institute and got a job as a shop manager. Friends in the Ministry of Commerce sent him imported clothes, which he sold at double the normal price. He shared his profits with his benefactors in the Ministry and his sales clerks, who would otherwise have informed on him. Even though he also had to give something to the Department for the Control of Thefts, he was left with enough to live quite handsomely. He was able to shop at stores for the privileged, take his vacations in sanatoriums for government officials, and see films restricted to the "servants of the people." All of Victor's friends—"tradesmen," he scornfully called them —came from a special stratum of Moscow society that included the Soviet bohemia and the offspring of government and party bosses.

In these circles everything was settled by telephone calls. If you wanted a ticket for Fellini's *La dolce vita* or *8½*, you called up the theater manager. "Comrade Ivanov? This is Petrov from the Ministry. Comrade Sidorov wants ten tickets in the fifteenth row. What do you mean, you don't have any tickets for the fifteenth row? Organize them! My secretary will pick them up." The important thing was to avoid mentioning your rank, to use the party jargon word "organize," and to indicate the row you wanted. The theater manager wouldn't raise a question.

Mikhaylovich laughed when I asked him why he was telling me things he could be put away for. "The KGB isn't interested," he explained. "The MVD knows but doesn't dare touch me. I didn't make my profits by swindling. I simply made use of the privileges permitted to the chosen few. If they tried to bring this up in court, they would put themselves away." In Victor's opinion, only the Politburo and the KGB could not be bribed. The Politburo had no need of "dirty" money, and KGB officers were severely punished for taking bribes.

Mikhaylovich had been sent to prison because a friend had betrayed him. The friend had a shop that was being audited, and he asked Mikhaylovich to lend him some inventory. When the auditor discovered goods manufactured on the sly in underground shops, the friend told on Mikhaylovich. In court he realized that he was ruining both Mikhaylovich and himself and tried to change his testimony. Mikhaylovich had an intelligent attorney who exploited the contradictions in the testimony and the violations of the law during the investigation, so Mikhaylovich was sentenced to only four years.

After he had spent a year at Butyrki, a currency speculator was caught who testified against him. Now Mikhaylovich had been brought to Lefortovo because the KGB does not trust the venal militia and Prosecutor's Office and keeps currency cases in its own jurisdiction. The KGB also handles serious economic cases in Georgia and Armenia, which are thoroughly permeated with corruption, embezzlement, and bribery.

Mikhaylovich was certain that the charge of currency speculation would not stick. "The businessman's first rule is not to mix different kinds of business. You have to specialize. All the more so since a lot of KGB and militia agents have infiltrated the currency speculators. They calmly make fortunes and send the militia information about various crimes."

Mikhaylovich and I alternated books with songs and stories about the sweet life. The library at Lefortovo was splendid, and in the six months I was there I read many fascinating books, some of which were nearly impossible to obtain outside. I read almost all of Gogol's novels, Sterne's *Sentimental Journey,* and many of Dickens's novels. My emotional perception of beauty became much more acute in prison, and Dickens, whom I had never liked, now revealed to me the beauty and sentimental humor of old England.

About a month after Mikhaylovich had joined me, the guards set up another bunk in the cell. "A stoolie," Mikhaylovich decided. A young man with a huge pile of books was brought in. "Livshits, Felix. Currency speculation," he introduced himself.

Mikhaylovich studied Livshits's indictment. "Why did you admit to so many operations?" he asked.

"My cellmate, Zubok, advised me to do so."

"Zubok? He's an experienced rogue and couldn't have advised such nonsense. The authorities stick on longer sentences for systematic operations and for a series of incidents than for the over-all sum involved. Zubok was assigned to give you that advice."

We got out the Criminal Code and found that what he said was so. "Zubok agreed to become a stoolie," Mikhaylovich explained. "He was given a stiff sentence and is hoping for an amnesty or a pardon."

We learned a great deal about the stoolies in Lefortovo by tapping out messages to other prisoners. Putting together all the information we obtained, we discovered about a dozen stoolies, all of them convicts with long sentences. The old-timers at Butyrki knew that a militia captain called "Gold Hand" or "Crooked Hand" (he had a crippled hand) was a stoolie. Although they warned the newcomers about Gold Hand, it was usually too late. He was always the first to meet a newcomer and would ask about his case and give advice. Many people were tricked by the "experienced zek." The old-timers tried repeatedly to do him in, but how could they succeed with only their bare hands?

Another inmate at Lefortovo was an Afghan student, related to the Shah, who had savagely murdered his father. (He was buried up to his neck, and his eyes were gouged out as men urinated on him.) The Afghan came to the Soviet Union to study and became a leftist. But his left-wing views did not stop him from speculating in currency. He was a greenhorn when he arrived at Lefortovo. Not knowing the law, he fell for the investigator's ruses and admitted everything. When experienced cellmates explained the law to him, he developed a fierce hatred of the Soviet Union, the KGB, and leftism, and he wrote complaints to the Shah. We could often hear his favorite curse from the corridor: "I'll fuck you in the nose like an enemy of the people!" "Like an enemy of the people" is a homosexual expression, but in his ignorance the Afghan ran it together with the other curse.

Livshits had had a cellmate who was an imbecile and a fascist. This cellmate and his friends had distributed at the Kremlin anti-Communist leaflets signed by the "Soviet Fascist Party." Livshits entertained himself by hypnotizing the imbecile and forcing him to dance. The cellmate was very fond of Livshits even though the leaflets had said, "Jews must be sent to gas chambers to stop them from smelling!"

All the inmates at Lefortovo admired Mykola Plakhotnyuk.[7] He had been strolling along the street in Kiev with an American girl in the summer of 1971. KGB agents never let them out of their sight. One of them came up to Plakhotnyuk and hit him in the face. Plakhotnyuk wrote a complaint, which was then used by psychiatrists as proof that he was insane and suffering from a persecution complex. He was sent to the Serbsky and now was waiting to be deported to a labor camp. Plakhotnyuk refused to speak Russian with the prison authorities. "Why am I being held in the Russian Republic? I demand my right to have an interpreter!"

One day in the exercise yard we saw "Yakir" written on the wall. Noticing my agitation, my cellmates poked fun at me. "Sakharov will show up tomorrow and Solzhenitsyn the day after." But I concluded that Yakir was in fact at the prison and wrote a greeting with my name and cell number on the wall. There was no answer.

Finally I was summoned to see a psychiatrist, a lady from the Serbsky Institute. She began by questioning me about sex, but I refused to answer. Then she asked about my background. "Your mother writes that you've been odd since school days."

"Show me her letter. Perhaps I can figure out what she means and explain the oddness."

"The investigator has the letter."

I imagine that Mother may have scolded me in a letter to relatives: "Lyonka never listened to me, and now he has been sent to prison." But it was very unlikely that she had been persuaded to "help" me.

The woman psychiatrist named several acquaintances who had also mentioned my eccentricities. One was a known informer, and another barely knew me. Before my arrest I had been visited by a certain Shevchenko, who introduced himself as a relative and a former deputy secretary of the party bureau at the Academy of Sciences. Shevchenko urged me to recant and offered to get me a job. I argued briefly about Czechoslovakia and the Ukrainian movement with him. Tanya quarreled with him because he claimed that Svitlychny had recanted while he was in prison in 1966. Although Shevchenko swore that a recantation by Svitlychny had been read at the Academy of Sciences, we knew this to be a vicious lie. When I asked Svitlychny, he told me that he had heard about the letter allegedly written by him. Phrases had been selected from the record of his interrogation and put together to sound like a recantation. Shevchenko left; I did not hear about him until he came up in the testimony during the interrogation and then appeared as a witness at my trial.

"Why did you become involved in anti-Soviet activities?" the woman psychiatrist asked.

"I was not involved in anti-Soviet activities."

"Well, then, political activities."

"I did not want to see 1937 repeated."

"But the cult has been done away with."

"Yet people are still imprisoned for their views, and workers and peasants continue to be underpaid."

"What are you striving for?"

"The democratization of the country."

After a long discussion about methods of democratization, the psychiatrist asked, "Do you know what will happen if we permit everything to be published?" And so we went in circles, while I resisted the urge to blow up and call her and Lunts fools and scoundrels. When I demanded a psychiatrist of my own, I was told that the investigator would decide.

The woman psychiatrist wrote down what I told her about my *samizdat* articles. I discussed only the ones that had been confiscated. She demanded that I summarize the contents, but I had forgotten some things.

"Why didn't you think about your family, your wife and children?" she asked. "This is a dangerous sign."

"I did think about them. Ask them."

"Well, they love you and therefore won't admit that you abandoned them to take up anti-Soviet activities."

I objected to the phrase "anti-Soviet activities."

"Your diary contains psychology, philosophy, literature, history, and God knows what else."

"The Program of the Communist Party of the Soviet Union states that the party wants people to be well balanced and well developed. I tried to follow the program."

"The diary was written before the program."

"That means I anticipated the program."

"You keep joking without considering the consequences for yourself. You've exposed yourself and your family to danger. This means that you are insufficiently responsive to your surroundings."

"Then the Bolsheviks demonstrated an even greater insufficiency."

"Do you consider yourself a second Lenin?"

"Lenin wasn't the only member of the Bolshevik Party. It's a strange situation. In school I was taught to be brave, principled, honest, and consistent. Now, when I try to apply these teachings, they are interpreted as a sign of mental derangement."

The psychiatrist quoted a passage from my diary in which I wrote that my head hurt and I would have to see a doctor.

"There's no such entry there," I said. "Let me see it."

"No, you may not."

"Then have my mother tell you about this period. My head started to hurt after I was hit by a streetcar."

"We've looked into this. The doctors wrote that they hadn't observed any mental aftereffects of the accident. But people are more honest in their diaries than they are with others."

The woman psychiatrist saw me for about twenty minutes on each of three occasions. In these senseless discussions she jumped from subject to subject, ignoring logic and dogma, constantly criticizing my eccentricities and lack of logic.

Felix Livshits, who was a psychiatrist, tried to figure out her method. Afraid that he might be a stoolie, I said little to him about how I planned to answer the questions. But in all the time we were together he never gave me incorrect psychiatric advice.

Livshits had two of his own books with him: a textbook on psychiatry edited by Morozov [8] and a collection of articles on "current problems in sexual pathology." I read the chapter on schizophrenia in the textbook. It was full of jargon and clichés, and the symptoms were vaguely defined. Nor could Livshits define Morozov's diagnostic methods. The fact that Livshits had such books indicated that he was a stoolie, but what were they trying to achieve through him? I found it very strange that a book on sexual pathology should be permitted in prison. After all, the authorities knew quite well about "séances."

Pages with love scenes were torn out from almost all the classical novels in the prison. Tolstoy's *Resurrection* was mutilated, and much of Maupassant was torn out. Reading such passages was called "holding a séance." Some prisoners would feign illness to spend a little time with a woman doctor and—this was the height of bliss—to touch her with a hand or foot. A woman guard would peer into a cell. "Aren't you ashamed of yourself for cursing so loudly that the whole prison can hear you?" The prisoners would respond by starting a séance. Stories about sexual escapades were séances, as were photographs of women pinned up on the wall. Combining sex and political protest, the inmates in one cell at Lefortovo hung a picture of Angela Davis and collectively masturbated as they contemplated her image.

Mikhaylovich's investigation came to an end. He had managed to refute the charges of speculation in foreign currency and was removed from the cell, so Livshits and I were left alone. I taught him to play many games, which we made out of paper and cardboard. He was a first-class player and beat me at everything except chess.

I made a mah-jongg set—it was my favorite game—out of cardboard, and Livshits became as enthusiastic about it as I. During one game the block warden rushed into the cell. "Why are you playing cards?" he shouted at us. Only dominoes, chess, and checkers were issued.

"We're not playing cards. This is Chinese chess," we replied.

"Aren't you satisfied with Russian games?" he asked, seizing some of the tiles and leaving.

I set about writing a complaint to amuse myself. Since Livshits was a Jew and I was a Ukrainian, I interpreted the statement about Russian games as a manifestation of great-power chauvinism. Chinese games were no more alien to us than Russian ones. If the guard was afraid that the game was Maoist, I hastened to refute this: mah-jongg is five thousand years old and probably more feudal than socialist. Hence it is not hostile in any way to the Soviet system.

Livshits also wrote a complaint, in which he parodied the discussion with the guard. I was afraid that he'd be thrown into solitary for writing the parody, but he got away with it. We never received replies to our complaints, but we were permitted to play our games in peace. The guards even learned various games from me and came to me for help when they were doing crosswords. They, too, were bored.

While we were amusing ourselves in this manner, the KGB psychiatrists were studying my answers. Finally I was called into the doctor's office. Professor Daniil Lunts, an old man with a sly and predatory look on his face, was sitting there. He immediately began to rattle off questions at me. They were not illogical, but I could not figure out the system behind them. I replied briefly and clearly because any imprecise phrase could be distorted. The authorities could distort precise answers, too, but why help them falsify? Lunts was more difficult to speak to than the previous psychiatrists. He quickly noticed contradictions and evasive answers, and there were ambiguities in my answers because I did not want to speak openly about all my views.

When Lunts asked what articles I had written, I cited my article about Babyn Yar, hoping that he had retained at least some Jewish feeling and that my attack on anti-Semitism would touch something in him. But Lunts was a pathological type, full of hatred, feared by

287

his relatives and co-workers. If he had not retained anything human, why should he have retained any national feelings? Babyn Yar did not interest him, and he completed the interview in about fifteen minutes.

"Why wasn't I given an inpatient examination?" I asked.

"We don't need one," he replied. "Your case is very simple."

"I demand my own expert."

"That's up to your wife and the investigator."

"But the investigator said that I and not my relatives have the right to demand my own psychiatrist."

"I didn't hear your conversation with the investigator."

Livshits decided that I had handled the interview properly when he heard my account. "The important thing in answering is to take a middle position. You mustn't be cheerful or sad. You mustn't be logical or illogical."

I laughed. "But isn't it also abnormal to be too close to the middle?"

The months passed, and I was not called out any more. Livshits and I joked and played games. I lectured to him on psychoanalysis and yoga, and he taught me about psychiatry. Finally the group of currency speculators to which Livshits belonged was brought to trial. When Mikhaylovich had studied their case, he had predicted, on the basis of his own experience, that Livshits would get no more than six years, and we were all certain of this. Livshits, however, hoped that he would get only four years. His attorney talked about five. The sentence staggered all of us. The ringleader was sentenced to fifteen years, a second fellow to twelve, and Livshits to ten. When Livshits was permitted to see his wife after the sentencing, he learned that the trial had been trumpeted in the press and the sentences had been so stiff because the ringleader had wanted to emigrate to Israel.

Livshits didn't recover until about a week after the unexpected sentence, but then our cell began to resound with laughter again, and the guards would come running in puzzlement at this laughter of victims.

Friction appeared between Livshits and me. One of our guards was a psychopath with sadistic tendencies. His face was so pathological that chills ran up and down my spine whenever he escorted me to the cell. Being a psychiatrist, Livshits quickly discovered the guard's sensitive areas and began to amuse himself at his expense. One or two words were enough to start the guard going. He would open the feed hole and shout abuse at us. But he was not nearly so clever as Livshits.

The guard would go on cursing until the whole block could hear him threatening to beat us. Finally the block warden would come running to put the rebels in their place. Livshits would be irreproachably polite with him, while the guard could not control himself and continued to shout threats. "I'll fuck you in the mouth! I won't give you any food! I'll tear your balls off!" Livshits would smile maliciously, give the guard a diagnosis, and suggest to the block warden that he summon Lunts to confirm it. I barely persuaded Livshits not to write a complaint. He wanted to continue his gloating and to suggest that the prison authorities were also psychos. I felt pity for the poor guard. Livshits was seeking revenge from him for the vileness of others. "You're a Tolstoyan," Livshits would tell me. "You should go into a monastery."

Livshits and I also entertained ourselves by telling funny stories, and we had a joke for every occasion. In 1971 many people who wanted to leave the Soviet Union were permitted to emigrate to Israel. A long series of "Zionist" anecdotes appeared then. These were stories about proud people, Jews who had straightened their backs and rid themselves of their feeling of being second-class citizens.

In one of these stories Rabinovich submits an application to emigrate to Canada. When he visits OVIR, the department that handles visas and in effect is a branch of the KGB, he is told that he can go. "I've changed my mind," Rabinovich replies. "I want to go to the United States." A week later he announces that he wants to go to Australia, then to Israel. Finally the bureaucrats at OVIR say to him, "Listen, Rabinovich, there's a globe in that room. Go in there and pick out a country to your liking." Rabinovich emerges three hours later. "Would you happen to have a different globe?"

We also kept busy by identifying figures in spots on the door, walls, and ceiling. Once, when Mikhaylovich was still with us, Livshits pointed to a spot on the ceiling just beside the light bulb. When I looked closely, I saw the Christ. He had raised his arms like the Madonna in the Cathedral of Saint Sophia in Kiev. This was a triumphant Christ, his suffering shining like an inner light. Mikhaylovich saw the Christ, too. Curiously enough, none of us mocked this epiphany of Jesus, although we ridiculed everything else. I still remember that cell as the one with the Christ on the ceiling.

My interest in games had not dissipated, but now it was more philosophical. In Marx's *Capital* I discovered elements in the theory of value and the descriptions of labor and capital that I could apply to games. Livshits and I tried out several of my games. I invented a new one, based on the transformation of a pawn into a queen. It proved to be cumbersome, but Livshits refused to help me improve it because it lacked elements of chance.

By questioning all my cellmates I managed to assemble a large collection of games played by criminals. Most of them were on a preschool level and in some respects were even more primitive because elements from outside the game—rewards, nicknames, praise, ridicule, jokes, passwords, and revenge—predominated in them. Fervor, inspired by non-game motives, was disproportionately important. The next step toward degradation is what is displayed by sports fans. The emotions of a child of five at play are in principle no different from those of a fan rooting for his team. Games based on plots and roles are corrupted into addicts' daydreams, bovine music that jangles the nerves instead of providing esthetic satisfaction. No wonder young people start fights at concerts. The quest for fashion, sensation, and titillating sport appears when culture is reduced to mechanized masturbation. A soulless culture is a game of substitutes, a culture of mechanized masturbation.

Although my fellow inmates could hardly have been called high-principled, I saw in them a profound love of life. We argued a great deal about values, though neither side was able to convince the other. They respected my principles but thought that I had missed the sweetness of life. I argued that their hedonism was superficial and irritating. They told me about the wealth of the "tradesmen" and the party elite and insisted that this was real life. "When you're dying, you'll regret the broads and the high-class restaurants you didn't have." "When *you're* dying, you'll regret the life you wasted on trivialities," I would reply. Nevertheless we all shared a love of life and a skeptical attitude toward everything, even the Democratic Movement, freedom, Communism, and Solzhenitsyn.

I narrated Solzhenitsyn's books from memory to my cellmates, who scolded me for remembering the plots badly. I was very sorry that I had not finished reading *August 1914*.[9] I had obtained it in 1971 but had read only the beginning when the owner of the copy reclaimed it. Now I had to reconstruct Solzhenitsyn's ideas from articles in *Literaturnaya gazeta*. Yekaterina Olitskaya, who had visited Tanya and me before I was arrested, loved Solzhenitsyn very much but was cool about *August 1914*. "How could a Tolstoyan justify his voluntary participation in the war of 1914 by saying 'I feel sorry for Russia'?" I, too, found such Tolstoyism strange. What was left of Tolstoy's teachings, his injunction not to kill?

Many of my acquaintances had reproached Solzhenitsyn with concealing anti-Semitism in the guise of naturalism, but I was always angered by these arguments. If Jews worked mainly as doctors or clerks in the labor camps, why does Solzhenitsyn not have the right to depict naturalistically what he has seen and to give a supply depot manager a Jewish name? Hushing up the large percentage of Jews in the Cheka would be anti-Semitic. It is only now that the Jews make up such a large percentage of those who oppose the regime, not because they are better than others, but because a persecuted people will naturally rebel. Anti-Semitism is not in the objective depiction of facts, but in the way they are interpreted and accented. There is a real danger in looking at the facts through the eyes of a chauvinist—Russian, Ukrainian, or Jewish.

If national grievances have to be discussed, it would be far more moral for everyone to speak only about his own people's offenses. We need an objective, noncondemnatory historiography that will help all nationalities free themselves from the bloody tangle of national enmities. What of it if the ancestors of the Mongolians oppressed our ancestors? Now if the Mongolians make Genghis Khan into a national hero, or if the Russians glorify Ivan the Terrible, or if the Ukrainians elevate Maksym Kryvonis, whose pogroms are often ascribed to Bohdan Khmelnytsky,[10] then the Mongolians will have to be reminded of Genghis Khan's crimes against Slavs, the Russians about Ivan's crimes against the Kazan Tatars, and the Ukrainians about pogroms. But even in this case it would be preferable if every nationality remembered its own "heroes" of slaughter and hatred.

Although relations between classes or nations cannot be discussed in the same way as relations between people, they do have an element in common. When two people quarrel, nothing good will come of it if out of rancor one of them stresses only the mistakes and failings of the other. If both are decent and intelligent, they will try to recognize their share in the quarrel and will honestly tell each other. The need for honesty with oneself is a platitude, but that honesty is continually forgotten in relations among nations.

Discussions on various subjects took up only a small part of the time at Lefortovo; for the most part my fellow inmates and I played games and read books. When I had finished reading everything I considered interesting in the library, I took whatever came to hand. In this manner I discovered Mikhail Prishvin. I had read Ivanov-Razumnik's high opinion of Prishvin's prerevolutionary writings,[11] but the postrevolutionary stories by Prishvin that I had read were so tedious that I doubted Ivanov-Razumnik's critical senses. Yet Prishvin's story "The Root of Life," which I first read at Lefortovo, exceeded all of Ivanov-Razumnik's praises.[12] I realized that Prishvin was *my* writer, closest to me in the problems he raised and the approach he took to culture and the individual, and I discovered a close affinity between Prishvin and Saint-Exupéry, all the more remarkable because they were distant in ideology and did not know of each other.

I had begun writing a series of letters to Tanya before I read "The Root of Life," because Fedosenko had promised that my letters and articles on game theory would be given to her after my trial provided they did not contain anything seditious. Afraid that I might be broken or turned into a madman in a *psikhushka*, I now hastened to tell Tanya my conclusions about life, culture, games, and human development in the form of literary and psychological criticism. In two of my letters I discussed Prishvin's "The Root of Life" and "A Drop of Water" and analyzed his concept of taming, which had earlier been introduced by Saint-Exupéry. Prishvin examined the psychology of relations between people and the various aspects of love and friendship. He established a link between the concept of culture and the humanizing of relations. All this can be found in Saint-Exupéry as well, but in different words.

After writing several letters about Prishvin's concept of taming, I approached the problem of culture from the viewpoint of purification and sublimation. I concluded that as a network of human relations, culture is a system of sublimations. Questions about the psychoanalytic interpretation of games, boorishness, love, taming, and laughter presented themselves to me as one problem of culture and anticulture. Both functions of culture—the humanization of relations among people and of the animal in man—are cursorily mentioned in Marx's *Economic and Philosophic Manuscripts of 1844* and in certain passages of *Capital*. Communism now became defined for me as a question of culture and a struggle against a boorish society that makes everything human boorish.

A second series of letters to Tanya dealt with the "fairy tale of love," that is, the positive function of ideals, fairy tales, and myths. I had written about the positive aspects of myth in 1970 in my essay "Moral Orientation." Prishvin and Saint-Exupéry supplied me with the artistic material I needed to define those aspects more precisely as the "fairy tale of love." I remembered that Stendhal's concept of crystallization dealt with the role of fairy tales in the development of love and the humanization of sexual relations, but his writings were not available in prison. Alexander Grin, however, was, and I found promising psychological material in his novels.

Galsworthy's *Forsyte Saga* also illuminates both aspects of culture

292

—the fairy tale of love and taming—in an original way. Galsworthy states, as does Prishvin, that the concept of taming must be opposed to that of appropriation. In taming, the self gives itself to another self, loves the other self for being different and having its own essence and value. Through this "gift" to another self, through a careful, solicitous, and respectful attitude toward the other, the self expands and transcends its boundaries. The tragedy of absolute solitude is partly resolved by culture—love, friendship, art, religion, and science. In giving itself away, the self acquires a world, another self, a friend.

The same need for self-expansion lies at the root of appropriation, but here the self encroaches upon the individuality and self-esteem of the other. In the fairy tale of the frog princess the appropriator burns her frog skin. In a similar tale about a swan princess the appropriation is expressed in a desire to devour the swan. Cain's murder of Abel, Michurin's dictum that man must seize Nature's bounties without waiting for her to grant them, breaking, burning, subduing—all these are forms of appropriation.[13]

In appropriating its surroundings, the self expands its physical body but kills the other self's individuality. It finds itself completely alone and thus disappears and becomes a no one. Legends about vampires who consume the psychic energy in their surroundings but themselves weaken more and more as they lose their libido give a mythological depiction of the appropriator's tragedy.

Fairy tales that depict a search for something missing or stolen often end with a marriage. The hero turns into a magus, a husband, a king, a saint, or a god. But the hero suffers before he marries. He finds himself pursued by the daughter, wife, or mother of the dragon he has slain. All the dangers that threaten him signify a swallowing and absorption of him. The wedding hymn of the Rig-Veda expresses the bridegroom's fear of the bride, a fear of being swallowed in marriage. One aspect of this is fear of the loss of virginity, which has no place in a patriarchal culture. The frog princess abandons her husband when he encroaches on her boundaries, represented by the frog skin.

In "The Root of Life," Prishvin connected the fairy tale about the swan and his own fairy tale about the deer flower with the myth of love in a generalized form. In "A Drop of Water," as well as in many nature sketches and philosophical parables, Prishvin defined the opposition between taming and appropriation, culture and boorishness. He established a link between love for the Other and creativity, between sublimation and its generalization. The point is not that she left you, but that she existed. If she has left, the search for her leads you to discover the beauty in nature, mankind, and culture, to expand the self, to discover art as a realization of the self, and to overcome solitude and death through creativity and love.

On September 15 I completed nine months in prison. According to the law, I could continue to be held for investigation only if the investigator, supported by the Prosecutor General, obtained a special decree from the Presidium of the Supreme Soviet. I addressed a statement to the Administrative Department of the Central Committee, to Prosecutor General Rudenko, and to the prosecutor in charge of supervising the KGB. (I hesitated for a long time whether to address the Central Committee, because this would mean recognizing de jure what exists de facto: that the party, and not the Soviets or the government, is the decision-making power in all matters.) I described how the investigation had been conducted and how psychiatric imprisonment had been planned for me since 1969. I demanded additional electrophysiological and biochemical tests, because mere questioning—especially when it was not objective—was not sufficient to determine a diagnosis. I also demanded that I have a representative included in the psychiatric panel and that an inpatient assessment be carried out.

In a separate statement to the warden of Lefortovo Prison I demanded that he explain why I was being held and asked whether the Presidium of the Supreme Soviet had granted permission.[14] The next day the warden came to my cell and announced that the investigator had already sent Prosecutor General Rudenko a request to continue holding me for investigation.

On September 17 I was summoned to the office of the prosecutor responsible for supervising the KGB. A group of people, among them Lunts and the woman psychiatrist who had interviewed me previously, were sitting in the room. A gray-haired man whose intelligent face made him stand out in the group explained to me that this second panel was from the Ministry of Health.

"And who are you?" I asked.

"I am Snezhnevsky." [15]

"Ah, yes, I've heard about you. Victor Nekrasov wrote a letter to you about Grigorenko and received a reply." [16]

"Yes, I sent him a reply."

"Why a second examination?"

"It's at the investigator's request."

"That's strange. The investigator is interested in having me declared a schizophrenic, and I doubt that the previous panel ruled me sane."

"But didn't you yourself want a second examination?" Snezhnevsky asked.

"Yes. An inpatient examination, with objective tests, and with the participation of a psychiatrist whom my wife or I could trust."

Snezhnevsky began to argue about objective tests and trust in psychiatrists. "Electroencephalograms don't prove anything," he insisted. "Nor does biochemistry."

I cited his own writings.

"But you yourself use structuralist methods," Snezhnevsky retorted. "In psychiatry the structure is composed of syndromes."

After arguing about structure and the objectivization of analysis, I asked, "But why isn't there a psychiatrist whom I can trust?"

"And why don't you trust us? After all, you don't know us."

"I know about you from *samizdat*. The intelligentsia is quite familiar with you, Morozov, and Lunts."

"The appointment of a psychiatrist is decided by the investigator. And he thinks that our panel is sufficiently competent."

"But there is a law that gives my wife and me the right to have our own representative at the assessment."

"I think that you're confused about the law and are misinterpreting it."

Snezhnevsky started to question me about the Democratic Movement and the Initiative Group. I wavered. Should I refuse to answer, in protest at the absence of my own psychiatrist? How would this help me? Without my participation they could write anything they wanted and even saddle me with a persecution complex or a "delusion of reference." If I replied to their questions, I could at least give answers that would contradict the diagnosis and could be used by a defense attorney. I therefore explained that the Democratic Movement was aiming to continue the democratic reforms begun at the Twentieth and Twenty-second Party Congresses. I did not consider myself anti-Soviet, because my friends and I were demanding the very things that were formally discussed at these congresses. The freedoms we asked for were granted by the Constitution.

"Then you think of yourself as a Khrushchevite?" Snezhnevsky asked. "You've written very critically about him."

"Yes, I have. But in the land of the blind the one-eyed man is king. Besides, I repeat that we are for the continuation of the half-hearted reforms begun by Khrushchev and against the rebirth of Stalinism."

"Where do you see Stalinism at present?"

I listed the invasion of Czechoslovakia, the illegal trials, and the persecution of people for demonstrating, circulating *samizdat*, and participating in the Ukrainian national revival.

"Then you're a reformist?"

"You want to ascribe a delusion of reformism to me?"

"We don't want to ascribe anything."

"Yes, I am for fundamental reforms in the USSR."

"And you think that a handful of *samizdatchik*s can reform the country?"

"No, everything will be determined by the development of the economy and of international relations."

"By fundamental reforms you mean permission to set up a multi-party system?"

"Not only that. This also means workers' councils and implementation of the Constitution."

"But the Constitution calls for a one-party system."

"Other parties are not formally banned."

"Just imagine what would happen if other parties were permitted!"

"How strange—the bourgeois countries are not afraid of their Communist parties, of Lenin's writings, or of *Pravda*. But in our country everything is feared. What sort of ideology is it that is afraid of other ideologies? And yet it boasts that it is invincible! More than fifty-five years have passed since the Revolution, and yet there's still a fear that the people will side with capitalism if they read a bourgeois thinker."

"What sort of works have you written in prison?"

"I've continued what my wife and I began before I was arrested. This includes the structural and psychological analysis of games. I hope that what I've written can be given to my wife so that she can show it to specialists. I want to continue this work in the *psikhushka*."

"Well, you know that you're going to be treated there."

"I still request that all my materials be given to my wife or me. The work I did before prison was favorably appraised by specialists, and my wife is a specialist in this field as well."

"They say you've invented some new games."

"Yes, I played them with my children and cellmates. They liked them."

"Very well. I shall pass on word to let you take all your materials with you."

The interview ended. Later I learned that on the basis of this discussion Snezhnevsky had given me a diagnosis of "ideas of reformism that have turned into a mania of inventiveness in the field of psychology." Hence he recommended that I be sent to an ordinary psychiatric hospital, rather than a special one. The next day I was shipped by convict train to Kiev.

At the prison in Kiev my cellmate was a burglar who specialized in robbing prosperous homes. He had been caught because of a prostitute who made frequent house calls to a government minister. She described the layout to my cellmate, and he robbed the apartment. When the militia questioned all the prostitutes who had visited the minister, she confessed. None of the stolen goods were found on the burglar, but foreign currency was discovered, and he was sent to prison as a currency speculator.

My new cellmate and I did not get along together. Our conversations and games led to quarrels, and we easily took offense at each other. He combined a contempt for the Soviet bourgeoisie with Soviet patriotism and anti-Semitism. No matter how much I argued that there are few Jews now in the upper crust of Soviet society, he continued to blame Jews for the venality of the regime. Quite depraved himself, he accused the children of Soviet bosses of being debauched by the West. ("That's where they get their narcotics, pornographic films, group sex, and other forms of debauchery.") When I tried to get him to define the difference between good debauchery and barbaric, Western debauchery, he was unable to answer. By comparison with Muscovite experts in debauchery he looked like a provincial amateur: what had become the fashion in Moscow was still unspeakable in Kiev.

The children of government and party bosses are intimately linked with the bohemian and criminal worlds. On the one hand they are satiated in a society of want; on the other they distrust the fine words of their parents, who often entertain themselves with pornography and whores. And there is also the rulers' desire to enjoy the fullness of power, to become hereditary rulers, not just kings for a day.

The Soviet bourgeoisie is changing from an elective into a hereditary caste. The privileges it enjoys and passes on to its offspring have no basis in law and depend on turnover at the top. The children of the bourgeoisie want either to become masters in their own right or to protest against their parents by becoming involved in crime, in fascist organizations, or even in the democratic opposition. (There have been cases where children of high-ranking KGB officials have stolen banned books and made them available for *samizdat*.)

The Kiev prison welcomed me with a surprise: many new books

had been purchased, among them Lermontov, Tychyna, Lesya Ukrayinka, Schiller, and Shevchenko. And Lenin had finally been permitted.

I began with Shevchenko. I was interested in his late period, when he turns to the prophets as he reflects on the future of Ukraine and compares her to Judea. An edict emancipating the serfs was expected at any moment, and he was writing about the Tsar's and landlords' hungry eyes. He did not trust the Tsar and expected him to forge new shackles for the people. And still he awaited a renewal of the earth, mocked the God of the Church, and dreamed of writing a Ukrainian *Odyssey*. His fate was to become a Homer, a bard, a blind man.

The aristocracy of some ancient race blinded nightingales to make them sing better. Our nightingales, the *kobzar*s, were blinded in battle.[17] To continue waging war with the enemy they became singers of laughter, tears, martial glory, and tender love for God, nature, and woman. They became the symbols of the Ukrainian spirit. Among them was the *kobzar* of *kobzar*s, Shevchenko. In 1935 the *kobzar*s were executed, and the remaining singers were forced to hymn the glory of Stalin and the party.

In prison I came across a two-volume collection of Tychyna's poetry. His strikingly musical *Solar Clarinets* depicts the Mother, the Madonna who blesses the dying Ukraine. Then the question arose for Tychyna: What do the people need, my sonnets and octaves or bread? The genius agonized and chose bread and collectivization. He renounced beauty for the sake of bread. But the collectivization brought with it an unprecedented famine: between five and ten million people perished, and God knows how many people were arrested for protesting. Fear of what was happening forced the former genius to shut his eyes, to blind himself, and to sing encomiums to terror. The singer of sunlight and beauty now romanticized the purges, the secret police, and Stalin. Then even that talent disappeared, and he became a government minister and a rhymester.

While I was in prison, I came across a newspaper with poems by Yevgeniy Yevtushenko. He was continuing his duplicitous behavior, writing seditious poems for *samizdat* and composing lofty odes to the party. Before my arrest I had written an article entitled "Quo Vadis, Yevgeniy Yevtushenko?" in which I accused him of writing cowardly civic poetry.[18] Drowning his conscience in drink, he courageously defended blacks and Chileans and held up foreign prisons to shame but did not say a word about Soviet prisons. Yevtushenko as a poet is dead, just like his many predecessors who toadied to the authorities.

In this system a talent dies if it does not refuse to submit to the authorities' demands.

When I had been thrown out of work, I got a job reading to a blind scholar named Shiryayev. He was working on a dissertation that dealt with the elimination of class distinctions between white-collar workers, laborers, and peasants in the Soviet Union. I would read newspaper headlines to him, and he would pick out what suited his collection of facts. Workers were becoming engineers, and teachers were going into the factories (because teachers' salaries are so low, I would say to him, but he did not listen). Shiryayev had no statistics to go by—only newspaper headlines and quotations from Lenin. I urged him to read Marx, but he refused.

Whenever an editorial in *Pravda* or a new speech by Brezhnev appeared, Shiryayev would change his theses to go with the times. But when he started to incorporate attacks against Dubček and other "opportunists" in his text, I was physically unable to write them down. "Have you read any Czechoslovak newspapers?" I asked him. "Have you read the Action Program or met any members of the Czechoslovak party?" Shiryayev was scandalized. "You can't believe everything so blindly after the Twentieth Congress!" I burst out. "A philosopher must think independently." As for the elimination of class distinctions, I cited the wages my mother was paid as a cook—sixty rubles a month—and the salary the Minister of Education received. My career with the philosopher came to an end. At my trial he testified for the prosecution about my anti-Soviet statements.

While I was studying the decline of Tychyna, I was summoned to see the attorney Krzhepitsky. He told me that he had been retained by my wife and that because I was being sent to a psychiatric hospital he would conduct the defense by himself. I told him that I was not prepared for such a conversation, but that in no way did I want him to admit any anti-Soviet tendencies in my articles; he was to argue that they are constitutional. He was also to state that my family and I were demanding a new examination with the participation of our own psychiatrists.

Hearing me use the word *psikhushka*, Krzhepitsky remarked, "Why do you, an educated man, use criminal slang?"

After this significant legal advice he became boring to me. I did not see him again.

On the anniversary of Lenin's birth my cellmate and I entertained ourselves with anecdotes about Lenin. We imagined the Mausoleum, that nightmarish pagan pantheon to the remains of the dead revolution, where robot soldiers change guard with inhuman motions as they stare unblinkingly ahead. A cult of a corpse celebrated with robots' rituals—what a symbol for killing an idea and turning it into a pagan religion!

In May I was transferred to another cell. My new cellmate was a hefty fellow who had been arrested for taking bribes, smuggling, and speculating in foreign currency. "Are you a political?" he asked me immediately. "I spent fifteen days here with one. Lisovy the philosopher.[19] He didn't like foul language and got rid of me."

My cellmate was tolerable at first. He read, and I worked on my theory of games. When he interrupted, I would ask him to wait an hour or two, but with each day he would let himself go more. "I have a certificate that says I'm a psychopath. I can do as I please!" He bawled obscene, idiotic ditties and gleefully related how he would rape the investigator's daughter and roast and eat his entire family. Then he began to make fascist speeches and to write a denunciation of his chums.

I told him that he was destroying himself. By testifying against his friends, he would provoke them to testify against him. "I realize that your chums are vermin like you," I said to him. "But why are you betraying them?"

"The Yid bastards will betray me no matter what I do," he replied.

After this exchange he became thoroughly insolent; not content with his obscene ditties, he passed wind and defecated right in the cell to spite me. After a month I could not take any more and demanded that we be separated. I spent the next week in solitary confinement.

20

THE MADHOUSE

On July 16, 1973, I was finishing B. G. Kuznetsov's *Einstein*.[1] I had read it before my arrest and thought it the best book about Einstein I had encountered so far. When I saw Einstein's face on the librarian's cart, I was so delighted that I forgot to look at the other books. I copied out from Kuznetsov passages about the "miracle" of magnetism, Einstein's "childishness," the emotional extension of his thought, his sense of beauty, his humor, his love for people, and his intellectual affinities with Dostoyevsky and Mozart.

Dostoyevsky wrote that beauty will save the world. "Will the dictatorships of monstrosities / retreat from the dictatorship of beauty?" Vasyl Stus asked. Alas, the Japanese fascists were connoisseurs of beauty, and the German fascists were not deterred from making use of Nietzsche's philosophy by its estheticism. There are lovers of beauty among Soviet fascists and KGB men as well. One KGB interrogator in Kiev knows by heart the poetry of Lermontov, Yesenin, Tychyna, and the Ukrainian poets of the 1960's.

Can science save the world? Yes, for without objective knowledge we shall hardly succeed in extricating ourselves from the apocalyptic "socialist camp" and the twentieth century as a whole. But science itself is becoming a myth as the Leviathan turns into falsehood.

The role of laughter, essentially, is to help us overcome fear, death, and everything deadening and dying. It has been said that Rabelais's laughter broke ground for the French Revolution. The Russian Revolution was accompanied by buffoonery and satire. Similarly, the jokes and laughter of the *samizdat* satirists are cleansing society of its prejudices. Galich's songs put an end to the dead ideology of the Soviet rulers. They make room for a new seriousness, a new struggle among living ideologies.

Both Ivan the Terrible and Peter the Great introduced carnivalization, but theirs was a carnival that mocked living people by degrading them and shedding their blood. At the same time as he allowed the *oprichnik*s to make merry at the boyars' expense,[2] Ivan banned secular songs, buffoonery, psaltery playing, dicing, and even chess. The merriment was imposed from above, and the laughter was degrading and sadistic. Stalin and Beria laughed just as sadistically. Their laughter did not set men free; it murdered them. Real laughter comes from below, from the people. It ridicules those who oppress them and deny them freedom.

Kuznetsov writes that the humor of Mozart and Einstein "flows into a broad and powerful stream of all-destroying and all-creating laughter." Bakhtin aptly calls it the "carnival culture." Laughter destroys the old and moribund and gives birth to the new. Is it proper to laugh at the old? Evidently it is, if the old claims "*Après moi le déluge*," if it drags what is being born into the grave, if it itself is a walking death. Popular culture provides the basis for a balance between traditions, which are so necessary to culture, and dogmas, which hinder life. The laughter of popular culture undermines the wisdom of the Sadducees and the hypocrisy of the Pharisees; it throws dirt at everything that degrades and oppresses man. What are the limits on laughter? If laughter in its totality engenders a dialectical attitude toward the world, then it, too, should be dialectical in both negating the old and creating the new. Otherwise it is reduced to a laughter of nihilism, cynicism, and madness.

Kuznetsov's book bore the stamp of the prison library, and a number had been written across the wrinkles on Einstein's forehead, like the convict number on Solzhenitsyn's forehead in one of the photographs that circulated in *samizdat*. I laughed at this farce, this tragicomedy of history. My laughter was a poor defense against my fear of a *psikhushka*.

"Get your things together," said the deputy warden as he entered my cell. "We'll look through them and return them."

"To Dnipropetrovsk? Already? What about the meeting with my wife that you promised?"

"You are going to the place that has been prescribed for you."

"The *psikhushka*?"

"You'll see."

"What about my letters, my articles? Call in Fedosenko! He promised to give them to my wife. There's nothing seditious in them! I want to continue my scientific work at the *psikhushka*. If you aren't going to give them to my wife, leave them with me."

"I don't handle these matters, but I do think that you'll get everything you need."

I gathered the letters to my family and the drafts and fair copies of articles on games, laughter, riddles, and fairy tales. In the box on the first floor guards took the papers and searched me, peering into my mouth, armpits, and anus. I couldn't have cared less about what was happening as long as they gave the papers to Tanya.

Soldiers walked in and searched me again casually—they trusted the prison guards. At the exit I was told to sign receipts stating that all my belongings had been returned to me. I objected: they hadn't returned a fountain pen, a book, a newspaper, and some clothes. The prison staff scurried around, looking for the items. The soldiers were getting angry. It was time to leave for the railway station. Finally someone called out, "We'll send everything on to you, Leonid Ivanovych! We never lose anything." I protested, but only weakly; the *psikhushka* was ahead of me, and I had to spare my nerves. It was apparent that nothing would be returned.

In the box in the Black Maria my leg again prevented me from sitting, and the ceiling was too low for me to stand. I peered through cracks and saw that I was in the parking lot at Lukyaniv Prison and criminal convicts were being picked up.

At the station guards with dogs counted off the prisoners. As always, I was placed between the men and the women. An hour, then two, three, and four passed. The prisoners begged to go to the lavatory, but this was not permitted at stations.

We moved out in the evening, and the night passed calmly. In the morning, a young girl asked for something unsalty to eat. I gave her my oranges and sausage, and we struck up a conversation. Her name was Nina.

"So you're a political," she said. "Good for you. They're all cocksuckers!"

"Are you in for Ukrainian affairs?" someone on my left called out.

"For all sorts," I replied.

"I used to distribute your leaflets in Lviv."

"Are you a political?" I asked.

"No, I'm a thief. Politics stinks."

"You gave those whores food!" another man called out. (The women's compartment cried out with indignation.) "How about giving me something?" He was an Armenian named Oleg from the Besarabka district of Kiev. He had been a thief and a currency speculator. My "political" acquaintance fell silent, but Oleg began to talk with the women. One of them was from the same part of Kiev, and they had mutual friends among alcoholics, thieves, and prostitutes. She and Oleg traded stories. But when he discovered that she was middle-aged, he lost interest and began to flirt with the girl to whom

I had given my oranges and sausage. "I've got a tenner hidden away here," he said to her. "I'll give it to the guard, and we'll go to the toilet together."

"What if he refuses?"

"As long as you don't refuse me."

"And what will we do?"

"We'll see."

Oleg negotiated with the guard, who put on an act but in the end agreed: ten rubles is a large amount for a soldier.

"Nina, hey, Nina!" Oleg called out. "It's all set up!"

"What's set up?"

"He'll let us out together."

"What for?"

"What do you mean, what for? We made a deal!"

Nina's friends gave her advice. She disagreed and seemed to be afraid of something. Oleg cursed. When toilet call came, the guards began with the women, who were noisier than the men. Nina was led out and was gone for a long time. Oleg gave vent to his anger. I couldn't understand what was going on, and when I finally guessed, I turned for confirmation to the older woman.

"Is he telling the truth?"

"What do you think?" she replied. I detected jealousy and disappointment in her voice. Why wasn't the soldier keeping *her* in the lavatory? She was also angry at Oleg. Why was he willing to pay ten rubles for a bitch who sold herself to a guard, but not for her? Yet I could understand Oleg, too. He was embarrassed to offer her money for sex after they had had such a touching conversation about mutual friends.

The women raised a din because they weren't being taken to the lavatory. When Nina was brought back, Oleg heaped abuse on her and promised to send word to the labor camp about what she had done. Nina remained silent. The women in her compartment would not speak to her.

When the train arrived at Dnipropetrovsk in the morning, we were all unloaded and immediately led to the bathhouse. Afterward I was taken to see a doctor, Ella Petrovna Kamenetskaya. "We'll soon cure you of your political delusion," she commented as she finished examining me.

"But you don't know yet what's involved!" I objected.

"Academician Snezhnevsky knows. He never makes a mistake."

The horror of the *psikhushka* had begun to grip me. The quarantine ward that I was taken to contained more patients than beds. I was assigned to be the third person on two bunks that had been pushed together. The other new arrivals were there already. Almost all of them were hardened criminals who had decided to fatten up on hospital rations and were malingering. "Don't talk to me," whispered Mykola, the "political" thief. "I'm faking. From the looks of him I'd say your neighbor is, too."

The thieves immediately took me under their wing. When the "imbecile" on my right smeared feces on his legs, they drove him away and gave me his spot. "Are you crazy?" they said to me when I protested. "You won't survive here if you bother with the louses. He's faking! He could at least have picked something more pleasant and not smelled up the air for everyone."

The orderlies were criminals serving short sentences for hooliganism, theft, or currency speculation. They were picked from the prison next door to the *psikhushka*, and most of them came willingly: instead of slaving away in a camp they could pass their time watching psychos. The thieves quickly came to terms with the orderlies and were allowed to do what they liked, because the orderlies were afraid of being sent to a camp and running across their victims. Their attitude toward the thieves extended to me as well. One orderly asked me if I needed anything. I questioned him about the regulations and the means used by politicals to fight the administration.

"There's complete lawlessness here," he explained to me. "If you fuck up with a doctor, a nurse, or an orderly, you're done for. They'll pump you full of drugs, and the orderlies will beat you and not let you go to the lavatory. All the politicals keep quiet, and so should you."

"What sort of drugs do they give the politicals?"

"All sorts. Some get more, and some get less. As long as they don't give you haloperidol."

I could see the effects of the potent sedative haloperidol on my fellow inmates and wondered why drugs were administered in quarantine. The patients' illnesses had not been diagnosed yet, and contraindications had not been established. One inmate was writhing in convulsions, head twisted to the side and eyes bulging. Another patient was gasping for breath, and his tongue was lolling. A third was screaming for the nurse and begging for a corrective to alleviate the physical effects of haloperidol. The drug was given in such large doses in order to reveal the malingerers and to break any resistance. My thieves became depressed. Now they were in for it. That very first day a criminal who had been simulating amnesia gave up and went to see Kamenetskaya to confess.

The next day was even more dispiriting. I awoke early to find two orderlies beating Oleg with all their might. Afraid of being punished with drugs, he did not resist and only muttered, "We'll meet up in camp! You'll be sorry!" The orderlies increased their blows.

"Why were they beating you?" I asked Oleg when they had left.

"I wanted to go to the lavatory for a smoke," he explained. We were allowed to go out for cigarettes only three times a day.

When I was sent to Kamenetskaya later in the day, she questioned me about my case: what had I written, to whom had I given it, and why had I been involved in anti-Soviet activities? I described my writings and denied that they were anti-Soviet. She listened inattentively and now and then made notes.

An orderly burst into the office. "A patient got excited and tried to beat me up!"

"Tell the nurse to give him sulphur," Kamenetskaya ordered.[3] When the orderly had left, she continued with me as if nothing had happened. "What was your wife's attitude toward your writing?"

"She didn't have any. She's not interested in politics."

"But she must have noticed that you were writing something. People came to see you. You traveled to Moscow, Lviv, and Odessa. Where did you get the money for this if you weren't working?"

"Friends helped me."

"Then you had an underground organization and a fund?"

"Are you an investigator or a doctor?" I snapped. "I shall reply to medical questions, but not to police questions."

"Very well. You'll answer all our questions if you want to be released from here."

The ward was in an uproar when I returned. The patient who had been prescribed sulphur had tried to hang himself in the lavatory. Kamenetskaya came to investigate. "So he wanted to hang himself? He won't get away with it!"

The thieves tried to explain to her that he had not beaten the orderlies: they had attacked him. Kamenetskaya summoned the thieves to her office and gave them sulphur and haloperidol. All the thieves except one admitted to being malingerers. The one exception, as I learned from talking to him, was genuinely deranged with megalomania and a persecution complex and thought that the camp bosses had sent him to the *psikhushka* because he knew their secrets. All my friends from the *étape* were sent to camps after being treated with drugs for several months, but the malingerers were released later than the genuine patient.

The orderlies came to Oleg to apologize. "We didn't know you're a real thief. We thought you were a psycho." That day our situation took a turn for the better. Our nicotine craving disappeared because the orderlies brought us tobacco, and they allowed our group to go to the lavatory at any time if Kamenetskaya and the nurse were not around. But I was depressed by the sufferings of my fellow inmates, who writhed in convulsions from haloperidol.

The political prisoners sent me a message advising that I admit to being insane and recant (only not in writing). I was surprised, because I had heard that some of them were very brave. They had been expecting me. Some months before, one of them had seen an order in a doctor's office: "Plyushch is not to be permitted to have contact with Plakhotnyuk." Thus the doctors had known that I was coming here even before the court had ruled to commit me.

The ward resounded with a din. A passive homosexual lay in a corner. He was given large doses of haloperidol and was frequently taunted by the patients and staff. "Did you like it?" orderlies would ask him about his relations with men. "Wasn't it painful? How was it the first time? Will you give me some?"

When I tried to defend the homosexual, my friends got angry at me. "What's wrong with you? Do you feel sorry for that queer, that stinking queen?"

He was in fact dirty, bedraggled, and pitiful. But we all walked around in torn underpants and shirts. At first I was embarrassed to be seen by the nurses, because I had no buttons or string to hold up the underpants. But then I thought angrily: You yourselves reduce people to shamelessness. Why should I be ashamed in front of you? Gradually I learned to ignore the nurses.

A new shipment of convicts was brought in. "There's a political from Kiev," the guards reported. I rushed to the hall and saw a familiar face with a Cossack mustache. It was Vasyl Ruban the young Kiev poet.[4] But why had he been sent here? His poetry was apolitical.

Kamenetskaya appeared in the hall. "I see you've met. Back to the ward! Orderlies, why did you let Plyushch come out into the hall?"

That same day I was transferred to the second floor. The inmates there immediately asked on what charges I had been sentenced. "Ah, a political! Plakhotnyuk was transferred out of here only today."

An old man introduced himself. "Maltsev. I'm a political, too. A citizen of the United States." Everyone called Maltsev "Mister." He suffered from a severe dissociation of consciousness but remained normal in some respects. He hated foul language and was polite in his dealings. Every day he wrote complaints to the Prosecutor's Office and the KGB, accusing the doctors of conspiring with his former mistress to poison him. Kennedy had been assassinated because of him, he claimed, and the militia had stolen all the gold he had smuggled from the United States. A relative brought Mister parcels. The orderlies took all the food in return, supposedly, for passing on his complaints. When an airplane flew over the *psikhushka*, Mister would wave a towel from the window and call out, "Americans! Drop atomic bombs on these fascists! Let this whole damn country go up in flames!"

I had barely become accustomed to this ward when I was transferred to the surveillance ward, which was intended for aggressive or severely ill patients. Here I met Boris Yevdokimov, a writer and a member of the NTS who had spent many years in labor camps under Stalin and worked as a journalist in Leningrad.[5] He was elderly and suffered from asthma and heart trouble. Yevdokimov's morale was quite low: he had admitted that he was ill and had confessed to his crimes against the state, but he had been told bluntly that he would not be released soon. I spent days on end sitting on his bed and talking about all sorts of things with him. We argued a great deal because our views were quite different, and the other politicals were amazed that we could be friends.

Yevdokimov's situation was particularly difficult because almost all the patients and staff treated him badly. "Why are you friendly with that fascist scoundrel?" Kamenetskaya asked me several times. She was very hard on him because of the Camembert his wife sent him. "You're an educated man," Kamenetskaya would say to him, "and yet you're so greedy. Your wife brings you rotten cheese, and you eat it." I tried to explain to her that Camembert is widely eaten in Western Europe, but she would not believe me. Realizing that she couldn't drive a wedge between us, Kamenetskaya ordered me transferred back to my previous ward. When Yevdokimov and I continued to meet in the lavatory and at meals, she told the orderlies to keep us apart. But the orderlies treated me as a political, and Yevdokimov and I gave them food from our parcels.

While Yevdokimov and I were still in the same ward, a nurse told the patients that we were Yids and anti-Soviets and were interfering with the patients' treatment. Only one patient fell for this. He shouted that our anti-Soviet conversations were keeping him awake.

The inmates called Kamenetskaya "Ilse Koch" or "Ellochka the Cannibal."[6] The height of her cynicism occurred when she sat on the head of a patient who had called her "Ilse Koch." She laughed at the nickname—"You see how the men are afraid of me!" She desperately wanted to be thought of as an intelligent person and boasted to Yevdokimov that she had bought a book by Erich Maria Remarque.

Yevdokimov nicknamed her "Remarque." She took revenge by prescribing haloperidol for him.

Like the other doctors, Kamenetskaya was harsh with informers but gladly used their services. The doctors did not care that many of the informers were lying. Since in theory they were not punishing but merely administering treatment, it was impossible to protest against their actions.

Patients who did protest were punished by being strapped to their beds for several hours or a full day, given increased doses of tranquilizers, and beaten by the orderlies. "Now, for that you'll get haloperidol," the nurses would say bluntly.

Sulphur was regarded as the worst punishment. After an injection of sulphur the patient's temperature would rise to 40° C; the site of the injection would be painful, and the patient could neither walk around nor lie down. Many patients developed hemorrhoids as a result of the sulphur injections. The doses would gradually be increased, then decreased. In Section 12, a course of treatment with sulphur usually involved ten to fifteen injections. Everyone spoke with fear about Section 9: the doses there were larger and a course involved twenty to twenty-five injections. (This was the section to which Plakhotnyuk had been transferred to keep him from meeting me.) Sulphur was never administered to me, because the authorities were afraid of my wife.

The Dnipropetrovsk hospital was not, properly speaking, a medical facility. First of all, it was called a "special psychiatric hospital" because the regime was particularly severe. Secondly, although sentences remanding prisoners to it referred to "releasing from guard," it was in fact a prison. The hospital and the adjacent prison were surrounded by a wall and barbed wire. Towers manned by guards with automatic rifles stood at the corners. In addition to the ordinary guards, we had over us criminal orderlies, nurses, and doctors, so that the security was even greater than in ordinary prisons.

Reveille was at six o'clock. As soon as tobacco and cigarettes (three teaspoons of tobacco or two to five cigarettes) had been issued, a trip to the lavatory was made. The patients were taken out by wards and often marched out two by two. They would fight for places in the lavatory, and those who had pushed their way through to the hole were urged on. The weaker patients were driven away. Some patients could not urinate when their turn came, having developed a neurosis of expectation. Fights would break out, and orderlies would rush in, beat the patients, and chase them out. There were six such trips a day. Smoking was permitted during three of them.

Meals were served three times a day. Before breakfast and lunch a patient appointed for the task distributed the food that patients had bought at the shop or received from home. The patients would stand in line or be sent out in groups of three to five. A nurse recorded how much each patient had received, in order to keep the orderlies from taking the food. Not permitted parcels from home, they were always hungry and would wait like birds of prey for the patients to receive food. "Do you have any sausage? Get me some canned goods and apples! And get some sugar for Vaska and me!"

Then the patient would have to conceal a can or a piece of sausage in his pocket under the nurse's nose. If a patient refused an orderly, he would not get his tobacco or be permitted to go to the lavatory outside the schedule. The patients also had to divide their food so that each orderly would get something from the two parcels that could be sent from home every month, the two parcels that could be received during visits from relatives, and the purchases at the shop. And it would be shameful not to give something to the patients who did not receive parcels from their families. Half the patients were in this category.

Some patients gave the orderlies all their food for the sake of permission to smoke. The doctors tried to catch the patients who were giving away their food. Section 9, to which I was transferred later, was raided one day, and many patients were caught short of the food they should have had. They were called in and threatened with sulphur to make them name the orderlies to whom they had given their food. Some patients complied. I was called in, too.

"To whom did you give your canned food?" Nina Nikolayevna Bochkovskaya, the director of Section 9, said to me severely.

"You know that I won't tell you," I replied.

"Aren't you ashamed of yourself? These scoundrels are robbing the patients. You insist on a just society, and yet you shield robbers."

I tried to justify myself. "The orderlies will steal as long as they have the power to limit lavatory visits and smoking."

"No, we'll issue regulations not to permit anyone to go to the lavatory without a nurse's permission."

"Then many people will develop bladder problems."

After breakfast or lunch we had an hour for exercise in the yard. The regulations called for two hours, but the authorities insisted that the exercise yard was too small. It would have been difficult in fact to send thirteen sections to it, so two or three sections were brought out together. In warm weather there would be a hundred men at a time in the yard. The ground was covered with vomit—the drugs made many patients throw up—and spittle. I went to the yard only to learn the latest news and to meet other politicals.

Bedtime was ten o'clock. The light of the bulb on the ceiling glared into my eyes all night.

Once a week we were permitted to write letters—all at the same time, in the midst of the unceasing noise—and issued reading matter. The library consisted of patients' books, most of which were such junk that I couldn't stand to read them.

We had showers once every week or ten days. The bathhouse was packed with patients, and three or four men would stand under one shower, pushing and fighting. So little time was allotted that those who couldn't fight their way through only managed to smear around the dirt on their bodies. The water was icy or boiling hot.

Once every few months the mattresses and pillows were shaken out and fumigated to kill insects. Many patients were too weak to carry out their mattresses, which were then piled by the orderlies on other patients. Tempers would flare, and curses would fly. The mattresses were beaten with sticks. It was necessary to find a place to beat out one's mattress, and many patients brought back their mattresses without having shaken them out.

I slept under the influence of tranquilizers and frequently would be awakened by shouts. Orderlies were beating a patient for insolent behavior. The patient would cry out that he wanted to go to the lavatory, but the orderlies would not permit it because he had no food to give them. A nurse would come running.

"Ivanenko, why are you being disorderly?"

"I want to go to the lavatory!"

"To smoke again!" the nurse would snap.

"No, to piss."

"Don't use foul language! You're lying, you want to smoke." If the nurse was kind, she would add, "All right, let him go. But make sure he doesn't smoke. His fingers are filthy with nicotine stains."

Someone would be loudly singing an obscene song. Another patient would sing an even more obscene one just as loudly. I could not avoid hearing the obscene doggerel, songs, and arguments or the stories about sexual escapades. "We dash into a Finnish village," one patient would relate. "Not a soul anywhere. Then I see a woman hiding. I pull out my pistol and point it at her. 'Lie down!' I tell her. She lies down." Then came all the details of the rape. I would listen with interest because the patient was an excellent storyteller. His

311

stories had a plot and revealed a good deal about the psychology of the people involved. He was particularly fond of relating how he had murdered his wife.

Tolya would go into a delirium. He would often start with a song, then proceed to screams and curses. His delirium involved rhymes. "Constitution, tution, tution, tution. Prostitution, tution, tution, tution . . ." For some reason everyone treated Tolya well. If he was not tied down when a fit came over him, he would head for the window to smash the glass or to the lavatory to break whatever came to hand. Then orderlies and guards would be summoned to tie him down, but he would continue to rhyme. "Tolya, tolya, olya, olya, olya. Medicine, medicine, dicine, dicine." The deliriums would last for hours. Tolya would be given injections and would gradually calm down. Sometimes he would have a delirium during the night, and then I couldn't sleep until it was over.

Occasionally I was called out for interrogation. The questions were always the same: what had I written, why had I written it, and why had I not thought about my family? "If you are to be released, you must help us understand your illness," Kamenetskaya said during one such interrogation. "Write an autobiography for us. Explain what motives led you to become involved in anti-Soviet activities."

"Is this to be a kind of confession, an intellectual autobiography?"

"Precisely. Don't be afraid. It's important for you yourself. You don't have to write about your friends or your relations with women. You're a Freudian, and yet for some reason you're embarrassed to speak about this."

"Now, that's exactly what I shall not write about because I consider it my personal affair. And I shall hardly write a confession. I can't be certain that it won't be used by the KGB."

"No, I've already explained to you that it's for the psychiatrists and not the KGB," Kamenetskaya insisted. "The KGB doesn't interfere in our business."

"All right, I will think about it."

"Do that. It's important for you to realize the error of your views. And the sooner we can cure you of them, the sooner you can return to your family. We are not asking you to reveal the anti-Soviet secrets of your democratic-nationalist movement."

I returned to the ward and told the other politicals about the proposal. Such proposals, I learned, were made only to political prisoners who were widely known. Those who wrote confessions were then interviewed by the doctors and forced to prove in writing that their ideas were senseless, illogical, and utopian. The recantations were accompanied by humiliation, and there were cases where such statements of self-abnegation were shown to relatives. Even then the KGB waited for a year or two before permitting the political to be released. Some political prisoners would write confessions without being asked to do so, but they were usually genuinely ill. Such confessions were the butt of jokes among orderlies, nurses, and doctors.

"Well, Ivanov, wouldn't you like to address the country on television?"

"No, Nina Nikolayevna, I was a fool."

"And now you're not a fool?"

"No, I've been cured."

"Are you certain that you've been cured?"

"Yes. I'm no longer interested in politics."

"And do you read newspapers?"

"Only the sports news." An interest in sports was taken as a sign that the patient had been cured of politics.

After my talk with Kamenetskaya I remembered my discussion with Vladimir Dremlyuga on Pavel Litvinov's birthday and my desire to write about what brings people to reject the Soviet system. All right, I thought, I shall have to write a confession of a child of these times when I leave the *psikhushka*.

I was finally permitted a visit from my wife. I had not seen Tanya for a year and a half and had a great deal to tell her. She also had much to tell me. Many of our friends had left the Democratic Movement out of fear. Others, for whom we had not had great hopes, proved to be brave and supported Tanya at the risk of trouble from the KGB. But many liberal orators and active *samizdatchiks* hadn't visited her even once. On the other hand, people who had not believed in *samizdat* and who had been apolitical learned to scorn danger for moral reasons or through respect for themselves.

Tanya hinted that Pyotr Yakir and Victor Krasin had behaved badly, which I found hard to believe. She also expressed doubts about Dzyuba's position. My own position had thus become shakier. Tanya realized this and said, "Are we drawing a distinction between ourselves and the people? We must go on for our sakes and for the people's sake, and not for the sake of our comrades in the movement. After all, the latter may prove to be unequal to the task."

Then Tanya asked me not to become embittered. She had noticed from my tone that I was full of hatred. I broke into laughter. Her request coincided with the goal I had set myself: to keep a cool head while my heart was full of both hatred and love. Tanya reminded me of an observation by Camus that I was very fond of: "A lengthy struggle for justice devours the love that gave birth to it."

I told Tanya that I wanted all my writings collected in one book under a pseudonym, so that I could continue the struggle. I asked her to get permission to obtain all the letters and articles that I had written in prison because I wanted her to carry on the work. She was refused, on the pretext that everything had been filed with my case history.

I also asked Tanya to bring me books on structural analysis, games, art, humor, and psychology. On her last visit, when she had not been allowed to see me on a pretext, she had brought me several books—a collection of Italian plays, a book by Martin Gardner on mathematical games, and Tove Jansson's story about the Moomin trolls.[7] I was called in for questioning.

"Why do you need a fairy tale by Jansson?" Kamenetskaya asked with astonishment.

"My son likes this story," I explained. I did not mention that I liked it, too: that would be a sign of infantilism. "He sent it to me."

"How strange! Complicated philosophical books that I can't understand a word of, and suddenly these children's books."

"I've studied child psychology, fairy tales, games, and riddles. This requires a complicated scientific apparatus. Do you see these formulas?" I said, showing her whatever came to hand to establish a connection between my childish interests and grown-up science.

But Kamenetskaya's suspicion of a schizophrenic return to childhood on my part remained with her, reinforced by my numerous books on Chinese culture, mythology, the morphology of art, and games. I had written a fairy tale about a mouse that lived in a reed. When Kamenetskaya read it and declared that she hadn't understood a thing, I explained that the fairy tale had been written especially for my son, not as literature. He would understand all the images. Kamenetskaya replied that she would not let the story go through because it might be needed for my case history. My son later replied to a letter in which I had outlined the fairy tale. He liked it.

"You see, my son understood the fairy tale," I said. "It's all based on a child's, and not an adult's, vision of the world."

Having written a second part of the fairy tale, I realized that I would not be able to complete it because the screams and deliriums around me prevented me from concentrating. It would also be difficult to write an optimistic ending, and the psychiatrists might take this as a symptom of my "illness."

During my three months in Section 12, two extraordinary events occurred. A patient tried to hang himself in the lavatory one night. He was discovered by accident. The orderlies beat him up and took away all the patients' handkerchiefs. Everyone mocked the potential suicide, who tried to excuse himself by saying that he could not stand such a life any longer.

On another occasion the patients in quarantine rebelled (the rebel spirit of the labor camps always exists in quarantine). When some of the orderlies beat up a juvenile, the thieves stood up for him and hit back at the orderlies. They were punished by being prescribed sulphur. Knowing that the drug would break down their resistance within a few hours, they barricaded the door to the ward with beds. While they were building their barricade, the strongest fellow came out brandishing a bench. He wielded it like a stave to keep off the orderlies and guards until he was seized and brutally beaten. The rebels smashed all the windows, cut up their chests and stomachs in the criminals' usual manner of protest, tore out the radiators, and threatened to throw them at anyone who broke through.

When the provincial prosecutor arrived, the prison authorities gathered outside the quarantine ward to open negotiations. The rebels demanded that sulphur injections and beatings by orderlies be stopped and that they be let off without punishment. The promise was easy to make. The rebels were all sent off to the prison and then split up among the sections.

All of us immediately felt the effects of the mutiny. Anyone who was overheard discussing the event or expressing satisfaction was prescribed a course of sulphur injections. Attempts were made to link me with the rebels, but unsuccessfully, even though I had passed on tobacco to them.

The day after the mutiny Kamenetskaya called me into her office. "You're being transferred to another section," she announced with an awkward smile.

"To Section 9?"

"Yes. Come now, why are you so gloomy all of a sudden? The treatment there is the same as here, and the orderlies are less high-handed. It's just that Plakhotnyuk has been demanding to be transferred to my section, and you'll be taking his place."

21

A PINEAPPLE FROM NEW YORK

In Section 9 I was placed in a high-security surveillance ward for aggressive and seriously ill patients. My ward contained between eighteen and twenty-one patients, though some surveillance wards held up to forty. The screams, the singing, and the fights between patients and orderlies never abated. I asked to be moved to a regular ward but had to await permission for a long time.

Although a radio blared from early morning until ten o'clock at night, the regular ward had its advantages. The patients were not violent, and it was possible to talk with them. Volodya, the young son of a philosophy professor, was keen on science fiction, and we discussed books and science. After two evenings of talk, he was transferred from the ward, cautioned not to have anything to do with me, and given stiff doses of haloperidol. I was asked why I had got involved with a boy who had murdered his brother.

"Can't I even talk with other people? Put me with just politicals," I replied.

"So that you can cook up plots?"

"What plots?"

"You know what we mean!"

Once I asked Volodya why in all this time I had not met a single thief, currency speculator, or murderer who had sincerely repented. Volodya never did understand that my question was directed at him as well. Whether they are sane, insane, or recovered, inmates never repent. Their only regret is that they concealed their traces poorly. They all have a justification for their crimes. "I only stole from the rich," one said. "Army officers, directors, and ministers." Another excused himself by saying, "The government steals from the people, and I steal from the government." And a third argued, "No one suffers from currency exchanges. I help make a transaction, and both parties are pleased."

Although the orderlies gave fewer beatings in Section 9, this was only because Nina Nikolayevna Bochkovskaya, the director of the section, held everyone in her iron grip. She is the one who should have been called Ilse Koch. Her voice was calm and assured, and her refined, cold face would light up occasionally with a contemptuous smile. By comparison with Bochkovskaya, Ellochka the Cannibal was simply a sexually obsessed hysteric.

Bochkovskaya refused to get involved in discussions with patients. She would dash into a ward and announce in a lifeless voice, "Petrov, you've been cursing the nurse again. Sulphur! Ivanov, I hear you've been masturbating. Haloperidol!" When an inmate complained about the pain, she replied, "That's all right. You'll stop and think about the sulphur before raping a girl again. You came here to be treated, not for a rest cure." To a patient who asked when he would recover she answered, "When I retire and you stop masturbating!" And to another inmate she said, "Your treatment is our business. We're paid for this. The sulphur will help you. Yes, it will hurt, but you're a man. You'll have to bear it. After all, you're being treated."

One old man called Bochkovskaya a Gestapo agent; she immediately prescribed a large dose of sulphur for him. He whimpered, groaned, and screamed with pain, making it impossible for the rest of us to sleep. "Leonid Ivanovych," he called out to me, "will I die?"

"No," I replied angrily. "People don't die from sulphur."

"Boys, will I die?"

"Shut up! You won't die!"

Mad with the pain, the old man smashed a window and tried to cut his throat. He was subdued and beaten up. Two days later someone noticed that his face had turned blue. A nurse took his pulse and summoned a doctor, who administered blood transfusions and oxygen. The old man was brought around after three days. Before administering sulphur, and such a large dose at that, Bochkovskaya had not bothered to check for contraindications.

Bochkovskaya obviously understood psychology and easily caught me when I tried to evade her questions. (I had no intention of telling her what I thought about the authorities and replied only to questions about my writings.) She made derisive comments about my letters to my wife and children: "kind words," "advice to the children," "dreams of joint work." To my surprise, she admired my favorite artist, Mikalojus Čiurlionis. Nevertheless, she reproached me for liking mentally disturbed artists: Ivanov, Vrubel, the later Van Gogh, and

Chagall.[1] When Tanya sent me Henri Perruchot's *La Vie de Van Gogh*,[2] Bochkovskaya forbade me to give it to the other inmates because it dealt with mental illness.

"Plyushch, why do you never say hello to us?" Bochkovskaya once asked me. "Is it a matter of principle with you, or is it your lack of breeding? You're an educated man. Just look at the books you read."

She conducted her interrogations in a sharp, derisive tone. "You're friendly with that murderer who killed two wives!"

"I wasn't friendly with him," I replied. "I simply listened to his interesting stories."

"How can you listen to such filth? You have a wife whom you call tender names in your letters, and yet you listen to this debauchery!"

"You yourself accused me of not talking to anyone except politicals. You separated Volodya and me because we talked about science fiction. With whom am I to talk? You give me few books."

Bochkovskaya did a good job of studying my letters to find my weak spots and thus occasionally succeeded in getting me to explode with anger. "Aren't you ashamed of yourself, calling me in for a political discussion?" I asked her. "The tranquilizers leave me barely able to think. I'm indifferent to everything, and any imprecise answer will be recorded as a sign that my condition is becoming more acute. And you'll be rewarded with money and vacations for absurd or illogical remarks on my part. I know you like art. Isn't love of beauty connected with love for people?"

"You're getting excited over nothing and misinterpreting my words. It is precisely because we love our patients that we must know what you're concealing, why you're so rude with the staff, and why you look away instead of saying hello. Have you decided to kill someone, or even yourself, to spite us?"

"You yourself encourage such ideas with your talk," I countered. "Why don't you practice psychotherapy instead of humiliating patients for every weakness and failing and threatening them with punishment?"

"You ought to write a report about all this."

"So that you can file it with my case history as evidence of my reformist mania?"

"You obviously have a persecution complex. You think the doctors are your enemies. Why don't you write your intellectual autobiography? Explain why you developed incorrect views in your youth, what books you read, whom you met, what you wrote, and how you've changed your mind now. Explain at length the mistakes in your previous views. Explain how you see our Soviet reality and your own anti-Soviet activity now. You have a morbid trait: you refuse to name other anti-Soviets. But that's all right. Those who need to know will learn who these people are. This Klara, for example. Who is she?"

"A stoker."

"That's not true. She writes very subtle observations about literature."

"Is a stoker incapable of appreciating literature?"

"Not so subtly."

"She was expelled from the university."

"You see, all your friends—Khodorovich, Gildman, Feldman—are anti-Soviet. How can we release you if you are immediately going to be in their company again and your delusions will be renewed? Stop corresponding with them. That will be a sign that you are recovering."

Lyudmila Alekseyevna Lyubarskaya was assigned to be my psychiatrist. Inmates told me that she had been the director of the hospital when it was established in 1968. Conditions were much worse at that time: patients slept on the floor, the orderlies savagely beat them, and several people were killed. Lyubarskaya was then demoted to an ordinary staff position and placed under Bochkovskaya.

Lyubarskaya was better than Bochkovskaya in that she was simply an ass and not a sadist. Her professional standards can be gauged by the reply she gave me when I asked why psychotherapy was not used at the hospital. "There is no use for psychotherapy in psychiatry," she announced. Lyubarskaya sincerely believed that a man who had renounced his career as a mathematician and exposed his family and himself to danger for the sake of politics (in which only politicians should be interested) must be abnormal. My wide-ranging interests were a clear sign of schizophrenia to her, and she conducted her interrogations from this position of normality and morality. "Write a statement of repentance," she would urge me. "Stop writing letters to your anti-Soviet friends and tell your wife to stop making trouble."

From the way Lyubarskaya spoke about Tanya I realized that she, and not I, was the chief psycho and enemy. The hospital staff was so afraid of Tanya that it even broke the regulation barring children under sixteen from visiting. Lyubarskaya asked me several times to make Tanya see reason. Otherwise she would be committed and the children would be taken away. I tried to make Tanya understand this, but I realized that I looked foolish: she was doing everything she could to rescue me, and I was interfering by advising her to keep quiet. In the end I gave up and let Tanya do as she saw fit.

319

Citing my younger son's interest in insects, rocks, fairy tales, and games, Lyubarskaya hinted that he was schizophrenic. When Tanya complained in a letter about something in our elder son's behavior and praised the younger son, Lyubarskaya told me that the elder was on the right track whereas the younger was schizophrenic. And when Klara Gildman wrote me affectionate letters, Lyubarskaya, claiming that she was my mistress, would not give them to me.

If I complained about the loud radio, Lyubarskaya would say, "You see, your anti-Soviet instincts can't take any more." If I failed to say hello to her, she accused me of being hostile. If I talked about the Soviet bourgeoisie, she claimed that I had an inadequate perception of reality. And if I objected to philistine attitudes toward social and political problems, she insisted that I suffered from megalomania and thought that I was Lenin.

When I found it difficult to concentrate on questions put to me and stopped arguing, Lyubarskaya commented, "Silence tactics. You've become embittered, withdrawn into yourself. And yet look at the glances you throw around: you'd kill us all if you had the chance."

I tried to smile. "I am against killing."

"Yet you talk to murderers and won't talk to us. Just look how much contempt and hatred your face shows! You're afraid to reveal your thoughts!"

The nurses in the hospital for the most part merely carried out the doctors' orders, although some liked to joke at the patients' expense and to shout at them. They treated me politely, apparently because an order had been issued not to speak to me. But some nurses whispered to me that they considered the inmates to be sane and advised us to pretend that we had improved. One nurse heard me talking to Tanya during a visit and afterward promised not to give me drugs. "I've understood everything," she said. "I feel sorry for you, but there's nothing more I can do."

The guards had also been cautioned not to speak to me, but they questioned me about Sakharov and Solzhenitsyn as they peered over their shoulders. The wife of one guard listened to a Western radio broadcast and announced to him, "If you don't leave that damn place, I'll divorce you!" The guard complained to us that his superiors wouldn't let him leave. We advised him to promise his wife that he would help the political prisoners in whatever way he could.

Several orderlies questioned me about the Democratic Movement and expressed their sympathy. On the whole, the orderlies were more humane than the guards with both the political prisoners and the genuine patients, mocking and beating only those inmates who toadied to the staff. Some orderlies warned us when a search was to take place and helped us to conceal tobacco and notes. Afterward they would return some of the confiscated goods to the owners. My letters, books, and cigarettes were almost always returned to me.

The inmates spent much of their time talking about sex, repeating the same obviously improbable stories, and the orderlies would stop by to listen and then contribute their own stories. They also amused themselves by taunting patients who wanted to go to the lavatory. "Have you had any women?" they would ask an inmate. "How many? What did you do with them? Dance a *hopak* for us.[3] No, that's bad. Do a boogie-woogie! Jump higher, higher!"

"What's that noise?" a nurse would call out.

"Petka wants to go to the lavatory. Shall we let him?"

"But he's just been there!"

"That's all right. He dances well. He wants to piss. Let him go!"

When the orderlies had tired of that game, they would goad two patients to fight. "He said that you're a queen!" "And he's a stinking faggot!" the other would retort. An exchange of obscenities would take place; someone would take a swipe, and the fight would be on. Sulphur would be ordered: the patients had "got excited."

Most of the inmates at the Dnipropetrovsk *psikhushka* were mentally deranged murderers, rapists, and hooligans. But there were also about sixty political prisoners, who were for the most part sane. These were people like Plakhotnyuk, Ruban, Yevdokimov, Lupynis, and Yatsenko,[4] who had been committed for "anti-Soviet activity," and also the border crossers—people who had tried to escape from the Soviet Union.

All the politicals were cautioned to avoid me. At times I was completely isolated from them, forbidden to go to the kitchen or the yard in case I might accidentally meet one of them. When I did go to the yard, I spoke mostly with Victor Rafalsky, a history teacher who had belonged to an underground Marxist group in Western Ukraine.[5] The group was discovered in 1954, and Rafalsky was sent from one psychiatric hospital to another until 1959. The Leningrad hospital diagnosed him as sane, but the Serbsky Institute insisted that he was schizophrenic. In the early 1960's Rafalsky was sent to the Kazan Special Psychiatric Hospital for five years because connections with an underground Marxist group in Kiev had been detected. He was rearrested in 1969, when a manuscript with a "nationalist deviation" that he had written a long time ago was found. Now, despite all his arguments that the book was old and that he hadn't given it to anyone to read, he was being held at the Dnipropetrovsk *psikhushka* as a schizophrenic.

A delirious patient in Rafalsky's section reported that Rafalsky, a former member of the Ukrainian Insurgent Army named Trotsyuk, and Vasyl Siry, a teacher who had been committed for trying to escape from the country by hijacking an airplane, were plotting an anti-Soviet conspiracy. Without being questioned about the charge, the three were given large doses of sulphur and sodium amobarbital, a central-nervous-system depressant used as a truth serum. They were brought back to their ward completely unconscious. Sulphur was contraindicated for Rafalsky. His health seriously deteriorated, and his usual cheerfulness disappeared. Later one of the doctors told him that he should not get involved with people like Trotsyuk and me.

Finally the doctors told Rafalsky that he had been cured. To be released he needed a guardian who would assume responsibility for him. His mother was living in a home for the aged in Leningrad and hesitated to ask any of her friends for fear of putting them in a spot. When a nurse at the hospital agreed to be Rafalsky's guardian, the administration threatened to fire her, and Rafalsky persuaded her to give up the idea. I suggested to Rafalsky that he take my friend Klara Gildman as his guardian. The director of his section looked at the name. "Aha, you want to flee abroad, to Israel! We know that this woman is Plyushch's protégée. You'll have to find a more suitable guardian." Rafalsky still has not found a suitable guardian.

Anatoliy Lupynis was treated well until he stole his case history and wrote a statement exposing the mendacious and illogical arguments of the panel that had certified him insane and demanding a second examination. The KGB then had a talk with Lupynis, and he was given a powerful new drug manufactured in the United States. A man of great courage, he caved in.

Mykola Plakhotnyuk was permitted by a doctor to keep notes, but the guards discovered them and reported Plakhotnyuk to the hospital administration. The doctor was given a party reprimand, and supervision of pens and paper was made stricter. But then the KGB, hoping to obtain testimony for new trials, came to question Plakhotnyuk. He refused to answer, citing his diagnosis of insanity. "That's all right," the KGB men replied, "we'll send you for a new examination, and you'll be ruled sane." Plakhotnyuk still refused to testify.

All the politicals were staggered when they heard Krasin's and

Yakir's perfidious confessions broadcast on the radio. Many were so shaken that they could neither think nor speak. Yevdokimov had expected something like this from Yakir, but I had not. How could Yakir, who had witnessed the farce of a trial that his father had been subjected to and the mockery that he and his mother had endured, utter such lies? I had thought that he would sooner commit suicide than betray his friends.

Then came the betrayals by Dzyuba, Seleznenko, and Kholodny.[6] Ukrainians were particularly wounded by Dzyuba, who had for years been a symbol of uncompromising Ukraine. We even wondered if he had been tortured. But Tanya explained his breakdown more simply when she came to visit: he hadn't wanted to leave his wife and daughter, whom he loved very much, and die of tuberculosis in a labor camp.

Bochkovskaya pestered me to write a similar confession.

"You yourself understand that people don't change their views so rapidly at my age," I explained. "Do you want me to write a false confession?"

"No, no. We know that you're a truthful man. But perhaps you'll think it over under their influence and will change your views."

Admitting to mental illness is a precondition for recovery. But when an inmate with whom I was friendly took my advice and announced that he was ill, Bochkovskaya said to him, "No, you are well, but you will stay here until you renounce your anti-Soviet views and stop talking to anti-Soviets." After the admission of illness a confession that one's activities have been harmful is required. The inmate must support his confession with proof that it is genuine, and he must substantiate why he considers himself to be ill. I handled the last point very carefully, saying that I was not a specialist and could not express an opinion about my own illness, particularly since I had not seen my diagnosis and did not know what I should be disputing. But even when an inmate proves to the doctors' satisfaction that he has been insane, the decision to release him is still made not by the doctors but by the courts, which can rule that he is in need of further treatment. In practice, of course, the KGB makes the diagnosis, prescribes the treatment (Tanya was told by the KGB that I would be given smaller doses of drugs if she kept quiet), and decides when the inmate has been cured and can be released.

A new victim of the regime's black humor had appeared on the ward. Kolya did not move at all when he was first brought in. At meals he would be propped up and fed with a spoon. In the lavatory he ate feces. Someone noticed that if you said "horse" in his ear, he would break out with loud guffaws. Orderlies, guards, and nurses came around to listen to his hysterical laughter.

Kolya changed as the weeks passed. He began to eat on his own and to laugh only in response to laughter. We noticed that he wanted sausage very badly.

"Do you want some sausage?" the guards and nurses would taunt him.

"Yes, yes! Where?"

"I'll bring it tomorrow!"

The next day Kolya would rush to the person who had promised sausage and with the joyous laugh of an imbecile call out, "Give it to me!"

When they were tired of the sausage game, the guards and orderlies threatened that they would go sleep with his wife. Kolya loved his wife and daughter very much and kept a drawing of his daughter with him. He cried and complained to the doctor. Then the guards and orderlies decided to feign rape, of which Kolya had a mortal fear. Several men would hold his arms and legs as another man dropped his pants and advanced on him. Kolya would scream and twist about, and everyone would roar with laughter.

Thus the days passed: hollering and interrogations by the doctors, pranks and beatings by the orderlies, and deliriums, cries of pain or desperation, obscene ditties, cursing, stories about sports, stories about sex, public masturbation, eating of feces, and scrounging for cigarette stubs among the used lavatory paper by the inmates. On New Year's Eve 1976 an orderly pulled the blanket off a patient and discovered that he had cut his throat. The other inmates were sent to the lavatory, and the doctors practiced their witchcraft over the patient all night. He was saved, only to be beaten by the orderlies. During a film showing a patient who had somehow obtained a nail stabbed another patient in the head. I called in the orderlies. Both patients were severely beaten.

When Mother came to visit, she was very upset because I had believed the psychiatrists' claim that she had written to the KGB about my eccentricities. Mother had never believed my stories about the life style and methods of the Soviet bourgeoisie, but now she finally realized what the Soviet regime is.

Tanya told me about the efforts Amnesty International, the International Committee of Mathematicians,[7] and Ukrainian organizations were making in my behalf. I was certain that it was all in vain, but I was also pleased that in some small way I was still part of the struggle. At one of her visits Tanya brought me a can of pineapple in syrup that someone had sent her from New York. That pineapple was shared by all the inmates as a symbol of the free world.

The tranquilizers and the daily sights deadened me intellectually, morally, and emotionally. The treatment and the regulations at the *psikhushka*, as I saw in my own case, were meant to break the inmate straightaway and crush his will to fight. In Section 12 I had been prescribed haloperidol in small doses. In Section 9 I was given two courses of insulin therapy. After each injection I was strapped down to my bed as if the doctors wanted to produce an insulin shock. Later I was given large doses of the tranquilizer trifluoperazine, both in tablet form—three tablets at a time, three times a day—and by injection. And when I developed erysipelas I was also given penicillin injections.

Although I tried to spit the drugs out when I could, they were killing my desire to read or think, and the mere idea of politics became thoroughly nauseating. My memory was slipping away, and my speech became jerky and abrupt. I was overcome by autism and misanthropy, and for days on end I lay on my bed and tried to sleep. The only thoughts that remained concerned smoking and bribing the orderlies for an extra trip to the lavatory. I even dreaded the visits I had longed for so desperately, because I was worried that Tanya might mention new arrests, and I did not want her to see my apathy and sleepiness or the dropsical swelling and convulsions that the drugs brought on. Visits from the children were particularly painful: I had to force a smile and try to make jokes.

I was increasingly afraid that my deterioration was irreversible and that I might help my torturers by going mad. Despair at the thought that there might be no end to this hell led many healthy patients to contemplate suicide. I, too, was losing my will to live. I maintained a grip on myself only by saying over and over: I must not become embittered; I must not forget; I must not give up!

During my last months at the *psikhushka* the attitude of the medical staff toward me changed for the better, and I encountered fewer taunts and insults.

"Would you like to be released now?" the doctors would ask. "What sort of job would you like?"

"Any job at all."

"Wouldn't you like to leave the country?"

"No. But if I had to choose between staying *here* and going abroad, I would prefer to leave."

I knew that Tanya was making efforts for us to emigrate, but I did not think this was possible. I only hoped that the authorities would release me from the *psikhushka,* and life in the West was beyond my imagination. I was no longer qualified as a mathematician. Were my writings on games worth anything? Would we be able to adapt to new living conditions and new values? All the good and the bad things I had heard about the West came to mind.

Bochkovskaya played on my uncertainty with all the refinement of an Ilse Koch. When I asked her point-blank whether I would be released soon, she replied that I had not been cured yet. Less than two weeks later, however, I was called to the director's office. Katkova, the head of the hospital division, and Babenko, the head of the prison division, were waiting for me. They announced with distress that my outer clothing was unsuitable and that they had bought pants and a shirt for me with hospital funds. The pants proved to be too small. Babenko ran out to buy new ones. These were also too small. He bought a third pair. I refused to put on the tie: they wanted to send me to the West dressed as a European. The stuff was put in a suitcase, also purchased by the *psikhushka.*

A sumptuous soup with meatballs was placed on the table for me. I was glad that I hadn't concealed in my cheek the list of sixty political prisoners I had drawn up with such difficulty over the previous months. I praised the soup.

"Aren't you given such servings of meatballs every day?"

"The cooks devour them before they get to us."

"Leonid Ivanovych, do you know where you're going?"

"To Kiev, I hope, to say good-bye to my relatives."

"No, you're going to the place for which your wife got a visa." They couldn't bring themselves to say "Israel."

"To the station at Chop? To Israel?"

"Yes."

I was driven to the airport and placed on an airplane. It landed at Mukachiv instead of Chop.[8] There, accompanied by plainclothesmen, I was allowed to walk about the town and say good-bye to Ukraine. I was held at Mukachiv for the rest of the day: they were limiting the time I would have for taking leave of my mother and sister. I arrived at Chop an hour before the train was to depart. Someone persistently photographed my family's happy reunion. We were delicately searched as the other passengers were indelicately kept waiting. Galich's poem ran through my head:

And when I come home, though it's February, nightingales will sing
That old melody, quaint and forgotten, sung into tatters,
And I will fall down, the conquered of my own conquest,
And buffet my head on your knees like a boat at the quay!
When I come home . . .

But when will I come home? [9]

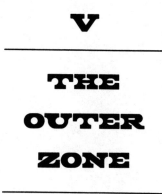

V

THE OUTER ZONE

by Tatyana Plyushch (Zhitnikova)

22

THE FIRST
TWO YEARS

Ministry of Internal Affairs   May 3, 1973
Ukrainian SSR

At about 11:00 P.M. on April 30 we were seized at the door of our residence by three persons—one wearing the uniform of a second lieutenant in the militia and the other two in plain clothes. Without giving us any explanation, they twisted our hands behind our backs and drove us to the Podil District Militia Station in Kiev.

There people who introduced themselves as Lieutenant Zhilinsky, Captain Filonenko, and Valeriy Smirnov (in plain clothes) announced that we looked like currency speculators and were suspected of concealing narcotics, weapons, and pornography in our handbags or clothes. We were subjected to body searches. The civilians who had brought us to the station served as witnesses.

After the search, the concoction about currency speculation was forgotten. The men demanded that a notebook be given to them, in return for which we would immediately be released. Otherwise we would be held for fifteen days for "resisting the authorities" and "attempting to conceal ourselves." When Zhitnikova objected that the charge was untrue, the men threatened that the "witnesses" would testify in court that we had used foul language, insulted officials, and refused to give evidence. When we stated that we would complain, Zhilinsky replied, "Complain all you like. The complaint will come to me no matter what."

The questions put to us by the militiamen and plainclothes agents concerned L. I. Plyushch (who is being detained in a KGB prison) and our walk around the city. Having confiscated the notebook, they gave us neither a receipt nor a list of the confiscated items. We did not get home until five o'clock in the morning.

This whole incident—from the boorish behavior to the strange questions—forces us to conclude that currency speculation was not the real reason for it. If we had not been in a militia station at the time, we would have concluded that we had been attacked by disguised criminals and would have complained to the militia immediately after being released. We request that you investigate the incident and take measures to insure that the said officials do not disgrace the uniform they have been entrusted to wear.

Tatyana Zhitnikova
Ada Plyushch

It is difficult to convey what those four years were like. How can I explain to anyone who has not lived in the "country of victorious socialism" what simple self-respect and a refusal to lie mean in a country where words and thoughts are crimes? The question of how to live arose for Lyonya and me when we first became aware of ourselves as persons. Gradually we formulated the only possible answer: to live with self-respect. That meant *samizdat*, which had to be typed and disseminated. Like-minded people had to be found, and we had to beat our brains all the time.

When it became clear that prison lay ahead, there was still only one answer. Nothing else was possible. To well-wishers who reproached us we would reply, "Yes, we have children. Yes, we know that we shall end up in prison. But we cannot save our children if we remain slaves and ruin their souls."

Hence we felt no fear when we found ourselves involved in the search of Ivan Dzyuba's apartment on January 14, but, rather, took everything as fitting. We had already experienced other searches and read the *Chronicle of Current Events*. We felt only anguish for Ivan. We wanted to help him in some way, to share his nightmare. He sat calmly, smiling and reassuring us.

The agents took me to the kitchen and told me to undress, but still I felt absolutely indifferent: they were not human beings. They probed the seams of my clothes, tore the label off my skirt, and pulled out the elastic from my underpants. Then they felt my hair, peered into my mouth, and forced me to squat. What were they looking for? Diamonds, *samizdat*? No, they knew quite well that they wouldn't find them there. (But they examined my handbag carelessly and overlooked a scrap of paper with information for the *Chronicle*.) All this was intended to intimidate and humiliate me. Later—at the police station and in Victor Nekrasov's house—when they searched me again, I always knew that they were looking for signs of fear.

When we were finally permitted to leave and rushed off to Ivan Svitlychny's, we found evidence of a pogrom there as well. Leonida, Ivan's wife, was sitting in a devastated apartment: the floor was littered with books that had been pulled off the shelves. For the next four years everything remained the same, as if the agents had just left. The door to Ivan's room was shut, and Leonida lived in a pocket-handkerchief space by the bed. You can understand how Leonida feels only when you see that still-shattered life.

That night I could not pull myself together to decide what to do. I watched with apathy as Lyonya burned his papers. In the morning we sent Lesyk to kindergarten and Dima to school. "If you come home from school and find a search going on, telephone Mother," we instructed Dima just in case.

Getting ready for work, I took with me our most precious belonging—an autographed photograph of Solzhenitsyn that he had given to Lyonya in 1969 in gratitude for his article, "Quo Vadis, Yevgeniy Yevtushenko?"

Toward the end of the day I was called to the telephone. "Mother, we have visitors," Dima said. My first thought was to warn our friends. I did not let myself think about what was happening at home. Somehow I managed to finish my lecture and then warned those friends whom I could reach by telephone. Thus my new life began. The boundary was sharp and clear: life before and after January 15. My last traces of fear vanished that day.

I was with Volodya Yuvchenko that day. One of those people who stay by their friends in all situations, he was a historian but had been fired from his teaching job a year earlier for being a "Tolstoyan" and for "propagating pacifism." He was not permitted to work with children and then was continually harassed because of his friendship with me.

Our last stop on the way home was at Alexander Feldman's. When we got there, we found a search going on. We managed only to exchange a few words with Sasha and to tell him who else was being searched. It became clear that a pogrom was under way. The searches and arrests went on for several days. A good deal of Jewish literature —articles and Hebrew textbooks—was confiscated from Sasha. He behaved firmly with the KGB: no discussions with the agents, only protests against the illegality. (His time had not come yet, and he was released three days later.) I demanded that Volodya and I be permitted to leave, because my children were waiting at home. The KGB men let us go quickly. There were so many searches being conducted that day, as I learned later, that they were not able to coordinate everything.

At home, there were two or three KGB men in every room. The friends I had warned had also come. Lyonya was exhausted, for the search had been going on since morning. Our friends were soon taken away by the KGB. Dima understood what was happening. Lesyk sensed that something terrible was going on, stared at the strangers with hatred, and refused to sleep.

Lyonya reassured me, insisting that he would hold out. He begged me to behave discreetly because I would be alone with the children. I had no thoughts and still could not believe that everything was over. At first the KGB men even forbade us to sit near each other, but later we ignored them and sat together until morning.

Toward the end, when they had written everything down, the KGB men began to confiscate our photographs. They took whatever they wanted, including photographs of my father and Lyonya's mother. They refused to explain when we asked why. "Get dressed!" the KGB men said to Lyonya.

All our belongings had been turned upside down. I looked for warm clothes. There were only three rubles in the house, but it was too early to go to neighbors and borrow more.

Lyonya and I said good-bye. The KGB men mumbled something reassuring and walked out with him. It was over. I lay down. I still had not fully realized what had happened.

The telephone rang. It was Lena Kosterin from Moscow, wanting to know what was happening. Then Pyotr Yakir called. "Tanya, remember that no matter what happens, we are always with you."

January, February, and March passed. Various people reported that they were being called in and questioned about Lyonya. The KGB was saying that he was "abnormal" and "just as mad as Grigorenko." At work I learned that someone at an executive conference had said that I was a "Zionist" and was leading "an antisocial way of life." What was I to do?

Prosecutor of the Ukrainian SSR   May 25, 1972

On May 24, 1972, Comrade Bortnychuk, the Director of the Office of Games and Toys at the Ministry of Education of the Ukrainian SSR, notified me that my previously planned official business trip to the Crimean Province has been canceled.

The administration has previously attempted to encroach upon my rights by canceling business trips to an international exhibition of toys and an All-Union seminar on toys in Moscow. In the second case, the administration and the KGB displayed a surprising coordination in their actions and jointly prevented my departure for Moscow.

But only now has the director of the office officially stated that my business trip is being canceled because I am being summoned for interrogation by the KGB and that I have been given a vote of no confidence as a methodologist. According to the director, I cannot go on official business trips or even continue working at the office.

Thus I have been given to understand that I can be dismissed from my job because of the arrest of my husband, L. I. Plyushch, in whose case I have been summoned as a witness by the KGB. I believe that such a threat is an attempt to blackmail me and to apply psychological pressure on me as a witness.

I demand that my right to retain my job be officially confirmed, and I request the Prosecutor's Office to assist me in this. Please attach this statement to my husband's case file.

T. I. Zhitnikova

The interrogations by the KGB began on May 11. "Tatyana Ilyinichna, here's a letter to you from your husband, but I cannot give it to you. Would you like me to read it?" the interrogator announced on the first day.

How the scoundrels had calculated everything! There hadn't been a word about Lyonya for four months, and I had agreed to come in for questioning only because I hoped to learn something about him. But how could I listen to this bastard reading *my* letter? "No, I don't want you to read it. Either give it to me or don't bother with it at all."

"Well, all right. I'll cover up several lines here, and you can read the rest."

The interrogations concerned the *samizdat* that had been confiscated: Where did it come from and who was reading it? Who visited us, and what did we talk about? At first there seemed to be no danger in saying that I was acquainted with Ira Yakir or Yuliy Kim. After all, they were friends. Claiming that I didn't know them would mean repudiating friends. Was I acquainted with them? Yes. Had they conducted anti-Soviet conversations? No, they hadn't. Had they brought anti-Soviet literature? No, they hadn't. What was my attitude toward them? Friendly.

But with every interrogation I realized more clearly that I was not doing the right thing. The KGB did not need the truth. It needed to establish that we were all anti-Soviet, to prove that because we knew one another, we were all enemies of the state. Even a positive statement about a friend would be turned against him and me. Thus I gradually developed a tactic of speaking as little as possible: "I don't know," "I don't remember," "No, he didn't read it," "No, he didn't give it to me." After a while I stopped admitting to being friends with anyone. My only consolation was that there was not a single word in my testimony on the essence of the charges.

Ministry of Internal Affairs   May 27, 1972
Ukrainian SSR
Committee of State Security
Council of Ministers

On May 27, 1972, First Lieutenant Yurechko summoned me for a talk at the Darnytsia Militia Station, where Captain Selekhov, the head of the station, and First Lieutenant Yurechko tried to force me to sign a statement that, on the dates of May 27, 28, 29, or 30, I would not visit public places in the city or go to the center of the city, except to go to work. If I contravened this demand, I would be charged with disturbing public peace. When I requested an explanation, Captain Selekhov replied that "the state is an organ of coercion" and all citizens are required to carry out its demands, particularly since this one came from both the militia and the KGB.

When I refused to sign the statement, which to my mind was insulting and illegal, the lieutenant refused to let me leave and threatened that I would be detained for fifteen days for resisting the authorities and would definitely spend those four days in a prison cell. After I unconditionally refused to sign such an unintelligible and unmotivated statement, I was permitted to leave, and the lieutenant told me to go for an explanation to the Republic KGB Office at 33 Volodymrska Street.

Such behavior by the militia gives me reason to expect illegal actions and deliberate provocations. I cannot be certain that I shall not be arrested on a pretext. I request that you investigate the actions of the said persons, explain what has happened, and protect me from arbitrary actions and violence.

T. I. Zhitnikova

Poor Dima, he was so frightened then! I had taken him with me so that at least one person would know where I was. Sasha Feldman had been taken away in exactly the same manner on the previous day, and his brother had been told that they didn't know where he was. Sasha was located only six days later, in a preliminary detention cell, where, according to the law, a person cannot be held for more than three days if charges have not been preferred. But what did the law have to do with it? Richard Nixon was expected in Kiev, and many people were summoned to the militia and required to sign promises or, like Sasha, simply arrested.

Comrade Roman Rudenko   June 4, 1972
Prosecutor General of the USSR

On May 25, 1972, Comrade Fedosenko, the KGB investigator conducting the investigation in the case of my husband, L. I. Plyushch (arrested in Kiev on January 15, 1972), informed me that my husband had been sent for a psychiatric evaluation. According to the investigator, the grounds for this were that my husband had been "ill a great deal," and "certain reasons" on the investigator's part. The parcel I brought for my husband was refused, and I was not told where he had been taken.

I have known my husband for fourteen years (we were married when he was nineteen) and thus am fully qualified to speak about his health. He was ill only in childhood, having suffered from tuberculosis between the ages of nine and fourteen.

Grounds for fearing a biased approach to my husband's case are provided by facts that occurred long before he was sent for a psychiatric evaluation. In February, Comrade Sur, a KGB official who was also involved in L. I. Plyushch's case, told F. A. Didenko, an acquaintance of my husband's, that the KGB had a letter from Plyushch's mother in which she wrote about her son's "eccentricities." In fact, she wrote no such letter and made no such statements to the KGB. One must suppose that the investigator wanted to hear about Plyushch's "eccentricities" and hence decided to prompt Didenko. At that same time, one of the witnesses in Plyushch's case (I know his name but am not mentioning it to avoid causing him trouble) was told that "Plyushch is just as mad as General Grigorenko."

All these facts force me to appeal to you not to permit any illegality in the course of investigating Plyushch's case (including the question of a psychiatric evaluation) and not to permit arbitrary actions in the disposition of his case.

T. I. Zhitnikova

Naturally I received no replies to these letters. The months of waiting stretched out. Lyonya was being held at Lefortovo Prison in Moscow, which I learned about only because parcels for him were accepted there. Rumors reached me that he had been ruled nonresponsible and would be sent to the psychiatric prison in Dnipropetrovsk, but telegrams and letters inquiring about the investigation were not answered. The investigation was closed in November. I found an attorney willing to accept the case, though he had no hopes, either.

In response to one of my letters I was summoned to the Republic Prosecutor's Office to see Maly, the director of the department that supervises the KGB. What supervision was there to talk about? My questions and demands were met with an incoherent reply. Maly read the results of the psychiatric evaluations.

I learned from him that there had been two. The first had lasted from June 12 to July 14, while Lyonya was supposedly at the Serbsky Institute, and was called an "inpatient examination." The chairman of the panel was Georgiy Morozov, and the members were Dr. Kachayev, Professor Lunts, and Senior Research Assistant Gartsev. Their diagnosis read:

The evidence in the case, the manuscripts, and the results of the evaluation indicate that L. I. Plyushch is suffering from a mental illness—sluggish schizophrenia. He has suffered since youth from a paranoid disorder characterized by messianism, reformist ideas, emotional disturbances, and an uncritical attitude toward his condition. He poses a danger to society, must be considered nonresponsible, and should be committed to a special psychiatric hospital.

The KGB questioned the diagnosis, however, and asked the Ministry of Health to set up a second panel, which included Andrey Snezhnevsky as chairman and Lunts, Morozov, and Anufreyev as members. Their diagnosis stated:

The patient is suffering from a chronic mental disorder of the schizophrenic type. The most prominent features of the illness have been its early beginnings and the development of paranoid disturbance involving elements of fantasizing and naïve opinions: this has determined his behavior pattern. Recent symptoms include the appearance of a delusion of inventiveness in the field of psychology: he has an uncritical attitude to what he has done. Constitutes a danger to society; needs treatment in a psychiatric hospital.

His condition has worsened since the first examination took place. . . . Some disturbance has become apparent in the emotional-volitional sphere (apathy, indifference, passivity); his constant concern with reformism has been evolving into a concern with innovation in the field of psychology. . . . He should be sent for compulsory treatment in a psychoneurological hospital.

From the attorney I learned that the second panel had recommended treatment in an ordinary psychiatric hospital. The attorney, who had seen Lyonya and said that he was holding up well, was absolutely convinced that Lyonya was sane, but he had no illusions.

The trial took place between January 25 and 29, 1973. On May 22 I addressed a letter to Nikolay Podgorny, Leonid Brezhnev, and Aleksey Kosygin:

. . . I have made every effort to keep the case of L. I. Plyushch within the confines of the law: I have appealed in person and in writing . . . to all possible authorities, including the Prosecutor's Office of the USSR and the Supreme Soviet of the USSR. But this has achieved nothing. I was deprived of every possibility of refuting the biased charges made at the investigation. I was not permitted to nominate a psychiatrist known to me as my representative on the psychiatric-evaluation panels. I was not informed of the times when these evaluations took place, nor was I given the opportunity to choose a lawyer during the investigation, although Plyushch has a right to this. I was not permitted to be present at my husband's trial. I still have not been given a copy of the verdict or even of extracts from it. I have been threatened on two occasions with repressive measures at militia headquarters. (In response to my indignation I was told cynically, "You can complain. Your complaints will all be dealt with by us.") I have not been allowed a single meeting with my husband (sixteen months have already gone by since his arrest). I have even been forbidden to write to him.

The Deputy Prosecutor of the Ukrainian SSR, Samayev, and the warden of the KGB prison, Sapozhnikov, officially stated to me, barely concealing their sadism, "You will never have a visit with your husband. Nor will anyone permit you to correspond with him. He's a madman. Why should you bother writing to a mental patient? Moreover, why bother to see him? What could you talk to him about? We don't want to see you here again!" A person who is capable of saying this to a woman about the father of her children is not merely hardened. He suffers from a pathological callousness and has eradicated everything human in himself.

My husband is completely sane. He was arrested not for anti-Soviet activities, but for views that differed from those of Samayev and Sapozhnikov. But for expressing views that were permitted after 1953 a person would have been shot before 1953. For expressing other views, which were permitted after 1964, a person could have been sent to a labor camp before 1964. Now someone in the KGB has invented an inquisitorial method of doing away with my husband without shedding blood. Samayev, Sapozhnikov, and others of that ilk do not see that their actions are illegal, and conceal their petty tyranny with phrases.

I have realized that if violations of the law can be committed with impunity in small things, they will inevitably lead to greater violations, which the transgressors will be forced to cover up with still-greater ones. If "expediency" is allowed to substitute for the law in even one case, then it will supplant the law in other cases as well.

Surely life in our society is now based on more humane and democratic principles than in the days before the Twentieth Party Congress. And I do not believe that what happened to my family is a necessity of state. I think that this injustice is attributable to certain people who have a mistaken idea of professional ethics!

Help us, or this wholly heartless, completely inhuman act will really take place—a sane man will be shut up in a special mental hospital. This fate, equivalent to the horrors of hell, is threatening my husband, my children, and myself in our own country, in the middle of the twentieth century.

One's situation becomes hopeless not when there is no help from anyone but when one despairs of asking for help. But it cannot be true that nothing in the world is considered sacred any longer.

Before this I had sent a long letter to the Chairman of the Supreme Court of the Ukrainian SSR in which I described how the investigation and trial had taken place and cited violations of the law.

. . . to assess L. I. Plyushch's mental health, testimony was taken from witnesses who were barely acquainted with him or had not seen him for the last five or ten years. Thus a witness named Shevchenko was summoned to the trial, although he had seen Plyushch only once, for all of one hour, as was witness Kolesov, who had known Plyushch intermittently in 1963, a time not relevant to the case at all.

None of the people called to testify has medical training, but at the same time four witnesses (S. E. Borshchevsky, A. A. Verkhman, A. D. Feldman, and V. E. Yuvchenko) who wished to give testimony and were well acquainted with L. I. Plyushch were not permitted to testify at the trial on the grounds that they were not psychiatrists.

I was not summoned to court, although I have known L. I. Plyushch for fourteen years and have a basis for speaking about his mental health. Nor was Plyushch's sister summoned, either by the investigators or by the court.

These letters were not answered, of course. Then came a talk with Investigator Kondratenko at the Darnytsia District Prosecutor's Office. I was taken there directly from work. The talk was "friendly" and almost cozy. Why was I refusing to testify in Victor Nekipelov's case (he had just been arrested) when I could be arrested for this? [1] Why was I linked with Zionism? The investigator read a long letter, supposedly from Israel. "You see how bad things are there?" he commented. (Three days later I received the invitation to come to Israel that had been sent to me.) Finally Kondratenko announced, "I understand your situation, your desire to ease your husband's lot. I might have tried to do the same thing. But I must caution you that the forms of defense you have chosen are not the right ones. After all, you have an ideological job. If you didn't behave this way, your husband's fate would be different."

On July 5 the Supreme Court of the Ukrainian SSR upheld the ruling to commit Lyonya to a special psychiatric hospital, but I was not informed that he had been sent to Dnipropetrovsk until July 23. The next day Tatyana Khodorovich and I were at the gate of the Dnipropetrovsk prison.

What official documents call a "hospital" is on the premises of the Dnipropetrovsk Province Prison. The area is surrounded by a stone wall topped with electrified barbed wire. Guards with submachine guns man the towers. The entrance is through a steel door with a peephole, along a narrow corridor, and past guards. Inside is another stone wall, also topped with barbed wire. In the distance the stone walls and barred windows of the old tsarist prison can be seen. This is the "hospital." In 1974 an official of the Soviet embassy in France told members of the International Committee of Mathematicians that it was a "hospital of an improved type, suitable even for academicians."

I would wait by the walls of this "hospital" for five or six hours at a time to get permission for a visit. The first time the guards turned me away on the pretext that Lyonya was in quarantine. They took the paper, pen, and photographs of the children that I had brought him. A doctor came out and, introducing herself as Ella Petrovna, Lyonya's psychiatrist, urged me to apply for benefits for the children (about twenty rubles a month). "I will never admit that my husband is ill," I replied, "and receiving benefits from you would mean admitting this." Later I learned that Lyonya had also refused the benefits.

The conversation gradually turned into an interrogation. How did I view Lyonya's "anti-Soviet activities"? Had I traveled to Moscow? Why? What sort of friends did we have? What sort of letters and documents had Lyonya and I composed together?

V. E. Makohin, Director   August 29, 1973
Board of Corrective-Labor Institutions
Ministry of Internal Affairs
Ukrainian SSR

My husband, Leonid Plyushch, is confined in the Dnipropetrovsk Special Psychiatric Hospital. Visits with him and talks with his doctor and the duty officer compel me to request that he be transferred to another institution.

The reasons for this are: My husband is not permitted to correspond with close relatives. Writing supplies are issued only on Sundays, and even these letters do not reach their destinations. During the six weeks he has spent at the hospital I have not received a single letter from him. He is also not permitted to read and make notes. This ban is determined not by medical considerations, but by the attitude of the people in charge of the regime. (This is how the duty officer explained it to me.)

Even if my husband is considered to be mentally ill (neither he nor I agree with this) on the basis of "ideas of reformism and messianism"—that is, on the basis of his attitude to social problems—there is no reason to prevent him from working on purely theoretical problems in his professional field, mathematics. It has been explained to me that according to the nature of his confinement my husband has the right to receive literature on the mathematical and psychological theory of games, the field in which he has worked in recent years.

341

My husband's appearance also left a depressing impression on me. His clothes are two or three times too large for him and are faded from washing. Since even clothes can help a man in his situation maintain a sense of his humanity, I draw your attention to this as well.

I am not requesting any exceptional conditions for my husband, only the ordinary regimen. I am afraid that someone is creating conditions for my husband devoid of ordinary compassion for people who have found themselves in a situation like my husband's.

I urgently request you to assist me.

Tatyana Zhitnikova

The appeal helped. I was allowed to send a pair of pajamas ("but only in dark colors") and then a second pair. Later I learned that the second pair was issued only for visits.

Lieutenant Colonel Pruss, the commandant of Institution Post Box YaE-308/RB (all military and penal institutions are numbered in such a fashion), called me in for a talk. "Examinations have revealed that your husband has a severe mental illness and must be treated," Pruss announced. "It is the duty of relatives to assist the doctors in this. Hence you must not bring him so many books. He finds them difficult to read and as time goes on will find them even more difficult. The books will lie there, and he'll get upset because he can't read them. And you should also not visit him so frequently."

On Friday, October 19, Dima and I arrived to see Lyonya. The visit was not permitted. "Plyushch has been transferred to another ward," we were told. "The patient in the adjacent bed came down with a severe infectious disease. Hence your husband is in quarantine. Try to come back on Monday. Perhaps the situation will have clarified by then, and you'll be permitted to see him."

Friday, Saturday, Sunday . . . What had happened? Why was Lyonya in another ward? It was clear that the quarantine was a fiction, a pretext for not letting us in. But why? Had something happened to Lyonya? To top it off, detectives never let us out of their sight. The friends with whom we were staying were good people. How could we bring the tails to them? But what were we to do? Where could we go?

At nine o'clock on Monday morning we were waiting at the gate. Permission for a visit was granted. Dima was allowed to come in, too, although previously he had been kept out because he was under sixteen. The visiting room was dark and narrow, with artificial lighting. The only window was blocked by a partition. Along the wall stood a long bench, in front of which was a waist-high barrier. At a distance of two and a half meters stood an identical barrier and bench, where the relatives were seated. Between the patient and his visitors sat a guard, sometimes two. They heard every word before the person for whom it was intended did.

I was still treated well: the authorities were so afraid of the information I brought Lyonya that I was almost always allowed to see him with only the guards present. Other prisoners did not have such privileges. Six or seven of them would usually be brought in together. For each patient there would be two visitors. The guards talked, too, giving advice and making warnings. The noise would get so loud that it was barely possible to hear what was being said. For the most part the patients were visited by their mothers, simple peasant women exhausted by the trip and confused by the city. In the midst of the uproar they related news, wept, and begged their sons to behave themselves. The sons frowned and eagerly asked about the outside world. In an hour or sometimes less, a command would be given, and the visitors would be let out through the barred door. Then the inmates would be led away.

Here, behind the partition, parcels were accepted and weighed on an antediluvian scale. Everything was strictly limited: a kilo of sugar, a kilo of fruit, a kilo of vegetables, three hundred grams of sausage, two or three cans of meat (they would be periodically banned and only canned vegetables or fish permitted), half a kilo of bread or rolls, ten cooked eggs, four hundred grams of butter, half a kilo of honey, half a kilo of sweets (but no chocolates), and half a kilo of tobacco (cigarettes were not permitted). From this list a parcel of five kilos could be put together.

Lyonya was unrecognizable when he was brought into the visiting room. I could see in his eyes that he was depressed and in pain, and he spoke with difficulty, in disconnected phrases. He often leaned back as though he sought support, and finally lay down. He found it difficult to breathe and unbuttoned his shirt with fingers that would not obey him. He began to have convulsions; his face was distorted by twitches; he could no longer control his arms and legs. He would pull himself upright, shuddering, his whole body tense, and then feebly collapse again. At times his hearing was gone. But he tried to speak, twitching and swallowing saliva. Convulsions seized his throat and affected his speech. Ten minutes before the end of the visit, he asked to be taken away.

Afterward I learned that he had been transferred to Section 9 ("the most terrible one in the prison," he had barely managed to whisper). Here he was kept in a ward with some twenty men, many of them violent, and given three injections of haloperidol a day.

I asked to see Lyonya's doctor. She introduced herself as Lyudmila Alekseyevna and refused to tell me her surname. "I haven't had time to become properly acquainted with Leonid Ivanovych and so can't tell you very much. I haven't noticed any signs of morbid philosophical preoccupation in him yet, but the patient has shown a tendency to mathematicize psychology and medicine."

I explained that Lyonya had been employed at an institute where he studied the use of mathematics in medicine and cited examples of mathematical applications in medical theory and practice.

"I am a doctor," Lyudmila Alekseyevna replied, "and I know that mathematics has absolutely no bearing on medicine. We doctors have no use for it."

"What drugs is my husband taking?" I then asked.

"Why do you need to know? We give him whatever he needs. You send him a lot of books. What does he need them for? He's ill!"

At the next visit Lyonya told me that he had felt very bad that day: he had been racked by continuous convulsions and kept jumping up and lying down. He had not slept almost the entire night.

> Ministry of Internal Affairs
> Ukrainian SSR
> Institution YaE-308/RB
> November 11, 1973, No. Zh-5

T. I. Zhitnikova
33 Enthusiasts' Street, Apt. 36
Kiev 252147

In reply to your letter of October 25, 1973, I wish to inform you that your husband is being treated in the hospital and the state of his health is satisfactory.

During your visit with him on October 22, 1973, he was in his usual condition, and there were no disorders in his speech and no convulsions. A doctor was present with you during the visit.

As for your husband's diagnosis and treatment, in accordance with the Regulations for Psychiatric Hospitals, relatives are given no medical information.

> Warden of Institution YaE-308/RB
> Pruss

More statements and more replies. From the Medical Department of the Ministry of Internal Affairs came a letter dated December 27, 1973:

Your statement about the deterioration in the health of your husband, L. I. Plyushch, has been examined. The information presented in your statement was not confirmed by investigation. During your visit on October 22, 1973, a doctor was present. Your husband did not have convulsions. He spoke freely, and there were no disorders in his facial expressions. Your husband's mental state requires continued treatment in a special psychiatric hospital.

Lyonya was growing worse and worse. The haloperidol had made his body swell up incredibly. Sluggish and apathetic, he barely managed to say anything during visits. He asked almost no questions. Everything seemed hopeless and senseless. No one was able to help.

Lyonya asked me not to bring books because he could neither read nor think, and he begged our friends to excuse him for not writing, but requested that they continue writing to him. "Letters are given to me only for reading and then taken away," he said. "They took away the photographs, too." Lyonya also asked that I try to get him transferred to Section 12, although he had said during my first visit that it was "terrifying here, so terrifying!"

During the visit the psychiatrist walked in and, smiling joyfully, wished us a happy holiday (it was the anniversary of the October 7 Revolution). I badly wanted to tell her what I thought of her, but I understood that I had to restrain myself: Lyonya was in her hands. "I am interested in my husband's diagnosis. Why is he being given haloperidol? Is he being given a corrective?"

"What corrective? Why do you need to know?"

"I know that he's being given haloperidol. That's precisely what caused the attack my son and I witnessed."

"Is Leonid Ivanovych complaining? Our relations with him are splendid. Isn't that true, Leonid Ivanovych?" Lyonya remained silent, but the look in his eyes gave a very clear answer. "As for your question, I shall not say anything either about the diagnosis or about the treatment."

I went to see Valentina Katkova, the head of the hospital division of the Dnipropetrovsk Special Psychiatric Prison, to ask that Lyonya be transferred to another section and permitted to have letters and photographs. Katkova told me in syrupy tones how splendid everything was here, how all the patients and relatives were satisfied, and how there were many applicants. "They don't really know," she remarked, "what people are here for, but they know we cure them. We belong to the Moscow school."

"Snezhnevsky's?"

"Yes, Snezhnevsky's," Katkova replied with pride. "We don't experiment here, you know. We treat everyone strictly according to established methods. Everyone is satisfied with our results. Even professors come to visit us."

I reminded Katkova of my requests.

"A transfer to his former section will be impossible, because that's our medical department," Katkova announced. "It's for people suffering not only from nervous disorders, but also from tuberculosis, ulcers, and liver diseases. We often transfer the patients. In any case, there's no room there now. We couldn't squeeze in even one more bed."

"And what about the letters and photographs?"

"As for letters, you know, when a lot of them pile up, they could become infested with cockroaches. We don't have cockroaches, of course, but anything could happen. The photographs? Well, all right, that's a modest request. And some letters, too. I'll try to arrange it. I think it might be possible to leave him a few."

Yes, this was Snezhnevsky's school. I already knew who he was.

February 14, 1973

Andrey Vladimirovich:

On January 29, 1973, the Kiev Provincial Court ruled that my husband, Leonid Plyushch, is nonresponsible and sent him for compulsory treatment to a special psychiatric hospital. The ruling was based on a psychiatric-evaluation report signed by you as chairman.

You may find it unpleasant to read this letter, but quite honestly, I am finding it even more difficult to write it. Please read it with an open mind.

I shall not speak about all the degradation of human dignity, the cynical disregard for the law, and the mockery to which my family was subjected during the investigation and trial because of your report. (If you are interested in a documentary presentation of the facts, you will find it in my appeal to the Supreme Court of the Ukrainian SSR for a review of the case.) I shall mention only what directly concerns your signature.

I venture to suggest that in this entire matter you were not independent. You merely carried out someone else's intention. From the first days of the investigation, employees of the KGB tried in every possible way to prompt the witnesses to speak about Plyushch's abnormality and eccentricities. The investigators chose compliant witnesses, most of whom we relatives and friends of Plyushch saw for the first time. But the KGB was certain that you would affix your signature to the report even without witnesses.

The KGB questioned me about my husband only after he had been sent for an evaluation. At the trial I was forbidden to testify or to represent my husband, who was not allowed to be present. The entire trial was held behind closed doors, and I was not permitted to enter. The court did not need witnesses who knew my husband. The most important testimony was your report. Thus the KGB used your signature to avoid giving my husband an open trial.

To err is human, but when an error causes torture and cruelty, it can no longer be called an error. What were you guided by, Andrey Vladimirovich, when you signed your name? After all, deviations from generally recognized norms, if they are not morbid, are not a sign of schizophrenia, even if the very convenient and elastic term "sluggish schizophrenia" is used. It is not for me to explain to you that social progress is the result of doubts and deviations from the norm which have become mass phenomena. The norm is a transient historical phenomenon. Radishchev, Chaadayev, the Decembrists, the Petrashevtsy, and religious zealots and revolutionaries gripped by *reformism* all doubted and deviated from the norm.[2]

To what expert conclusion would you come if you examined a man who had decided to become a tramp and to tempt people with salutary allegories and to promise them heaven if they perfected themselves inwardly? Conclusions about a deviation from the norm, a messianic mania? Yet this is exactly what Jesus Christ did.

What if a man, old enough to be satisfied with his accomplishments, disappeared mysteriously from his home, leaving behind wife and children, in order to protest against the established norms? Would you call this a deviation from the norm or an uncritical attitude toward his actions? Yet this is what Tolstoy did!

And what about a man who gives up material security and a beloved job and suddenly decides to perform charitable work in Africa? Would your expert report conclude that this was a sign of naïveté in his judgment? Is this how you, the personification of normality, would characterize the great Albert Schweitzer?

So what were you guided by, what standards of normality did you apply when you ascribed messianism, reformism, an uncritical attitude, and naïveté to my husband? How did Plyushch deviate from the norm you so zealously defend?

I met my husband when he was nineteen (he is now thirty-three). We have two children, the elder thirteen and the younger seven. I love my husband; I love him more than you can comprehend. I am grateful that this man came into my life. He was arrested on January 15, 1972. Since then I have not been permitted to see him. My husband has been taken away from me; my children have been deprived of their father.

My husband is good, honest, and intelligent. Having known him for fourteen years, I have every reason to assert that he is absolutely normal and sane. He possesses the noble virtue of never letting others think for him. In all his thoughts, words, and actions he is guided exclusively by his conscience. Everyone who knows him will confirm this.

Your signature hurled this man into a *special* psychiatric hospital where he will be imprisoned for life. You know as well as I what this means for a completely healthy man. Why, in the name of what, did you decide to crush and destroy my husband? What lofty ideals were you guided by? Surely it wasn't the seventy-three rubles of court costs extracted from

Plyushch, which include the fee for your report? Where did you find such a complaisant conscience? Where did you obtain the moral right to condemn a sane man to be completely isolated among mental patients and totally defenseless against arbitrary actions? For this is worse than prison, hard labor, or death. How did you dare do this, you who have taken the Hippocratic oath? Were you not prey to any doubts? Were you not afraid of being choked by the tears of Plyushch's children? You are my husband's hangman!

My only question is whether you are a hangman deliberately. I still have a vestige of hope that you are not aware of what you have wrought. If this is so, you will do everything within your powers to ensure that after the review of his case (about two weeks are left) Plyushch will not be thrown into the abyss you have prepared for him with a scribble of your pen.

If my letter should not reach you, I shall try to draw it to your attention with whatever other means come to hand.

Tatyana Zhitnikova

I know the letter reached its destination, for in reply I was sent an acknowledgment that Snezhnevsky had received it. Other letters reached their destination, too: they were all meant for the KGB. The address on the envelope did not matter. I knew this and placed my hopes on it. There was no other choice. At each visit Lyonya looked worse and worse.

Then came an answer to my letter. A friend whom we loved very much acted as an intermediary between me and the KGB. The ultimatum was quite firm: either I stop writing and appealing to the public for help or things would become worse. The most terrible thing was not the ultimatum from the KGB—that was quite natural —but that our friend had given me the message and himself urged me to negotiate with the KGB.

My first response was: *No! Not for anything! No deals with government bandits!* But then what about Lyonya? Could I answer this way? I was here, but he was in the *psikhushka*. Should I talk to him, ask his advice? Did I have the right to make him shoulder this decision? He was holding out, not agreeing to any offers; would I stab him in the back?

No, no! I could never agree to negotiate with them, even if I discarded all the moral principles that forbade me to participate in their crimes: simple logic insisted that one does not make deals with gangsters, who have neither principles nor honor. And government gangsters aren't even aware of logic. No! That was the only possible answer.

Yet Lyonya was growing worse and worse: he had swelled up to incredible proportions and no longer spoke at all when I visited him. I tried to cheer him as I wondered how to hold back my tears and not let him know how terrible he looked. When his mother visited him, I had to support her, too: Lyonya must not see her tears. Life turned into endless waiting, and I alternated between despair and wonder at what else they had done to him.

On January 4, 1974, I went to visit Lyonya with my friend Tanya Chernysheva.[3] I didn't have the strength to come away from the visit alone, with nothing but the thought that I was leaving Lyonya again in that nightmare. Tanya patiently waited for five hours in freezing weather. Not even permitted to see Lyonya through the bars in the corridor, she was forced to stand outside and only managed to look through the peephole. After that none of my friends was able to see Lyonya. The guards kept everyone out, and a Tommy-gunner would block the peephole with his back.

Never before had I sensed so clearly what the warmth of friendship means. My dear sister Tanya Chernysheva, how the KGB dragged her about, how many admonitions she was subjected to! Why was she associating with such bad people? Did she know what she was letting herself in for? Not a fighter, an oppositionist, or a dissident, she had only one answer: "I will continue to go and help. People are suffering, and I must be with them."

23

THE SECOND
TWO YEARS

The doorbell rang on January 17, 1974, a sound so ordinary that I didn't even shudder. The KGB had come to search.

The search was carried out in a quiet, homey fashion. The agents even gave me a note to justify my absence from work, referring to an "investigatory action." I could see that it involved Nekrasov. When the KGB men found his book *In Life and Letters*, with the dedication "To Lyonya Plyushch, with love and respect," they rushed to telephone someone and get instructions. I had to warn people in Moscow: a film and the essay "Moral Orientation," which were also confiscated in this search, were being prepared for a book about Lyonya that would be sent abroad. Besides, I wanted to share the news and hear friendly voices. Then I went off to Nekrasov's to learn what had happened to him and to tell him about the confiscated book.

I discovered the tails behind me immediately. Something serious must be up. At Nekrasov's house, I peered through the keyhole: how strange, stacks of newspapers were piled in the hall and the light was on.

"Ah, Tatyana Ilyinichna! Have they finished with you already?" A plainclothesman was standing at the door. "Why have you come here? Wasn't your own search enough for you?"

The agents had come to Nekrasov's at eight in the morning. His books and papers had been turned upside down, and there were so many KGB men in every room that I could barely locate the Nekrasovs. I was taken into the kitchen, and a witness was seated beside me. The young girl was embarrassed: the people here hardly looked like criminals, and there were so many books. The KGB men settled in for a long stretch. They had brought Thermoses with them and were drinking tea.

After a while the Nekrasovs were permitted to enter the kitchen, and we sat down to eat and talk. KGB men kept coming and going. A superior poked his head into the kitchen. "Ah, Zhitnikova! What are you doing here?"

A young girl wearing the uniform of a KGB ensign arrived. "You serve in the KGB?" Galina Victorovna, Nekrasov's wife, asked. "So young and pretty? Aren't you ashamed?"

RECORD OF A PERSONAL SEARCH

Ensign Tomashevskaya, employee of the KGB, on the instructions of Major Kolpak, Senior Investigator for the KGB, in the presence of witnesses . . . in Apt. 10, 15 Khreshchatyk Street, Kiev, occupied by Citizen Victor Platonovich Nekrasov, in accordance with Articles 184, 188, and 189 of the Code of Criminal Procedure of the Ukrainian SSR, performed a personal search of Citizen Tatyana Ilyinichna Zhitnikova, born in 1937, residing at 33 Enthusiasts' Street, Apt. 36, Kiev, who arrived at the apartment of Citizen V. P. Nekrasov at 15 Khreshchatyk Street, Kiev, where a search was being conducted at the time.

Citizen T. I. Zhitnikova entered the said apartment at 16:10. During the personal search of Citizen T. I. Zhitnikova nothing was discovered or confiscated. The search lasted from 17:35 to 18:05.

Four women worked for half an hour: one poked the seams in my clothes and peered into all my orifices, while the other three watched silently so that they could state that "nothing was discovered or confiscated."

Now the shadowing was open and round-the-clock. When I looked out the window at work, I saw a car putting in its hours just as I was.

On January 20 I was sent on a business trip to the Crimea. The assignment was an ordinary one: to monitor educational work in kindergartens, observe the teachers' methods, and read a paper at a seminar for preschool teachers in Yalta.

I was met at the station in Simferopol by local education officials, and we set out for Yalta in the car of the first secretary of the district party committee. The secretary's wife, who ran a kindergarten, was also going to the seminar. Our car was immediately followed by another. When we stopped in a lane in the new section of the town, I noticed that our tail was gone. I was amused and wondered what would happen.

Leaving the town, we drove into the mountains toward a pass. At the peak was an automobile inspection station. Our car was waved over. The secretary's wife was indignant: the militia knew the license plates of the local officials and should not have stopped the car. "That's not the militia," our driver explained. "It's the KGB. They

351

asked me who would be in the car, and I told them." My traveling companions cheered up and made jokes, but I knew what was happening. In a few minutes the car that had got lost caught up with us, and we were allowed to proceed.

At the hotel I was given a room in a corridor with only one exit, with a strange girl, rather than with my colleagues. I worked normally that week. I'd go off to a kindergarten, and the agents would follow. Here, on the crooked little streets of towns nestled in hills along the coast, empty of holidaymakers, there was no attempt to conceal the surveillance. I came to know all seven detectives by sight.

My colleagues introduced me to two men on business trips with whom they had become acquainted. On January 27, the next-to-last day of the trip, my colleagues invited their new friends and me to a restaurant. Unfortunately I still cannot reveal how I learned about the provocation. I have no documents here, and the reader will have to take my word.

The idea was primitive: get me drunk, have me found in a hotel room with a strange man, and accuse me of being a prostitute. In the Soviet Union there is a very strict rule that you cannot be in a hotel room with a person of the opposite sex after 11:00 P.M. The rule is enforced with particular severity in seaside towns. This is the authorities' way of controlling prostitution, which supposedly does not exist under socialism.

During the dinner I discovered that my colleagues were involved in the operation. Now I understood why the senior one had unexpectedly left Yalta and then come back.

After dinner my colleagues invited their friends and me to one of their rooms. Before we got there, one of the women had disappeared. The remaining four of us went into the room, and an ominous silence settled over us. My colleagues and their male friends were trembling (I suppose the men were not professionals, either). One of them made an absurd excuse, seized his companion by the hand, darted out of the room, slammed the door shut, and locked it.

It had all happened too quickly for me to feel fear. Dashing to the door, I began to bang on it with all my strength. I must have made a great deal of noise, because the man returned and unlocked the door. He muttered something, but I ran past him to my room and flung myself on the bed.

I did not sleep that night. Nor did my roommate. I had come to understand during the last week who she was. Her explanation for being in the town in an Intourist hotel was absurd, her attempts to question me awkward. Besides, the careless manner in which my belongings were put back in place after being searched spoke for itself.

Despair seized me. I was alone and helpless. I saw how easy it is to break a person. My only reassurance was that total strangers had taken a risk and warned me.

In the morning I telephoned Tatyana Khodorovich in Moscow and told her the whole story. She immediately agreed to meet me in Dnipropetrovsk, where the train from Simferopol would stop.

At two o'clock in the morning on January 30 I was waiting for Tatyana at the railway station. Militiamen appeared, and I sensed that something was up. When Tatyana walked in, I immediately ran to her. The militiamen surrounded us. "Tatyana Sergeyevna, come with us."

"Where, what's wrong?" she asked.

"Come with us. We have to talk with you. We're going to the militia station."

Their office was on the station grounds. Tatyana was carrying a bag: she had brought canned food and sausage (which couldn't be obtained in Kiev) for Lyonya, but they did not permit her to send him the food. She was led into a room. I was kept out, then told a few minutes later to go into the adjacent room. A militiaman stood at the door to keep me from leaving. I could hear Tatyana's voice. When I realized she was being taken away, I darted past the guard. The car was pulling off. Where were they taking her?

That night it seemed to me that all my strength was gone. During the last two weeks there had been the search, the incident in Yalta, and now the arrest of Tatyana. In the morning I was not permitted to visit Lyonya: he was in "quarantine." The explanation struck me as odd. I had sent a telegram inquiring about a visit, and at the prison I was told that an answer had been sent to me. A telegram was, in fact, awaiting me when I returned to Kiev, but it had been dispatched at 11:40 A.M., and I had been at the prison at 10:00 A.M.

Back in Kiev, I did not have the strength to go home and face the children. Instead I went to see Ilya Goldenfeld. He was a professor of physics who had given Lyonya a job at his laboratory a year before Lyonya was arrested. After Lyonya's arrest Goldenfeld and I became close friends. I could always find support and consolation in his home.

Goldenfeld and I went to the telegraph office. Thank God, the danger was over for now! Tatyana had been put on a plane to Moscow and forbidden to visit Dnipropetrovsk, on the pretext that the city was closed to foreigners and she was acquainted with foreigners.

In the evening I had a visit from a superficial acquaintance who told me confidentially that Lyonya had been examined and would continue to be held. His condition was grave. My acquaintance had also learned that a decision had been made to arrest me. What was this? Another provocation?

To finish talking about provocations, I shall tell about one that occurred soon after. The aim was the same: to compromise and blackmail me.

One evening I stopped by Nekrasov's. He and his wife were away, and Ilya Goldenfeld was staying at the apartment. We sat talking late into the night. The doorbell rang in a familiar manner. Militiamen and witnesses were at the door. "We've had a report from the neighbors that there's a drinking bout going on and suspicious characters are hanging around." They checked our documents. Everything was in order. Nevertheless, a record was drawn up that Goldenfeld and I had been alone in Nekrasov's apartment at night. It was horrible to think that the state could do with me as it wished. A bastard in a militia uniform had the right to break in on me at any time. Goldenfeld had applied to emigrate to Israel and had been expelled from the party and sacked from his job. We thought then that the incident was part of his emigration ordeal, but the next day an anonymous caller informed his wife of his "immoral behavior." Channels were found to send word to Lyonya in the *psikhushka* as well.

The KGB drew my parents in, too, asking them to exert influence on me. Until then I had told them very little, but now I informed them of what had happened in the Crimea. When my father went to inquire, he was told, "She shouldn't visit restaurants!" Threats were made to my parents that my children would be taken away. They were already being attentively observed at school, and Lesyk had even been followed on the street.

The February visit took place. Lyonya's condition was unchanged. He was being given insulin. I wrote a letter to Nikolay Podgorny, requesting permission to emigrate. In lieu of an answer, my father was called into party headquarters and told about the letter. Again threats were made to take away the children.

I learned that Andrey Sakharov had sent an appeal for Lyonya to the West.

Comrade Yuriy Andropov
Chairman of the KGB

On July 16 I applied to you requesting that you assist my family in leaving the country. The answer was a talk at the Provincial KGB Office with Comrade A. V. Bondarenko, who told me that the KGB is not the competent authority for my request.

This answer does not satisfy me, for a number of reasons. The investigation by the KGB ended with the commitment of my husband, Leonid Plyushch, to a psychiatric prison, due to the bias with which the investigation was conducted from its very inception (before any evaluations had been made).

In March and May, Comrades M. S. Davydenko and A. V. Bondarenko, officials of the Provincial KGB, explained to me quite clearly that Plyushch's situation depends entirely on my behavior. I should stop appealing to various organizations, which would end the public demand for Plyushch's release. Plyushch was transferred in April to another cell, where he was given insulin instead of haloperidol. ("You see how we've kept our promise," Davydenko said to me.)

At the same time various provocations against me were undertaken. This includes the search in connection with case number 62, about which I know nothing at all. There was also a provocation intended to make me appear a woman of easy virtue in my colleagues' eyes. In a talk with my father, officials of the KGB did not deny knowledge of this incident. Naturally, provocations also include the customary shadowing and the ban on publishing my work.

My husband's confinement and treatment in a special prison are also made contingent upon his accepting proposals that have little to do with medicine. It has again been suggested to him that he make a public statement like the ones by Yakir and Krasin and admit that all his actions in defense of human rights were anti-Soviet. In reply to a question why Plyushch was being treated, his psychiatrist stated, "He must change his views."

Plyushch's so-called treatment in a special prison, in which a sane man is being injected with mind-destroying drugs, and the situation of my family are no doubt connected with the KGB.

My husband and I have thoroughly considered the question of leaving the country. Therefore I am again turning to you for assistance in canceling Plyushch's compulsory treatment and permitting my family to leave the country.

I sent the application for an exit visa to the municipal OVIR. The procedure calls for a reference from one's place of work, but I decided to quit my job. I had made up my mind about leaving the country and had to concentrate all my energy. Moreover, the double life I led was becoming intolerable: attending political lectures that attacked "nationalists" and "Zionists," parroting official propaganda, remaining silent when Solzhenitsyn and Sakharov were reviled, and then coming home in the evening to read Solzhenitsyn and retype

Sakharov's letters for *samizdat*. I felt easier as soon as I had resigned. Now I would look for manual work that had nothing to do with ideology.

Early in August Lyonya stopped receiving insulin. Toward the end of this treatment he had been in a preshock state. Instead he was given trifluoperazine, which made him sleepy and sluggish but was preferable to insulin or haloperidol. His cell was stuffy, and his exercise was limited to an hour a day. He washed his underwear and pajamas in the sink and dried them on his bed. When I offered to bring him linen more often, he refused: government issue was preferable because it was changed occasionally. I asked about his fellow inmates. "I feel very sorry for them," he replied. The doses of trifluoperazine were constantly being increased, and by now he was getting forty-five milligrams a day. His eyes were in bad shape, and he could read only with difficulty.

Director of the Medical Department   December 16, 1974
Ministry of Internal Affairs
Ukrainian SSR

My husband, Leonid Plyushch, has been confined in the Dnipropetrovsk Special Psychiatric Hospital since July 15, 1973. His condition has taken a sharp turn for the worse since November 29, 1974, because of the inadmissibly large doses of trifluoperazine that he is being given. Since similar injections of haloperidol a year ago led to an almost complete loss of vital activities—he could not speak, read, write, or move about—I am afraid that attempts are being made to reduce him to a similar state.

My fears were fully confirmed on December 13, when the director of the institution suggested that I appear the next day. But on December 14 I was not permitted a visit. Nor did I see Lieutenant Colonel Pruss because, as the medical staff informed me, he had left on an urgent business trip. Not one of the reasons cited for refusing me a visit seems likely. Something else does seem likely: my husband has again been reduced to such a state that there is a reluctance to let me see him. My certainty is reinforced by the fact that I have not received a single letter from him during the last month.

Since I have applied recently for permission to leave the country, I view my husband's present condition as the KGB's answer to my legal right to emigrate and as blackmail and intimidation. I view this as the practice of keeping hostages: my husband is in the hands of the MVD, an organization that is not accountable to anyone. My three years of experience in struggling for Plyushch's release and defending his rights and dignity confirm this.

I remind you: Plyushch suffers from tuberculosis, and his health, which was poor before imprisonment, has been completely destroyed by his confinement in prison and the special psychiatric hospital. The drugs with which he is being injected are intended for severe forms of schizophrenia.

Mentally Plyushch is completely healthy. But even the false and unsubstantiated diagnosis given to him at the Serbsky Institute—a "sluggish form of schizophrenia"—does not require such cruel "treatment."

Neither you nor your subordinates can guarantee a successful outcome with such drugs and doses. I am afraid now not for my husband's health, but for his life.

I demand a visit immediately, within the next few days. Otherwise I will charge the staff of the Dnipropetrovsk Special Psychiatric Hospital with the deliberate murder of my husband, Leonid Plyushch.

T. Zhitnikova

There was no reply.

On December 20, 1974, I wrote the Prosecutor of the Dnipropetrovsk Province, petitioning him to institute criminal proceedings against the medical staff of the hospital, specifying that my husband was being subjected to premeditated destruction of his mental and physical health.

At the same time I wrote to the International Association of Jurists and the World Psychiatric Association.

I am appealing to these organizations because it is a question now not of human rights, but of quite specific violations of laws concerning jurisdiction and health which are accepted throughout the civilized world, including the Soviet Union.

I do not doubt that there are in the Soviet Union attorneys who could represent my interests in court and honest psychiatrists who understand how absurd the diagnosis and how criminal the so-called treatment are. But the state organizations I am charging are beyond the reach of ordinary public institutions. This is a closed world, impenetrable to knocks and cries. This is the only reason I am turning to the international public and to international organizations.

My goal is the implementation of my entire family's legal right to emigrate. Emigration, as an official of the Kiev OVIR stated officially, will be possible only if Leonid Plyushch is free. But he can be *freed* only if he is ruled to be sane or recovered. Thus everything again comes down to the events in Dnipropetrovsk.

I have concluded that Leonid Plyushch's condition has taken a sharp turn for the worse on the basis that open and round-the-clock surveillance of me has been resumed. The resumption coincides with a refusal to grant me a visit. This means that the authorities want to intimidate me, understanding what conclusions I shall draw from the refusal to permit me a visit. They want to force me to be silent. Thus the MVD is openly admitting Leonid Plyushch's difficult situation.

I have been placed in a situation where all my actions come up against the actions of the MVD, because both OVIR and the special psychiatric hospitals are run by it. I want to break this vicious circle and am asking for help. I am stating with full responsibility that it is a matter of a human life.

T. Zhitnikova

The answer came quickly, again through an intermediary. Andropov's deputy proposed that I apply for guardianship. Then, he said, we could talk about a discharge. A more concrete answer was promised right away. At times there was even talk that Lyonya might possibly be released toward the end of January; "possibly" sounded almost like "certainly."

Although the department that was making promises seemed very impressive, I knew that it was trying to stall me. After we arrived in the West I learned that the authorities had only wanted to procrastinate: the question of Lyonya was the hundredth or so item on the agenda for the meeting between Leonid Brezhnev and Gerald Ford at Vladivostok. Once Soviet-American friendship had again been "strengthened" and Ford had left, things remained just as they had been.

Nevertheless, I decided to follow the advice given by my "wellwisher" at the KGB and apply for guardianship. I went around to the various departments and discovered that it was not so simple. I would have to file a statement with the court that I recognized my husband to be mentally ill and requested to be entrusted with guardianship over him. Even this would not settle the question: the authorities could rule Lyonya insane on the basis of my statement and still not grant me guardianship because of my political unreliability and parasitism.

The following is from Tatyana Khodorovich and Yuriy Orlov's samizdat article, "Leonid Plyushch Is Being Turned into a Madman. For What Purpose?"

A half-hour visit on February 10, 1975. (The visit has been permitted even though a quarantine has been declared. Why?) Leonid Plyushch is brought in. His face is swollen and covered with red spots, the result of a recent attack of erysipelas. But the important and frightening thing is his empty, unexpressive eyes, the complete absence of emotion, and the indifference and sluggishness. His lifeless eyes do not show emotion even at the sight of his wife.

Plyushch is silent. He does not say anything and does not even ask questions about his children.

"Do you feel bad?"

"Everything's all right."

"Do you have heart pains?"

"Everything's all right."

"Do you have a fever?"

"Everything's all right."

This is not Plyushch! This is a mentally ill man. Is his state reversible? Will he become himself again?

From his curt replies, which he gives only when questions are put to him directly, his wife learns that he continues to be held in a ward for violent mental patients. He does not go outside for exercise. It's cold, and he doesn't want to: "Everything is difficult." He cannot read or write letters. He lies in bed all the time and sleeps a great deal. He takes three tablets of some drug twice a day.

After the visit Tatyana Zhitnikova has a talk with head physician Pruss. "We have transferred your husband to a surveillance ward because his mental state has deteriorated."

"How has this deterioration manifested itself?"

"You yourself complain that you don't get any letters from him. He doesn't want to write. That's a sign of deterioration. And there's also his sluggishness. You've seen that yourself just now." (So that's why they permitted a visit during quarantine!)

"But this condition appears only after he is injected with drugs! Besides, should a 'sluggish' person be kept with aggressive patients?"

"We are not required to give you an account of our actions, treatment, or diagnosis. We have our instructions."

At home a reply from Popov, the Deputy Director of the Medical Department of the Ministry of Internal Affairs of the USSR, is awaiting Zhitnikova. "We wish to inform you that the mental health of your husband has in fact somewhat deteriorated. Because of this he was placed in a surveillance ward (it is not a cell, as you call it). His confinement in this ward poses no danger to his life or health. His treatment is being carried out according to medical indications. The doses of drugs are prescribed for him in accordance with his mental and physical state and cannot produce any deterioration in his health. You regularly receive information about his health during visits and talks with the doctors."

After the visit I wanted to go straight to Moscow. When I arrived at the station in Dnipropetrovsk, there were no tickets for the Moscow train. Two others were due in three hours. This time I had come with Tamara Levin, a close friend from Kharkiv who had wanted to see Lyonya. We walked through the streets, shivering in the cold, shadowed by the usual detectives. I had come to recognize them on sight.

When Tamara and I decided to go to a movie to warm up, one of the women detectives got in line behind us for tickets. "Shall we go see a movie?" Tamara said, turning around to her. "Yes," the woman replied gladly. She was cold, too. We could at least go into a café from time to time, but she had to hang around by the door.

Thus I was not surprised when I saw detectives join Tamara and me in the line for tickets to Moscow. The only strange thing was that the cashier took a long time to issue our tickets. The train was about to leave when she said apologetically (we could see that she didn't understand what was going on), "I'm sorry, but I've been told not to sell tickets for some reason." We realized that we were not being permitted to go to Moscow. We would have to go home.

I decided that I must get to Moscow and appeal directly to the MVD. In view of what had happened in Dnipropetrovsk, I planned to take a bus that went only as far as Oryol and then make my way to Moscow by other means. Klara Gildman bought the tickets. She had volunteered to go with me "just in case." We played our parts like characters in a crime novel. I went to the bus without any luggage (Klara had everything) to make it appear that I was seeing her off, and got on at the very last minute. The KGB men who had followed me in a car all the way from home were left behind with looks of dismay. But this was not a Simenon or a Christie. As it left the city, the bus was stopped at an automobile inspection station. A traffic controller and a plainclothesman got on and walked toward us without hesitation. "Let's go, Tatyana Ilyinichna!"

"Why?"

"Let's go. We'll explain everything."

"I will not get off! I have a ticket and I must go! I see no reason for you to stop me." I asked the men for identification. The plainclothesman was a captain in the militia.

"You must understand that the bus will not leave until you get off," he said. "People are getting fidgety because of you. Get off!"

It was true that the passengers were fretting. At first they were nonplussed: why was a woman being taken off the bus? When I began to protest loudly, one passenger even supported me. "Yes, really! What right do you have? She has a ticket!" But time was passing, and the bus stood still. After an hour it became apparent that the bus would not move until I got off. Consulting with Klara, I decided to leave. Why should other people be inconvenienced? The trip to Oryol would take all night, and tomorrow was a working day.

When Klara and I got off the bus, we were led to the traffic control booth. Again I asked what grounds the militia had for taking me off the bus. "You have to show up at the militia station tomorrow," came the reply. "There's a summons waiting for you at home."

"But I left the house just an hour ago, and there was no summons." I was driven home. There I discovered that a militiaman had in fact just delivered a summons.

At the militia station the next day I was given a grilling. Why wasn't I working? What money was I living on? I was handed a piece of paper to sign, a warning that if I did not get a job within two weeks, I would be charged with parasitism.

In March Lyonya's condition remained unchanged. Besides being apathetic and sleepy, he was now very swollen. He was still in the surveillance ward and was still being given drugs. He tried to cut himself off from his surroundings. This aloofness would come over him now even during visits, and he would stare ahead with empty eyes. At such times he did not hear or see anything. I would have to call him again and again to make him come to.

I could not take any more. Cautiously I urged Lyonya to write a statement with a carefully worded admission that his articles were a "deviation from the norm." But Lyonya said firmly, "I will not write anything for them."

At the Prosecutor's Office in Dnipropetrovsk, to which I was finally summoned, I was told in no uncertain terms that no criminal proceedings could be instituted against the hospital's medical staff. A medical commission chaired by Professor Blokhina, who had been assigned by the Ministry of Health to head a permanent commission at the hospital, had investigated Plyushch's treatment and had not found any violations. (At my next visit Lyonya told me that there had been no commission and no one had examined him.)

The prosecutor then informed me that Lyonya had been given a new diagnosis: "schizophrenia, paranoiac type." He had also heard of articles about Plyushch in the French press. "I advise you to appeal to Soviet authorities instead of Western newspapers. Otherwise you might be charged with slander."

I made another trip to Moscow and went with Yuriy Orlov to the Medical Department of the Ministry of Internal Affairs.[1] There I submitted a petition to transfer Lyonya to another hospital and to stop treating him with tranquilizers until the Kiev Provincial Court had examined the question of compulsory treatment.

That day Yuriy and I also visited Academician Snezhnevsky. He did not know who we were and, confused by Yuriy's titles of doctor and professor, let us in. He was forced to read my letter.

361

April 7, 1975

Andrey Vladimirovich:

On October 12, 1972, a psychiatric panel at the Serbsky Institute of which you were a member, diagnosed my husband, Leonid Plyushch, as suffering from "sluggish schizophrenia." Neither I, Leonid Plyushch's wife, nor his mother and sister nor any of his relatives, friends, acquaintances, or former colleagues believed that the diagnosis issued at the Serbsky Institute was professionally conscientious or scientifically reliable. We interpreted the diagnosis as a sentence for a politically inconvenient dissenter issued by a biased organization and carried out by complaisant doctors. . . .

The treatment being given Leonid Plyushch is criminal from the point of view of both international and Soviet psychiatric norms. In ordinary psychiatric hospitals—those which are not subordinated to the MVD—"sluggish schizophrenia" is not treated with tranquilizers. I deem this premeditated deviation from established norms to be a monstrous torture by drugs. The aim of this "treatment" is to produce the symptoms of schizophrenia.

Your colleagues have achieved their aim: Plyushch is losing his memory, ability to work, and interest in books, science, and friends, all of which comprised the true meaning of his life before his confinement and even in the inhuman conditions at the Dnipropetrovsk Special Psychiatric Hospital before he was subjected to lengthy and intensive "treatment." I have received a notification from the Medical Department of the Ministry of Internal Affairs of the Ukrainian SSR that Plyushch's condition has deteriorated. The only conclusion I can draw is that the deterioration is a result of the "treatment," and the only conclusion an honest psychiatrist can draw is that the deterioration is none other than a neuroleptic syndrome that disappears whenever the treatment with neuroleptics is stopped. Plyushch is being "treated" in order to make him ill, and he is ill because he is being treated.

Now I am demanding not justice but logic. There is a limit beyond which injustice turns into open cynicism, which flouts man's rights and dignity and endangers the very existence of such concepts. Representatives of the "most humane profession" have exceeded this limit: for them it is not the diagnosis that determines the treatment, but the treatment that determines the diagnosis.

I am filing a statement with the Kiev Provincial Court requesting that the forcible treatment be ended, and I demand your immediate intervention. As the recognized head of the Soviet psychiatric school and as an author of the diagnosis condemning my husband to life imprisonment in a psychiatric prison, you bear complete moral and professional responsibility for all that has happened.

I demand that Plyushch stop being pumped with drugs until the court has issued a ruling. The next medical commission must see a man and not the effect of drugs which have been savagely used on him.

Snezhnevsky promised us that he would ask Georgiy Morozov, the director of the Serbsky Institute, to send his experts to Dnipropetrovsk immediately. But no commission ever visited Lyonya.

Yuriy and I also appealed to a press conference about Lyonya, held in Paris on April 23. The International Committee of Mathematicians and Amnesty International, which had organized the conference, had been leading a campaign for Lyonya's release for the last two years.

ON THE INTERNATIONAL DAY FOR LEONID PLYUSHCH, APRIL 23, 1975

I consider it necessary to publicize several incidents on Leonid Plyushch Defense Day:

(1) On April 9, 1975, Leonid Plyushch's wife and I visited the Medical Department of the USSR Ministry of Internal Affairs. In the course of a lengthy discussion an executive of the department stated, "You are acting in the worst interests of Plyushch himself. Would he really be better off sent to a labor camp?"

(2) That same evening, we visited Professor A. V. Snezhnevsky at his apartment. During an emotional discussion he posed the following staggering question: "Would Plyushch have been better off if he had been given seven years in a strict-regime labor camp?"

(3) Plyushch's wife, Tatyana Zhitnikova, was told once again through intermediaries that the methods of Plyushch's forcible treatment depend directly on her behavior. If she stops appealing to world public opinion, Leonid Plyushch may be transferred from the special psychiatric hospital to an ordinary hospital after a year or eighteen months. Otherwise, things will get worse for him.

I believe that these facts speak for themselves. I can only repeat what. I told Professor Snezhnevsky: *similar methods were condemned by the Nuremberg Tribunal.*

Professor Yuriy Orlov

Nearly three and a half years have passed since my husband was arrested. Of these he has spent one year in prison and the rest in the Dnipropetrovsk Special Psychiatric Hospital. He remembers the prison as a paradise lost: there he could talk and read, and, most importantly, he was not being "treated."

Two books about Plyushch have been published in the West. Articles have been written, and signatures have been gathered. Psychiatrists and

363

members of associations that defend human rights have telephoned from various countries. Strangers have written letters full of compassion and understanding. I have not felt abandoned in my battle with a huge government apparatus which is capable of taking away my children and my freedom just as it has taken away my husband.

This attention has not been the important thing. Each time that I learned about a new action in defense of Plyushch I thought to myself: Now they'll let him go. If they don't let him go, they'll at least stop the torture and give him a breather. They'll stop and think. If not from compassion, then for the sake of their reputation and moral authority. Is it worth arousing the indignation of five hundred French mathematicians for the sake of one insufficiently loyal citizen? It turns out that the Soviet state has its own conception of détente, reputation, and moral authority. It has one reply to everything. I submit complaints, statements, requests, and documents to every possible Soviet authority, from a district court to the Central Committee in Moscow, but Plyushch continues to be treated. International organizations and the press speak out in his behalf, but Plyushch continues to be treated.

Leonid Plyushch, "the mathematician Plyushch," as he is called in Western radio broadcasts, the Plyushch about whom books and articles have been written, whose letters and essays have been published, the Plyushch whom his children, relatives, and friends knew, that Plyushch no longer exists. Instead there is an extremely sick, exhausted man who has been driven to the brink of endurance and is losing his memory and his ability to read, write, and think.

Those who are killing him with their own hands know that they are committing a crime. Previously it had seemed to me that I was dealing with obedient bureaucrats who were not fully aware of their actions. Now I am convinced that they know exactly what they are doing. Everyone knows—from the doctors at the Serbsky Institute who sent a man whom they knew to be sane to be tortured by madness, to the captain who ordered a guard with a submachine gun to cover the peephole in the door so that my friend would not see what they had done to Plyushch.

My situation is agonizing. My children have been harassed and live in constant stress and fear. Every time I come home, I see their pale, drawn faces—they are afraid that I will disappear the way their father did. Our circle of friends is growing smaller. We are outcasts, marked people. Associating with me means displaying a fortitude of which few people are capable. Everyday life with its joys and woes continues around us. We have been excluded from it, crossed out, for there is nothing more terrible for my fellow citizens than the stamp of "political unreliability" that the KGB has given me.

There is no "Plyushch case." This is a case of human freedom and dignity. What can we expect tomorrow if the world becomes accustomed to the persecution of free thought and to the immorality and impunity of a state that is responsible for the fate of humanity? What can we hope for? To what kind of tomorrow are we condemning our children? Don't think of us. Think of yourselves. My terrible today may become a tomorrow for a vast number of people if you lose heart, if it seems to you for even a second that your efforts to save reason and conscience are fruitless.

Plyushch did not want too much: to live in his country and to be of benefit to it as a creative and therefore free man. He was sent to a madhouse. I have made every possible effort to prove his sanity. An absurd undertaking: those who punished him with madness knew as well as I that he was sane. What I thought was a mistake was in fact a premeditated crime. Now I say: Yes, he is ill, terribly ill. He must be saved from something even worse than illness—death.

I have nothing more to hope for in this country. Now all my efforts are directed at getting my application for emigration accepted by the relevant institutions. But they have an unassailable logic: they cannot accept my application while my husband is undergoing medical treatment. The prison where he is being "treated" is subordinated to the same Ministry of Internal Affairs as the office that handles emigration.

I am boundlessly grateful to all the mathematicians abroad and to everyone who is concerned about Plyushch's fate. But I also understand why Plyushch's Soviet colleagues are silent. They are deaf to injustice, as if the drugs that are making Plyushch deaf have an effect on them as well.

Let me be given back my husband, ill as they have made him, and let us then be allowed to leave this country. The right to emigrate is the only right I am demanding.

T. Zhitnikova

At the end of April Lyonya's sister went to visit him. She returned horrified and desperate. He had developed erysipelas again, and his nose was so swollen that it covered half his face. His temperature was 38.9° C. The trifluoperazine had been stopped for several days, and now he was being given injections of penicillin. His condition was acute: he walked into the visiting room with difficulty and did not talk or ask questions. His mood was depressed; he had no hope of leaving prison.

The KGB again talked to me through intermediaries, making promises and threats. But I had fully realized that the authorities had no intention of letting Lyonya go. They only wanted to avoid protests from abroad.

From July 1 until September 3 Lyonya was "treated" with trifluoperazine and insulin. However, the doctors apparently did not intend to take things as far as inducing an insulin shock, for not once was he strapped to his bed. He remained dispirited and pessimistic: "I shall never get out of here!"

In May an American congressional group visited me.[2] The congressmen arrived at two o'clock in the morning to ask questions about Lyonya and to console me. They couldn't even imagine how encouraged I was to see people from an almost unknown country. It was a striking contrast to the following morning, when I went to work and was abused with foul language.

By then I was working as an agent for a photo studio, going from house to house to obtain orders for reproductions of photographs. I had got the job illegally, lying about my education when I applied for it, since there is a regulation that people with higher education cannot be accepted for menial positions.

The months passed, without any change in Lyonya's situation. I had stopped believing that change was possible. It was more obstinacy than any real hope that made me continue to send letters to the West. I learned that the International Committee of Mathematicians would be organizing a mass meeting for Lyonya in October. But what news could I give them? There were no changes, no sensations, nothing to shock the world with.

One evening three French attorneys who represented the International Committee for the Defense of Human Rights visited me.[3] They asked about Lyonya and explained that they wanted to visit the Ministry of Internal Affairs. We decided to go together.

At the Ministry we were told at first that all the officials had left on urgent business trips—the minister himself had even been sent abroad—but then we managed to get through to the director of the Medical Department of the Ministry, which oversees the Dnipropetrovsk Special Psychiatric Hospital. We got to see him solely because the Medical Department had only one unguarded entrance—the main entrance to the Ministry was guarded, and a pass was required—so that Lieutenant Colonel Vashchenko could not avoid us by running out a back door. Even I, who had grown accustomed to the Kafkaesque Soviet system, found the conversation extremely curious. By then I was so familiar with the way officials talked that I was able to write down the discussion in shorthand so that the attorneys could take it to the West.

QUESTION: Every person has the right to choose a doctor, or to have one chosen by relatives. Plyushch's wife considers it essential for her husband to be examined by other doctors.

VASHCHENKO: I regard this as distrust of Soviet specialists. We have specialists who are known abroad. Our system does not permit outside people to act as observers.

QUESTION: As attorneys, we do not understand how in that case the principles of the Declaration of Human Rights are implemented in the Soviet Union and ask that this be explained.

VASHCHENKO: How can a doctor be chosen if the patient is in a hospital?

QUESTION: If a person cannot make the choice himself, there are relatives. Could you explain how this is done here?

VASHCHENKO: We have doctors at the hospital and other doctors as well. Otherwise the result is that distrust is expressed.

QUESTION: There are a number of highly qualified specialists in the Soviet Union. Who are they? Give us their names.

VASHCHENKO: Yes, that's true. We have famous specialists, and they are known abroad.

QUESTION: We would like to select a doctor from among Soviet psychiatrists to examine Plyushch.

VASHCHENKO: Why should *you* choose? We can appoint a doctor ourselves.

QUESTION: Name some well-known psychiatrists.

VASHCHENKO: I am not prepared to answer. I don't understand why someone should choose a doctor for us.

QUESTION: Could you tell us the names of the doctors who are treating Plyushch?

VASHCHENKO (after some hesitation): Yes, I can, but at the end of the day.

QUESTION: We have an invitation for Plyushch and his family, and also for Yevdokimov, to come to France for treatment. What methods can you suggest for legal emigration?

VASHCHENKO: There are the Ministry of Foreign Affairs and the Ministry of Health.

QUESTION: May we deliver these invitations personally?

VASHCHENKO: No, they're patients, and a special decision is needed from the medical commission, which will decide the question of departure.

QUESTION: Tell us, do you consider Plyushch ill?

VASHCHENKO: Yes, he's ill.

QUESTION: The Soviet Union does not have a law forbidding one to see a patient. May we see Plyushch?

VASHCHENKO: If the patient's condition permits.

QUESTION: Please explain, why may we not see the patient?

VASHCHENKO: These people are mentally ill. They have different conditions.

QUESTION: But this contradicts the laws of the Soviet Union! Is there a law that forbids one to see a patient?

VASHCHENKO: You may visit if the patient's condition permits. You're tourists and must have a permit to go to Dnipropetrovsk.

QUESTION: We don't have one, but even so, why may we not see Plyushch if his wife has asked us to do so?

VASHCHENKO: You may, if the state of his health permits.

QUESTION: What specific features of Plyushch's state do not permit us to see him?

VASHCHENKO: I cannot say in this specific case.

QUESTION: Could you call Dnipropetrovsk and find out whether Plyushch's state permits him to be seen? His wife saw him on September 3 and found his state suitable for visits. If that is so, find out whether we may go to Dnipropetrovsk with Plyushch's wife. The same thing for Yevdokimov. Please find out about his condition and whether we may see him.

VASHCHENKO: All right, I will find out all this. (We agree to come back at the end of the day.)

QUESTION: We also request that you find out in Dnipropetrovsk the name of the doctor who is treating Plyushch, as well as the names of the doctors in the panel that is to examine him in October.

VASHCHENKO: Very well, I will find out everything. I will telephone Dnipropetrovsk by five o'clock.

At five o'clock:

VASHCHENKO: Plyushch's state of health has not changed since his wife saw him on September 3. His attending physician is a psychiatrist with fifteen years of experience. He's been reconfirmed and has a first-category rating. His name does not need to be known.

QUESTION: Is the doctor's name a state secret?

VASHCHENKO: He's an experienced and learned doctor, and his name is of no importance. You are not official persons and therefore must apply to the Ministry of Foreign Affairs. I am not seeing you officially.

QUESTION: As attorneys, we consider ourselves to be official persons, as are you. You are wearing a uniform, and we have come for a meeting with you at an official institution. Besides, the lieutenant colonel in charge of the reception room at the Ministry of Internal Affairs sent us to you in the Medical Department of the Ministry.

VASHCHENKO: You are not official persons, and I am not replying in this case. I can name the doctor if Plyushch's wife asks me, but she has not asked me this question.

ZHITNIKOVA: Please tell me the name of the doctor who is treating Plyushch.

VASHCHENKO: I will not name the attending physician.

QUESTION: Since this is your official duty, who else besides you can reply?

VASHCHENKO: You should be interested in what sort of a doctor he is— whether he's experienced or not. Plyushch's attending physician is a specialist with a long service record. His name is not important.

QUESTION: Throughout the world, including the Soviet Union, an attorney defends the interests of people who have turned to him. Plyushch's wife has turned to us as attorneys, and it is important for us to know the doctor's name.

VASHCHENKO: I have told you already. You are tourists and have no right to ask questions. There is a bar association, and the conversation must not be conducted in the manner in which you have done so. Your medical questions have been answered.

QUESTION: We represent the public opinion of a country that has friendly relations with the Soviet Union. We have many contacts with colleagues in the Soviet Union. We are well acquainted with and take an interest in the state of medicine in the Soviet Union. Plyushch's name is widely known in the West. Five hundred mathematicians have signed an appeal in which they expressed alarm about his condition. We are struck by the fact that we have not received answers to simple questions about Plyushch. We will continue to follow his case intently.

YATSENKO (Deputy Director of the Medical Department, present at the second meeting) : We are grateful for your high opinion of Soviet medicine. You have received answers to your medical questions and can receive answers to your remaining questions from the proper organizations.

QUESTION: We have three more questions. One, what is known about Yevdokimov's condition?

ANSWER: He has been provided with the proper care and, considering his illness, is doing well. His condition does not call for alarm.

QUESTION: Two, if Plyushch's condition is satisfactory, why does he have to remain in the hospital?

ANSWER: His mental state is satisfactory, but as a patient he has to remain there.

QUESTION: Can we take Yevdokimov's condition to be the same as Plyushch's?

ANSWER: There will be a medical panel to decide this question.

QUESTION: Three, we have submitted invitations for treatment of Plyushch and Yevdokimov in France. Have you received such papers?

ANSWER: We have not received them. The question of such treatment is decided by the Ministry of Health of the USSR and the Ministry of Foreign Affairs.

QUESTION: What organization is competent to handle such a letter?

ANSWER: We are not competent to decide such a question.

QUESTION: Can you give us the address of the Ministry of Foreign Affairs?

ANSWER: We have no connections with the Ministry of Foreign Affairs and do not know their address. (The Ministry of Foreign Affairs of the Ukrainian SSR is located five hundred meters from the Medical Department of the Ministry of Internal Affairs.)

QUESTION: We are struck by the fact that you do not know the address of the Ministry of Foreign Affairs. We shall have to send invitations to all the ministries until they reach the right one. Is that normal? Is there any hope that Plyushch and Yevdokimov will come to France?

ANSWER: I cannot answer such a question. It is not within our jurisdiction.

QUESTION: May medicine be sent to Plyushch and Yevdokimov?

ANSWER: If it is required in the treatment and if it corresponds to the State All-Union Standard—that is, the standard by which we purchase drugs abroad.

QUESTION: What do you make of the fact that such preparations as halo-peridol and insulin are used in Plyushch's treatment? Aren't they very harmful?

ANSWER: These are accepted drugs in the Soviet Union. We read the literature and know that they are used abroad as well. And in France, too. If you don't know this, then you have not been reading your medical literature. (Rising) I have answered all the questions.

The absurdity of this discussion dismayed the French, but I found it thoroughly natural. In the Soviet Union, crimes, courts, and executioners are all anonymous, and only the victims have names.

The message I addressed to the mathematicians turned into a kind of summing up of my views on the society in which I lived and my place within it. I titled the letter "Torture by Time (October 1975)." [4]

On this day, which has been named for my husband, Leonid Plyushch, I turn to you with immense gratitude and infinite sorrow. Looking back at the terrible three and a half years Leonid Plyushch has spent in prison, and thinking about the cheerless future, we ask ourselves the same question over and over: Why has the state inflicted such torment on one man? Why has a husband been torn away from his wife, a father from his children, and a friend from his friends? For whom has it been necessary that after our trips to the Dnipropetrovsk Special Psychiatric Hospital every two weeks we conclude that the physical strength of the man dearest and closest to us is being sapped by unceasing torture with drugs, a brilliant mind is growing dim, and the passionate interest in life that was the very essence of Leonid Plyushch's personality is being dulled? Why has Leonid Plyushch been condemned to a slow death, and why have we been condemned to be impotent witnesses?

At first it seemed that the authorities wanted to force Leonid Plyushch to renounce his convictions, to cancel his past, to repent of his "sins" publicly, and to obtain absolution by entreaties. But these attempts were fruitless: Leonid Plyushch stood his ground and refused to engage in a dialogue with his tormentors.

We think now that an answer to our question can be found in the length of Leonid Plyushch's imprisonment in the special psychiatric hospital and in the obvious ridiculousness of such imprisonment even from the point of view of the absurd diagnosis to which he was condemned. The authorities are not simply taking vengeance on Leonid Plyushch for his staunchness, fortitude, and loyalty to his convictions. Plyushch, his family, and his friends are being tortured by time. We are being inured to the notion that what is happening to us is natural, legal, and normal, that things must be this way and cannot be otherwise.

Our country finds it perfectly natural and legal that a sane, gifted man, at one time full of inexhaustible social energy, is marking his thirty-sixth birthday not in the circle of his family and friends, but in a cell with twenty-eight murderers, maniacs, and pathological criminals. Personal social activity is considered dangerous in the Soviet Union as soon as it exceeds the boundaries of recognized dogma. Those who are socially dangerous must be isolated. This is the unwritten law, and Leonid Plyushch was convicted on its basis.

The future will show whether yet another scientific experiment is being conducted on Leonid Plyushch: it is both interesting and scientifically important to know how long a normal mind can hold out when it is ceaselessly attacked by huge doses of drugs that are usually administered to the mentally incapacitated.

But there is no doubt that a social experiment is being carried out in which Leonid Plyushch and all of us are the subjects. We are being taught to feel that we are odd men out, renegades whose very step is dangerous and who are granted an unheard-of mercy when we are allowed to be at large. Even simple relations with us are made difficult because they demand a courage of which few are capable: an acquaintanceship with us can turn at any moment into a crime in the eyes of the KGB.

The Soviet leaders sign documents in Helsinki, and a district militiaman stops Leonid Plyushch's sixteen-year-old son on the street and asks, "Who are those scum gathering at your mother's?" He has in mind American congressmen and French attorneys who have come to visit. The Declaration of Human Rights, détente, and Helsinki are not for us. The torture by time continues.

This is why we are so immeasurably grateful to all the people who defend conscience, thought, and the right to emigrate from a country where life has become intolerable. Every intervention from the outside, every voice ringing out in our defense, regardless of whether it achieves an immediate practical result, is a breach in the terrible psychological and social isolation to which we have been condemned. This is all that inspires hope. This is all that helps us live.

Tatyana Khodorovich and I jointly signed the letter. Ready to lay down her life for her friends, Tatyana Sergeyevna took our sorrow to her heart and treated our children as her own from the very first days after the arrest. Threats, blackmail, searches, a disconnected telephone, surveillance, nights in the Moscow-Dnipropetrovsk train, and cold, rainy days by the walls of the Dnipropetrovsk prison all became a part of her daily life. Later she stood outside more prison walls: in Odessa, when Vyacheslav Igrunov was arrested, and in Moscow, when

371

Pyotr Starchik was incarcerated. Again and again she took up her "anti-Soviet activities"—telling the truth about her country. No one in this world is dearer or closer to us than she.

Time passed. A panel examined Lyonya and again decided to extend his treatment. I knew that the protests in the West were not subsiding, but by now I was almost completely indifferent. I felt gratitude and had absolutely no hope. But could I stop? Could I remain silent? Should I write? Where? I tried writing to the officials at the USSR Ministry of Health, reminding them of the discussion at the Medical Department of the Ministry of Internal Affairs in Kiev. I asked in the letter that Lyonya be released for proper treatment and cited the invitation from France, although it had never reached me. The result was the same as always: silence.

On November 26, 1975, I received a curt notice: I was to come to the Ministry of Health of the Ukrainian SSR. I went, taking along Vitaliy Skuratovsky for support, although I expected nothing more than a formal reply. In the Department of External Affairs a bureaucrat announced, "The Ministry of Health of the USSR has called us and asked us to tell you that your request to leave the country has been granted. We've already been in touch with OVIR. Go over there, and they'll tell you what to do."

I don't remember how Vitaliy and I reached the OVIR office or what we talked about. I only knew that the news was too good to be true. At the OVIR office I was received by an official known to all the Jews of Kiev. How much woe this faceless man in an MVD colonel's uniform has inflicted! It was he who had mocked me a year before, saying that he would not accept my application until Lyonya had been "cured." Now the official was polite, affable, and loquacious. "Here are the applications for you and your sons. Fill them out, pay the fee, get your documents together, and bring everything to me."

"But what about Plyushch?"

"I don't know anything about that. Fill out the applications first, and then we shall tell you what to do. The question of your husband will be decided later. The leadership is thinking about it."

What did this mean? What were they thinking about? It was clear that the question had been settled if OVIR had been instructed to process the application. What was I to do? Go see Lyonya? I couldn't go to him until December 1: the weekend was coming, and visitors were not permitted at the prison on Saturdays and Sundays. (This was done to reduce visits, especially from a distance.)

I began to dash about, collecting the necessary documents. At the same time the OVIR officials began to act strangely: appointments were postponed from day to day. In Dnipropetrovsk no one seemed to know about the decision, or perhaps the director only pretended to ignorance. To make things worse, Pruss was transferred at this time, and his replacement was setting up a new system. Parcels were regulated more strictly, and one could sense that an "educated man" had taken over: on his lieutenant colonel's uniform he wore two badges indicating that he had degrees in both medicine and law. His replies consisted of stock phrases. "I don't know anything. When instructions come, we shall inform you." Lyonya continued to receive trifluoperazine and was still in the same cell.

Finally I managed to see the director of the OVIR office and demanded a definite answer about Lyonya's visa. (The papers for my sons and me had been accepted.) He did not give me a clear answer this time, either—"The leadership is deciding this question"—but he did try to blackmail me. "Why do you send news abroad? The leadership might not like this. Keep in mind that such behavior may slow down the decision instead of speeding it up."

In the last days of December I sensed that the "leadership" had made its decision. Now the OVIR employees tried to get in touch with me. By December 29 the only thing left was to obtain signatures on the documents we had been permitted to take with us and to get the visas.

But we were approaching the New Year's holiday, and none of the offices had any time for me. When I arrived at the notarial office, the only place in Kiev where certified copies could be made, the employees had just received their New Year's bonus: eggs, herring, canned meat, and buckwheat. They knew how people who are leaving depend on them. No one else could do their job—retyping and certifying the documents attesting to allegiance to the Soviet state. When I asked them to make my copies, they said curtly, "Come back tomorrow."

"But I can't come back tomorrow. I have to get my visas in the morning."

"We don't care. Besides, who will give them to you tomorrow? You'll get them after the New Year."

"But there are still three hours before closing time, and I'm first in line."

"You won't get anything today."

I called the director of the OVIR office, and he issued an order. He must have been very persuasive, because the director of the notarial office told the clerks to put away their bonuses and handle my papers. The typists were perplexed. Why such a rush, and why was I so important?

The same thing happened the next day at the Ministry of Justice, where I merely needed to have our birth certificates and diplomas stamped. Although I arrived at opening time and was the only visitor in that department, I was told to come back for the papers at the end of the day. Again a call from the OVIR director solved the problem, and within fifteen minutes I had my papers in hand.

This OVIR "assistance" continued right until the end. I traveled to Moscow in a train for which I had never before been able to obtain a ticket, and on New Year's Eve, when it's almost impossible to leave Kiev.

On the last day of our last year as Soviet citizens, I obtained visas through Austria and visas to Israel from the Dutch embassy, which handles Israeli affairs in Moscow.

Head of family: Tatyana Ilyinichna Zhitnikova.
Member of family: Leonid Ivanovych Plyushch.
Purpose of trip: permanent residence.
Destination: Israel.
Valid for exit from USSR: until January 10, 1976
  and for reentry into USSR until: _____
  through border points of the USSR open to passenger movement at: Chop.
Issued: December 30, 1975.

Thus was I officially notified that we were no longer Soviet citizens and did not have the right to return home. I even had to pay nine hundred rubles for each of us for the privilege of giving up Soviet citizenship.

Although everyone had been making haste and I could see that there were strict orders to throw us out quickly, things became uncertain again in the new year. On January 3, 1976, OVIR suggested that I take clothes to Lyonya in Dnipropetrovsk. When I arrived, I had an ordinary visit. Lyonya was the same as before. I cautiously told him that everything had been settled and the visas were in my hands. I had naïvely assumed that he would be released to me now, but I discovered that they only wanted the clothes. Again the director told me that he knew nothing. Lyonya had just been examined by a panel, and a court would be deciding whether he could be released.

My head was spinning. I ran to the Provincial Court. "By what law?" I shouted. "I have the visa in my hands. Leonid Plyushch is no longer a Soviet citizen! We have to leave the Soviet Union by January 10!"

The prosecutor examined the visa and said nothing. Everything was quite logical: an illegal conviction and an equally illegal release. Usually the procedure is quite strict. A medical panel must rule that the patient is sane, after which a court decides whether he can be released. Then comes a lengthy process of drawing up guardianship. The whole business can drag on for years as people who have recovered continue to be kept in cells with madmen while they await review of their case.

But the state machine can turn in a different way. As he handed the visas to me, the director of the OVIR office said, "Put in your application, and we shall assume that everything is in order. Just write a statement that you are asking to have a panel appointed. I'll send this statement to Dnipropetrovsk. I can do it more quickly."

Thus I never did learn whether Lyonya had been set free by a court. And I had petitioned for a hearing for so long, writing mountains of statements to every possible department. Yes, everything is decided according to law: the law of lawlessness.

I did not hand over the clothes I had brought. "I don't want to take part in your charade," I said at the prison. "Send Lyonya abroad in what he's wearing now."

The tickets to Chop were also sold to us at the request of OVIR. At first Lyonya's mother and sister were refused tickets, and I had to raise a stink to get them.

All our friends who could get the day off came to say good-bye. The taxis in which they rode from our apartment to the railway station were escorted by KGB cars. The coach was surrounded by a ring of militiamen and then, farther away, a ring of plainclothesmen. My mother and father were there. Would I ever see them again?

At Chop we were led into a room reserved for Intourist and asked not to leave the station grounds. The lieutenant in charge of us explained that he did not know when the airplane from Dnipropetrovsk would arrive. We spent the day waiting at the station, in an Intourist restaurant that had been opened just for us. I was surprised that no other emigrants were to be seen. Later, in Bratislava, we met a group of people from Ukraine who had come on the same train from Chop. They had guessed who we were when their customs inspections were handled very quickly. The lieutenant advised me to buy tickets for Vienna. I said that I would not get them until I saw my husband.

At nine o'clock in the evening Lyonya was led in. He could barely

375

walk and was being supported by plainclothesmen. We rushed to him. A photographer from Tass, the Soviet news agency, began to take pictures. Lyonya was dressed in fancy new clothes. I tore the clothes off him and threw them in the agents' faces. "Get out of here!" I screamed. "I don't want to see you any more!" They tried to say something but then left us alone. We redressed Lyonya. All his old things were too small for him. I had seen him bloated and swollen so many times, and yet it had never occurred to me that he would need larger clothes. But how could I accept what they had given him? I threw out the clothes along with the suitcase they had so solicitously provided. They had thought of everything and had even given Lyonya a tie, a tie clip, and—for a shirt with buttoned cuffs—cuff links.

Afterward we calmed down a bit. Lyonya sat shivering beside his mother and sister. The boys were crying. Their father had been unable to dress himself, and they had had to help him. The lieutenant came in, suggested that I go get tickets, and warned that the train was leaving in an hour.

Then the men who had accompanied us walked in again. One of them, a doctor from the Dnipropetrovsk hospital, gave me a piece of paper to sign. It stated that I was assuming guardianship of Leonid Plyushch and was promising that he would not engage in "antisocial activities." I curtly told the doctor that I would not sign anything and demanded that the agents take their photographer and go. Lyonya got excited and begged me to calm down. When I had subsided, the doctor made another proposal. "We anticipated your response and have prepared a second statement. Sign whichever version you like." I crossed out everything concerning any kind of activities and wrote that Plyushch had been entrusted to me as his guardian. The photographer energetically recorded the scene.

An officer in the border guards came in and announced that it was time to go. Escorted by soldiers, we went to the customs office, which had been cordoned off. Lyonya was shown one last mercy: after he had been searched, he was permitted to spend with his mother the few minutes during which the children and I were examined. Then the guards came again and took us straight to the coach. A few minutes later the train for Vienna started. The last we saw of our homeland was border guards and plainclothesmen.

AFTERWORD

by Leonid Plyushch

Although I am still a Marxist by conviction, my faith in the Soviet Union was shattered in 1956. How can I forget that millions have been murdered? That whole nations have been decimated culturally and physically? That all the hopes of the Revolution have been shattered? That literature and art have been ground into the dirt? That scientific progress has been halted? That lies and terror prevail and freedom is completely absent? How can I overlook the dissidents who are hounded from their jobs and whose families go hungry? And most importantly, how can I ignore the trumped-up trials, the labor camps, the prisons, and the *psikhushkas*, where inmates are mocked and tortured and political prisoners have their minds destroyed?

One of my fellow inmates at the Dnipropetrovsk *psikhushka* was a good-natured working-class boy who had been sent there for a trifle. He had never been interested in politics, but now his face twisted with anger whenever a political subject was mentioned to him. "Pinochet is doing the right thing!" he would declare. "All these Communists and socialist-liberal scum should be drowned in their own blood!" He was not the only one to have been instilled with such views in the *psikhushka*. Listening to them, I promised myself that I would not become a slave to my hatred and desire for revenge.

Yes, existence determines consciousness, but this does not mean that a person must become a slave to his individual existence. If I am struck from the left, I must stop to see whether it is leftists who are hitting me and think how to reply to them. Freedom is a necessity that my consciousness has become aware of and accepted. It is a duty to myself as a self-aware person, a way of living that I have chosen in given conditions and with my given possibilities.

At a rally in defense of Soviet political prisoners in New York, I mentioned torture in Chile.[1] Afterward an acquaintance from the

Soviet Union came up to me. I had thought of him as one of the steadiest people in Moscow. He even considered himself to be a Christian. Now he was choking with hatred. "Isn't Russia enough for you?" he asked. "Why do you bother with Chile? What do you know about it?"

Why should Chilean torture be regarded as more agreeable than the torture in Soviet *psikhushkas*? Why should the West believe our testimony about the *Gulag* if we refuse to believe the Chileans? They have less reason to believe us, because deception is easier in the USSR and they can learn more readily about atrocities in Iran or Uruguay than in the Soviet Union.

The Peruvian Trotskyist Hernan Cuentas told me how happy he and his comrades in prison had been when they read about my release in government newspapers. The report had been published by their enemies. How were they to know that I would later support them and not their government, that I would not conduct fascist propaganda? I am very pleased that our International Committee Against Repressions was able to help in the release of Cuentas and his attorney.

By supporting the trumped-up trials of the socialist opposition in Czechoslovakia, Angela Davis was virtually inciting the Americans to carry out witch hunts. I am certain that she supports the *Gulag*, but I was pleased when I heard in prison that she had been acquitted. Now I support the demand to free Jose Luis Massera, the secretary of the Uruguay Communist Party, although he is most probably a protégé of Brezhnev. The police broke Massera's legs and trumped up charges that an arms cache had been found at his home. The Uruguayan government must permit an international committee of jurists to investigate the charges of torture and other barbaric practices by its police.

Before World War II, the Gestapo, the GPU, and the NKVD cooperated in perfecting the science of torture. Eugenia Ginzburg points out in *Journey into the Whirlwind* that German Communists who had been in the hands of both the Gestapo and the NKVD wondered who had taken lessons in torture from whom. During the Slánský trial, the Czechoslovak security forces were instructed by both Soviet advisers and ex-Nazis.

Torture and lies do not become more humane if they are practiced in the name of Christian salvation or the Communist ideal. They have the faculty of irradiating throughout the countries that resort to them, of turning the torturers into beasts, and of contaminating them with the psychoideology of torture: an eye for an eye,

a tooth for a tooth. In a poem entitled "After My Interrogation,"
Victor Nekipelov wrote:

> No matter what spittle-covered wall I stand at,
> I will sing without bowing my head.
> I curse all the torture chambers of this world,
> Be they in Santiago, Athens, or Moscow.

Torture in Chile, Greece, or Iran cannot be divorced from persecution in Ukraine, Armenia, and Georgia; *psikhushka*s in the Soviet Union foreshadow psychiatric prisons in the West. The world
is one: both bondage and freedom are indivisible.

NOTES

CHAPTER 1

1. The KGB, or Committee for State Security, is the Soviet security service and secret police. It was previously known as the Cheka, GPU, and NKVD.

2. During World War II, eight small nationalities, including the Crimean Tatars and the Volga Germans, were charged with pro-Nazi sympathies and forcibly shipped to eastern Siberia and the Sino-Soviet frontier. About one-third of the million and a half people deported died during the first year. The eight nationalities have now been officially cleared of the charges, but many people are still not permitted to return to their homelands.

3. The kulaks were prosperous peasants who were denounced by the party for having excessive wealth or for refusing to join collective farms. In Ukraine and the neighboring Kuban region millions of them died in the artificial famine with which the collectivization campaign of the early 1930's climaxed, and most of the rest were scattered throughout the Soviet Union.

4. The Komsomol, or Leninist Young Communist League, is a mass youth organization that assists the authorities in conducting programs in sports and military training. It operates an extensive system of political schools and study circles and publishes more than a hundred newspapers and some forty magazines. The main function of the Komsomol is identifying activists and recruiting them into the party.

5. Nikolay Ostrovsky (1904–36): Russian novelist, author of the popular *How the Steel Was Tempered*, a largely autobiographical novel about young Communists in the Civil War. Alexander Fadeyev (1901–56): Russian proletarian writer known for his novel *The Young Guard*, about resistance behind the German lines during World War II; as General Secretary of the Writers' Union from 1946 to 1955, he helped exile or execute many writers. Maxim Gorky (pseudonym of Aleksey Peshkov, 1868–1936): Russian writer and revolutionary whose novel *Mother* has been proclaimed the model of socialist realism.

6. Vladimir Mayakovsky (1893–1930): famous Russian poet and playwright who died by his own hand, probably because of both political pressure and a complicated personal life.

7. Khrushchev's speech is available in Bertram Wolfe, *Khrushchev and Stalin's Ghost: Text, Background, and Meaning of Khrushchev's Secret Report to the Twentieth Congress on the Night of February 24–25, 1956* (New York: Praeger, 1957).

CHAPTER 2

1. The virgin-lands campaign, begun by Nikita Khrushchev in 1954, involved bringing under cultivation some seventy million acres of arid lands in the Asiatic parts of the Soviet Union.

2. Yakiv Sikorsky (born 1904): worked as a schoolteacher in Odessa from 1926 to 1956, then became a professional novelist, but has failed to win significant recognition.

3. Vladimir Ilyich Lenin, *Materialism and Empirio-criticism: Critical Comments on a Reactionary Philosophy*, third revised edition (Moscow: Progress Publishers, 1964).

4. Gleb Maksimilianovich Krzhizhanovsky (1872–1959): member of the Communist Party from 1893, active in the prerevolutionary Bolshevik underground, later Vice President of the Academy of Sciences of the USSR, member of the Central Committee of the party, and director of the Energy Institute of the Academy of Sciences.

CHAPTER 3

1. Vasiliy Aksyonov (born 1932): began his career as a doctor, then published *Colleagues* (1960), which won the admiration of conservative critics and was made into a film in 1963. Aksyonov's novellas *Starry Ticket* (1961) and *Half-way to the Moon* (1962) aroused great controversy for their use of slang and portrayal of the *stilyagas*. For the latter novella see Patricia Blake and Max Hayward (eds.), *Half-way to the Moon: New Writing from Russia* (New York: Holt, Rinehart and Winston, 1964; Anchor, 1965).

CHAPTER 4

1. Stanisław Lem (born 1921): Polish author, philosopher, and physician who has gained international fame through his numerous works of science fiction, satirical fantasy, and detective fiction. Arkadiy (born 1925) and Boris (born 1933) Strugatsky: brothers who have been jointly writing science fiction since the mid-1950's and have achieved great popularity among both the masses and the intellectuals throughout the Soviet Union. Their novel *Hard to Be a God* has been translated by Wendayne Ackerman (New York: Seabury, 1973; London: Eyre Methuen, 1975).

2. Mikhail Vrubel (1856–1910): Russian painter who won little recognition in his own lifetime but inspired the Russian avant-garde of the next twenty years. Nicholas Roerich (1874–1947): Russian painter and stage designer who lived in the United States and India after 1920. Mikalojus Čiurlionis (1875–1911): Lithuanian painter and symphonic composer.

3. Bernard Kazhinsky: Soviet pioneer in psychic research, author of *Biologicheskaya radiosvyaz'* [*Biological Radio Communication*] (Kiev: Akademiya Nauk USSR, 1962).

4. Eduard Naumov (born 1932): biologist who headed a parapsychological laboratory in Moscow and lectured widely on ESP. In March 1974 Naumov was found guilty of charging unlawful admissions to illegal lectures and sentenced to a two-year term in exile. Kazhinsky and Naumov are discussed in Sheila

Ostrander and Lynn Schroeder, *Psychic Discoveries Behind the Iron Curtain* (Englewood Cliffs, N.J.: Prentice-Hall, 1970), and Naumov figures in Henry Gris and William Dick, *The New Soviet Psychic Discoveries* (Englewood Cliffs, N.J.: Prentice-Hall, 1978). For *samizdat* texts on Naumov see Arkhiv Samizdata, *Sobraniye dokumentoo samizdata*, Nos. 1806–10 (AS 1806–10).

5. Leonid Vasilyev: chairman of the department of physiology and head of a parapsychological laboratory at Leningrad University.

6. French journalists reported in 1959 that ESP had been used to communicate between shore and the U.S. atomic submarine *Nautilus*. The U.S. Navy has consistently denied these reports.

7. There is a chapter on Ryzl in Sheila Ostrander and Lynn Schroeder, *Psychic Discoveries Behind the Iron Curtain*, pp. 332–47.

8. Valentyn Moroz (born 1936): leading Ukrainian oppositionist, sentenced in 1966 to four years of labor camp; rearrested in 1970 and sentenced to six years of prison, three years of labor camp, and five years of exile. His writings, including the essay "Report from the Beria Reserve," are available in *Report from the Beria Reserve*, edited and translated by John Kolasky (Toronto: Peter Martin Associates; Chicago: Cataract Press, 1974) and in the fuller but less smoothly translated *Boomerang*, edited by Yaroslav Bihun, introduction by Paul L. Gersper (Baltimore: Smoloskyp Publishers, 1974).

9. Nikolay Bulganin (1895–1975): Prime Minister under Khrushchev, dismissed in 1958 for having supported the "antiparty group" (see note 22 on p. 384) in 1957.

10. V. I. Lenin, *The State and Revolution* in *Collected Works* (Moscow: Progress Publishers, 1964), Vol. 25, pp. 381–492.

11. Yevhen Sverstyuk (born 1928): leading literary critic in the early 1960's, dismissed from his job in 1965 for outspoken statements, sentenced in 1973 to seven years in labor camps and five years of exile. His major writings are available in Ievhen Sverstiuk, *Clandestine Essays*, translated and with an introduction by George S. N. and Moira Luckyj (Cambridge, Mass.: Harvard Ukrainian Research Institute, 1976).

12. Karl Marx, *Economic and Philosophic Manuscripts of 1844*, edited and with an introduction by Dirk J. Struik, translated by Martin Milligan (New York: International Publishers, 1964). Also in Karl Marx, *Early Writings*, introduction by Lucio Colletti, translated by Rodney Livingstone and Gregor Benton (New York: Vintage, 1975).

13. Lev Tolstoy, *A Confession, The Gospel in Brief, and What I Believe*, translated and with an introduction by Aylmer Maude (London: Oxford University Press, 1961).

14. Lev Tolstoy, *The Kreutzer Sonata*, translated by Isai Kamen (New York: Vintage, 1957).

15. Sergey Yesenin (1895–1925): Russian poet who wrote about the disappearance of an idealized countryside and the romantic appeal of the Revolution. In his final years he led a life so debauched that it has become a legend.

16. Victor Rozov (born 1913): Russian playwright best known for *Eternally Alive*, which was filmed in 1956 as *The Cranes are Flying*.

17. Konstantin Paustovsky (1892–1968): Russian writer who won enormous popularity and respect for his lyrical and romantic fiction and his preservation of personal and artistic integrity. His most remarkable work is the autobio-

graphical *Story of a Life*, which ranges from the turn of the century to the early 1930's.

18. Alexander Grin (pseudonym of A. S. Grinevsky, 1880–1932): Russian writer of mystic and fantastic fiction.

19. Ivan Svitlychny (born 1929): a translator from French and author of articles on contemporary Ukrainian poetry, persecuted for protesting against political arrests in 1965. In April 1973 he was sentenced to seven years in labor camps and five years of exile.

20. Antoine de Saint-Exupéry, *The Little Prince*, translated by Katherine Woods (New York: Harcourt Brace Jovanovich, 1943).

21. Mikhail Prishvin (1873–1954): Russian writer loved by millions of Soviet readers for his observations of nature, his ethnographic lore, and his poetic and philosophic meditations.

22. In 1957 Khrushchev's colleagues conspired to demand his resignation, and Khrushchev found himself in a minority at a meeting of the Central Committee's Presidium. He insisted, however, that the Presidium did not have the right to decide his future; that was the right of the much larger Central Committee. In the latter, Khrushchev's opponents (Molotov, Malenkov, and Kaganovich) were outvoted, labeled the "antiparty group," and rusticated to minor jobs.

23. Fyodor Raskolnikov (1892–1939): Vice Chairman of the Kronstadt Soviet in 1917, commander of the Baltic fleet, and ambassador to several countries. Summoned to Moscow in 1938 because his memoirs of the October Revolution had brought him the label of "enemy of the people," Raskolnikov fled to France and wrote an open letter expressing his revulsion against Stalinism. He died a few weeks later, probably assassinated by Soviet agents. The entire letter has circulated widely in *samizdat*, and excerpts were published in *Problemy istorii KPSS*, December 1963. See also *Samizdat I: La Voix de l'opposition communiste en U.R.S.S.* (Paris: Editions du Seuil, 1969), pp. 92–101, and Roy Medvedev, *Let History Judge* (New York: Alfred A. Knopf, 1971; Vintage, 1973), pp. 256–57.

24. Iona Yakir (1896–1937): party leader, Red Army officer in the Civil War, and commander of the Kiev Military District; arrested during Stalin's purge of the army and shot on charges of treason.

CHAPTER 5

1. See Michael Glenny (ed.), *Novy Mir: A Selection, 1925–1967* (London: Jonathan Cape, 1972).

2. At least five English translations of Solzhenitsyn's *One Day in the Life of Ivan Denisovich* have appeared: Max Hayward and Ronald Hingley's (New York: Praeger; Bantam, 1963); Ralph Parker's (New York: E. P. Dutton; London: Gollancz, 1963; Penguin, 1973); Thomas P. Whitney's (New York: Fawcett, 1963); Bela Von Block's (New York: Lancer, 1963; Lodestone, 1973); and Gillon Aitken's (New York: Farrar, Straus & Giroux, 1971).

3. Vladimir Dudintsev (born 1918): Russian writer, of mediocre talent, who created a furor when he published *Not by Bread Alone* (New York: E. P. Dutton, 1957), which attacked Soviet bureaucracy by depicting an inventor who carries on an eight-year struggle against the system. The novel was at first greeted as a sign of the post-Stalin "thaw" and then roundly condemned in official criticism.

4. Nina Kosterin (1921–41): killed during World War II as a Soviet guerrilla. Her diary, first published in *Novy mir* in December 1962 and then frequently

reprinted, is the Soviet equivalent of *The Diary of Anne Frank*. An English translation by Mirra Ginsburg is available (New York: Crown, 1968).

5. Aleksey Kosterin (1896–1968): spent three years in tsarist jails, then seventeen (1938–55) in Soviet labor camps. After his release he published a few of his stories and essays—often severely censored—in the Soviet press. He also became active in the Democratic Movement, representing, along with Petro Grigorenko and Ivan Yakhimovich, its Marxist wing, and was a notable champion of the Crimean Tatars and Volga Germans in their attempts to return to their homelands.

6. Petro (Pyotr) Grigorenko (born 1907): a major general in the Red Army and a lecturer on cybernetics at the Frunze Military Academy, he was demoted to private, ousted from the party, and committed to a psychiatric hospital after he denounced anti-Semitism, criticized Khrushchev, and formed the Union of Struggle for the Revival of Leninism. Grigorenko was released in 1965 and became a leader of the Democratic Movement, for which he was recommitted from 1969 to 1975. Permitted to leave the country in 1977, he settled in the United States.

7. The eulogies and speeches at Kosterin's funeral are available in George Saunders (ed.), *Samizdat: Voices of the Soviet Opposition* (New York: Monad Press, 1974), pp. 281–323.

8. Ilya Ehrenburg (1891–1967): Russian novelist, poet, and journalist who lived abroad for many years before finally settling in Russia in 1941. After Stalin's death he occupied the vanguard of liberalization, and his novel *The Thaw* (1954) gave its name to a new trend in Soviet literature. His memoirs have played an important part in acquainting the younger generation with the history and culture of the century. See his *Selections from People, Years, Life*, introduction and notes by C. Moody (Oxford: Pergamon Press, 1972).

9. The campaign against Jews in Stalin's last years involved the liquidation of Yiddish cultural institutions and the arrest and execution of prominent Jewish figures, for whom the code phrase in the official press was "rootless cosmopolitans." The campaign climaxed in January 1953, when nine Kremlin doctors, six of them Jews, were accused of having conspired with the U.S. and British intelligence services to murder Soviet leaders. The press whipped up diatribes against "murderer-doctors who have become monsters in human form," but the campaign collapsed when Stalin died in March 1953. Had Stalin not died, however, mass deportation of Jews might well have taken place.

10. Yevgeniy Yevtushenko (born 1933): Russian poet who achieved a great deal of international publicity with verses that dealt, within prescribed limits, with the aspirations of the younger generation. See his *A Precocious Autobiography*, translated by Andrew R. MacAndrew (New York: E. P. Dutton, 1963).

11. Alexander Yesenin-Volpin (born 1924): son of the poet Sergey Yesenin (see note 15 on p. 383), taught mathematics but found himself at odds with the authorities for his outspoken political views, and between 1949 and 1968 was confined five times to psychiatric institutions. Permitted to emigrate in 1972, he now lives in the United States. See his *A Leaf of Spring* (New York: Praeger, 1961).

12. Victor Nekrasov (born 1911): Russian writer who spent most of his life in Kiev. After studying architecture and drama, working in the theater, and serving in the army, Nekrasov turned to literature, and in 1947 won the Stalin Prize for his novel *In the Trenches of Stalingrad*. Until Khrushchev denounced "On Both Sides of the Ocean" he was a firmly established writer, but then experienced

increasing difficulties. He emigrated in 1974 and settled in France. "On Both Sides of the Ocean" is available in Patricia Blake and Max Hayward (eds.), *Halfway to the Moon: New Writing from Russia,* pp. 181–228.

13. Ivan Drach (born 1936): one of the most gifted of the younger Ukrainian poets, Drach has also published translations and screenplays. Vitaliy Korotych (born 1936): after studying medicine and working as a doctor, Korotych turned to literature, editing a youth magazine and publishing poetry, travel essays, and translations. Mykola Vinhranovsky (born 1936): studied acting and cinematography, appeared in Alexander Dovzhenko's film *Chronicle of the Fiery Years* (1961), and has worked as a director at the Kiev Studio, but is better known as a poet and writer of children's books. See *Four Ukrainian Poets: Drach, Korotych, Kostenko, Symonenko,* translated by Martha Bohachevsky-Chomiak and Danylo S. Struk, edited and with an introduction by George S. N. Luckyj (n. p.: Quixote, 1969), and Ivan Drach, *Orchard Lamps,* edited and with an introduction by Stanley Kunitz (New York: Sheep Meadow Press, 1978).

14. Velimir Khlebnikov (1885–1922): Russian poet who established futurism, a seminal movement in Russian art of the twentieth century, with David Burlyuk (also an associate of Mayakovsky), and attempted to rebuild Russian poetry with radical linguistic experiments.

15. Having met Lilya Brik and her husband, the publisher and critic Osip Brik, in 1915, Mayakovsky entered into an extremely close relationship with them. Several of Mayakovsky's love poems were dedicated to Lilya and published by Osip. Despite many emotional storms the relationship endured until Mayakovsky's suicide in 1930.

16. Mikhail Lermontov (1814–41): Russian romantic poet in the mode of Byron who spent much of his life as an officer in the army and was killed in a duel; best known for his novel *A Hero of Our Times* (1840). Lesya Ukrayinka (pseudonym of Larysa Kosach, 1871–1913): Ukrainian poet whose greatest achievement is a series of dramatic poems, often with Biblical or historical settings. Her masterpiece *The Forest Song* (1911) is based on Ukrainian folklore.

17. *The Protocols of the Elders of Zion* was concocted by Russian secret service agents in 1895. Purporting to be minutes of clandestine meetings of Jewish leaders in the 1890's (a time that coincided with the first World Zionist Congress), the apocryphon discussed a Jewish conspiracy to take over the world through the Masons. It was widely disseminated after World War I in many languages and versions.

18. Korney Chukovsky (pseudonym of N. V. Korneychukov, 1882–1969): eminent Russian writer who is highly regarded for his many portraits of Russian writers, his popular books for and about children, and his translations of English literature.

19. Vladimir Vysotsky (born 1938): popular Russian stage and film actor and *chansonnier* whose songs circulate widely in *samizdat.*

20. Iryna Avdiyeva (born 1904): studied and acted in Les Kurbas's Berezil Theater 1921–24, then worked as a graphic designer. Les Kurbas (1887–1942): leading Ukrainian stage producer, founder of the Berezil Theater, where he staged expressionist performances of *Macbeth,* Georg Kaiser's *Gas,* Upton Sinclair's *Jimmy Higgins,* and above all Mykola Kulish's major plays. Attacked by the party for formalism and nationalism, Kurbas was arrested in 1933 and died in a labor camp.

21. Taras Shevchenko (1814–61): painter and poet, born a serf, whose poetry

had an enormous effect on the Ukrainian national movement. In 1847 Shevchenko was arrested for membership in the Brotherhood of SS. Cyril and Methodius, a radical group that advocated the abolition of serfdom, an end to religious and national hatred, and the establishment of a democratic union of Slavic peoples. Sentenced to penal servitude in Central Asia, he returned after ten years with broken health and died shortly after. His first collection of poems was called *Kobzar* (*The Kobza Player*, 1840), and the title has been given to his collected poetry as well.

22. Pavlo Tychyna (1891–1967): symbolist poet whose first collection, *Sonyashni klarnety* (*Solar Clarinets*, 1918), established him as the outstanding Ukrainian poet of this century. Tychyna's poetry of the 1910's and 1920's is marked by a pantheistic vision of the universe as a cosmic harmony. In the early 1930's, however, he submitted to party pressure and geared his poetry to official requirements, for which he was rewarded with high government honors. Mykola Kulish (1892–1942): playwright whose major plays, *The People's Malachi* (1928), *Myna Mazaylo* (1929), and *Sonata Pathétique* (1930), established a new era in Ukrainian drama when they were staged by Les Kurbas at the Berezil Theater. Kulish was arrested in 1934 on charges of nationalism and formalism and died in a labor camp. See Mykola Kulish, *Sonata Pathétique*, translated by George S. N. and Moira Luckyj (Littleton, Colo.: Ukrainian Academic Press, 1975). Alexander Dovzhenko (1894–1956): Ukrainian film maker widely regarded as one of the world's greatest directors. He was increasingly hampered by political restrictions after 1930 and was able to complete only eight feature-length films, which include his major works, *Zvenyhora* (1928), *Arsenal* (1929), and *Earth* (1930). See Alexander Dovzhenko, *The Poet as Filmmaker: Selected Writings*, edited, translated, and with an introduction by Marco Carynnyk (Cambridge, Mass.: The M.I.T. Press, 1973). Fedir Krychevsky (1879–1947): Ukrainian painter and teacher, brother of Vasyl Krychevsky (1873–1952), who designed the sets for several of Dovzhenko's films. Anatol Petrytsky (1895–1964): Ukrainian painter, graphic artist, and stage designer. Unlike many of his contemporaries, Petrytsky was never arrested and continues to be revered in the Soviet Union, but some of his work was destroyed for failing to conform to socialist realism. Mykhaylo Boychuk (1882–1939): notable Ukrainian painter who combined Byzantine, pre-Renaissance, and Ukrainian folk-art elements in a monumental style known as Boychukism. Arrested in 1937, Boychuk died in a labor camp, and all his work, except for some small paintings, was destroyed. Ivan Padalka (1897–1938): Ukrainian painter and graphic artist, pupil of Mykhaylo Boychuk. Charged with "nationalist formalism," he was executed in 1938, and most of his work was destroyed.

CHAPTER 6

1. The agronomist Trofim Lysenko (1898–1976) denounced the genetic theory of heredity as reactionary and advanced his own theory that one can manipulate the inheritance of physical characteristics in plants by controlling their environment. With Stalin's approval, Lysenko led a campaign to silence his critics. Discussion of his claims was banned, and many reputable scientists were sacked from their posts or even arrested. Khrushchev continued to support Lysenko's charlatanry, and it was not until after Khrushchev's dismissal in 1964 that the hold of Lysenkoism over Soviet genetics and agriculture was weakened.

2. The letter was seized by the KGB at the time of Plyushch's arrest in 1972 and is not available in the West.

3. Accounts of the strike in Novocherkassk appear in Michel Tatu, *Power in the Kremlin* (London, 1969), p. 115; Albert Boiter, "When the Kettle Boils Over," *Problems of Communism*, 1964, No. 1, pp. 33–43; and John Kolasky, *Two Years in Soviet Ukraine* (Toronto: Peter Martin Associates, 1972), pp. 191–92. They are summarized in M. Holubenko, "The Soviet Working Class: Discontent and Opposition," *Critique*, No. 4, Spring 1975, pp. 5–25.

4. Lenin, *Collected Works*, Vol. 25, p. 420.

5. *Loza* means "vine," and *plyushch* means "ivy." In Russian or Ukrainian script, both are words of four letters. The essay has not reached the West.

6. "Idolocracy" was coined by the Russian philosopher Nikolay Berdyayev (1874–1948) to indicate a government based on idols. Plyushch means here that the ideals on which the state was founded have been turned by the rulers into idols. The popular masses, however, continue to believe in the ideals and thus instinctively express their protest against the rule of idols.

7. Wanda Wasilewska (1905–64) was a Polish writer who lived in the Soviet Union after 1939 and was frequently elected to the Supreme Soviet and awarded government prizes.

8. In the strict sense, Banderites are members of a faction of the Organization of Ukrainian Nationalists headed by Stepan Bandera (1900–59), which maintained wide-scale armed resistance to Soviet rule during and after World War II. In the Soviet political lexicon, however, the word has been broadened into a pejorative for all Ukrainians suspected of nationalism.

CHAPTER 7

1. Yuli Daniel (Nikolai Arzhak), *This Is Moscow Speaking and Other Stories*, translated by Stuart Hood, Harold Shukman, and John Richardson, foreword by Max Hayward (New York: E. P. Dutton, 1969; Collier, 1970), pp. 85–86.

2. Pavel Kopnin (1922–71): Russian philosopher whose main work concerned gnosiology, logic, and scientific method. Appointed director of the Institute of Philosophy of the Ukrainian Academy of Sciences in 1962.

3. Victor Glushkov (born 1923): Ukrainian mathematician, Vice President of the Academy of Sciences of the Ukrainian SSR, winner of the Lenin Prize for 1964, and editor of a two-volume *Encyclopedia of Cybernetics* (Kiev, 1973).

4. Mykhaylo Klokov (born 1896): as a botanist Klokov has written extensively on the flora of the Ukrainian steppes and is the author of a *Guide to the Flora of the Ukrainian SSR*. Using the pseudonym Dolengo, he has also published poetry since 1920.

5. The fiction writer Mykytenko (1897–1937), the critic Koryak (1889–1939), and Klokov-Dolengo were members of VUSPP, the All-Ukrainian Union of Proletarian Writers, which was established by the party in 1926 and which waged a fierce and indiscriminate campaign against writers who refused to accept direct party control of literature.

6. Rasul Gamzatov (born 1923): Avar (Daghestani) poet who began publishing in 1937. *Moy Dagestan*, translated by Vladimir Soloukhin, was published in Moscow by Molodaya Gvardiya in 1968. Shamil (1798?–1871) was the Imam of Muridism, a Moslem sect that waged holy wars against infidels, and the leader for twenty-five years of guerrilla resistance to Russian forces in the Caucasus.

The legend of Shamil as a military hero was actively propagated in the Soviet Union before World War II. In 1950, however, the party reversed its stand on Shamil and declared that Muridism was a reactionary religious movement and an instrument of Turkish and British expansion, and that the annexation of the Caucasus to Russia was a progressive move. Shamil was denounced as a reactionary leader with no popular support, and historians who had written positively about him were labeled "bourgeois nationalists."

7. Volodymyr Sosyura (1898–1965): extremely popular Ukrainian lyric poet who was frequently attacked for being insufficiently party-minded. His poem, of which only excerpts were published in the 1920's, deals with Ivan Mazepa (1639–1709), the Ukrainian Hetman who joined forces with Karl XII of Sweden to regain Ukrainian independence, which had been lost after the Treaty of Pereyaslav with Muscovy in 1654. The Swedish-Ukrainian forces were defeated by Peter the Great at the Battle of Poltava in 1709, and Karl and Mazepa fled to Turkey. Russian and Soviet propaganda has consistently castigated Mazepa as an archtraitor who attempted to undermine Russian-Ukrainian friendship.

8. Dzyuba's speech on Symonenko's thirtieth birthday, January 16, 1965, is available in John Kolasky, *Two Years in Soviet Ukraine*, pp. 253–58.

9. Cesar Roux (1857–1926): Swiss surgeon.

10. Konstantin Fedin (born 1892): Russian novelist whose best-known work, *Cities and Years* (1924), deals with the problems of intellectuals in times of revolution. A translation by Michael Scammel is available (New York: Dell, 1962).

CHAPTER 8

1. Victor Krasin (born 1929): economist who served time in labor camps under Stalin, active in the Initiative Group for the Defense of Human Rights (see note 15 on p. 397). Arrested in December 1969 on charges of parasitism, Krasin was sentenced to five years' exile.

2. Boris Pasternak, *Doctor Zhivago*, translated by Max Hayward and Manya Harari (London: Collins and Harvill; New York: Pantheon, 1958).

3. Andrey Sinyavsky (born 1925): prominent Russian writer and critic who published in the Soviet Union under his own name and in the West, beginning in 1956, under the pseudonym Abram Tertz. Arrested in September 1965 and tried, along with Yuliy Daniel, in February 1966, Sinyavsky was sentenced to seven years in a labor camp. He was released in June 1971 and in August 1973 emigrated to France, where he has been lecturing on Russian literature at the Sorbonne. The letters he wrote to his wife from the labor camp have been published as *A Voice from the Chorus*, translated by Kyril Fitzlyon and Max Hayward, with an introduction by Max Hayward (London: Collins; New York: Farrar, Straus and Giroux, 1976). He has also published *V teni Gogolya* [*In the Shadow of Gogol*] (London: Overseas Publications Interchange and Collins, 1975) and *Progulki s Pushkinym* [*Strolling with Pushkin*] (London: Overseas Publications Interchange and Collins, 1975). Yuliy Daniel (born 1925): published his work abroad under the pseudonym Nikolay Arzhak. Tried with Sinyavsky, he was sentenced to five years in a labor camp. In July 1967 he was transferred to Vladimir Prison for joining other prisoners in a protest against the authorities' highhandedness. After his release Daniel was not permitted to return to Moscow, and he settled in Kaluga. For a full account of the Sinyavsky-Daniel case see *On Trial: The Soviet State Versus "Abram Tertz" and "Nikolai Arzhak,"* trans-

lated, edited, and with an introduction by Max Hayward (New York: Harper & Row, 1966).

4. Sergo Paradzhanov (Paradzhanian, born 1924): Armenian director who worked at the Kiev Film Studio. *Shadows of Forgotten Ancestors*, based on a novella by the Ukrainian writer Mykhaylo Kotsyubynsky, won sixteen prizes at international festivals and initiated a poetic or folkloric trend in Ukrainian film. Professional envy and Paradzhanov's outspoken defense of persecuted intellectuals prevented his completing any subsequent projects except for the remarkable (but little-circulated) Armenian film, *Sayat Nova*. He was arrested in December 1973 on charges of homosexuality and trafficking in art objects and sentenced to six years in labor camps. He was reported to have been released in January 1978. See Antonin J. Liehm (ed.), *Serghiej Paradjanov* (Venice: La Biennale di Venezia, 1977) and Marco Carynnyk, "Sergo Paradzhanov in Prison," *Journal of Ukrainian Graduate Studies*, Vol. 3, No. 2, Spring 1978, pp. 47–55.

5. Ivan Dzyuba (born 1931): Ukrainian critic whose political polemics and literary articles made him a leader of the Ukrainian opposition, for which he was frequently attacked by the party and threatened with expulsion from the Writers' Union. In 1972 Dzyuba was arrested and held for interrogation for almost a year, despite poor health. In March 1973 he was tried and sentenced to five years' imprisonment and five years' exile.

6. Lina Kostenko (born 1930): gifted Ukrainian poet, frequently charged by official critics with "formalism" and "detachment from Soviet reality." She ceased to be published in the mid-sixties, when she sought to gain admission to the closed trials in Kiev and Lviv and appealed for publicity and judicial fairness, and reappeared in print only in 1977, with *Nad berehamy vichnoyi riky* [*On the Shores of the Eternal River*] (Kiev: Radyansky Pysmennyk). Lyubov Zabashta (born 1918): Ukrainian poet, playwright, and writer of children's books. Oles Berdnyk (born 1927): popular and prolific Ukrainian science-fiction writer. He was in the labor camps from 1949 to 1955 and came into open conflict with the authorities again in April 1972, when his apartment was searched by the KGB and *Literaturna Ukrayina* attacked his well-attended lectures on space travel and futurology. Since then Berdnyk has written numerous appeals to the West and been active in the Ukrainian Helsinki Monitoring Group.

7. Article 62 of the Criminal Code of the Ukrainian Republic (equivalent to Article 70 of the Criminal Code of the Russian Republic) is frequently used to charge political dissidents. It states in part: "Agitation or propaganda carried on for the purpose of subverting or weakening Soviet authority or for the purpose of committing individual especially dangerous crimes against the State, or circulating for those purposes slanderous fabrications which defame the Soviet State and social system, or circulating, preparing or keeping for the same purpose literature of such content, is to be punished by deprivation of liberty for a term of from six months to seven years, with or without an additional period of exile for a term of from two to five years." (E. L. Johnson, *An Introduction to the Soviet Legal System* [London: Eyre Methuen, 1969], p. 154.)

8. The "Appeal of the 139," so known because of the number of signatories, is available in Michael Browne (ed.), *Ferment in the Ukraine* (London: Macmillan; New York: Praeger, 1971; New York: Crisis Press, 1973), pp. 191–96.

9. Mykola Amosov (born 1903): Ukrainian surgeon, corresponding member of the USSR Academy of Medical Sciences since 1961, and prolific writer on biocybernetics and thoracic surgery: *Regulyatsiya zhiznennykh funktsiy i kiber-*

netika [*Regulation of Vital Functions and Cybernetics*] (Kiev: Naukova Dumka, 1964); *The Open Heart*, translated by George St. George (New York: Simon and Schuster, 1966); *Modeling of Thinking and the Mind*, translated by Leo Finegold (New York: Spartan Books, 1967), and *Notes from the Future*, translated by George St. George (New York: Simon and Schuster, 1970).

10. Alexander Galich (1919–77): Russian playwright (ten of his plays have been staged in the USSR) and film maker who became widely known in the early 1960's as a writer and singer of songs. Their topical nature and sharply satirical orientation led to persecution by the authorities, and Galich was forced to emigrate in 1974. His poems, translated by Gerry Smith, are available in *Index on Censorship*, Vol. 3, No. 3, Autumn 1974, pp. 11–28, and the anthology *Kontinent* (Garden City: Anchor, 1976), pp. 25–34.

11. Alexander Bogdanov (pseudonym of Malinovsky, 1873–1928): Russian economist and philosopher, expelled from the Bolshevik Party in 1909 for revisionism. In a long series of studies Bogdanov speculated on new forms of organizing society, culture, and labor. He spent the last years of his life in the appropriately visionary post of director of an institute for the "struggle for vital capacity" and died after an experiment involving transfusions of his blood.

12. Gavriil Tikhov (1875–1960): Russian astronomer whose major work involved astrometrics and spectrophotometrics; considered to be a founder of astrobotany and astrobiology.

13. Vasiliy Fesenkov (born 1889): Russian astrophysicist and astronomer, author of numerous books on cosmogony.

14. Vladimir Propp (1895–1970): Russian philologist and folklore expert whose *Historical Roots of the Fairy Tale* and *Morphology of the Folktale* (Austin: University of Texas Press, 1968) have exerted a strong influence on contemporary structuralism.

15. Lev Vygotsky (1896–1934): Russian psychologist who investigated developmental psychology, education, and psychopathology. Dmitriy Uznadze (1886–1950): Georgian psychologist. His theory of set (*ustanovka*), or nonconscious nervous activity, has been promoted as a Soviet alternative to Freudianism and serves as a point of departure for Plyushch's essay "Moral Orientation" in Tatyana Khodorovich (ed.), *The Case of Leonid Plyushch*, translated by Marite Sapiets, Peter Reddaway, and Caryl Emerson (London: C. Hurst; Boulder: Westview Press, 1976), pp. 131–42. Nikolay Vavilov (1887–1943): Russian plant breeder and applied geneticist who headed the opposition to Lysenko's charlatanry (see note 1 on p. 387). Labeled an "enemy of the people" and a "Trotskyite-Bukharinist diversionist," Vavilov was arrested in 1940 and sentenced to death. The sentence was commuted to ten years' imprisonment, but Vavilov died in prison. Nikolay Koltsov (1872–1940): prominent Russian pioneer in genetics and cytology. His eugenicist views of the early 1920's were used as a pretext by Lysenko's followers in the late 1930's to persecute him along with Vavilov.

16. Mikhail Bakhtin (1895–1975): influential Russian formalist and structuralist critic, author of the seminal study *Problems of Dostoevsky's Poetics*, translated by R. William Rotsel (Ann Arbor: Ardis, 1973). Bakhtin's provocative *Rabelais and His World*, translated by Helene Iswolsky (Cambridge, Mass.: The M.I.T. Press, 1968), deals with laughter and its manifestation in folk rites and carnival festivities and has inspired the title of the present book. Alexander Vvedensky (born 1904) and Daniil Kharms (born 1905): Russian absurdist writers whose work was almost unknown in their lifetimes. They were arrested just before

World War II and died in 1941 or 1942. Their stories have been collected and translated by George Gibian in *Russia's Lost Literature of the Absurd: Selected Works of Daniil Kharms and Alexander Vvedensky* (Ithaca: Cornell University Press, 1971; New York: W. W. Norton, 1974).

17. Mikhail Lomonosov (1711–65): Russian scientist, founder of Moscow University, man of letters, and grammarian.

18. Dmitriy Mendeleyev (1834–1907): Russian chemist who established the periodic law in 1869. Alexander Butlerov (1828–86): Russian chemist. Nikolay Lobachevsky (1792–1856): prominent Russian mathematician, founder of non-Euclidian geometry.

19. Konstantin Tsiolkovsky (1857–1935): Russian pioneer in aerodynamics, rocketry, and the theory of space travel. Regarded as a crank in his own time, he laid the foundations for much of the later work in these fields.

CHAPTER 9

1. Bulat Okudzhava (born 1924): poet, balladeer, and (more recently) novelist. Okudzhava's resounding fame comes from his performance of his antibureaucratic, anti-Stalinist, and pacifist ballads on stage to the accompaniment of his guitar. Eager listeners have made hundreds of tapes, several of which have been released as phonograph records in the West.

2. Kuo Mo-jo (1892–1978): Chinese writer, scholar, and revolutionist. Head of the Chinese Federation of Literature and Arts, vice chairman of the National People's Congress, a member of the party's Central Committee, and President of the Academy of Sciences, he was publicly humiliated during the Cultural Revolution.

3. Dmitriy Merezhkovsky (1865–1941): Russian symbolist novelist, poet, and critic. Violently opposed to the Bolsheviks (whom he called "boors"), Merezhkovsky emigrated in 1919 and subsequently adopted a near-fascist position.

4. Club of Creative Youth: set up under the auspices of the Writers' Union in 1962–63 and headed by the poet Vitaliy Korotych, the group was disbanded after about a year and a half of activity.

5. Fedir Ovcharenko (born 1913): Ukrainian chemist, head of the Science and Culture Department of the Central Committee of the Ukrainian party from 1956 to 1968, ideological secretary from 1968 to 1972.

6. Available in two English translations: *Cancer Ward*, translated by Nicholas Bethell and David Burg, two volumes (London: The Bodley Head, 1968 and 1969), one volume (New York: Farrar, Straus & Giroux, 1969; Penguin, 1971; Bantam, 1972). *The Cancer Ward*, translated by Rebecca Frank (New York: Dial 1968; Dell, 1973).

7. *Candle in the Wind*, translated by Keith Armes and Arthur Hudgins, introduction by Keith Armes (London: The Bodley Head and Oxford University Press, 1973).

8. The two extant translations of *The First Circle* are by Thomas P. Whitney (New York: Harper & Row, 1968; Bantam, 1969) and Michael Guybon (London: Collins and Harvill, 1968; Fontana, 1972). *Lenin in Zurich*, translated by H. T. Willetts (New York: Farrar, Straus & Giroux, 1976; Bantam, 1977).

9. *Cancer Ward* (Penguin edition), p. 474.

10. Book 5, Chapters 3–5, of *The Brothers Karamazov*.

11. Aleksey Yermolov (1772?–1861): Russian general who fought in the Napo-

leonic Wars and was commander in chief of Russian forces in the Caucasus from 1816 to 1827. The Decembrists: aristocrats and army officers who conspired to replace the autocracy with a democratic system. The armed rebellion they mounted in 1825 was crushed, but the episode is important as an early chapter in the history of the Russian revolutionary movement.

12. Nikolay Marr (1864–1934): Russian Orientalist who played a role in linguistics similar to Trofim Lysenko's in biology. Supported by the party, Marr denied established language groups in favor of a ubiquitous evolution of four basic sounds that could be related to the different stages of a people's material development. Marr's ruinous influence on Soviet linguistics ended when he was denounced by Stalin in 1950.

13. Vladimir Yermilov (born 1904): critic who caused Mayakovsky much grief with his doctrinaire and ignorant attacks on Mayakovsky's play *The Bathhouse.*

14. The Uniates, or Eastern-rite Catholics, are Ukrainians who have been in union with Rome since 1596 but who maintain their Eastern liturgy and customs (married priests, for example). After World War II the church was forcibly united with the Russian Orthodox Church, and its remnants in the underground have been hounded with particular severity.

CHAPTER 10

1. Solzhenitsyn's "The Easter Procession" is available in *Stories and Prose Poems,* translated by Michael Glenny (New York: Farrar, Straus & Giroux; London: The Bodley Head, 1971; Bantam, 1972; Penguin, 1973).

2. In August 1961 a dissenting group within the officially recognized Union of Evangelical Christian-Baptists (ECB) formed an "Initiative [Action] Group for the Convening of an Extraordinary All-Union Congress of the Evangelical Christian-Baptist Church in the USSR" (hence the popular name *initsiativniks*). Led by Presbyters Aleksey Prokofyev, Gennadiy Kryuchkov, and Georgiy Vins, the *initsiativniks* broke with the ECB in protest against government infringements on religious freedom. Despite harsh persecution, this reform Baptist group has become by far the best organized and most active of the contemporary protest movements in the USSR.

3. *Stories and Prose Poems* (Bantam edition), p. 194.

4. "Diabolism" is used here to translate *besovshchina*, which means both "diabolism" and the complex of ideas associated with Dostoyevsky's "pamphlet-novel" *Besy* (translated as *The Devils* or *The Possessed*).

5. Boris Dyakov, "Povest' o perezhitom" ["The Story of My Experience"], *Oktyabr'*, 1964, No. 7, pp. 49–142; reprinted as a book (Moscow: Sovetskaya Rossiya, 1966) .

6. The White Guards: members of various military formations, including Denikin's and Vrangel's, that opposed the Bolsheviks in the Civil War. Andrey Vlasov (1900–46): Red Army commander who was captured by the Germans in 1942. Disillusioned by his experiences under Stalin, he headed a formation of captured Soviet soldiers in German uniform known as the Russian Liberation Army. After Germany's defeat, the Allies repatriated these troops to the Soviet Union. Vlasov and his officers were executed in August 1946, and the rank and file were dispatched to labor camps. See Jürgen Thorwald, *The Illusion: Soviet Soldiers in Hitler's Armies,* translated by Richard and Clara Winston (New York: A Helen and Kurt Wolff Book, Harcourt Brace Jovanovich, 1975).

7. Eugenia Semyonovna Ginzburg, *Journey into the Whirlwind*, translated by Paul Stevenson and Max Hayward (New York: A Helen and Kurt Wolff Book, Harcourt Brace Jovanovich, 1967).

8. Nikolay Tikhonov (born 1896): Russian poet, influenced by Khlebnikov, Mayakovsky, and Pasternak, whose ballads are characterized by a kind of revolutionary romanticism.

9. Nikolay Yezhov (1895–1939): secret-police official, People's Commissar of Internal Affairs 1936–38.

10. Osip Mandelstam (1891–1938): brilliant Russian poet who was arrested on Stalin's order in 1934 and sent to a labor camp. He has been recently discovered and widely translated in the West. His wife's memoirs of him are a remarkable literary work in their own right: Nadezhda Mandelstam, *Hope Against Hope*, translated by Max Hayward, introduction by Clarence Brown (New York: Atheneum, 1970) and *Hope Abandoned*, translated by Max Hayward (New York: Atheneum, 1974).

11. Vasyl Stus (born 1938): gifted Ukrainian poet and translator (particularly of Rilke) whose work stopped being published in the Soviet Union when he became active in the opposition movement in 1965. Arrested in 1972, Stus was sentenced to five years in labor camps and three years of exile. He is reported to be in extremely poor health, and some six hundred poems and translations that he wrote in camp have been confiscated and destroyed by the authorities. His essay on Tychyna has not reached the West.

12. Ivan Dzyuba, *Internationalism or Russification? A Study in the Soviet Nationalities Problem*, second edition (London: Weidenfeld & Nicolson, 1970; New York: Monad Press, 1974.)

13. *Ibid.*, p. 74.

14. Sholem Aleichem (pseudonym of Sholem Rabinovitch, 1859–1916): Yiddish writer, a founder of modern Yiddish literature, whose numerous stories, sketches, and novels deal largely with small-town life in tsarist Russia. Perets Markish (1895–1952): Yiddish poet and playwright whose epic works depicted Jewish heroism. Markish was arrested and executed in a Stalinist purge of a large group of Jewish writers.

15. Babyn (Babiy) Yar is the ravine on the outskirts of Kiev where the Nazis massacred some 200,000 people, most of them Jews, during their occupation of Ukraine. The Soviet authorities' refusal to put up a monument on the site and to admit that Babyn Yar was a Jewish tragedy was a burning political issue.

16. See "Babyi Yar Address by Ivan Dzyuba" in Abraham Brumberg (ed.) *In Quest of Justice: Protest and Dissent in the Soviet Union Today* (New York: Praeger, 1970), pp. 200–04; and "Ivan Dzyuba's Speech in Babyn Yar" in Vyacheslav Chornovil (ed.), *The Chornovil Papers* (New York: McGraw-Hill, 1968), pp. 222–26.

17. Borys Antonenko-Davydovych (born 1899): respected Ukrainian writer, member in the early 1920's of the Ukrainian Communist Party, which opposed the Bolsheviks, then of the Kiev writers' group MARS, of which all the members were arrested in the early 1930's and some executed. Antonenko-Davydovych was sent to the labor camps and did not return to writing until 1956. In recent years he has been attacked by official critics and blacklisted by the KGB for his support of the opposition movement. Trofym Kichko's *Judaism Without Embellishment* (Kiev: Academy of Sciences of the Ukrainian SSR, 1963) depicted Judaism as fostering hypocrisy, bribery, greed, and usury and linked Zionism, Israel, Jewish

bankers, and Western capitalists in a world-wide conspiracy. After extensive protests, including sharp statements by Western Communist parties, the authorities in Moscow denounced the book in a vaguely worded resolution that only pointed out some "mistakes" in the presentation and failed to charge the book with being anti-Semitic.

18. *Kul'turnyky* and *halushnyky* or *khutoryany* in Ukrainian.

19. Erast Binyashevsky (ed.), *Ukrayins'ki pysanky* [*Ukrainian Easter Eggs*] (Kiev: Mystetstvo, 1968).

20. Vladimir Soloukhin (born 1924): Russian writer whose stories, verse, and essays display a lively talent; a singular proponent of resurrecting old cultural values, including the restoration of churches and icons. See his *Searching for Icons in Russia*, translated by P. S. Falla (New York: A Helen and Kurt Wolff Book, Harcourt Brace Jovanovich, 1972).

21. Iryna Steshenko (born 1898): a granddaughter of the writer Mykhaylo Starytsky and an actress in the Berezil Theater in the 1920's, she has extensively translated Western drama into Ukrainian.

22. Oksana Ivanenko (born 1906): editor of children's magazines and translator and author of numerous books for children.

23. *The Insulted and the Injured* is Dostoyevsky's first longer novel, published in 1861.

24. Mikhail Katkov (1818–87): Russian journalist and a leading spokesman of reaction. Prince V. P. Meshchersky (1839–1914): reactionary adviser to the Tsar and opponent of popular education. Konstantin Pobedonostsev (1827–1907): Russian jurist, civil servant, and political philosopher who advocated unrestricted autocracy and was largely responsible for the government's repressive policies toward religious and national minorities.

25. Shigalev is a doctrinaire theorist in Dostoyevsky's *The Possessed* who argues that man can be happy only if his freedom of choice and action is restricted. He proposes that nine-tenths of humanity be turned into a herd and the remaining tenth be granted absolute freedom and unrestricted powers over the rest.

26. Truman Capote, *In Cold Blood* (New York: Random House, 1965; New American Library, 1971), p. 362.

27. Eduard Rozental, "Khippi i drugiye" ["Hippies and Others"], *Novy mir*, 1971, No. 7, pp. 182–204.

28. The Fourth Congress of Soviet Writers was convened in Moscow on May 22, 1967. Solzhenitsyn, who was not invited to attend, prepared some 150 copies of his open letter, mailing them to arrive just before the Congress opened. An early translation appeared in the New York *Times* on June 5. A later version is available in John B. Dunlop, Richard Haugh, and Alexis Klimoff (eds.), *Aleksandr Solzhenitsyn: Critical Essays and Documentary Materials* (Boston: Nordland, 1973; New York: Collier Books, 1975), pp. 541–49. The text has also been included in the Bantam edition of *One Day in the Life of Ivan Denisovich*, pp. v–x.

29. Georgiy Vladimov (born 1931): Russian writer, author of a *samizdat* novel *Vernyy Ruslan* (*Faithful Ruslan*, 1964), which is an original contribution to the voluminous literature on labor camps: the hero of the novel is a watchdog that has been released from its job. For Vladimov's letter to the Fourth Congress of Soviet Writers see Leopold Labedz (ed.), *Solzhenitsyn: A Documentary Record*, second edition (Middlesex: Penguin, 1974), pp. 123–25.

CHAPTER 11

1. See "To World Public Opinion" in Pavel Litvinov (ed.), *The Trial of the Four: A Collection of Material in the Case of Galanskov, Ginzburg, Dobrovolsky, and Lashkova, 1967–1968,* English text edited and annotated by Peter Reddaway (New York: Viking, 1972), pp. 225–27.

2. Abram Terz (Andrey Sinyavsky), *Fantastic Stories,* translated by Max Hayward and Ronald Hingley (New York: Pantheon, 1963). Yuli Daniel, *This Is Moscow Speaking,* pp. 75–134. Victor Velsky is a pseudonym for the author of *The Confession of Victor Velsky.* For "My Apologia," a section of *The Confession,* see Michael Scammell (ed.), *Russia's Other Writers: Selections from Samizdat Literature* (New York: Praeger, 1971), pp. 185–216.

3. Pyotr Yakir (born 1923): son of Iona Yakir (see note 24 on p. 384), he was arrested, at the age of fourteen, after his father's execution and confined to labor camps for seventeen years. He became active in the Democratic Movement during the 1960's. See his *A Childhood in Prison,* edited and with an introduction by Robert Conquest (London: Macmillan, 1972).

4. The NTS (Narodno-Trudovoy Soyuz, or Popular Labor Alliance) is an organization of anti-Soviet Russian émigrés with headquarters in Frankfurt and Paris.

5. Pavel Litvinov (born 1940): a grandson of Maxim Litvinov, the Soviet Foreign Minister and ambassador to the United States, sentenced in 1968 to five years' exile for his involvement in the Democratic Movement; now lives in the United States.

6. L. Plyushch, "Pis'mo v redaktsiyu *Komsomol'skoy Pravdy* o dezinformatsii v svyazi s protsessom Ginzburga, Galanskova i dr." ["Letter to the Editors of *Komsomolskaya Pravda* about the Misinformation around the Trial of Ginzburg, Galanskov, and Others"], January 1968. AS 48. Translated as "To the Editors of *Komsomolskaya Pravda*" in *The Trial of the Four,* pp. 332–35; as "The Thermidorians Fear the Truth" in *Samizdat,* pp. 268–72; and as "Open Letter to the Editors of *Komsomolskaya Pravda*" in Tatyana Khodorovich (ed.), *The Case of Leonid Plyushch,* pp. 3–6.

7. The *Chronicle of Current Events* is produced in typescript every two to four months by an anonymous and changing group of human-rights activists. The first eleven issues appeared in English in Peter Reddaway (ed.), *Uncensored Russia: Protest and Dissent in the Soviet Union* (London: Jonathan Cape; New York: McGraw-Hill, 1972). Subsequent issues have been published in English by Amnesty International in London.

8. Anatoly Marchenko, *My Testimony,* translated by Michael Scammell, introduction by Max Hayward (New York: E. P. Dutton, 1969; with a new appendix, Penguin, 1971).

9. Heorhiy Pukhov (born 1916): Ukrainian computer specialist, employed at the Kiev Institute of Cybernetics since 1959, member of the Ukrainian Academy of Sciences since 1967, has published numerous works on analog computers.

10. Yuliy Kim (born 1936): graduated from the Moscow Teachers' College and worked as a teacher in Kamchatka and Moscow until he was dismissed for his role in the Democratic Movement. Kim is a popular underground composer and singer and has also written—under a pseudonym—songs for plays and films.

11. Ilya Gabay (1936?–73): teacher and editor whose poetry circulates in *samizdat.* He was an active member of the Democratic Movement and committed

suicide as a result of frequent arrests and interrogations. For the letter by Yakir, Kim, and Gabay see Abraham Brumberg (ed.), *In Quest of Justice: Protest and Dissent in the Soviet Union Today* (New York: Praeger, 1970), pp. 157–62.

12. Valeriy Pavlinchuk (1937?–68): scientist at the research center in Obninsk, where the first Soviet nuclear-power station was built in the 1950's. Pavlinchuk was expelled from the party and dismissed from his job in the spring of 1968 for his *samizdat* activity. Shortly before he died, he sent an open letter to Alexander Dubček, supporting the new political course in Czechoslovakia. Friends and sympathizers who attended his funeral were subjected to reprisals. The "Letter of the 224," also known as the "Letter of the 170" because of the original number of signatories, is available in *The Trial of the Four*, pp. 254–57.

13. Vladimir Dremlyuga (born 1940): worker from Leningrad who was sentenced to three years in labor camps for his part in the demonstration in Red Square in August 1968; now lives in France.

14. Larisa Bogoraz (Bogoraz-Bryukhman, born 1929): philologist who has taken part in numerous demonstrations and written, with Pavel Litvinov, a famous appeal "To World Public Opinion." She was exiled for four years to the Irkutsk region for her part in the Red Square demonstration. Formerly married to Yuliy Daniel, she is now the wife of Anatoliy Marchenko.

15. Grigoriy Podyapolsky (1926–76): a geophysicist at the Institute of Earth Physics in Moscow, he was also active in the human-rights movement. He was a founding member of the Initiative Group for the Defense of Human Rights and later joined the Moscow Human Rights Committee, and he was the author of a book of poetry, *Zolotoy vek* [*The Golden Age*] (Frankfurt: Possev-Verlag, 1974).

16. Yuriy Eichenwald (Aikhenvald, born 1930), a teacher of literature as well as a poet and translator, and his wife, Valeriya Gerlin (born 1930?), also a teacher, spent time in Stalinist labor camps. They were fired from their jobs in April 1968 for signing the "Letter of the 224" but were reinstated after filing appeals. A transcript of the teachers' meeting at which Gerlin was criticized is available in *Politicheskiy dnevnik, 1964–1970* [*Political Diary, 1964–1970*] (Amsterdam: Herzen Foundation, 1972), pp. 361–75, and in Abraham Brumberg (ed.), *In Quest of Justice*, pp. 340–49.

17. Grigorenko and Kosterin's letter to the Budapest Conference is in *Mysli sumasshedshego: Izbrannye pis'ma i vystupleniya* [*Notes of a Madman: Selected Letters and Speeches*] (Amsterdam: Herzen Foundation, 1973), pp. 103–26.

18. Translated as "Persecution of Young Dissenters Is Adventurism" in *Samizdat*, pp. 263–67. Biographical information about Yakhimovich is available in Grigorenko's "My Friend and Comrade, Ivan Yakhimovich," *ibid.*, pp. 346–51.

19. Led by such prominent Bolsheviks as Trotsky, Zinoviev, Kamenev, and Bukharin, the Left Opposition of the 1920's and 1930's was destroyed in the Stalinist purges but gave rise to the world Trotskyist movement. Documents of the Left Opposition are available in George Saunders (ed.), *Samizdat: Voices of the Soviet Opposition* (New York: Monad Press, 1974); there is also a study by Robert Vincent Daniels, *The Conscience of the Revolution: Communist Opposition in Soviet Russia* (Cambridge, Mass.: Harvard University Press, 1960; New York: Simon and Schuster, 1969).

20. Ninety-nine of the 4,500 workers at the Praga automobile factory in Prague sent a letter to *Pravda* (July 30, 1968) approving the presence of Soviet troops in Czechoslovakia. The Soviet press then alleged that the signatories were being persecuted and cited this as evidence of counterrevolutionary activity.

21. Rudolf Slánský (1901–52): Secretary General of the Czechoslovak Communist Party from 1946. In a wave of purges throughout the Soviet Union and Eastern Europe, Slánský (along with thirteen other defendants) was tried in November 1952 on charges of spying for Britain and Israel and executed. Eleven of the fourteen accused were Jews, whereas a number of arrested gentiles were not placed in the dock, and the whole affair had an unmistakably anti-Semitic flavor. For an account of the trial by one of the defendants, see Eugen Loebl, *My Mind on Trial* (New York: A Helen and Kurt Wolff Book, Harcourt Brace Jovanovich, 1976).

22. Ludvík Vaculík (born 1926): prominent Czech writer, author of "Two Thousand Words," the manifesto of the Prague Spring, and of several widely translated novels. The documents referred to are available in Andrew Oxley, Alex Pravda, and Andrew Ritchie (eds.), *Czechoslovakia: The Party and the People* (London: Allen Lane, The Penguin Press, 1973), and Robin Remington (ed.), *Winter in Prague: Documents on Czechoslovak Communism in Crisis*, introduction by William E. Griffith (Cambridge, Mass.: The M.I.T. Press, 1969).

23. Ludvík Svoboda (born 1895): Czech army officer, Minister of Defense 1945–52, President of Czechoslovakia from April 1968.

24. Andrei Sakharov, *Progress, Coexistence, and Intellectual Freedom* (New York: W. W. Norton, 1968). Also available in *Sakharov Speaks* (New York: Vintage, 1974), pp. 55–114.

25. Rollan Kadiyev, a physicist from Samarkand in Uzbekistan, and Zampira Asanova, a doctor also from Uzbekistan, were prominent activists both in the Crimean Tatar movement and in the Democratic Movement.

26. Petro Shelest (born 1908): First Secretary of the Communist Party of Ukraine from 1963 until his demotion in May 1972.

27. Zinoviya Franko (born 1925): granddaughter of the prominent Ukrainian writer Ivan Franko, active in the Ukrainian movement until her arrest in 1972. She was released after publishing a recantation (*Radyanska Ukrayina*, March 2, 1972; *Index on Censorship*, Vol. 1, No. 2, Summer 1972, p. 143).

28. Andriy Malyshko (1912–73): popular Ukrainian poet.

29. Borys Paton (born 1918): Ukrainian metallurgist and specialist on welding, member of the Soviet Academy of Sciences and President of the Ukrainian Academy since 1962.

30. Daniil Lunts (born 1911): forensic psychiatrist, head of a section concerned with assessment of political offenders at the Serbsky Institute, and high-ranking officer (probably a major general) in the MVD or KGB. The Professor V. P. Serbsky Institute of Forensic Psychiatry: established in Moscow in 1921, defined by the *Great Soviet Encyclopedia* as the "central Soviet scientific research institution for the investigation of theoretical and practical problems of forensic psychiatry." It also functions as an assessment center for forensic cases from all over the country, and many of the dissenters who have been subjected to psychiatric commitment have passed through it.

31. Natalia Gorbanevskaya, *Red Square at Noon*, translated by Alexander Lieven (London: André Deutsch, 1972; Penguin, 1973).

32. Genrikh Altunyan: lecturer on radio technology at the military academy in Kharkiv, member of the Initiative Group for the Defense of Human Rights. In July 1969 Altunyan was expelled from the party, dismissed from the academy, and discharged from the army for signing letters of appeal, then arrested on a

charge of anti-Soviet agitation and propaganda and in November 1969 sentenced to three years in a labor camp.

33. "Free Medical Aid": Russian text, dated March 1968, AS 153 and in *Posev* 6, 1969, pp. 43–54. English extracts in *The Times*, July 9, 1970. "Letter to Yu. V. Andropov, Head of the KGB" in *The Grigorenko Papers: Writings by General P. G. Grigorenko and Documents on His Case*, introduction by Edward Crankshaw (London: C. Hurst; Boulder: Westview Press, 1976), pp. 75–88.

34. Milovan Djilas, *The New Class* (New York: Praeger, 1957). A. Avtorkhanov, *Tekhnologiya vlasti* [*The Technology of Power*] (Frankfurt: Possev-Verlag, 1959). Published in English as *Stalin and the Soviet Communist Party: A Study in the Technology of Power* (New York: Praeger, 1968).

CHAPTER 12

1. Yekaterina Olitskaya, *Moi vospominaniya* [*My Reminiscences*] (Frankfurt: Possev-Verlag, 1970).

2. The scene occurs in *Journey into the Whirlwind* on pp. 112–13.

3. Zinaida Tulub (1890–1964): Ukrainian novelist; arrested in 1937, she spent many years in labor camps.

4. Vasiliy Aksyonov, *Liubov' k elektrichestvu: Povest' o Leonide Krasine* [*Love of Electricity: A Story About Leonid Krasin*] (Moscow: Izdatel'stvo Politicheskoi Literatury, 1971).

5. Ilse Koch: wife of a notorious Nazi extermination-camp commandant, known for her brutality and ferocity.

6. Pierre Teilhard de Chardin, *The Phenomenon of Man*, translated by Bernard Wall, introduction by Julian Huxley (London: Collins; New York: Harper & Row, 1959; Harper Torchbooks, 1965).

7. Mikhail Bulgakov (1891–1940): Russian dramatist and novelist whose writings have only recently evoked wider interest; author of *The Master and Margarita, Heart of a Dog*, and *Diary of a Country Doctor*. Nikolay Mikhaylovsky (1842–1904): Russian sociologist, journalist, and literary critic who was connected with the terrorist group Narodnaya Volya and articulated the ideology of liberal populism. Victor Chernov (1873–1952): leader of the Social Revolutionaries.

8. Nestor Makhno (1884–1934): leader of an anarchist guerrilla movement in Southern Ukraine during the Civil War, emigrated to Paris in 1921.

9. Mykhaylo Hrushevsky (1866–1934): a historian and statesman opposed to the Bolsheviks, Hrushevsky was deported from Ukraine in 1931 and died in circumstances suggesting murder.

10. Yuriy Kotsyubynsky (1895–1937): son of the Ukrainian writer Mykhaylo Kotsyubynsky, ambassador of the Ukrainian Soviet Republic to Vienna, 1921–23, counselor of the USSR embassy in Vienna, 1923–25, and prominent party and military leader until his death in the purges.

11. The Solovetsky Islands in the White Sea are the site of monasteries where opponents of the Tsar or the Orthodox Church were imprisoned from the Middle Ages on. Soviet labor camps existed on the islands in the 1920's and 1930's.

12. Franz Koritschoner (1892–1941): founder of the Austrian Communist Party, took refuge in the USSR and died a victim of the purges. Clara Zetkin (1857–

399

1933): German Social Democrat active in the socialist and feminist movements, a founder of the German Communist Party.

13. Dzyuba was sentenced in March 1973, after nearly a year of interrogation, to five years' imprisonment and five years' exile. When *Literaturna Ukrayina* (November 9, 1973) published his recantation, the Presidium of the Supreme Soviet of the Ukrainian SSR granted him a pardon so that he could work on an "extended critical analysis of *Internationalism or Russification?*" Yakir, who had been arrested on a charge of anti-Soviet activity in June 1972, was placed on trial along with Krasin in August 1973. The KGB's pretrial interrogation had broken the two men, and they turned state's evidence against their friends. Both defendants pleaded guilty, and Yakir stated that reports of psychiatric persecution of dissenters in the Soviet Union were "libelous." At an official press conference several days later Yakir again denied that psychiatric abuses occur in the USSR.

14. For Nekipelov's account of his psychiatric assessment see *Institute of Fools: Notes from the Serbsky Institute*, edited and translated by Marco Carynnyk and Marta Horban (New York: Farrar, Straus & Giroux, 1979).

CHAPTER 13

1. Funded by the United States government, Radio Liberty broadcasts to the Soviet Union.

2. The Alexander Herzen Foundation, in Amsterdam, publishes manuscripts written in the USSR that cannot be published there because of censorship.

3. Alexander Feldman (born 1947): Jewish activist from Kiev who emigrated to Israel in July 1977, after serving a sentence of three and a half years. Jean-Paul Sartre, *Anti-Semite and Jew*, translated by George J. Becker (New York: Schocken, 1948).

4. Yevgraf Duluman: author of *Ideya boga [The Idea of God]* (Moscow: Nauka, 1970), *Sovremenny veruyushchiy [The Contemporary Believer]* (Moscow: Izdatel'stvo Politicheskoy Literatury, 1970), and *Dukhovna kultura i relihiya [Spiritual Culture and Religion]* (Kiev: Academy of Sciences of Ukrainian SSR, 1972).

5. Plyushch's contribution to the *Chronicle* can be found in *Uncensored Russia*, pp. 301–06. See also Moshe Decter (ed.), *A Hero for Our Time: The Trial and Fate of Boris Kochubievsky* (New York: Academic Committee on Soviet Jewry and Conference on the Status of Soviet Jews, 1970).

6. The demonstration in Pushkin Square on January 22, 1967, was against new articles in the Criminal Code which made the disturbance of public order and the spreading of slanderous inventions about the Soviet Union punishable offenses. See Pavel Litvinov, *The Demonstration in Pushkin Square*, translated by Manya Harari (Boston: Gambit, 1969).

7. Alexander Ginzburg (born 1936): prominent human-rights activist, imprisoned from 1960 to 1962 for editing the *samizdat* journal *Syntaxis*. Arrested in January 1967 for compiling a *White Book* about the trial of Sinyavsky and Daniel, he was sentenced the following January to five years' imprisonment. After his release he served as head of the Russian Social Fund, which aided political prisoners and their families, and helped found the Moscow Helsinki Monitoring Group. Arrested in February 1977, Ginzburg was convicted in July 1978 of anti-Soviet agitation and propaganda and sentenced to eight years in a labor camp and three years in exile.

8. Mustafa Dzhemilyov (Abduldzhemil, born 1943): Crimean Tatar activist.

Fired from his job in 1962 and then expelled from an agricultural institute in 1965 for discussing Crimean Tatar history, he was first arrested in 1966 on a charge of draft evasion and sentenced to one and a half years in a labor camp. Moving to Moscow as a Crimean Tatar representative, Dzhemilyov joined the Initiative Group for the Defense of Human Rights and denounced the invasion of Czechoslovakia. He was arrested in September 1969 for "slandering the Soviet state," tried along with Ilya Gabay in January 1970, and sentenced to three years in a labor camp. In June 1974 Dzhemilyov was rearrested for draft evasion and sentenced to another year in a camp. Just before this term ended he was resentenced to two and a half years in a labor camp. See Andrei Grigorenko, "Mustafa Dzhemilev," *Survey*, No. 4 (97), Autumn 1975, pp. 217–22.

9. Leonid Petrovsky: grandson of Grigoriy Petrovsky, an Old Bolshevik and Chairman of the Ukrainian Central Executive Committee until he was disgraced in 1939, and son of Pyotr Petrovsky, a prominent Bolshevik who died in the Stalinist purges. Leonid Petrovsky is the author of a letter objecting to the rehabilitation of Stalin. Both English and Russian texts can be found in *Za prava cheloveka* [*For the Rights of Man*] (Frankfurt: Possev-Verlag, 1969), pp. 45–98. He also signed the "Appeal to World Communist Conference in Moscow" and a letter protesting the trial and sentencing of the demonstrators in Red Square. For the latter action he was expelled from the party and then forced to resign from his job as historian and archivist "at his own request."

10. Translated as "Appeal to World Communist Conference in Moscow" in *Samizdat*, pp. 370–72.

11. The Initiative (or Action) Group for the Defense of Human Rights in the USSR was founded by fifteen dissidents in May 1969. The group set itself the task of bringing abuses of human rights to public attention, and its first act was an appeal to the United Nations Commission on Human Rights, referring to a "particularly inhuman form of persecution: the placing of normal people in psychiatric hospitals for their political convictions." Subsequently Natalya Gorbanevskaya, Vladimir Borisov, Yuriy Maltsev, and Leonid Plyushch, all founding members of the Initiative Group, were themselves interned in psychiatric hospitals.

12. Arkadiy Levin (1933–77): design engineer who signed the Initiative Group's documents as a supporter. He was arrested in December 1969 and sentenced, in April 1970, to three years in a labor camp.

13. Nicholas Berdyayev, *The Origins of Russian Communism,* translated by R. M. French (London: Geoffrey Bles, 1937).

14. Oles Honchar (born 1918): Ukrainian short-story writer and novelist, and high-ranking official in the Ukrainian Writers' Union, member of the Central Committee, and winner of several government prizes. English excerpts from *Sobor* [*The Cathedral*] (Kiev: Radyansky Pysmennyk, 1968), translated by Marta Olynyk, in *Journal of Ukrainian Graduate Studies*, Vol. 1, No. 1, Fall 1976, pp. 51–61.

15. "Lyst tvorchoyi molodi Dnipropetrovs'koho" ["Letter from the Creative Youth of Dnipropetrovsk"], *Suchasnist'*, 1969, No. 2, pp. 78–85. Reprinted with additional documents as *Molod' Dnipropetrovs'koho v borot'bi proty rusyfikatsiyi* [*The Youth of Dnipropetrovsk in the Battle Against Russification*] (Munich: Suchasnist', 1971).

16. Sverstyuk, *Clandestine Essays*, pp. 17–68.

17. Yuriy Ilyenko (born 1936): Ukrainian film maker, cameraman for Parad-

zhanov's *Shadows of Forgotten Ancestors*, then director of four films that introduced a surrealistic panoply of mythological and folkloric motifs: *Saint John's Eve* (1969), *White Bird with a Black Spot* (1971), which dealt with the establishment of Soviet rule in Western Ukraine, *In Spite of Everything* (1972), a Soviet-Yugoslav coproduction about the Montenegran national hero Petar Negosh, and *To Dream and Live* (1974), which wove together World War II and the present.

18. Mykhaylo Braychevsky (born 1924): historian who has published several respected monographs on medieval Kiev. He wrote *Annexation or Russification?* in 1966 and submitted it to the Ukrainian Academy of Sciences, but it was rejected and circulated only in *samizdat*.

19. See "Kratkaya zapis' sobraniy provedennykh v Khar'kove" ["An Abridged Transcript of Meetings Held in Kharkiv"], AS 662; and "Kratkaya zapis' zasedaniya Komiteta partiynogo kontrolya pri TsK KPSS i dvukh predshestvuyushchikh besed" ["An Abridged Transcript of the Meeting of the Party Control Committee of the CC CPSU and of Two Preceding Discussions"], *Posev: Spetsial'nyy vypusk*, No. 5, 1970, pp. 45–48.

20. The Ukrainian Insurgent Army, or UPA, was formed by the Organization of Ukrainian Nationalists in 1942 to fight for an independent Ukraine. It continued guerrilla actions in the Carpathians against Soviet and Polish forces until the middle 1950's.

21. "Anonimnoye pis'mo 'dorogomu drugu' ot rusifitsirovannogo ukraintsa o natsional'nom voprose v SSSR" ["Anonymous Letter to a 'Dear Friend' from a Russified Ukrainian About the Nationalities Question in the USSR"], Ufa, June 5, 1968. AS 280.

22. Plyushch's article has not reached the West.

23. The Code of Criminal Procedure gives an accused the right to demand that a judge or prosecutor disqualify himself if he is involved in the case, is related to someone involved in the case, or has a personal interest in the case.

24. The article has not reached the West.

25. The Chukchi are a Siberian Americanoid people with a population of 12,000 (1964), largely in the Magadan Province of the Russian Republic. The Kamchadal are a Paleo-Asiatic people inhabiting southern Kamchatka. The Nentsi, or Samoyed, are a Finno-Asian people scattered to the Far North. The Yakut are a Turkic people with a population of 250,000 (1964), largely in the Yakut Autonomous Republic in northeast Siberia.

26. The Komi and Mordovians speak languages related to Finnish and live, respectively, in the Komi and Mordovian Autonomous Republics within the Russian Republic.

27. Volodymyr Vynnychenko (1880–1951): Ukrainian novelist and socialist politician who emigrated to France in the 1920's.

28. Petro Konasevych-Sahaydachny (died 1622): Ukrainian Cossack leader.

29. Leonhard Euler (1707–83): Swiss mathematician and physicist who lived in Russia 1727–41 and 1766–83.

30. Ilya Glazunov (born 1916): Russian painter who enjoys official recognition and has written several books on Soviet art.

31. Chornovil's documents are available in *The Chornovil Papers* (New York: McGraw-Hill, 1968).

32. Mykhaylo Osadchy, *Cataract*, translated, edited, and annotated by Marco Carynnyk (New York: A Helen and Kurt Wolff Book, Harcourt Brace Jovanovich, 1976).

33. Yuriy Larin (born 1936): son of Nikolay Bukharin (1888–1938), the prominent Bolshevik theoretician, founder of the Comintern, and editor of *Pravda* who led the list of twenty-one defendants in the trial of the "Anti-Soviet Bloc of Rights and Trotskyites" in March 1938. In recent years Larin has been making repeated efforts to have his father's name cleared of the charges. See his article in the New York *Times*, July 7, 1978.

34. Ihor Kalynets (born 1939): extremely gifted Ukrainian poet most of whose poetry has been available only in *samizdat*. Active in defense of arrested Ukrainian intellectuals, particularly Valentyn Moroz, Kalynets was arrested in August 1972 and sentenced on charges of anti-Soviet agitation and propaganda to six years' imprisonment and three years' exile. His wife, Iryna Stasiv-Kalynets (born 1940), was arrested early in 1972 and sentenced in July to an identical term.

35. The Borotbist Party, named after its organ *Borot'ba* (*The Struggle*), emerged in 1918 from a split in the Ukrainian Social Revolutionary Party. The Borotbists accepted the Soviet platform but insisted on the independence of the Ukrainian Republic. The party was dissolved under pressure from the Bolsheviks, and many of its members later died in the purges.

CHAPTER 14

1. Anatoliy Levitin-Krasnov (born 1916): church activist and writer, imprisoned 1949–56. Arrested in September 1969 and held under investigation for nine months. Rearrested in August 1970 and sentenced to three years of imprisonment. Emigrated soon after his release in 1974.

2. A. Krasnov (Levitin), "Svet v okontse. K arestu gen. Grigorenko" ["A Light in the Window. On the Arrest of General Grigorenko"], May 24, 1969. AS 269.

3. Oleg Bakhtiarov: medical student from Kiev who was arrested under Article 62 of the Ukrainian Criminal Code in August 1969, at which time much Ukrainian and Russian *samizdat*, including Plyushch's writings, was confiscated. Plyushch's apartment was also searched in connection with the case, and he was twice called in for interrogation. In February 1970 Bakhtiarov was sentenced to three years in a labor camp.

4. "Babiy Yar" in *Vestnik Iskhoda*, No. 2. AS 1085.

5. Lyudmyla Semykina: artist who, with Panas Zalyvakha, Alla Horska, and Halyna Sevruk, designed and produced a Shevchenko stained-glass panel for Kiev University. The panel was destroyed on party orders, and in May 1964 Semykina was expelled from the Artists' Union. Subsequently reinstated, she was again expelled after signing the "Appeal of the 139 to Brezhnev, Kosygin, and Podgorny."

6. Alla Horska: took part in the design and production of the Shevchenko stained glass, for which she, too, was expelled from the Artists' Union. She was expelled from the Union a second time and frequently called in for questioning by the KGB after signing the "Appeal of the 139" and numerous other protests.

7. Halyna Sevruk: artist who took part in the design and production of the Shevchenko stained glass and signed the "Appeal of the 139," for which she was expelled from the Artists' Union.

8. Ostap Vyshnya (pen name of Pavlo Hubenko, 1889–1956): popular Ukrainian satirist and humorist who was sentenced in 1933 to ten years in a labor camp.

9. Maximilian Voloshin (1877–1932): Russian poet who at first exalted the

Revolution but ceased writing when he found that his increasingly mystical outlook was incompatible with subsequent events.

10. Yuliy Daniel, *Stikhi iz nevoli* [*Verses from Bondage*] (Amsterdam: Herzen Foundation, 1971). Partly available in Yuli Daniel, *Prison Poems*, translated by David Burg and Arthur Boyars (London: Calder and Boyars; Chicago: J. Philip O'Hara, 1971).

11. In his polemic with Dzyuba, "In the Midst of the Snows," *Report from the Beria Reserve*, p. 103; *Boomerang*, p. 79.

12. Yemelian Pugachov (1726–75), a Don Cossack, led a wide-scale popular revolt in 1773. Following the defeat of his forces he was handed over by his own men to the government and executed in Moscow.

13. I. P. Kalyayev (1877–1905): Social Revolutionary who assassinated Grand Duke Sergey, Governor General of Moscow, in 1905.

CHAPTER 15

1. Yuriy Maltsev (born 1933): translator from the Italian who was committed to a psychiatric hospital for a month in October 1969, shortly after he joined the Initiative Group. In 1974 he emigrated to Italy, where he lectures on Russian literature. He has also written a survey of Russian *samizdat* literature, *Vol'naya russkaya literatura* [*Free Russian Literature*] (Frankfurt: Possev-Verlag, 1976).

2. Tatyana Khodorovich: linguist who worked at the Russian Language Institute of the USSR Academy of Sciences until she was dismissed in 1971 for her *samizdat* activity and membership in the Initiative Group. In 1974, Tatyana Velikanova, Sergey Kovalyov, and Khodorovich distributed to reporters a new issue of the *Chronicle of Current Events*, which had ceased to appear in October 1972 because of KGB repressions. Khodorovich has also compiled *Istoriya bolezni Leonida Plyushcha* (Amsterdam: Herzen Foundation, 1974), translated by Marite Sapiets, Peter Reddaway, and Caryl Emerson as *The Case of Leonid Plyushch*. Permitted to emigrate in 1977, Khodorovich now lives in Paris. Anatoliy Yakobson (born 1935): literary scholar and translator, member of the Initiative Group, and author of a book about Alexander Blok, *Konets tragedii* [*The End of a Tragedy*] (New York: Chekhov Publishing House, 1973). Yakobson left the Soviet Union in 1973.

3. Vladimir Yevgenevich Borisov (born 1943): electrician from Leningrad who was interned from 1964 to 1968 in a psychiatric hospital. After his release he became a founding member of the Initiative Group, whereupon he was rearrested on a charge of "defaming the Soviet state and social system," ruled insane, and recommitted for five years. During this time he resorted to prolonged hunger strikes to win better treatment for his fellow inmates and himself. In December 1976 he was once again interned for two months.

4. In Pushkin's poem *The Bronze Horseman*, an equestrian statue of Peter the Great towers over Saint Petersburg.

5. Les Kurbas's Berezil Theater, which had been under heavy party attack for several years, was finally purged in October 1933 at a session of the Board of the People's Commissariat of Education which ended in Kurbas's dismissal. To avoid arrest Kurbas moved to Moscow (where he had been invited to stage *Othello* at the Maly Theater and *King Lear* at Solomon Mikhoels's State Jewish Theater), but he was arrested on December 26, 1933, and was sentenced the following May to hard labor on the White Sea Canal.

The campaign of vilification that began after the publication of Pasternak's *Doctor Zhivago* in Milan in 1957 was quickly stepped up when Pasternak was awarded the Nobel Prize for Literature on October 23, 1958. On October 27 a meeting of the Writers' Union was summoned at which Pasternak was expelled from the Union. Although he informed the authorities that he was turning down the prize, on October 31 a general meeting of the writers of Moscow was held with the aim of approving the decision to expel him from the union. Vladimir Soloukhin's remarks were typical of the tone:

[*Doctor Zhivago*] is the deliberate championship of individualism to be expected from an internal émigré. . . . The entire book is a weapon in the cold war against communism. . . . He will be able to tell [the Americans] nothing of interest, and after a month they'll throw him away like an empty eggshell or a lemon which has been squeezed dry. This will be the main punishment for the act of betrayal he has committed.

The whole matter is discussed and extensive excerpts are quoted in Olga Ivinskaya, *A Captive of Time*, translated by Max Hayward (Garden City, N. Y.: Doubleday, 1978), pp. 251–61.

6. For Solzhenitsyn's letter to the Secretariat of the Writers' Union see *Solzhenitsyn: A Documentary Record*, pp. 222–24.

7. Vyacheslav Bakhmin (born 1947): fourth-year student at the Moscow Institute of Physics Technology. The *Chronicle of Current Events*, No. 11 (*Uncensored Russia*, pp. 418 and 420), reports that Bakhmin was arrested on November 20, 1969, but released after spending ten months under investigation.

8. Vladislav Nedobora: engineer from Kharkiv who supported the Initiative Group's appeals. He was arrested on November 27, 1969, but released three days later. He was soon rearrested, however, and in March 1970 was tried along with Vladimir Ponomaryov on charges of "defaming the Soviet state and social system" and sentenced to three years in a labor camp.

9. Alexander Kalinovsky, an engineer from Kharkiv, and his wife, Veronica, supported the appeals of the Initiative Group, for which they were condemned at meetings at their place of work.

10. Olga Iofe (born 1950), an economics student, and Irina Kaplun (born 1950), a linguistics student, were arrested in December 1969, apparently because they had been preparing protests against the celebration of Stalin's ninetieth birthday. (They had already run into the KGB in 1966, when they had distributed anti-Stalinist leaflets.) Kaplun was released after ten months, but Iofe was sent to the Serbsky Institute, diagnosed as a chronic schizophrenic, and committed to the Kazan Special Psychiatric Hospital until July 1971. Excerpts from her father's account of the conditions in which she was held are in *The Case of Leonid Plyushch*, pp. 92–95.

11. Quentin Hoare and Geoffrey Nowell-Smith (eds.), *Selections from the Prison Notebooks of Antonio Gramsci* (London: Laurence and Wishart, 1971).

12. Vladimir Ponomaryov (born 1933): engineer who was arrested in December 1969 after signing a letter about the arrest of Petro Grigorenko and appeals by the Initiative Group to the United Nations Human Rights Commission. He was sentenced in March 1970 to three years in a labor camp.

13. *The Grigorenko Papers*, pp. 133–52.

14. Roy A. Medvedev, *Let History Judge: The Origins and Consequences of Stalinism*, translated by Colleen Taylor, edited by David Joravsky and Georges Haupt (New York: Alfred A. Knopf, 1971; Vintage, 1973).

15. The letter is not available in the West, but a summary was published in

the *Chronicle of Current Events*, No. 12 (London: Amnesty International Research Department, 1970).

16. Mendel Beilis: Jewish workman in Kiev who was accused of murdering a Christian boy to use his blood in a ritual. Although a judicial inquiry produced no evidence of Beilis's guilt and it was apparent that the boy had been killed by a gang of thieves to which his mother belonged, high officials engineered a case against Beilis to divert popular dissatisfaction and strengthen the autocracy. Beilis was held in prison for over two years until international protests forced the authorities to give him a trial. The trial, which took place in October 1913, was heavily rigged in favor of the prosecution. The jury consisted of uneducated Ukrainian peasants who had been exposed to anti-Jewish incitement before the trial. The judge, a known anti-Semite, hampered the defense, tried to influence the jury, and assisted the witnesses for the prosecution. Despite all this, the jury found Beilis not guilty, and the government grudgingly dropped its case.

17. Like the *Chronicle of Current Events*, the *Ukrainian Herald* is published in typescript by an anonymous group that has set itself the task of reporting as completely and objectively as possible on government abuses of human rights. Seven issues of the *Herald* have reached the West, of which the following have been published in English: *Ukrainian Herald IV* (Munich: ABN Press Bureau, 1972); *Ukrainian Herald, Issue 6,* introduction by Yaroslav Bilinsky, translated and edited by Lesya Jones and Bohdan Yasen (Baltimore: Smoloskyp Publishers, 1977); and *Ukrainian Herald, Issue 7–8: Ethnocide of Ukrainians in the U.S.S.R.*, introduction by Robert Conquest, translated and edited by Olena Saciuk and Bohdan Yasen (Baltimore: Smoloskyp Publishers, 1976).

18. Sergey Kirov (1889–1934): a high party official in Leningrad whose murder, quite possibly on Stalin's orders, was used as a pretext to step up repressions.

19. Mikhail Saltykov (pseudonym Shchedrin, 1826–89): Russian novelist whose sketches of tsarist Russia satirized officialdom, the nobility, and the rising capitalists.

20. Pyotr Chaadayev (1794–1856): Russian philosopher who was declared insane and placed under house arrest when an excerpt from his main philosophical effort, *Philosophical Letters*, was published in a Russian journal.

21. Uttered in 1934, Gorky's remark was used by Stalin as a justification for his mass purges.

22. Otto Bauer (1881–1938): leading theoretician of the Austrian Social Democratic Party.

CHAPTER 16

1. In 1965 and 1966 Drach personally applied to party and government authorities for an explanation of the arrests of political dissenters, tried to gain admission to their supposedly open trials, and signed collective letters to the authorities, asking for an explanation and appealing for publicity and fairness. For the previously mentioned "Appeal of the 139" Drach was expelled from the party, of which he had been a member since 1959. Pressured to dissociate himself from "bourgeois nationalists," Drach finally published in *Literaturna Ukrayina*, on July 22, 1966, a vituperative rebuttal to an émigré critic's interpretation of his poetry (Bohdan Kravtsiv, " 'Protuberantsi sertsya' i kredo Ivana Dracha" ["*Protuberances of the Heart* and Ivan Drach's Credo"], *Suchasnist'*, 1966, No. 1,

pp. 5–25). Drach was then readmitted to the party and took to writing versified lampoons against "bourgeois nationalists."

2. Vladimir Borisov (1945?–1970): worker with a higher education in literature who founded the Union of Independent Youth with the aim of promoting socialist democracy. He was interned in May 1969 in a psychiatric hospital in Vladimir—only "for investigation," though he was given injections there. Released in July after public pressure, he was rearrested a month later, charged with "defaming the Soviet state and social system," and sent for a psychiatric examination, at which he was declared insane. In May 1970 he hanged himself in the hospital wing of Moscow's Butyrki Prison.

3. Julius Telesin: Jewish mathematician who lived in Moscow until 1970, when he left for Israel. Telesin has contributed a foreword to Peter Reddaway's *Uncensored Russia*, pages 43–51.

4. Boris Tsukerman: author of numerous *samizdat* writings, including a biography of Petro Grigorenko.

5. *Izvestia* attacked Hájek as a "counterrevolutionary," on September 4, 1968. See AS 1056 for Tsukerman's reply.

6. "Moral Orientation" is available in *The Case of Leonid Plyushch*, pp. 131–42.

7. David Elkin (born 1895): Ukrainian psychologist, professor at Odessa University since 1934, whose work concerns memory, perception, and the senses.

8. Under the Soviet "antiparasite law," it is a crime to "avoid socially useful work" and to "lead an antisocial, parasitic way of life." A person who refuses employment proffered by his district Executive Committee may be punished with correctional tasks or deprivation of freedom for up to one year.

9. Zhores A. Medvedev and Roy A. Medvedev, *A Question of Madness*, translated by Ellen de Kadt (London: Macmillan, 1971; Penguin, 1974).

10. Zhores A. Medvedev, *The Rise and Fall of T. D. Lysenko*, translated by I. Michael Lerner (New York: Columbia University Press, 1969; Anchor, 1971).

11. The Human Rights Committee was later joined by Igor Shafarevich and Grigoriy Podyapolsky and became affiliated with the International League for the Rights of Man in New York and the Institute for the Rights of Man in Strasbourg. For a statement by the committee see *Sakharov Speaks,* edited and with a foreword by Harrison E. Salisbury (New York: Alfred A. Knopf, 1974), pp. 218–21.

12. The Homin Choir was a volunteer group founded in the 1960's that set about reviving Ukrainian folk music and customs, including caroling and spring and summer choral rituals. In 1969 the ensemble was attacked for "bourgeois nationalism" in its repertoire, and its members were subjected to reprisals. The group was disbanded in September 1971, and its leader, Leopold Yashchenko, was expelled from the Composers' Union. For details of the reprisals see the *Ukrainian Herald, Issue 6*, pp. 130–38.

13. Alexander Galich, "Pamyati B. L. Pasternaka" ["In Memory of B. L. Pasternak"] in *Pokoleniye obrechyonnykh* [*Generation of the Doomed*] Frankfurt: Possev-Verlag, 1972), pp. 114–16. Translated for this book by Gerry Smith.

14. Alexander Serhiyenko (born 1932): expelled from medical school in 1967, then fired from his job as art teacher for his speech at Alla Horska's funeral. Arrested in January 1972, Serhiyenko was given a closed trial in June, at which the main charges were making notes on Dzyuba's *Internationalism or Russifica-*

tion? (the court took this to mean that he had edited the book and was therefore a coauthor), criticizing the Soviet intervention in Czechoslovakia, and mentioning the Ukrainian right to self-determination. He was sentenced to seven years in labor camps and three years in exile. He is reported to be in very poor health (pulmonary tuberculosis), and Soviet dissidents have made numerous appeals on his behalf. A detailed account of his case has been provided by his mother, Oksana Meshko, in a letter addressed to Amnesty International (*Suchasnist'*, 1976, No. 4, pp. 82–95).

15. Ivan Hel (born 1937): active participant in the Ukrainian movement who spent three years (1966–69) in labor camps for disseminating *samizdat*. He was arrested again in 1972 on charges of "anti-Soviet agitation and propaganda" and sentenced to ten years in labor camps and three years in exile. The text of his final statement to the court at his second trial has been published in *East-West Digest*, Vol. II, No. 8, April 1975, pp. 311–14.

16. Vasyl Stus, *Svicha v svichadi* [*A Candle in a Mirror*], edited by Marco Carynnyk and Wolfram Burghardt, with an introduction by Marco Carynnyk (Munich: Suchasnist', 1977), p. 37.

17. The eulogies at Horska's funeral appeared in *Ukrainian Herald, IV*, pp. 7–30.

18. A summary of Mikhaylov's "Thoughts on the Liberal Campaign of 1968" can be found in *Chronicle of Current Events, No. 17* (London: Amnesty International Publications, 1971), pp. 93–96, and in *Samizdat*, pp. 446–52.

19. "Slovo natsii" ["Word of the Nation"], *Russkaya mysl'*, November 26, 1971, and AS 590.

20. Vladimir Bukovsky (born 1942): prominent Russian writer and human-rights activist. First arrested in May 1963 for circulating Milovan Djilas's *The New Class* and confined in a Leningrad psychiatric hospital until February 1965. Rearrested in December 1965 for helping to plan a demonstration in defense of Sinyavsky and Daniel, he was confined without trial to a psychiatric hospital for six months. He was arrested again in January 1967 for organizing a demonstration against the arrests of Galanskov, Ginzburg, and others and sentenced to three years in a labor camp. Continuing his activity in defense of human rights, Bukovsky collected material on the political misuse of psychiatry. He was arrested for the fourth time in March 1971 and sentenced the following January to seven years in labor camps and five years in exile. While in a labor camp Bukovsky and Semyon Gluzman compiled a *Manual on Psychiatry for Dissidents* (*Survey*, Winter/Spring 1975, pp. 176–98; published as a pamphlet in London, 1976, by the Working Group on the Internment of Dissenters in Mental Hospitals). On December 18, 1976, Bukovsky was released in exchange for the Chilean Communist Luis Corvalan. He now lives in England. See his *To Build a Castle: My Life as a Dissenter*, translated by Michael Scammell (New York: Viking, 1979).

21. *The Grigorenko Papers*, pp. 126–32.

22. Gabriel Superfin (born 1943): Russian literary scholar, signer of letter in defense of Ginzburg and Galanskov (*In Quest of Justice*, pp. 164–69). He was arrested in July 1973 and in May 1974 sentenced to five years in labor camps and two years in exile. The main charges against him were signing the letter about Ginzburg and Galanskov, editing and sending abroad Edward Kuznetsov's *Prison Diaries* (New York: Stein & Day, 1975), editing and distributing the *Chronicle of Current Events*, and making corrections to Peter Reddaway's *Uncensored Russia*.

23. Alexander Pushkin (1799–1837): died from a wound he received in a duel with an officer in the Horse Guards, d'Anthes, who had been spreading scandalous rumors about him.

24. Alexander Griboyedov (1795–1829): Russian dramatist, killed during disturbances in Persia, where he was a diplomat.

25. "Pochemu ya ne podpisal Stokgol'mskoye vozzvaniye" ["Why I did not sign the Stockholm Appeal"], AS 2614.

26. Anatol Lupynis (born 1937): Ukrainian poet, imprisoned from 1956 to 1967 on a charge of "anti-Soviet agitation and propaganda," during which time he staged a two-year hunger strike (he was kept alive by force-feeding). On May 27, 1971, Lupynis recited a poem at a meeting in honor of Taras Shevchenko. He was arrested a few days later and in January 1972 was tried on the same charge as before. Declared to be schizophrenic, he was sentenced to an indefinite term in the Dnipropetrovsk psychiatric prison.

27. Alexander Galich, "Kaddish" in *Pokoleniye obrechyonnykh*, pp. 288–300. Translated for this book by Gerry Smith.

CHAPTER 17

1. Ivan Rusyn (born 1937): a geodesist who was arrested in August 1965 and sentenced the following March to one year in a labor camp. In 1968 he signed the "Appeal of the 139." For a description of him in the labor camp, see Osadchy's *Cataract*, pp. 90–91.

2. The Soviet Prosecutor's Office, or Procuracy, is charged with ensuring the observance of the law by all persons and authorities and thus, in theory at least, supervises the actions of KGB investigators.

3. Mykola Kholodny (born 1939): Ukrainian poet whose verse circulated widely in *samizdat*. He was expelled from the university in 1965 and detained briefly in 1966.

CHAPTER 18

1. Jan Palach: Czech student who burned himself to death in January 1969 to protest the Soviet occupation of Czechoslovakia. Janusz Korczak (1878–1942): Polish writer and educator who died in the gas chambers at Treblinka with two hundred of his pupils.

2. Danylo Shumuk (born 1914): revolutionary, member of the Communist Party of Western Ukraine, imprisoned by Polish police 1935–39. After fighting in the Red Army, 1941–43, Shumuk joined the Ukrainian Insurgent Army. He was arrested in 1945 and imprisoned for ten years. In 1957 Shumuk was given a second ten-year sentence for writing his memoirs, *Za skhidnim obriyem* [*Beyond the Eastern Horizon*] (Baltimore: Smoloskyp Publishers, 1974). In January 1972 Shumuk was arrested once again when the second volume of his memoirs was discovered; in July he was sentenced to ten years in labor camps and five years in exile.

CHAPTER 19

1. Pyotr Stolypin (1862–1911): Russian statesman, Minister of the Interior in 1906, Prime Minister from 1906 to 1911.

2. Volodymyr Zatonsky (1888–1938): prominent Ukrainian Bolshevik who died in the Stalin purges.

3. Alexander Herzen (1812–70): prominent Russian journalist and radical thinker, publisher of the muckraking émigré journal *Kolokol* [*The Bell*], which had much influence in Russia. Herzen's masterpiece is his book of memoirs, translated by Constance Garnett as *My Past and Thoughts*, six volumes (London: Chatto & Windus; New York: Alfred A. Knopf, 1924–27). In 1968 both publishers brought out a four-volume revision of Garnett's translation by Humphrey Higgens.

4. Vacys Sevrukas (born 1937): Lithuanian sociologist and philosopher. Arrested in January 1972 on a charge of connections with the *Chronicle of Current Events*, he was held in a psychiatric hospital in Vilnius until July 1973. Sevrukas emigrated in the autumn of 1974 and now lives in New York.

5. Zinoviy Krasivsky (born 1930): Ukrainian writer and teacher who was arrested in 1967 for involvement with the journal of the Ukrainian National Front, a clandestine group established in 1964 with the aim of liberating Ukraine. Krasivsky was sentenced to five years in prison, seven years in a camp, and five years in exile. In December 1971, while at Vladimir Prison, he was charged with circulating his poems and sent to the Serbsky Institute, where he was ruled nonresponsible and committed to a psychiatric hospital.

6. Yuriy Belov (born 1941): Russian journalist who served a labor-camp sentence (1964–67) for a political offense. In 1968, after writing a book entitled *Report from Darkness*, he was sentenced to five years in camp for trying to send the book abroad. Transferred to Vladimir Prison, Belov was charged with "agitation in prison," sent to the Serbsky Institute, ruled nonresponsible, and committed to a psychiatric hospital.

7. Mykola Plakhotnyuk (born 1936): Ukrainian physician arrested in January 1972 and charged with anti-Soviet agitation and propaganda for his involvement in *samizdat*. Sent to the Serbsky Institute, he declared a hunger strike in protest against the conditions. His diagnosis was "schizophrenia with persecution mania, periodically nonresponsible," and in November 1972 a court committed him to a special psychiatric hospital with trial on recovery, a procedure not foreseen by Soviet law. At last report Plakhotnyuk was still at the Dnipropetrovsk hospital, suffering from a disease of the lungs.

8. Probably the Russian edition of G. V. Morozov and I. M. Kalashnik (eds.), *Forensic Psychiatry* (White Plains, N.Y.: International Arts and Science Press, 1970).

9. *August 1914*, translated by Michael Glenny (New York: Farrar, Straus & Giroux, 1972; Bantam, 1974).

10. Maksym Kryvonis (died 1648). Cossack colonel during Bohdan Khmelnytsky's uprising against Polish domination.

11. R. V. Ivanov-Razumnik (1878–1946): Russian literary critic and sociologist. An implacable foe of Marxism who espoused populist ideas, he spent many years in both tsarist and Soviet prisons and labor camps. His account of his imprisonment is available in *The Memoirs of Ivanov-Razumnik*, with an introduction by G. Jankovsky, translated and annotated by P. S. Squire (London: Oxford University Press, 1965).

12. Prishvin's "The Root of Life" is available in *Ginseng: Root of Life*, translated by G. Walton and P. Gibbons (London: Putnam, 1936), *The Lake and*

the Woods (New York: Pantheon, 1951), and *The Larder of the Sun*, translated by W. Goodman (New York: Viking, 1952).

13. Ivan Michurin (1855-1935): Russian biologist and plant geneticist who developed some three hundred fruit and berry hybrids.

14. Soviet law stipulates that the preliminary investigation of a case must be concluded within two months, although extensions up to nine months may be granted by a provincial or republican prosecutor. After that a suspect may be detained only if the Presidium of the Supreme Soviet has granted special permission.

15. Andrey Snezhnevsky (born 1904): prominent Russian psychiatrist, director of the Institute of Psychiatry of the Academy of Medical Sciences, and author or editor of several textbooks on schizophrenia. Snezhnevsky's extremely broad definition of schizophrenia has come to dominate Soviet psychiatry, and he is a vehement defender of Soviet psychiatrists against charges of abuses.

16. Nekrasov's letter (written in late 1971) and Snezhnevsky's reply were confiscated from Nekrasov by the KGB. Nekrasov discusses the matter in a second letter to Snezhnevsky which serves as an introduction to Vladimir Bukovsky and Semyon Gluzman's *A Manual on Psychiatry for Dissidents*.

17. The *kobzars* were itinerant minstrels, often blind, who supported themselves by begging for alms as they performed historical songs and ballads to the accompaniment of the *kobza*, a lutelike instrument of Turkish origin. *Kobzar* was also the title of Taras Shevchenko's first book of poetry, and the term is often applied to Shevchenko himself.

18. The article has not been published in the West.

19. Vasyl Lisovy (born 1937): lecturer at Kiev University and research associate at the Institute of Philosophy, arrested in July 1972 for writing a letter of protest against the arrests in Ukraine the previous January. In November 1973 Lisovy was found guilty of anti-Soviet agitation and propaganda and sentenced to seven years in a strict-regime camp and three years in exile.

CHAPTER 20

1. B. G. Kuznetsov, *Einstein: Zhizn', smert', bessmertiye* [*Einstein: Life, Death, Immortality*] (Moscow: Nauka, 1972).

2. The *oprichniks* were the rulers of an administrative division in Muscovy established by Tsar Ivan IV in 1565 in an effort to gain control over the boyars. The term was also applied to the Tsar's bodyguards, who were renowned for their savagery and led a wave of extermination of his enemies.

3. A one-percent sterile solution of purified sulphur in peach oil, known as sulphazin, was widely used for various psychiatric disorders in the 1930's, but it fell into disfavor when it was shown to have no therapeutic value. Its continued use in the Soviet Union for punitive purposes has been cited by many dissenters.

4. Vasyl Ruban (born 1942): Ukrainian poet whose work ceased to be published in the early 1970's, considered nationalistic. Arrested in 1972, Ruban was ruled nonresponsible in 1973 and committed to the Dnipropetrovsk Special Psychiatric Hospital.

5. Boris Yevdokimov (born 1923): Russian journalist who was arrested in 1971 on a charge of "anti-Soviet agitation and propaganda" for publishing articles in the émigré press. Ruled nonresponsible, he was committed to the Leningrad

Special Psychiatric Hospital, then in September 1972 transferred to the Dnipropetrovsk Special Psychiatric Hospital, where he is reported to be suffering from asthma, heart trouble, and high blood pressure.

6. Ellochka the Cannibal is a vulgar and greedy character in *The Twelve Chairs*, a satirical novel by Ilya Ilf (pseudonym of Ilya Fainzilberg, 1897–1937) and Yevgeniy Petrov (pseudonym of Yevgeniy Katayev, 1903–42).

7. Tove Jannson: popular Finnish children's writer, author of numerous books on the Moomin family of trolls.

CHAPTER 21

1. Alexander Ivanov (1806–58): prominent Russian painter, best known for *The Appearance of Christ to the People* (1837–57).

2. Henri Perruchot, *La Vie de Van Gogh* (Paris: Hachette, 1957). The Russian translation was published in Moscow by Progress Publishers in 1973.

3. A Ukrainian folk dance that involves ingenious leaps and squats.

4. Vyacheslav Yatsenko (born 1948): student at a shipbuilding institute in Mykolayiv, sentenced to a year in prison for attempting to cross the Finnish border. In 1973 he was charged with "defaming the Soviet state and social system" and ruled nonresponsible. Rearrested in May 1975, he was charged with circulating anti-Soviet letters, ruled nonresponsible at the Serbsky Institute in the autumn of 1975, and committed to the Dnipropetrovsk Special Psychiatric Hospital.

5. Victor Rafalsky (born 1920?): writer and schoolteacher in Western Ukraine. Arrested in 1954 for belonging to a clandestine Marxist group, he was interned until 1959, undergoing six psychiatric assessments, three of which (in Leningrad) found him responsible and three of which (at the Serbsky Institute) found him schizophrenic and nonresponsible. In 1962 Rafalsky was rearrested for having links with a Marxist group and for creating "anti-Soviet" literary works and was committed to a psychiatric hospital for two years. He was arrested once again in 1968, when an "anti-Soviet" novel of his was found, and was committed to the Dnipropetrovsk Special Psychiatric Hospital.

6. Several dozen people, including Leonid Plyushch, were arrested in Ukraine in the sweep of January 1972. Of these, Leonid Seleznenko (a petroleum chemist born in 1934), Mykola Kholodny, and Zinoviya Franko were released after they gave in to KGB pressure, publishing statements of repentance and testifying against their colleagues.

7. The International Committee of Mathematicians for the Defense of Yuriy Shikhanovich and Leonid Plyushch was founded in Paris in January 1974. After the July 5, 1974, release of Shikhanovich, a Jewish mathematician who had been committed to a psychiatric hospital for his *samizdat* activity, the Committee continued its efforts on behalf of Plyushch.

8. Mukachiv is a town about forty-five kilometers from Chop, which is a railway center near the Soviet border with Hungary and Czechoslovakia.

9. *Kogda ya vernus'* [*When I Come Home*] (Frankfurt: Possev-Verlag, 1978), p. 139. Translated for this book by Gerry Smith.

CHAPTER 22

1. Victor Nekipelov was arrested on July 11, 1973, and charged with "disseminating deliberately false and libelous material, defaming the Soviet political and social system." In May 1974 he was sentenced to two years in a labor camp.

2. Alexander Radishchev (1749–1802): prominent Russian writer, philosopher, and social critic. He was at first condemned to death and then banished to Siberia for *A Journey from St. Petersburg to Moscow*, which harshly criticized Russian autocracy, serfdom, and bureaucratic inefficiency. An English translation by Leo Wiener, edited by Roderick Page Thaler (Cambridge, Mass., Harvard University Press, 1958) is available. The Petrashevtsy: members of an underground radical group in Saint Petersburg headed by Mikhail Petrashevsky. The circle was discovered by the police in 1849, and the most active members, among them Dostoyevsky, were at first condemned to be executed and then exiled to Siberia.

3. Tatyana Chernysheva: student of philology who signed the "Appeal of the 139."

CHAPTER 23

1. Yuriy Orlov (born 1924): physicist and prominent human-rights activist who has signed numerous appeals in behalf of repressed dissidents. A founder of the Soviet chapter of Amnesty International, Orlov also founded and served as chairman of the Public Group to Promote the Implementation of the Helsinki Accords in the USSR. He was arrested in February 1977 in a crackdown on the Helsinki monitoring groups and in May 1978 sentenced to seven years in labor camps and five years in exile.

2. Representative Christopher Dodd of Connecticut was heading a group sent by the House Judiciary Committee to visit Kiev, Moscow, and Leningrad.

3. The attorneys were Jean-Marc Varaut, Jean-Michel Pérard, and François Morette. See *Le Figaro*, September 18, 1975, for Varaut's account of their visit.

4. Tatyana Plyushch's message was to a rally organized in Paris on October 23, 1975, by the International Committee of Mathematicians in Defense of Leonid Plyushch.

AFTERWORD

1. The rally was held on March 27, 1976, and was sponsored by the Committee for the Defense of Soviet Political Prisoners. The speakers included Michael Harrington, Henry Jackson, Edward Koch, Simas Kudirka, Pavel Litvinov, and Leonid Plyushch.

INDEX

418